# STAND UP THAT
# MOUNTAIN

The Battle to Save One Small Community in
the Wilderness Along the Appalachian Trail

## JAY ERSKINE LEUTZE

Scribner

New York  London  Toronto  Sydney  New Delhi

Scribner
A Division of Simon & Schuster, Inc.
1230 Avenue of the Americas
New York, NY 10020

To my Shirley, Erskine, Leutze, and Bordley families

The story of the southern mountains is told in her face. The crepe-soft skin is laid over stone-hard bone. She's as white as February snow, but her blue eyes smolder.

I ask her, "Where did they come from, your father's people? When did they come into these mountains?" I want to hear about her ancestors. The Cherokee side and the Scots-Irish kin, the old-timers who came here to hide or scratch dirt or seek a wage felling timber. I want to hear about her wire-thin Appalachian grandmothers, who walked these steep ridges, these wildflower slopes.

But she can't call it up. Either she can't remember or she won't. Maybe all the stories were lost in her youth, when she lived hard, drank hard. All she will tell me is "My grandfather shot his own sister in the potato patch over a piece of land. I guess that's what you're wanting to hear." She shakes her head and laughs at her bloodline, her own destiny. Then she hardens. "You'll be sorry you ever knowed me."

"I'm already sorry," I say, lying. It's how we talk.

Ollie Ve Cook Cox. She married a man named Carpenter, bore a son, but that's all she'll say of that man, and there's no point asking for any more. Later, she married Dallas Cox, from over in Tennessee, so now she's Ollie Ve Cook Cox. Ollie Ve. Say it Ollie *Vay*.

She worries one raw hand into the other.

"Tell me about all of them," I try one last time. "I'll put it in a book. You trust me, don't you?"

She only shakes her head softly. "Son, you ain't mountain. I'm *mountain*. That's all the hell I am and you wouldn't never understand."

She is right. But I will try.

# PART I

# Chapter 1

For me, this is how it started. With a phone call.

"My name is Ashley Cook and I'm calling about Paul's crusher."

The woman spoke rapidly, as if seizing an opportunity that might pass. "I got your name from a lady up on Yellow Mountain."

"Who? Which lady?"

"Beth, I believe it was."

Beth Langstaff? My mind tried to find a reference. Witt Langstaff and his wife had bought the pastureland down the hill from me, below my pond. Beth. Must be Witt's wife, I thought.

"Is everybody okay? Is Witt okay?"

"Well, not everybody." The woman's voice was high and tight, like the first string on a guitar. "Paul pulled a shot over at the rock crusher and it cracked the foundation on our house. We've got a police report on it. I called that lady and she called her husband, who is off somewhere working, and that man said I should call you, because Paul has run all over the mountain, and you being a lawyer . . ." She stopped to regroup. "See, Paul and Richard Whitehead—you probably know him—and James Vance, we call him Nasty, they work for Paul, and he has violated the mining law in ten different ways. At least ten. I haven't counted it up, not yet. Now they want to put in a gravel conveyor that would be on a seventy-nine-foot tower." Ashley Cook's words came out in a torrent, but her tone was clear and her intelligence obvious. Her accent was faint, country, but not overtly *mountain*, and I wondered if she was making an effort to conceal it. She said she was a Cook. I knew the Cooks from up on Little Horse Creek, but she didn't talk quite like

2

them. She sounded as if she had moved away from here and come back, had tried to forget how to talk mountain.

"I heard it," I said.

"Heard what?" She'd gotten tangled up in her own telling.

"When they pulled that shot. When they blew that first chunk out of the mountain."

"Don't you live up on Birchfield Creek somewhere?"

"I live up on the mountain."

"And you heard it all the way up there?"

"Yes."

"That's interesting," she said, as if this were an important part of a puzzle she was piecing together. Now she muffled the receiver and relayed my words to some audience: "He says he heard that shot all the way up on Yellow Mountain!"

Yes, I had heard it. I was working at my desk when the air went wild with an explosion on Belview Mountain. The sound swept up the east slope of Big Yellow and screamed over the house. I sat up. Nearly levitated. One of the dogs, Biscuit, rose from a deep sleep and let loose a fusillade of barks. I expected every tree on the ridge to lie over flat, for feathers to fly from birds, but once the sound passed, everything stood as it had.

"Tell me about the gravel conveyor," I said. I wasn't sure what to make of any of this just yet, but this woman had seized my attention.

She paused. I detected in her tone that she was less than impressed that I did not immediately understand the significance of a seventy-nine-foot conveyor tower.

"Do you want to talk to Aunt Ollie?" she asked suddenly.

I didn't know if I did or not. In my brief moment of consideration, the phone was passed on to Aunt Ollie.

"I hope we're not a-botherin' you," said a new voice, "but, son, we got big trouble, Mr.—"

"You can call me Jay."

"All right, Mr. Jay. We need help. We're killed."

This voice I knew. The Cooks have been rooted in Avery County for as long as history or memory records. They are mountain people. Hard people with birdy faces who live high up on the cold creeks. Either hard drinking or hard churchgoing, the Cooks and Taylors I knew growing up were wraithlike. They grew potatoes and a little bit of corn, cabbage. They hacked at the slopes to try to get the earth to give something back. Some of them carpentered for a living, others worked horses, in timber, and one of them was married to a man who ran a sawmill down below our house when I was a boy. They talked in the singsong trill of the deep hollers. I asked Aunt Ollie how she was kin to my neighbor Stella Thomas, who was born a Cook.

"She's my sister. My half sister. See, my father got married twicet."

"Okay." I had heard that before.

Aunt Ollie took a deep breath. "We're in trouble," she said before pausing. Was she smoking? She might have paused to pull on a cigarette. "We're barely hanging on. Paul's killing us."

"All right. But who is Paul?"

"Oh, Jesus, son!" she exclaimed at my lack of knowledge. "Paul owns that rock crusher over across from my house. He's killing us. You don't know Paul Brown?"

"Paul Brown," I said, scrambling to repair my credibility. "Clark Stone Company. I know of him."

"Well, you're going to know Paul real good before this thing is over. Because he's going to pull that whole mountain down."

"So I hear. What can I do for you?"

"What we need for you to do, if you'll do it, is to come to the county-commissioner meeting. I don't know if we need a lawyer, or a preacher, or a damn undertaker, but Sam Laws has got this thing all lined up the way he wants it. Thing is, doesn't Avery County have a Ridge Law?"

"North Carolina has a Ridge Law," I said. "I don't know about the county."

"Well, if I'd knowed what to do, I'd've already done it." She nearly said *I'd've already did it,* but she corrected herself. I made a note of her efforts in this regard. "We can't get a lawyer because Paul has them all bought off already. He's got a lawyer on a retainer, that's what I heard. Ashley, she's read everything on the books, but Paul don't care one thing about any laws, and he's wanting to get a variance for his conveyor tower and hit seventy-nine feet tall. And the commissioners are all a bunch of damn dogs, some of them anyway. You might know some of them."

"Who is Ashley?" I asked, treading furiously to keep up.

"That's who you were just talking to. Ashley Cook. She's read everything in print and on the Internet, too. All the mining laws they ever passed. She's my niece."

I heard a question raised from beyond her. A son? Husband? Aunt Ollie now relayed the question. "Dallas says, don't a seventy-nine-foot conveyor violate the Ridge Law? We're killed if it don't. *Hayull.*"

"It might."

She drew in her breath again. "Well, I'm honest I don't know what to do. You got to forgive me. I got your name and I told Dallas, that's my husband—everybody calls him Curly on account of his hair, I'm sure you've heard of him—and he said we had to call somebody to do something about this, because Paul, he's coming in here like a Scud missile. And luckily Ashley, she got your name." Aunt Ollie felt the need to explain, for which I was grateful. "Well, what happened was, Dallas asked a man, and he said to call Witt Langstaff from up on Yellow Mountain 'cause he's madder'n hell about Paul. And his wife, Mrs. Langstaff, she said she would have to call him where he was a-workin', and then she called me back and she give me your number. Can you help us?"

# Chapter 2

B ack in the summer of 1999, before I got the call from Ashley and Aunt Ollie, which was the last summer of the twentieth century, I had educated myself on the subject of the Clark Stone Company and their rock crusher. Or I thought I had. I had certainly not put myself on a first-name footing with Paul Brown.

I was working in the garden on a June day, trying to make a warm place where tomatoes would ripen, even at this elevation, when I became aware of the distant snarl of a chain saw. The sound rose and fell with breezes and seemed to race nearer when the air stilled. The pitch dropped and intensified as steel teeth plunged into the hardwood forest, into maple, beech, and oak. It was not unusual to hear a chain saw running. Not in the least. I run my own STIHL saw to cut my firewood, to drop snags and widow-makers, and to clear brush. In early November, when the Christmas-tree harvest begins, you hear chain saws running all over Avery County, all through the mountains. But this was summer. And this sound never seemed to die. All that day, then into the next. And the one after that. Sometimes it was a team of them. More than two. As many as four, from the chorus it formed. This wasn't anybody getting in firewood. Somebody was clearing land down in the valley, or across the gap. A lot of land. Occasionally I felt, as much as heard, the percussive rip of a big tree leaving the canopy and crashing to the forest floor.

The dogs didn't like it. I have a pair of yellow Labrador retrievers, Biscuit and Maggie, mother and daughter. Maggie is oblivious to much that goes on around her, but her mother is another story. While Maggie drowses the day away, until it's time to eat, Biscuit is alert to everything in her broad zone of interest. She was affronted by these damn chain saws. Every few minutes she would lift her pretty square head, aggravated anew, and nearly prepared to defend against something. *What was it?* We set out walking.

Sound plays tricks in thin mountain air. This sound seemed to fall from the sky, seemed to rain, but instinct told me to head down. Witt, who had first put Ashley and Ollie in touch with me, had cut a dozen trees for the cabin he was preparing to build on his place and I'd heard the saws on that day. Maybe he was cutting some more. His pasture was long and steep, one in a series that goes from my house all the way down the east face of Big Yellow Mountain, all the way to the valley floor and the North Toe River.

First I walked through the big, flat meadow by my house, my mother's land, to see if I could see any timber clearing from there. From her land on a summer day I can see almost every west- and north-facing slope for thirty miles. On a clear day, in the winter, the eye travels seventy miles, all the way to the mountains that rise over Asheville, well beyond the Blacks and the Craggies. On this day I saw no fresh clearing, just a million acres of soft, blue mountains. I dove into the cool forest, shedding elevation. Five minutes walking had me near the end of Chestnut Oak Ridge. As I broke out into the clearing of Witt's upper pasture, my eye sought the familiar vales and ridges. Big Haw. Grandfather. Jonas Ridge. A few shiny jewels were set deep into the green, the window glass of vacation houses peering back at the mountain on which I stood, a few granite outcrops, and the orderly rows of Christmas-tree fields, but mostly just treetops. But now, as I took a couple of long steps into the clearing, I saw it, right there, on the nearest-facing ridge, right up under me. There, on Belview Mountain, the green fabric was rent in a terrific diagonal scar across the face of Hartley Ridge. It was so close, so tight up under the flat, that I hadn't seen it from my house, higher on the mountain.

I live in a mature hardwood forest, the most biodiverse temperate forest on the planet. From my house to the backside of Grandfather Mountain, a span of ten miles, a hiker encounters more species of hardwood trees than grow on the entire continent of Europe. In 1898, John Muir, the father of American conservation and the founder of the Sierra Club, came into these mountains. Upon seeing Grandfather Mountain and the surrounding peaks, he famously remarked, "Here is the face of heaven come to earth." Scientists say the cure for cancer will be found in the countless species of fungi here or in the pituitary gland of one of our rare salamanders. One hundred years after the timber companies stripped most of the Southern Appalachians bare building Charlotte and Knoxville and Johnson City, everything they could reach with the technology of the day, the forest has come back with a vengeance. The trees are now, once again, of harvesting size, and the timbermen with their sawmills and skidders are coming back into the region. But we're far from the big roads, nearly forgotten along the Tennessee line, and the saws will get here last.

The scar I now beheld was no regular timber harvest. These days even the least reconstructed timber company leaves a few trees standing, a few per acre, for erosion control, as seed trees. Some even follow Best Management Practices, the protocol promoted by staff here in the Appalachian Ranger District of Pisgah National Forest. Standing where I stood, my gaze fell into a deep orange wound, raw earth. I did the rough calculation for figuring the size of the clearing and came up with about four football fields, or four acres. Roughly. My eye snagged on splintered timber sprawling haphazard in a mess. It suggested the landing path of a downed airliner. And seeing it, my ear registered a new family of sounds in addition to the persistent screech of the saw blades. Add the throaty rumble of dozers. A trackhoe hitting rock and the flutter of a Jake brake.

I stared hard and my mind fastened on the likely explanations. It could be a road, swinging up and across Hartley Ridge, to the summit of Belview Mountain. But I hadn't heard anything about a road project. Where would it go? There was already a road to Newland, the county seat, just down the hill by the river, and if the county wanted to speed the route to town, it would surely widen and pave the Old Toe River Road before building a new one over the heights of Belview. It could go to Mountain Glen, I reasoned, a local golf club on the other side of the Sawdust Holler. But their boundary didn't come over this way, this far south. Did it? It could be a new development of summer homes, either woodsy cottages, or trophy homes for the Charlotteans and Floridians who come to the mountains in waves to escape the heat. Or it might be the path for a powerline. But it looked most like a road. And if it was, it was going to be a big one. But what was the big flat area going to be? A cloverleaf interchange? A clubhouse? A Walmart superstore? The big, shiny kind with a gas station and an auto shop?

After dinner I called Witt at his home down in South Carolina. Though I had known him for some years, and we regularly came upon each other on hikes and on the road we shared, we had never had occasion to speak on the telephone.

"What's up?" he said breezily, possibly wondering why in the world I would be calling.

I reported to him what I had seen from his pasture and was met by a stony silence, then these words: "You've just about ruined my dinner." His voice was flat, understating his concern.

Witt is a consultant and a nature photographer. He runs a small business coaching managers on leadership and teamwork. He earned his degree in forestry, worked for a time in forest management out West, then served as an executive with a paper-products company in South Carolina. But I could never imagine him in an office, in a suit. He was made to climb up and down steep hills. Raised on the other side of the mountains, in East Tennessee, he has spent his life hiking, fishing, and camping. His love of the outdoors has given him the aura of bristling good health, bestowed on him the glow of an extended youth, and provided him a genial disposition. My father raised me with snatches of wisdom including this one: "You'll meet very few assholes on trout streams or walking in the woods." Witt Langstaff proved the dictum.

For ten years he had been buying land below my place, preparing to build a log cabin. While neighborly by nature, he didn't care to have anybody living too close to him. He is not a neighborhood sort of person. So whenever anybody has had land to sell joining one of his boundaries, Witt buys it, eagerly adding to the buffer for his future home. Back when he started putting his piece together, even ten years ago, land around Avery County was cheap. Some of it he got for $800 an acre, some for $1,000, while some of it cost him more.

The prior fall, satisfied he had accumulated sufficient privacy that he would never encounter the smoke from another man's fire, he had made the clearing for a cabin. Trees he felled he sent to the local mill for finishing into flooring and paneling.

It was Witt's habit to string a hammock between two sugar maples and sleep that way as he made plans for his cabin. To make sure the spot felt right. Not a spade in the dirt would he turn until he was certain how the sun poured into the clearing in the morning, exactly where the shade would fall in the afternoon. The view from his place was sweeping, taking in nearly all of Avery County, from Hump Mountain and Beech Mountain around to Grandfather, out to the Linville Gorge, and the weaving spine of the Blue Ridge. Looking down the pasture to the south, Witt could see Squirrel Creek and the Toe River Valley, the waters coursing away toward a meeting with the Cane. Near his camping place, down a faint trail through the woods, he also prepared a "getaway spot," on a shady knoll risen above a crystal springhead. He dug a hole for the cold water to pool, and this served as his refrigerator. Witt was the only guy I knew who drove three hours from home to get to his mountain retreat, then needed almost instantly to dive deeper into the woods for a more perfect sense of solitude. My kind of guy. "It's my getaway from my getaway," he explained.

One evening we sat in front of his campfire and he told me to lie down in the hammock. I did as instructed.

"See?" he said happily.

"See what?"

"You can't see a single electric light!" he exclaimed. And it was true. I looked down the long valley of the Toe River and saw nothing but soft mountains stacked in layers of night shadow.

From the spot he had picked, Witt was insulated from all that was ugly and modern. His consuming passion was to shed the sights and sounds of civilization, the noise and clutter of Hartsville, South Carolina. He traveled for work and wanted a refuge from airports and highways. He had just about made it to his place of perfect solitude. But now here was this construction project I was telling him about. A massive earthmoving effort on the nearest ridge to his pasture, a potential resort development. Either that or a road or an airport. A Walmart superstore.

He tossed around the options. "It's got to be a development. You think it's a resort?"

"Probably. I don't know. There's a big flat area."

"How big?" he pressed, hoping that it wouldn't be too big.

I couldn't lie. "Real big. Four football fields. Roughly."

"Can you find out what it is and let me know? I can't get up there until next week."

"I can try."


My education had begun innocently enough. Before the call from Ashley, before I knew anything of gravel conveyors and county commissioners and variances, I had chased down a few suspicions and worries on my own. If you want to know anything around here, in this part of the Toe River Valley, in the little settlement everybody calls Dog Town, you ask our postmistress, Louise Buchanan. Louise is a Vance, who married a Buchanan, which means she is kin to almost everybody between Big Horse Creek and Little Horse Creek. Kin to the Youngs and the Tatums and the Hughes. Which is to say, practically all the two-legged folks you're likely to meet.

So I went to see Louise. After collecting my mail, and picking some squash out of the box she filled daily with the excess from her summer garden, I turned to my great concern. "What's that up on the hill, Miss Louise? Are they putting in a truck yard?"

"On the hill?"

"Up on Belview." I nodded up the road, toward Cranberry Gap.

"Aw, that?" she sang in her Dog Town swing. "Son, that's Clark

Stone's rock crusher." She reported this news without emphasis, as if it were any other piece of news handed out in the course of her day.

I adopted her sense of ease over the news, outwardly. But her words went right through me. *A rock crusher.*

I had been hearing about the crusher for a while, a reference dropped into casual conversation in the grocery store, or in town—Paul Brown was putting it in Sawdust Holler, or he was putting it down near the old iron mine. I had heard a man at the hardware store lament, "They give Paul *pyore hayull* over his crusher down at Cranberry. They run him off." But I was loath to confess I didn't know what a rock crusher was, exactly. I assumed it was a machine for processing river stone for the construction trade. With a boom in building on the other side of the county, around the resorts in Linville and Banner Elk, the roads had become littered with small-time sellers of rock for retaining walls and chimneys. A lot of that rock came out of the rivers. I had seen rock hoppers, big metal bins used for separating small rocks from big, smooth from ragged, down by the North Toe River in Plumtree and on down to Spruce Pine. But that didn't sound like "crushing" to me. It sounded more like *sorting.* Plus, the clearing on Belview was high up on the hill, not down by the river. Clark Stone's *rock crusher.* That's what Louise said.

I decided to ask for a little more information. "When you say rock crusher—"

"They say that's going to be the biggest surface mine in western North Carolina. Right here in little old Dog Town!" Louise marveled over the long odds of it.

I called Witt.


I made it my business to learn all I could about rock crushing, mining, and all I could about Clark Stone Company. And Mr. Paul Brown, too.

Mr. Brown came from a line of prominent community leaders in Watauga County, the neighboring county to ours. His family ran a prosperous country store and gas station in Cove Creek. Paul excelled at business, but he had a rough edge. Still, over the years, he had turned out to be an enterprising chamber-of-commerce type. He turned unimproved land into a paving business and a shopping mall. He developed a golf course across the state line in Tennessee. Word was, he was sitting on thousands of acres of raw land on Stone Mountain. Ask anybody in this corner of the state and he or she will tell you that Paul Brown is the richest man in the mountains, or maybe even west of Winston-Salem, all the way to the middle of Tennessee. Nobody can name anybody richer, and they have tried. So they say.

In addition to all his other business interests, Brown had, since 1986, owned Clark Stone Company, Avery County's local gravel quarry, which for decades sat on a small mountain near Linville, on the other side of the county from where I live. When he bought Clark Stone and their mining equipment, Brown took over a thirty-acre permit to mine gravel. There his crew drilled, blasted, and crushed granite into gravel for construction bond, eating away at the upper reaches of the mountain. And for most of those years, he did so in utter anonymity.

Linville, with its bark-sided cottages and rustic summer estates, is a sylvan hamlet of old Southern money. Its reason for being is peace and quiet, a cool salve for the spirit for those escaping the heat and thrum of city life. Paul Brown's mining operation, while nearby, was situated on a west-facing slope, angling away from the forested pocket of Linville, and had therefore caused little impact on its neighbors. Except for the periodic rumbling of gravel trucks, and the abundance of rock dust that sometimes hung in the air, most Linvillians paid Paul Brown little mind. But as the county grew, the need for rock grew, and the truck traffic grew, too. As the work at the quarry sped up, alarms went up in Linville and other nearby towns, Montezuma and Pineola. Suddenly having a quarry so nearby seemed a hindrance to the good life.

Controversy flared in 1993 when the Linville folks succeeded in having the mighty state Department of Transportation construct a $4 million bypass to steer truck traffic away from their lodge and golf course. Word was, the gravel trucks and the increase in heavy-construction traffic was playing hell with putts and drives on the golf course and spoiling the bridge games and lunches on the mossy patios of the Linvillians.

Political pressure was applied in all the right places down in Raleigh, the distant state capital, and the shiny new bypass was carved through a dense forest on the far side of a ridge, at a blessed remove from the nearest wicker chaise.

After the bypass boondoggle faded from memory, Paul continued doing a good business. Linville itself had changed little over the years, but all around it, the eastern side of Avery County was experiencing explosive growth. Now, the county leaders had a grand project in mind, one that would impact Paul Brown and change the fabric of the county forever. A project that would put Paul and Ollie Cox—and me—on a collision course.

For years, when the summer residents of Linville and the members of the Grandfather Mountain Golf and Country Club fell ill, they traveled home, to Charlotte or Birmingham or Savannah to seek care, preferring the long journey to a dose of local medicine. But more and more, the summer residents were stretching "the season" into October, even November. Some installed baseboard heaters in the big, drafty cottages. They started coming up in May and staying on through Thanksgiving.

All around Linville the ridges began sprouting expensive vacation homes built by a different kind of retiree. Florida license tags are a familiar site on the Blue Ridge Parkway and throughout the North Carolina mountains. A Realtor friend explains, "The Yankees who could afford it all went to Florida in the 1970s. But it is too hot in the summer in Boca Raton and they miss the change of seasons, so everybody that can afford a summerhouse heads north in June. But they never make it all the way back home to New Jersey and Connecticut. They like North Carolina because it's only halfway back to where they came from." These *half-backs* seemed to have unlimited supplies of cash for their second and third homes. Brassy new developers set up in local courthouses to search the titles on large tracts. They deployed massive grading equipment to carve roads and golf fairways out of the tops of mountains that had lain unmolested for a billion years. They ran ads in the *Wall Street Journal* and the *Miami Herald* touting views of unspoiled scenery, even as they spoiled the very scenery they boasted of. Gates went up down by the main roads, all framed with stonework and manicured plantings. A strange affection for artificial waterfalls expressed itself in many forms, each more elaborate and expensive than the last.

The entreaties, the comely invitations, worked. People came as if on a tide, plunking down cold cash for million-dollar fairway homes and Italianate castles perched on rock cliffs.

I try to imagine their reaction to their new surroundings. Avery County has always lagged the rest of the state in personal income in a region that has always lagged the nation. It has been, since European settlement began in the 1700s, a hardscrabble land of subsistence farming and insularity. Lyndon Johnson famously used images of Appalachia to highlight his War on Poverty, so stark were the scenes of deprivation. Barefoot children stirring dirt, frigid winds tearing at all that was ramshackle, hungry-eyed women and long-faced men staring darkly at the camera. In the last decades of the twentieth century Appalachia's fortunes had risen a little, with better health care and expanded services to the poor and universal electrification, and some of its people had moved out of the tacked-together houses and into the crisp modernity of mobile homes. Others had turned land into money by entering the profitable Christmas-tree and shrubbery industry. But mostly the region was still poor. Outside the resort areas, Avery County was. The high-school-dropout rate was high. Teenage pregnancy, illiteracy, and other markers of poverty were stubborn and more or less unchanged by the War on Poverty and other plans to lift people up. Old refrigerators, sofas, and mattresses tumbled down the slopes into the county's main drainage, the Toe River. I have cast trout flies around tires, dishwashers, and discarded cinder blocks in streams that are otherwise heartbreakingly lovely. The stereotypes of Appalachia—ignorance, slovenliness, violence—are unfair, and overplayed, but they are not wholly baseless, either.

Louise Buchanan reflected the general view of the native-born when the subject of newcomers came up. "They aren't here for five minutes before they start complaining about how we've done this or that, or how we've not done it right. Well, what did they come in here for if they don't like it?"

The affluent newcomers to Avery County liked the long-distance views, and the relief from the sweltering heat in the rest of the South, but found nearly everything else to be lacking. They found the local grocery store dirty and understocked. They thought the local builders and service people were slow, functioning on "mountain time." The local police were colorful, charming in a backward sort of way, but ineffective and unsophisticated.

Perhaps most alarming, they found the two local hospitals to be staffed with—of all things—people who talked like and even looked like *mountain people.* Mountain people were fine for bulldozing roads, and placing rocks in artificial waterfalls, but possibly not for dispensing pills and drawing blood. So a group of go-getters who had accomplished a great many things in the places they came from decided something had to be done to address the deficiencies in their Appalachian retreat. First the hospital facilities—and the staff—were subtly derided as "underperforming" and "in need of attention" by the folks who evaluate such things in preparation for change. After all, the doctors and nurses had degrees from schools the civic-minded newcomers had never heard of. Of course there was a grain of truth to all they said. Some real needs were not being met in addition to the perceived shortcomings. The county had no dialysis center, no orthopedic surgeon to repair broken hips, no cardiac-care unit. So the clamor for a new hospital with state-of-the-art facilities grew. Soon a Hospital Corporation Board was formed and $20 million was raised at cocktail receptions and black-tie parties on the eastern side of the county.

What did all this have to do with Clark Stone Company and Paul Brown and Ollie Cox? In midsummer of 1996, the Linville Resorts company notified Brown that his lease at the Linville mine site would not be renewed. The site of the Linville quarry would instead soon be home to a new multimillion-dollar, state-of-the-art acute-care hospital. Where rock had long been crushed, wounds would now be bound up, arteries repaired, joints replaced.

As the planning for the new hospital took shape, Clark Stone's drag-lines and weight scales and drilling equipment came down the little unnamed mountain. The foreman's trailer, the front-end loader, the hoppers and screens, were piled on lowboys and inched down the steep slope. It all had to go to make way for the parking lots and splashy examining rooms and the wellness center. For the spacious lobby with upholstered furniture and coffee tables fluffed with copies of *Architectural Digest.*

And Paul Brown went hunting a new source of rock.

One of the fundamental truths of every county in every part of the country is that he who controls the gravel supply, the road bond, wields enormous political power. Rock. Granite for gravel. I had given it little thought, but crushed stone is central to much of what we do in modern society. It is spun into asphalt for road improvements, it is used in ditching, erosion control, and parking-lot construction. Stream-bank restoration. Gravel is laid down for house foundations. It all starts with a quarry dug out of the ground, and without it life as we know it would grind to a swift, muddy halt. So when Paul headed out of Linville looking for a new quarry site, he went with best wishes from the county leadership and the people who make things go.

Paul's first stop in his search for good rock was ten road miles away, to the west, in Cranberry. Population, not many. This side of the county, the side hugging the Tennessee line, had not seen the development pressure that the Linville area had. No resorts sprung up near the Tennessee line. No timber-peg mansions loom over golf fairways in Carpenter's Bottom or Gooseneck or Lick Log. No grocery stores or video-rental stores in Dog Town. No stores at all, really. This side of the county was still a place of vast forested tracts of land, some of it owned by the US Forest Service, some owned by conservation organizations seeking to protect the rare ecosystems and globally significant biodiversity of the towering mountains. And it is still home to the rarest breed of all: the mountain people, the nearly forgotten folk whose ancestors built simple homes out of lumber they milled themselves.

Homes that still stand, rickety but proud, perched above the creeks that tumble off the slopes. Home to the Cooks and the Taylors and the Vances. And home to me, too.

The little town of Cranberry had seen mining before. Magnetite, the magnetic mineral used in compasses and to line steam boilers, was first discovered at the base of Hump Mountain in 1789. During the Civil War a twenty-two-mile-long vein of iron ore was discovered running from the North Toe River all the way to the base of Roan Mountain, deep into the Tennessee country. The Confederacy mined the seam furiously between 1861 and 1865, as matériel for the war was in great demand. Miners tunneled into the seam using steam-powered drills and handlines.

When I was a boy, a trip to the open throat of the Cranberry Iron Mine was filled with fear of the unknown. There wasn't anybody around; the old equipment lay twisted and rusting, a ruin set back off the main road. A friend and I would go down there to hunt ball bearings, each as precious to us as a bolus of sterling. We expected to find bodies in the caverns or, more thrilling yet, a last Confederate deserter holed up, living on newts and buckeyes, or a rogue band of Cherokee, hiding from the government. The more realistic possibility was coming upon a bootlegger making white lightning, hiding his cooker from the sheriff.

Upon vacating the Linville site, Paul intended to set up his crusher at the entrance to the old Cranberry Mine and pull the mountain down around it. But there were two problems with this plan. For one thing, few people in the little settlement of Cranberry wanted to live near the dust and noise of a rock crusher. Mountain people, it turned out, didn't like the prospect of a parade of gravel trucks and earthmoving equipment rumbling past their homes any more than the golfy set in Linville did. They didn't want their dinners, their naps, and their Wednesday-evening church services interrupted by blasting and raining earth.

Their sentimental attachment to peace and quiet was a thin defense in the face of progress and the economic might of Paul and his crusher. With the full blessing of the county leadership, Clark Stone Company started moving equipment into Cranberry and made preparations to tear into the granite runs. But the good people of the little crossroads town didn't roll over. They spoke out in their churches. They wrote letters to the editor. They contacted the state Division of Land Resources in the Department of Environment and Natural Resources to complain about the noise and the dust that would be visited upon their pleasant way of life, and they raised alarms over water supplies that would surely be disrupted by the blasting of granite and the copious amounts of groundwater required for the washing of rock. But fights with mining companies generally all end the same way, from the Appalachians to the Ozarks to the banks of the Bighorn. Letters to the editor opposing the mine were met head-on by letters from those who supported it, those who wanted the jobs. Those who saw progress in the form of more and better roads. And the community leaders were squarely for it, for they were no worse and no better than community leaders everywhere else who worship at the altar of expanding tax bases. They were business-minded adherents of the notion that it is our manifest destiny to cover every inch of this good green earth with taxable assets, subdivisions and shopping centers—the man-made. All of which require an unending supply of crushed rock.

The second problem with Paul's plan was buried deep in the North Carolina General Statutes, in the Mining Act of 1971. The act sets up certain guidelines for the permitting of mining operations. It calls for different agencies of the state to evaluate proposals before issuance of permits to ensure that mining operations will not, for example, cause undue disruption to a school or damage a site of archaeological significance. The act calls for a series of public hearings where concerns may be raised. Hospitals get special protection, as do streams and publicly owned parklands. The statute has no protections against truck noise. Loss of property value and peace-and-quiet get no mention at all. But some animals do. In the case of the Cranberry Iron Mine site, Paul had the exceptional bad fortune to run into a protected class of critter: the Virginia big-eared bat. The tiny flying mammal is known to roost in two places in Avery County: high atop the granite peaks of Grandfather Mountain, and deep in the abandoned tunnels of the old Cranberry Iron Mine. So rare is the diminutive creature that in 1994 it was granted protection under the federal Endangered Species Act.

The fight brewing over the proposed operation at Cranberry came to an abrupt end with surprise winners: the Cranberrians and a little airborne member of the order Chiroptera measuring about four inches long and weighing in at 0.4 ounces.

Seeing he was licked, Paul loaded up his equipment and put Cranberry in the rearview mirror. I did not see him go, cannot say that I paid an awful lot of attention to the battle over the Cranberry Mine, except to say that I am generally comforted when local efforts to beat back powerful outside forces succeed. I did not know Paul Brown or any of his crew, but I imagine them defiant and annoyed as the equipment was readied to haul off the site. Done in by a bat and a small band of hardheads and nature lovers who failed to appreciate the value of crushed stone.

Sometime in 1998 Paul's convoy of steel hoppers and grinding heads, and trusses and belts, rumbled five miles up the hill to the north side of Cranberry Gap, to the mouth of the Sawdust Holler. Here the procession made a sharp left turn up an old logging road. Up the faint way the circus train of crushing equipment went, up along the banks of Cranberry Creek.

A pristine tumble, Cranberry Creek is high enough up the mountain to hold the frigid water that supports the rare *Salvelinus fontinalis,* the native speckled trout—which isn't a trout at all, but an arctic char, left behind when the Wisconsin ice sheet retreated northward twelve thousand years ago. These headwater streams in their undisturbed state are increasingly rare in the South as development and timbering warm the waters by letting sunlight fall on the forest floor, leaving ever more creeks unable to support the imperiled speckleds. But Cranberry Creek was still wild, still cold. Here Paul's crew began clearing land, making preparations for his second go at relocation.

Mining in North Carolina is defined as *the breaking of the surface soil in order to facilitate or accomplish the extraction or removal of minerals, ores, or solid matter.* The law requires a mining permit from the Division of Land Resources *before* the surface of the soil can be broken. But Paul didn't apply for a mining permit in Sawdust Holler. He just started clearing land, started digging, started *mining.*

When the state officials who regulate such activity found out what Paul was doing, probably alerted by some concerned neighbor or an alarmed trout fisherman, they paid a visit to the Sawdust site. What they found was cause for concern indeed. Paul's crew had built his haul road right up the creek bed. Not up along the creek, and not across the creek. *Up the creek bed.* They had steered a four-ton grader into the waters of a designated trout stream and pushed the very waters out of the way. The report showed more damage farther up the creek. There the crew had cleared—"disturbed"—2.2 acres of land, or roughly two football fields' worth. All of this without obtaining, or even seeking, a permit to mine.

The inspectors evaluating the Sawdust Holler site were properly horrified, as horrified, anyway, as state officials in the Division of Land Resources get. After conducting a review, the state authorities issued a Notice of Violation. Clark Stone Company was instructed thusly: "Immediately halt the above mentioned mining operation until you have obtained a valid permit from this Department." Paul was informed that the fine for mining without a permit was $5,000 a day, just in case he wanted to press his luck. This was tough stuff, the long regulatory arm of the state reaching way up into a dark holler in Avery County to enforce a rule drafted over 200 miles away in Raleigh.

Rather than simply apply for a permit at the Sawdust site, Paul moved on yet again. No one has said why. Was there little rock up that holler? Was Paul spooked by the presence of the sainted brook trout? I do not know. I only know that he left in a hurry and that he wasted little time in his hunt for yet another place to set up his crusher.

This time he did not go far. He moved his equipment farther up the main road, deeper into the back country, to the site I saw from Witt's pasture. Here was 151 acres of lush hardwood forest long owned by Robert Putnam, a Floridian.

Paul negotiated a lease with Putnam for a term of ninety-nine years. That was a start. But because Putnam's land did not have any frontage on the paved road, Highway 19E, there was no way to get the rock down from the mountain to the buyer, and there was no way even to move the equipment onto the leased parcel. Then, in November of 1999, Paul put down earnest money to buy twenty-five acres of road frontage from Charles Smith. Deed stamps show that Paul paid Smith $225,000 for the tract, a figure that alarmed those familiar with the local real estate market. Land on this side of the county more commonly went for $2,000 an acre. Maybe $3,000 if it had a long-range view or a bold stream with trout. Not *ten*. And this just for an access road. Looking back, this seems a gesture of desperation. Paul was eager, maybe frantic, to get working.

Upon securing access that winter, the Clark Stone crew began constructing a haul road. This haul road traversed the Smith tract and snaked up the mountain to the Putnam tract. Such a hurry was Paul in, though, that he neglected to apply for a Department of Transportation Driveway Connecting Permit to tie into a US roadway, as required by law.

By late spring, the crew had cleared the large flat area I had come to know, the processing area, and started reassembling the crushing equipment there. They pulled the first shot of dynamite to make a spot to set the primary crusher jaw, an area several times the size of my house. Despite the earlier brushes with agency authority in Cranberry and in Sawdust Holler, Paul's operation still functioned very much on his terms. At the time they began construction of the plant equipment, in addition to lacking a Driveway Connecting Permit, there is no record of Clark Stone having received, or even having applied for, an Avery County building permit.

Paul had learned one thing from his experiences at the old Cranberry Mine site and up in Sawdust Holler, though. Or at least someone in his operation had. On March 1, 1999, Clark Stone company submitted to the state's Division of Land Resources an eighty-one-page application seeking a mining permit to break the surface soil in pursuit of minerals on a 151-acre site. In pursuit of rock. The application was signed by Paul Brown and by his surveyor and engineer, Randy Carpenter. On May 14 the Division of Land Resources sent Paul a letter notifying him that his application had been found to meet the requirements of the Mining Act. Clark Stone Company was thereby issued permit number 06-09. At last Paul had his green light, his license to crush rock, his permit to tear into the broad granite shoulders of Belview Mountain.

## Chapter 3

I don't take a newspaper—there is no delivery up Birchfield Creek and I get my news from the radio—so if Ollie had not told me about the County Commission meeting, I would not have known anything about it. But now I was excited by the prospect. The unfolding of Paul's fate was a spectacle I intended to witness, and, if at all possible, to steer.

Most states have "bad actor" provisions on the books. The bad actor provisions are meant to identify serial offenders of permit conditions and environmental regulations. After running afoul of the Virginia big-eared bat and the violations in Sawdust Holler, it looked as if Paul might be pushing his luck yet again. Was he in danger of becoming a bad actor in the eyes of the state's regulators? Ollie Cox said something on the phone about having pictures of the seventy-nine-foot conveyor structure. Was it possible that Paul was now violating North Carolina's Mountain Ridge Protection Act with his plant equipment? And if he was, surely the county or the state would move to stop him, I reasoned.

I made my way through the short hallways of the county's new Courthouse Annex. Everybody in the building was wet from a downpour, and the smell of puddles on vinyl tile and damp cotton clinging to flesh mixed in an unfortunate aromatic slurry with the cloying pine-cleaner scent typical of public buildings. I turned the corner at the entrance of the meeting room and came face-to-face with my team. Before me stood Ashley, Ollie, Dallas, and Freddy. The first one I noticed, the one I could not look away from, was Ollie. I could have picked her out of a lineup as a Cook. She was pure Little Horse Creek. Kin to Ollises and Taylors. Sharp, bold features, trim and fierce, with straight platinum hair. A woman of fifty years. Or sixty. It was hard to say. Her green, ankle-length slicker dripped water on the floor. She stepped forward, a leader. "I'm Ollie Cox," she said apologetically. "And this is my family. What a damn mess."

I introduced myself and was immediately drawn into a whispered chorus of confidential information. They put documents and photographs into my hands. They laid out violations of the Mining Act, specific allegations, in lurid detail. Something about burning down houses without a burn permit. Pulling a shot without a seismograph on-site. The part about building a haul road "without any say-so from the Department of Transportation." All the information flew into my head and swirled around with the hard facts I already knew.

Today's meeting, Freddy said, might be a sham, with Sam Laws, the chair of the commission, pulling the strings and up to his old tricks.

"That's Sam," Freddy said brightly, as if the threat presented by Paul and his allies was both predictable and in some way delicious.

Who was Freddy? I wondered. How did he fit into this family unit? Oh, yes. Ollie's son. Ashley's cousin.

I had asked a local attorney to join me. I have a law degree, as I'd told Ollie, or Ashley, one of them, but I was not admitted to the bar and did not practice. I wanted the insight of a qualified practicing attorney. I introduced Bill Cocke to the others I had only just met myself. They knew him, by reputation, though he didn't know them.

Ollie looked to me. "You do the talking," she said. "I can't say nothing to the commissioners. I'm already killed."

Dallas, Ollie's husband, shook his head over his wife. "You've not ever had the least trouble getting your words out, Ollie, by God."

"What should I say?" she implored.

I didn't have any idea. "Talk about your foundation," I said.

She started to tell me all about the house they were building across the road from the mine site. When Paul's crew pulled the big shot, the first blast, to set the primary crusher jaw in a notch in the mountain, Ollie said it moved all the ground around their new house, putting a crack in the foundation. She was talking about the same shot I'd heard from my house. The one that sat me up and so tormented Biscuit.

Freddy wanted to round out my understanding. "And they pulled that shot without a seismograph on-site like they were supposed to. It's all in the Mining Act. You can ask Ashley."

"Don't tell me," I said, overwhelmed and impressed at the flurry of accusations. "Tell the commissioners."

"They weren't going to let you speak," Ashley said breathlessly. "I signed you up. They tried to cancel the whole meeting, they were going to go into secret session, on account of Richard. That's what they always do. But I raised hell on them. I hope I spelled your name right."

Ashley. I turned my attention to Ollie's niece. She was the one who'd called me on the telephone. But how could this be her? This was a child. Thirteen? Fourteen? Was this the same woman on the telephone, the one who knew everything there was to know about the Mining Act? And who was Richard?

Now Dallas answered one of my questions. "Son, Ashley knows this thing up and down." He clasped a big hand on the girl's shoulder. "You got any questions on Paul, on Sawdust, on anything, you just ask her. She told me we had to have the World Wide Web put into the house, and now she looks at that thing all day long. She's one of those child geniuses. Oh, and you can call me Curly."

Ashley beamed, proud. She cocked her hip and tore into a series of violations of the Mining Act committed by Paul Brown. "Do you know who Bill Beck is?" she asked me.

"No."

"Well, he's out of the Asheville office, with the state, they call it the ARO for Asheville Regional Office. And we have evidence on him."

"I'd say he's been paid off," said Freddy, who appeared to be scanning the hallway behind me, distracted. "That's what they typically do. Pay everybody off so they don't have any trouble."

"There's no telling how much money Paul has paid the people down in Raleigh," Ashley said. "Listen, Aunt Ollie took a picture of Bill Beck standing by Paul's Jeep, and then he got into the Jeep and rode up on the hill with him." When I did not immediately respond to this rock-solid indictment, she pressed me. "What do you make of that?" A furious search for a photo of Bill Beck with Paul ensued. They rifled through a three-inch stack of snapshots. "Do you think state officials should be riding around with the owner of a mine when they are supposed to be inspecting the mine for violations?" When I did not offer an immediate reply, Ashley answered her own question: "I don't. Oh, and we take pictures of everything."

Ashley laughed now, as if to confess that this was all a little bit weird.

"Okay" was all I could say. I was still swimming hard, trying to catch up.

"That's when Paul buys them off, Ashley," Freddy said. "He can't give them their salary out in broad daylight. It wouldn't look right, so they just hop in the car together and then Paul starts passing out the big denominations."

Freddy was joking. Sort of. If this speculation was the best we had, it didn't seem very convincing to me.

We went in and sat.

Just before the meeting began, I went up to the county manager to make sure I was on the speaking list. Don Baker wore an expression of boredom and fatigue common to public officials. He had spent too much time under fluorescent lights, in meetings.

"You going to get to everybody today?" I said with exceedingly good cheer.

"I don't know if we will. With all this press."

I looked around. The meeting room did seem surprisingly full. "What's going on?"

The county manager stared in disbelief. Was I really so dumb? "Sheriff."

I had forgotten. Our sheriff, Richard Buchanan, had just been indicted on charges that ranged from stealing from prisoners to discharging his firearm into an occupied vehicle. The State Bureau of Investigation was crawling all over the county. Word was that the FBI was coming in, too. Press crews from Winston-Salem and Asheville and Charlotte had picked up the scent, more hillbilly doings up in Avery County, and they were packing in to gawk at the spectacle.

"I'd like to speak on the Putnam Mine," I said.

"The what?" Mr. Baker asked blankly.

"The Putnam Mine. Paul Brown."

Baker looked at me coolly. "Well, let your conscience be your guide." An unmistakable note of warning was in his remark, an invitation delivered as a threat.

"I intend to."

Sam Laws was a perennial officeholder. He was always either sitting as a commissioner or gearing up for another run. The narrow roads of the county were plastered with old and new signs proclaiming his willingness to serve the people. I had already picked up from my new best friends that Sam Laws was not for us. Rather he was against us. Also that he was Dallas's boss, which made this whole matter pretty ugly.

After a prayer, in which a commissioner implored our Lord and Savior Jesus Christ to grant the commissioners wisdom, and an offering of humble thanks for the privilege of living in these beautiful mountains that our Lord made with His own two hands, the chair made a motion that the discussion concerning Sheriff Richard Buchanan be held in a separate session. The motion was seconded hungrily, by more than one commissioner, and the meeting proceeded with issues more mundane: salary disputes and tax receipts and the HVAC system at the elementary school. The press groaned, and some members of that august estate packed their notebooks and cameras and made to leave.

When it was my turn to speak—during the designated time on the agenda for "public speaking"—I approached the podium to address the commissioners. Chairman Laws sat up in his chair and tipped himself forward when I spoke, the better to hear. I talked about the nuisance the mine would create. How I woke up every morning to the sound of drills, and backup beepers, and the falling of trees. How you could see the excavation from everywhere you went around Dog Town, my side of the county, and up on the mountaintops.

"I'm not getting you," said the chairman. He rubbed his ear with a pawlike hand, as if he had a burr in it. I had succeeded only in boring him with my inconsequential concerns. He chatted with another commissioner as I took another swing.

I explained how the Appalachian Trail crosses Hump Mountain, how the treeless mountaintop openings, the grassy "balds" unique to the area, afford views of three states, how the Trail's course ensured a hiker would travel directly toward the Putnam Mine for a mile or more, and how the sounds of the drilling and crushing would destroy the experience of being in that place. Laws appeared not to hear me so I picked another, more sympathetic-seeming commissioner and I pressed on, speaking only to her. I spoke of how the damage to Belview Mountain, as visible as it was, would reflect poorly on the county and the state. I wrapped up by noting my concern that a seventy-nine-foot conveyor tower would not only spoil the scenery from the Appalachian Trail, it might, possibly, violate the Mountain Ridge Protection Act, which was enacted to protect the state's prized scenic vistas.

The commissioners sat in stultified silence. Phyllis Forbes made a note in her notepad. Jake Owens seemed to chew on something. Gum?

"Did you say th'Appalachian Trail?" Sam Laws said suddenly.

"Yes, sir," I replied, jolted to attention.

"Well, I don't know anything about th'Appalachian Trail," he declared, demonstrably pleased with his ignorance of the subject. "And we cain't do nothing about that anyways." His voice came out of him as an affronted squeal, forced perhaps through a tight passage, and coming out of a man of his considerable girth, the effect was alarming. As if he were putting me on.

He unfolded his hands and scratched something out on a sheet of paper that was on the table before him. And that was that.

He scanned the agenda and asked, "Any more public speakers?" I was done.

Ollie rose next. "I would like to publicly—," she said, halting before completing her request. She was nervous. She was, after all, addressing her husband's boss. She was unfailingly polite as she described the damage to her foundation and the strain Paul had put her family under. I noticed that she looked mostly at the floor as she spoke, as if ashamed of having to do what she was called to do. As if this were a spectacle she wanted no part of.

But she continued, "We can't sleep, and Ashley, she's about got asthma, and now we've got rock dust in our water from all the drilling. I think that blast may have ruined our water for good."

Commissioner Laws, our longtime community leader, and serial candidate, was wholly unimpressed. "We sure do thank all you people for coming today," he said, dismissing us. "We like to hear what our citizens have to say, don't we?" He polled his fellow commissioners, all of whom nodded agreement. Still, our time was up, and the matter closed.

Or nearly so.

After the meeting, a reporter found me in the hallway. I was speaking with Doug Hall, the county attorney, and Bill Cocke. Doug Hall was underlining, with a yellow highlighter, a passage from the county ordinances for lawyer Cocke. "If you wanted to sue the county, on the crusher, you might want to cite this," Hall said, turning the passage bright gold with the damp instrument. I read over his shoulder. The passage read in part, *Inappropriately located and/or designed tall structures detract from the scenic environment and threaten the economic welfare or certain businesses and adjacent property values.* Then Doug Hall stunned me. "I think you might have a decent lawsuit on your hands," he said. It was a purely strange moment, being led by the nose to the grounds for a lawsuit by the lawyer who would have to defend the county should such a lawsuit eventuate.

I was still trying to process that exchange when I turned to meet Scott Nicholson, a reporter with the *Mountain Times,* a Boone newspaper.

"What were you saying in there, about the Appalachian Trail?" he asked. "What mine did you mean?" A smallish guy with a stringy beard and an academic bearing, he looked like a learned fiddle player. He was preparing to jot notes.

I repeated what I said in the meeting, but, sensing Scott's interest, I warmed to the subject. Suddenly, I was a defender of the Appalachian Trail, of Trail values and the sanctity of public lands. I was taken aback because I thought the Mountain Ridge Protection Act would be our hook, would draw notice to our grievance, if, indeed, there was to be a hook and a grievance. After all, Avery County is where the Ridge Law was born. In 1983 a developer had built a ten-story condominium tower atop Sugar Mountain, much to the horror of nearly everyone whose eyes were unlucky enough to land upon it, which is to say nearly everyone not encumbered by macular degeneration, glaucoma, or outright blindness. It was visible from everywhere in the county. From every pretty place. It loomed up over the lovely forested slopes like, well, like a massive concrete condominium tower. It was an unwelcome addition to the otherwise pristine viewshed, a dog turd in the middle of a flower bed. Local people who were already disgusted by the explosive growth in the resort industry, the traffic, the aggressive newcomers crowding the aisles of the grocery stores, were now enraged at the sight of this monument to greed. Likewise the tourists themselves, some of whom had driven hundreds of miles to climb Grandfather Mountain to take in the famous views, or those who roamed the peaks of the Roan Highlands, were dismayed to confront, among the soaring ridges, the detestable sight. Bumper stickers blared STOP SUGAR TOP and even the more aggressive DROP SUGAR TOP. Even as the construction crews were erecting it, people of goodwill raced to the NC General Assembly and demanded legislation to keep such an affront to the sensibilities from ever occurring again. The landmark bill limits construction of buildings over forty feet tall from high-elevation ridges. Since that day, claiming a Ridge Law violation was usually sufficient to set off alarm bells and draw press attention. But Scott Nicholson wasn't asking questions about the Ridge Law.

"What do you want to know?" I asked.

"Tell me everything about it," he said. "There's a story in here somewhere."

The interest Scott Nicholson showed did something to me. A cog turned in my mind. The Appalachian Trail ran across Hump Mountain, just a steep climb up the slope from Ollie's house. I had not thought of the issue in quite this way before, but I got a warm glow inside when I realized that topography had blessed my new friends with a pretty powerful backyard neighbor: a unit of the National Park Service, possibly the most famous footpath in the world.

Every year thousands of hopeful souls throw fifty to seventy pounds of gear on their backs and start walking from Georgia to Maine. They follow in the footsteps of a visionary urban planner named Benton MacKaye, who foresaw the end of wild forestlands in the eastern United States. In 1921 MacKaye wrote an article titled "An Appalachian Trail: A Project in Regional Planning." In it he proposed creation of a trail where suburbanites in a crowded nation could escape to the woods for a day or for several months for a wilderness walk. For decades the Trail existed informally, as shorter paths were knit together, linking parklands and remote ridges, often crossing private land where landowners gave assent. Trail clubs were formed and a conference was convened to oversee the ambitious plans to acquire sufficient land and build the trail-bed along the way.

In our neck of the woods the planners for the Trail and the local trail club had worked since the 1950s to secure a route across the stunning grassy balds of the Highlands of Roan.

The existence of grassy balds is a puzzle. Well below the elevation of the tree line, grassy balds are treeless expanses on the summits of some mountains. A number of theories seek to explain them. The one with the most currency among scientists of our era is Peter Weigl's megaherbivore theory. In short, Dr. Weigl, and his colleague Travis Knowles, propose that the balds are treeless because of grazing by woolly mammoths, bison, elk, and, eventually, cattle. The balds were likely opened by some disturbance, wind and ice or forest die-off, then kept open by grazers. There is no evidence that Native Americans or European settlers opened the balds on purpose, as some have posited. Nor is there any real evidence of fire in the landscape, though lightning strikes are common. The elevation band from four thousand to six thousand feet in the Southern Appalachians is a moist place indeed, and that probably rules out fire as a major factor in the creation of grassy balds. While we cannot know for certain how the balds first formed, ample evidence suggests that they have been bald for a long time. Soil builds relatively quickly in grasslands, rather slowly in forests, and depth tests indicate that the soils on the Southern Appalachian grassy balds are considerably deeper than the soils in the forest just off the edge of the mountaintops.

The best evidence that the balds have been bald for a long time—at least since the end of the last ice age—lies in the inventory of plant life found in the openings. Arctic plants—cinquefoil and oat grass—persist on some balds to this day. These northern plants would have arrived in these locations ahead of the Wisconsin ice sheet, which moved down as far south as Pennsylvania between 2 million and 12,000 years ago. Plants such as these do not travel quickly. They would have moved ahead of the advancing glaciers and thrived in the frigid-air regime. They would likely have been found in other open areas in the South at one time. But in a warming climate these species persist only at the highest elevations. And only in openings.

Hearing of these remarkable summit grasslands, botanists from France, Scotland, and New England scoured the Roan landscape in the late-eighteenth and early-nineteenth centuries looking for rare plants. In the first years of the nineteenth century François André Michaux, son of the Botanist to His Majesty, the King of France, retrod his famous father's footsteps through the area, noting the unusual bald on Yellow Mountain—"the only one not stocked with trees," in his field notes. Asa Gray, the father of American botany, made frequent visits to the mountain in search of the elusive *Shortia galacifolia,* which he eventually saw, decades after he first searched for it on Roan Mountain, when it was discovered by an amateur herb collector. Dr. Gray's repeated visits were not in vain, however, as his wife would later reflect on her pleasure at seeing the breathtaking bloom of the six-hundred-acre Catawba rhododendron garden, and his nieces delighted in wagon rides through the primitive backcountry. Gray was not alone in making frequent visits to the Roan. The procession of famous visitors was long, once being described as "an almost continuous scientific convention." A fascination to botanists and early explorers, grassy balds are also beloved by hikers and bird-watchers and by modern-day photographers and painters. The openings afford long-range vistas in an otherwise heavily wooded landscape. Indeed a tourism industry developed in the mid-1800s to take advantage of the splendor and the cool summer climate. A large hotel, The Cloudland, was erected at Tollhouse Gap in 1885, and travelers from across the country came to gaze upon the wondrous bald mountaintops and take in the air. I recounted some of this history for the county commissioners but they seemed uninterested. Grassy balds and inspiring vistas drew more acclaim from European botanists and sightseers in the 1800s than from local officials in 1999, it seemed.

Efforts by conservation groups to protect the rare species of the balds and to locate the Appalachian Trail atop the summits have paid off, though critical tracts remain unprotected. From the 1940s to the present, over nineteen thousand acres have been set aside to secure the Trail route and buffering lands, a playground for scientists from around the world and for mere ramblers alike.

In 1968 the National Trails System Act designated the Appalachian Trail a National Scenic Trail, giving the footpath the status of a congressionally authorized unit managed by the Department of the Interior. In legal terms, Paul Brown's crusher might as well have been going in next to Yellowstone, or Yosemite. The ramifications of this happy coincidence were being born in me even as the hallways were clearing after the meeting of the county commissioners.

After we left the courthouse we stood around the parking lot and recounted the meeting.

Ollie said she was "madder'n hell" with the way Sam Laws ignored us, and I was unimpressed. Outside the meeting room she was restored to herself. Her eyes sparkled with the fight.

"Sam art not to treated you like that," she said. "I thought you were going to strip a gear, but you just let him go. I get all aggravated and can't keep from cussing and flying mad."

"I wasn't trying to be cool," I said. "I was just trying to finish up before they threw me out."

"That was typical Sam," Freddy said, leaning in. Out here in the parking lot, in the light, I could see Freddy's resemblance to his mother, to Ollie. The pellucid skin, the bright eyes. A birdlike intensity.

"Really? How does he keep getting elected?"

Ashley grabbed me by the arm, bracing me like an old friend, and said, "You know what he does, don't you?"

"Sam Laws? He's a county commissioner. What else does he do?"

They all laughed. Ollie had to tell Freddy, who was moving toward their car. "Jay don't know what Sam does for a living," she hooted. They jockeyed for the right to be the one to fill me in. Ashley won. "Sam Laws is the biggest rock hauler in the county. He's got crushed rock running through his veins."

Ollie picked up the ball. "But I'll be damned, I never seen our little, round commissioner squirm like that. You got him scared."

Ashley again: "The commissioners were all watching you talking to the reporters. And Sam, he was about to bust a artery."

I made to protest. I hadn't caused Sam or any of the commissioners the least discomfort. I had failed utterly to make a case that Paul was a serial bad actor or that the county ought to take action to stop him. I tried to explain that. But Ollie only shook her head and smiled. A legend was born for her. In me, of all people.

I was exquisitely unworthy of Ollie's high estimation. To her I was a lawyer with connections in the middle of the state. And I had money, big money, or else how could I live at the top of Birchfield Creek, in a house with long-range views, for that didn't come cheap. But she didn't know the whole story and I was not prepared to tell it to her. She didn't know that I had no interest in being a lawyer or having connections in the middle of the state. She did not know that I had left the middle of the state behind, left job offers in law firms, severed my connections with the well-connected. I had, instead, to the astonishment of my family and those who knew me best, embarked upon an experiment in living. I had stepped out of the fast track, slipped out of the mainstream, to live by myself in the back of beyond. To fish and hike and read. To write novels that stood little chance of publication. Ollie didn't know that I had not bought the house I lived in—the summer place of my childhood—with "big money," but rather had ended up owning it out of a divorce settlement when my parents' marriage ended. She didn't know that I had a law degree but had decided not to practice law, that I failed the bar exam the only time I took it. It was too long a tale to share there in the parking lot of the Courthouse Annex. I couldn't bring myself to say it plain: that I had walked away from a promising career path and a good job to write and think and live a simple life. It sounded ridiculous spoken out loud, even to me. And it sounded self-indulgent whenever I recounted the pleasure I derived from drinking water from my spring or told of the joy I took when I worked in the sun or when I built things out of wood. Such professions of my faith tended to draw blank stares. So I would not tell Ollie my story yet. She would learn it, but in pieces, over years. I was not who she thought I was, but here we were.

Ashley asked me to come to their house for supper and I accepted. They lived on the second floor of a defunct auto-repair shop at the head of the Cranberry Gap, right under the excavation site for the mine. The place still smelled of crankcases and oily tools. The house they were building, the one with the cracked foundation, was just across the road, right next to the home of Ollie's brother, and just up the hill from the trailer where her mother lived. The Cooks used to own a lot of the land around Dog Town and Cranberry Gap. They were a big family and they looked back on a time when they were land rich. But now the Cooks and many of the other old families were reduced to small parcels hugging the roads and creeks. Timber interests, the Forest Service, and real estate investors owned the valuable ridgetops. Ollie explained that they had been working on the new house for two years. Freddy and Curly were doing the work themselves, in their spare hours, at night and early in the morning, whenever Curly wasn't out doing maintenance on the county vehicles and Freddy wasn't doing auto paint and bodywork. The space they called home for now was one vast room that served as bedroom, living room, dining room, and kitchen. It measured forty feet by thirty feet, and they had divided it off into smaller areas by hanging sheets and bedspreads. Every corner, every flat place, was heaped with belongings.

Ashley fell all over herself apologizing. "It's an awful mess but we're moving across the road to the new house one of these days, so we're not incentivized to clean it up," she said in her own unique way of talking, a combination of self-conscious formality and teenage experimentation.

We stood at a window and looked across the road to the new house. The house was dried in, with shingles on the roof, and doors and windows installed, but it still lacked siding. Freddy was a collector of Hillman cars, a British make rebranded by Chrysler before they were mothballed in the 1970s. He had a dozen of them, in various states of ruin, arrayed about the yard. To some, the rounded bonnets and open trunks might have amounted to junk. To Freddy they were a gold mine of possibilities—and parts.

We settled in and they told me about the building we were in. Their landlord was Mr. Paul Brown, who, when he bought the Charles Smith tract for his access road, had also come to own everything on it, including the old auto shop and apartment. If you made this up, nobody would believe it.

"Paul?" I managed. "Our Paul?"

"Why, yeah," Freddy said as if all things are not only possible, but likely. "We haven't had any trouble out of Paul. He's just as nice as he can be. You know, for a damn snake."

"You don't want to get him mad is all," Ollie said. "He'll cuss you up and down. But I'm honest, Dear Ol' Dad, he never give me no problems a'tall, has he, Ashley?" This was the second time I had heard this nicknaming. I thought back to the first time I talked to Ashley. She had asked me if I knew "Nasty." Now I asked Ollie about it. They all laughed. Ollie called Paul Brown either Pawl, Dear Ol' Dad, or Droopy, owing to, as Ashley said, "the skin on his face is real bad to sag." Ollie had to pile on. "He's the awfullest-looking man there ever was. God, he's droopy." Usually, though, he was just Pawl. Who is Nasty? I asked. "James!" they all replied, dissolving in laughter. James Vance, the site foreman. I asked them why they called him Nasty.

"Have you ever seen him up close?" Ashley asked.

"He's awful dirty," Curly said, laughing. "He's a good boy, James is, I like him, but, well, he's pretty nasty."

"No, you wouldn't want to share a spoon with him," Freddy added.

Now Ollie decided it was my turn to get nicknamed. "Listen here,

Little Buddy," she said, sizing up my six-foot-four-inch frame. "If you want to be in the band, you got to get a nickname. Just like Dear Ol' Dad and the rest." I offered no resistance. Little Buddy it would be.

Ashley tried a new angle by way of obtuse explanation. "You don't seem like the kind of person who knows anything about scanners and digital technology," she said summarily.

I looked at her blankly, not following, which she took as an answer to her question.

She continued, "Anybody who is speaking on a cordless phone anymore is putting themselves at risk of having their conversation listened in on. And that's just using standard scanning technology. The nine-hundred-megahertz phones are better, but I still wouldn't trust them if I was you. So," she said at length, letting me figure it out, "anytime we call you, it would be helpful if we just used nicknames, especially on a cordless phone, which you should never talk on anyway. On account of we don't want anybody knowing what we're talking about. Especially if it's about Paul and the crusher."

"People really do that?" I asked.

They all busted out laughing and I had my answer.


We settled in on a huge sectional sofa that nearly made a complete square. They pushed soft drinks and Little Debbie cakes on me. They wanted to tell me everything. They told me stories of Paul cussing his employees, right beneath their window, out on the haul road. They had some of these episodes on videotape and they'd be happy to show them to me if I wanted to see for myself. They told me of more outrages perpetrated by Bill Beck out of the Asheville Regional Office. I was filled in on the circus endemic in the county. Everybody knew about the long-running feud between Snowball Clawson and Nub Taylor, our clerk of court, but I got the background story on the famous murder of my neighbor Nod Buchanan. And the untold tale of how poor Jerry Lee Buchanan had lost the will to live after Vietnam. Ollie had the rundown on the further adventures of my neighbor Sparky, too, aka David Sparks, who couldn't seem to stay out of trouble. *Sparky keeps having people die where he's at,* Curly lamented. The Cox clan seemed to know everything about everybody between Elk Park and Spruce Pine, especially when it came to fights and hard feelings and broken relations. After a while they asked the question I always get asked eventually: *Didn't Rob Thomas shoot your daddy a long time ago up on Yellow Mountain? Shot at him,* I said, *but he missed,* proud that my own family figured into their narrative of local happenings.

Mostly I was interested in what they knew about the crusher, and about Paul. I learned that they videotaped or photographed nearly everything they saw out their windows. When the primary crusher jaw went up the hill on a lowboy, they got it on tape. When Bill Beck from the Asheville Regional Office came to conduct an inspection, Ollie recorded his every move, until he went up on the mountain out of her view. When the blasting company got locked out at the haul-road gate, Ashley had the pictures to document it.

Ashley was teaching me—the Happy Luddite—how to use the Internet on her computer in the corner of the room, was demonstrating how she found the North Carolina General Statutes online, when Ollie hurled an oath.

"What's the matter?" I asked.

At least two of them, but maybe all four, replied in unison "Tony."

Tony was coming across the road.

"Who's Tony?" I asked.

"Don't say anything," Ashley instructed. "He'll be drunk. He's my daddy."

Ollie added, "And that makes him my brother. What a damn mess."


Tony Cook was a character around the county. For many years he ran the Linville Fish Camp, a breakfast-and-lunch place. He was outspoken, hard-drinking, and a fool. Everybody called him Gomer, and he seemed to embrace the identity, not quite realizing it was meant to be unflattering. He was unusually unattractive. His broad face had a smashed quality, as if it had been rearranged in a fight. He had a full head of black hair, curled in what appeared to be a perm, and a bushy mustache over a scowling set of lips. I had known his reputation for a long time. You heard his name around the county. He was running for county commissioner that very election cycle. His slogan appeared on his business card: FROM THE COURTHOUSE TO THE WHITE HOUSE, I WILL FREE AVERY COUNTY, I DON'T WANT ANY COUNTY PAY! An old story about Tony goes this way. In grade school the teacher could take no more of Tony's talking back, his disrupting the class, so she rapped on her desk and announced. "Tony Cook, I can't take it anymore. I'm giving you a zero for today." At this, Tony rubbed his head and replied, "Well, that's better'n nothing, ain't it?" There's another. As a grown man, Tony was working in a resort in the little town of Banner Elk. He happened to pass through the lobby at the precise moment the spaceship *Challenger* exploded into tentacles of smoke, setting off profound grief across the land. As the staff and patrons of the resort crowded around the television, as they stared in horror at the image on the screen, Tony alone dared to speak: "Well, if you was dumb enough to strap your ass to a rocket ship, you might just get it blowed off." He liked to tell that one on himself, liked to retell it, keeping it alive. But not until this moment did I connect Gomer Cook, Tony, with his sister Ollie and the Cox-Cook clan. And only now did it sink in that Gomer Cook was the father of lovely, whip-smart Ashley. One would never guess it.

He stomped heavily up the wooden steps from the old garage space to the living quarters.

We all said some hellos and Tony fell into a chair.

"Jay's a lawyer," Ollie said.

"Aw?"

"You ort to seen him a-tellin' Sam about the Appalachian Trail," Curly said. "Son, Sam was tied in knots."

"Appalachian Trail?" Tony scoffed.

"Not really," I said, responding to just one of the puffs in a string of serial exaggerations I was now used to hearing.

"You a lawryer, huh?"

"Not really," I repeated. "I have a law degree. I'm a writer."

"A book writer?"

"I guess so. I'm writing a book."

"Aw. Is it a damn good'un?"

"I hope so."

Tony glared at me through swimmy eyes. "So you're a book writer and a lawryer." He had moved past the questioning phase.

"I went to law school."

In that case, Tony had something to show me. He dug around awhile in his pockets, then he came over to me. He leaned over my shoulder, smelling of rancid cologne and motorcycle grease. I could barely smell the liquor. He unfolded a sheet of paper and offered it to me, a handwritten document of some sort.

"I want my house back," he said. My bafflement must have been apparent because I was hit with a blizzard of history. I learned that Tony, as much as anyone else, had started the fight I had stepped into. Back in the summer, after the haul road was cleared and Paul's equipment started arriving on the Putnam tract, Tony wrote letters to the head of the North Carolina Division of Land Resources complaining of dust, damage to his spring, and damage to the structure of his house. Between August and November he had penned nine complaints and sent them off to Raleigh. "Paul was coming in here killing us," he said.

But then, in December, Tony had stopped writing letters. Ollie explained this sudden twist. "One day Dear Ol' Dad paid Tony a personal visit and waved a check in front of his nose," she said, derision dripping from her. "And Tony here took the bait. He signed Paul's check and he cashed it at the damn bank."

Tony had sold his house, the little gray-and-black pile just across the road, to his sister's arch-enemy. But now he wanted it back.

"Why did you sell it?" I asked the obvious question.

"I can't live near any crusher," he said as if wounded. "I've got bad lungs, and he's done ruined [*rurent*] my water. I can't live without my water so I sold it to him. You can't lick Paul."

The recriminations in the air filled the space. Ashley burned at a low boil just off my elbow.

"Well, now what?"

41

"I want you to tell me if that's legal." He shook an unsteady finger at the paper in my hands. "How it got sold. I don't b'lieve he can do what he done."

I wanted a moment to read the paper, to consider the question more closely, but Tony removed it from my hand and put it back in his pocket.

"What is it?"

"It's a contract's what it is. It's wrote up."

"Well, what does it say?"

Now Ashley filled in the details. "In exchange for him selling his house to Paul, he agreed not to ever speak ill of Paul Brown or Clark Stone Company again."

I remembered just enough from my contracts classes to recall the bones of a written contract. A meeting of the minds, consideration, a signature.

"Is it dated and signed?"

It was dated and signed by Tony Cook and Paul Brown.

Tony seemed to sink deeper in his chair. "See, he bought me out and said I can't fight the crusher no more if he give me my price. But that takes away my constitutional rights, don't it? I don't believe you can take away a man's constitutional rights to speak out. Not in America."

"I think you can contract away your right to speak," I said, uncertain.

"Well, I want my house back. Paul stole it. I ort to shoot that son of a bitch."

Freddy couldn't help himself. "I believe you just violated the terms and conditions of your contract."

I picked up the inquiry. "What did he give you for it?" I wanted to hear him say it.

"Hunnert thousand."

I was taken aback. Tony's house on the other side of the road was little more than a falling-down shed with a couple of blocky additions. Black trim. A paint-peeled shack by the side of the road. For some reason Paul was dropping tall piles of banknotes in Cranberry Gap, trying to keep everybody—or at least Charles Smith and Tony Cook—happy.

I tried to remember more law, anything from my courses in contracts

42

and property law that might be relevant here. "Did he hold a gun to your head?"

"Hunh?"

"Were you under duress and forced to sell it to him?"

"I was high on pills," Tony said helpfully.

Ashley couldn't take any more. "You're a dumb ass," she said with the dismissive venom that is the specialty of fourteen-year-old girls.

Tony paused and smiled wide. "No, I ain't. I'm one rich sunvabitch is what I am. And you ort not talk to your daddy like that. It's ugly."

The next day I drove down to the middle of the state to learn more about Paul's mining permit. Ashley had asked me what my intentions were. "Are you going to go down there and pull Paul's permit?" she asked, right impressed. "Yeah," I'd said, "I'm going to go down there and pull it," because apparently that's what you call it when you go to the Division of Land Resources and ask the secretary to let you have a look at a permit. You *pull* it.

The Division of Land Resources regulates the mineral wealth of the state. Its mission includes mitigating sediment flows in state waters and the imposition of erosion-control plans for developers and municipalities. It promotes the wise use of public and private land resources, protects geologic features, does mapping, and runs dam-safety programs. It issues mining permits and polices the terms and conditions of issuance.

The agency is housed in the Archdale Building, the tallest building in Raleigh. It is also notable as the second-ugliest building in the state. Its height serves to amplify its unpleasantness. It looms like a flesh-colored tombstone at one end of a grassy mall. Its windows seem like an afterthought and barely permit light into the functional interior.

I was sitting in a bath of fluorescent, yellow wattage in a conference room on the sixth floor, with the bulging Putnam Mine file open before me, trying to familiarize myself with Paul's mining permit, when an angular man with a tidy white beard leaned in the door to ask if he could be of any assistance. I didn't know if he could. My eyes met his for an embarrassing instant.

"I'm Charles Gardner."

I knew the name. The letters Tony wrote, about his water, the dust, the blasting, were all addressed to Charles Gardner, director of the division. Ashley had warned me that he was unresponsive, that he had buried their complaints in some paper pile she could not imagine. Freddy had shared with me his suspicion that Charles Gardner was in somebody's pocket. Ollie called Charles the head *knocker* down in Raleigh. "Oh, God," she'd said when I reported that I was going to Raleigh. "Banging around down there you're liable to run into the head knocker himself, Mister Charles Gardner. Don't tell him you know me," she pleaded. When I told her that was my objective, to run into Charles Gardner, she stared straight at me. "You ain't afraid of nothing, are you?" Maybe, I thought, that's all I have to offer. I might lack credentials, and I had no idea how to stop Paul Brown from pulling down Belview Mountain, but I was not afraid. Not yet anyway.

I introduced myself and explained, in brief, what I was doing.

"I'm looking through here to get a sense of how this permit got issued."

"Which permit?" Gardner asked.

"The Putnam Mine. Up in Avery County."

"Well, I issued it. Maybe I can help you."

"Maybe you can, but I don't even know what I'm looking for."

"Well, when you figure it out, just let me know."

I sought to hold his attention for just one more moment. "Mr. Gardner, I'm trying to figure out if there is anything in here that would afford protection to the Appalachian Trail."

There was a distinct and deep pause. A hole opened in the stale air, and I felt my wind sucked into it. It would have been helpful if the HVAC system had stalled, if the lights had flickered, to ratify the unease I felt at that moment. My mind whirred.

"Why?" Gardner's bright eyes went flat.

"Because this mine is right next to the Appalachian Trail at Hump Mountain, right in front of a natural overlook at Houston Ridge."

The next thing the director of the division said surprised me. He had been leaning forward slightly. Now he stood straight. "When you're

44

finished here, I wonder if you would come down to my office, at the end of the hall, and tell me a little bit more about that."

I said I would, and Charles Gardner excused himself.

I spent an hour or so reading. I photocopied the permit application. I hadn't found anything obvious, a few misstatements on the application, the faulty identification of the river basin the mine was located in, and an obvious misrepresentation on the second page: *Will the operation involve the washing of stone? No.* It didn't make any sense. Even I knew that quarries wash crushed stone with water. Ashley had told me to look for that one.


Gardner's office was slightly less gloomy than the other offices on the floor. I stood outside his door in an anteroom. His secretary barely acknowledged me. She looked as if she had been sitting there, at her desk, since 1978.

Right behind me came a slim, brush-cut man of thirty years. I nodded at him.

Gardner wrapped up a phone conversation and ushered us in.

"Jay, I've asked Tracy Davis to join us if that is all right with you. Tracy is the state geologist."

"Sure." I nodded my assent, unable to fathom the grounds for any objection.

We visited for a couple of minutes, sniffed about like dogs. We talked basketball, weather. In my conversations with Ollie and with some of my friends in the conservation community whom I had quizzed before heading for Raleigh, I had been told that Charles Gardner was immovable, fierce in his defense of the extraction industry. I had been told that the Division of Land Resources was a creaking bureaucracy full of overworked, underpaid public servants who had little incentive to take risks or to buck the special interests. I had found out that the gravel industry is a powerful bunch that usually get their way, and that any environmental weaknesses I found in the Mining Act were probably the result of the gravel-industry drafting position papers that had worked their way into the statute through lobbying. That our Mining

Act was weak by design. None of what I heard was inspiring or in the least bit encouraging. But here I was, loafering around on the sixth floor of the Archdale Building, grinning in Charles Gardner's office, talking hoops.

I figured I was either making pretty famous progress or I was being humored.

Mr. Gardner convened our meeting and we all sat. "Jay, I'd like you to repeat what you said to me down in the conference room. For Tracy's benefit."

Sensing an opportunity that might not come again, I described how the Appalachian Trail winds around the broad shoulder of Grassy Ridge, then drops into Yellow Mountain Gap, right along the ridge, tracing the North Carolina state line with Tennessee, and how it leads the Maine-bound hiker over the famous bald tops of the eastern extreme of the Roan High Massif. I described the views in all directions, Roan High Knob, and the Iron Mountain Range in Tennessee; Mount Rogers and the Grayson Highlands in Virginia; Grandfather Mountain, Hawksbill, Table Rock, and Mount Mitchell in North Carolina. "You can see the Smokies, to the west of Asheville, from the Roan on a clear winter day," I said. "That's about seventy miles." I described what I know of how the landscape came to be protected by the Southern Appalachian Highlands Conservancy and The Nature Conservancy, and the federal government. I laid out the importance of the Appalachian Trail and the Overmountain Victory Trail to the cultural history and economy of Avery County. I described how the preliminary clearing of the mine site had already spoiled the quiet atmosphere for the hiker, how the construction racket had broken the wilderness solitude with the sound of trucks, compression-release engine brakes, and backup beepers. I threw in a riff on the Mountain Ridge Protection Act and laid out what I knew of Paul's seventy-nine-foot conveyor tower. My dissertation was exhaustive and thoroughly amateurish, full of *uh*s and *er*s and the kind of circular reasoning and repetition that is the purview of the passionate.

When I finished, Charles looked first at Tracy and then at me. He chose his words with care. "I can assure you, Jay, if I had known that the Appalachian Trail was as close to the quarry as you say it is, if it is, I would not have issued a permit. We don't like to do that."

This was not what I expected out of Charles Gardner. I expected cool evasion. Or outright hostility. Television-exposé-style door-slamming, perhaps.

Given that Gardner was listening and had not tossed me out, I carried on. I told about Ollie and Curly, about their new house and how their foundation was cracked by the blast from the initial clearing of the mine site, and how there was a police report on file confirming that.

Gardner nodded as I spoke. He reached into a file folder next to his desk and pulled out a stack of papers. He let me run a little, then interrupted, "These are letters from Tony Cook. They're in the public record. You're welcome to have a look at them."

Tony's letters! It turned out they were not buried under the streets of Raleigh. They were in a file in a credenza next to Charles Gardner's desk.

Mr. Gardner sat back in his chair. He thought for a moment and his eyes seemed to search the ceiling. He turned to Tracy. "Tracy, what did we hear from the Appalachian Trail folks at the hearings?"

Tracy's eyes fluttered, an involuntary response I would come to know. "There weren't any hearings on the Putnam Mine."

Gardner nodded and a thin smile was born on his face. "Okay."


I was driving between Charles Gardner's office in Raleigh and my sister's house in Durham, still buzzing from my impromptu meeting with the head knocker, and suddenly I had a terrible thought. *Was the excavated area as visible from the Appalachian Trail as I had said it was?* I had told the commissioners that a hiker would travel "directly toward the Putnam Mine for a mile or more." And now I had told Charles Gardner the same thing. I was sort of surprised at the traction it had gotten. But I had not seen the clearing from Hump Mountain since—well, I couldn't remember if I had seen it from the summit of Hump Mountain at all. I had walked that stretch of Trail—the two easternmost balds—since I was five years old. I knew every rise and fall and rock outcrop. And Belview Mountain is due east of the point where Houston Ridge shears off to the south on Big Hump. But what if the mine site was low enough down the slope of Hartley Ridge that William Cable's cow pasture blocked the view from the long ridge? I didn't think it was likely, but if I was wrong, I had just wrecked my credibility before our fight could even get started. I stopped at my sister's house and fed the dogs. Then I got back into the truck, and I drove straight home to the mountains, four hours, and fell into bed.

The next morning I flew out of the bed at sunup, threw some lunch in my backpack, and took off walking. I tore up the steep slopes to the summit of Big Yellow. It was a classic winter morning, bright and frigid, and every blade of bald grass had an ice flag pointing to the south, telling of a northerly wind. When I got to Little Hump, I was pleased that I could see Paul's clearing from the place where the spur trail joins the Appalachian Trail. But from this vantage, three miles from the site, the clearing looked small and it was hard to make out vehicles and other equipment in the long, flat opening. I carried on, braced for the hour of hard climbing ahead of me. Hoofing up the backside of Hump Mountain, I nearly managed to convince myself that the mine was going to be too low on Belview to be visible from the top. I felt sick. My heart slammed in my ears. Finally, I broke out onto the top of the broad, bald peak. And there it was. Along with dozens of ridges and tops, a hundred folds and graceful curves, and the magnificent backdrop of Grandfather Mountain, the mine site was wonderfully, horribly visible. I felt giddy, a combination of ecstasy and revulsion. Given the inclination of the footpath and the lay of the land, the Putnam Mine site could not be more visible. And the effect on a hiker could not be worse. If anything, I had undersold the impacts to Gardner and to the county commissioners. From this spot on the prized Trail the impact on a hiker seeking solitude and pristine vistas would be profound. And I was shamefully grateful for that.

I snapped a couple of pictures to satisfy myself, then I headed back to the house. I took a shower, got right back in the truck, then drove four hours reversing the previous day's journey to resume an effort that now seemed infinitely more urgent.

My mother had just gotten an Apple computer with an Internet connection, so I made her house my base for the next two days. Using the skills Ashley had taught me, I found the website for the Appalachian National Scenic Trail. I quickly found a whole stable of advocacy groups that fight for conservation causes. I had been leading hikes in the mountains for the Southern Appalachian Highlands Conservancy and The Nature Conservancy for seven years as a volunteer land steward so I already had contacts in those groups. The new groups I found had heroic, bold names: Appalachian Voices, Blue Ridge Defense. I scored e-mail addresses for the Carolina Mountain Club and the vaunted Tennessee Eastman Hiking and Canoeing Club. I spent most of a day on the telephone, talking to hikers, conservationists, lawyers, and activists. Soon I had a list of six contacts who showed some interest, some concern about the Putnam Mine. But nobody was offering to hire an attorney or to press the matter with the state.

I called my neighbor Witt to see if he could think of any other organizations.

"What about the Appalachian Trail Conservancy?" I asked. "They're the ones with the authority. This should be their fight. They're the big dog."

"I already tried," Witt said. "After you called me, I called them. Back in the summer. But they didn't think it was going to impact the Trail."

Still fresh off my hike, I erupted, "It's right in front of the Trail!"

But Witt didn't need convincing. Now he recounted his dealings with the Appalachian Trail folks.

When I'd first called to tell him what was happening on Belview, Witt called the group's regional office, in Asheville, to see what they were going to do to protect the Trail from the Putnam Mine. He was told, politely, that the mine would not have any significant impact on the Trail, and besides, even if it might have some impact on hikers using that section, the permit had already gone through; the Appalachian Trail Conservancy could do nothing even if they wanted to. Having become intimately familiar with the openings in the forest cover from his land, but not from Big Hump, Witt accepted their assessment that the impacts on the Trail would be minimal, and he and I then started to think of what else we might do to address the worst of the impacts of the mine. Now I was struck by the thought that maybe the Appalachian Trail Conservancy had not seen the excavation from Big Hump, either. Maybe none of their board members or regional representatives had stood at the rocky knot at the summit and looked out over Cranberry Gap since Paul had arrived in the neighborhood. Surely, if they had seen what I had seen, they would be moving on this, doing whatever it is they do when the experience of using a section of the Appalachian National Scenic Trail is set to be derogated for future generations. At least I thought they would.

The next morning I was watching the clock, eager for it to turn to nine so that I might resume contacting potential allies. Witt was sending me some of his pictures, too, overnighting them for morning delivery, and I was eager to greet the deliveryman. I had to get back to the mountains, but I wanted to get in a couple more calls before I left the middle of the state, maybe drop by the offices of a couple of the big conservation groups headquartered around Raleigh to ask for assistance, to seek guidance. To beg attention to this cause.

What I found was sobering. Everyone I spoke to professed an abiding, nearly holy, affection for the Appalachian Trail, and I heard murmurs of recognition when I mentioned the Roan Highlands and Hump Mountain. But none of the big conservation groups had much stomach for addressing emergent threats to the lands they were all trying to protect. Some groups offered to put me in touch with other groups. Some told me that they didn't have the resources to get involved in costly battles and sent me on my way. One exception, the North Carolina chapter of the Sierra Club, had a staff lobbyist, and their executive director said she would look into my claims if I would get her more information.

Before I left for the mountains I had one more idea of a potential ally, though it was a long shot. I presented myself in the reception area of the offices of the North Carolina chapter of The Nature Conservancy. As the owners of the nature preserve on top of Big Yellow Mountain, The Nature Conservancy might, I thought, take a position. While the mine would not directly affect the species on the preserve, would not throw fly rock as far as its boundaries, the impact on the experience of visiting the preserve would forever be changed if Paul Brown succeeded in pulling down Belview Mountain. As the largest nonprofit conservation organization in the world, their support could, I figured, move, or in this case, save, mountains.

In my role as a land steward for both The Nature Conservancy and Southern Appalachian Highlands Conservancy, I had hosted photographers and led curious scientists to populations of rare wildflowers and unique habitat at the top of the mountain. A generation of conservationists had used my restroom on their way to see the best example of a Southern Appalachian grassy bald in the world. Occasionally, prominent donors to the organizations wanted to see the summit and experience the Canadian climate. Recognizing the usefulness of large donations, I had gladly served as a guide and docent. I was a member and a supporter of the mission, and ordinarily my ideas were welcomed by the statewide chapter. But The Nature Conservancy has made its mark buying and stewarding land, not by making enemies of government agencies and industry. I had already been rebuffed by their regional director for the Southern Blue Ridge Mountains project area. She had responded to my e-mailed request for assistance with a curt reply: "This issue is not one that The Nature Conservancy will tackle. I wish you luck." This had stung, but now I wrote it off. Maybe I had been unclear about the threat posed to the experience of visiting the preserve on Big Yellow. Maybe I had caught my contact on a bad day. Rather than circle back and try to win her over, I was now aiming higher. I wanted to show Witt's pictures to Katherine Skinner, the chapter's executive director. At the very least she could tell me where to focus my attention.

Katherine is the most visible figure in the state's conservation movement. She is feared and respected in nearly equal measure. She is hailed for signature accomplishments protecting hundreds of thousands of acres across the state, and she is regarded as impossible, imperious, sometimes all in the same breath. If you're interested in conservation in North Carolina, your journey will eventually lead to Katherine's door.

When she approached me, in the reception area of her office, she already had her hands in the air, waving me off.

"I don't want to hear about it," she said in her blatant eastern–North Carolina drawl.

Astonished but unbowed, I made to protest. She didn't know what I was going to say. I hadn't even gotten to introduce the purpose of my visit.

But she knew enough from the message I had left on her voice mail. "We're not getting mixed up in your legal fight."

I endeavored to get a word in. "I just want to show you these pictures," I said in exceedingly good cheer. "As a volunteer steward on Big Yellow, and—"

"I don't want to see them." She was smiling, but she was dead serious.

Katherine was tough, but I was on a mission. I would have to talk fast and be smart. "I've been talking to newspapers and other conservation organizations. If a newspaper is going to write a story on the mine, I'd like to refer them to you," I said as quickly as I could. "I'm trying to make sure you have something coherent to say."

Skinner raised her eyebrows at the word *coherent.* This was not going well. "I'm not going to talk to the *News and Observer.*"

"What are you going to say when they call?"

"I'm going to say, 'No comment.'"

That's when I saw it. Fear. Katherine Skinner, the North Carolina chapter of The Nature Conservancy, was afraid of what a fight like this could do. And I understood. I was disappointed by the reception, but I understood. There I was, mad with the pending fight, driven crooked by the injustice I saw. I was tired from a couple of sleepless nights, from my last hike and my long hours of research, and my eyes jittered in their sockets from staring at the computer screen. Katherine saw this, this fervor, this fatigue, and must have feared her organization's getting dragged in with the likes of me. We would work together on other projects, but not on the fight to save Belview Mountain.

At one time I had understood as well as anyone why land trusts and conservancies need to project this spirit of cooperation, need to keep a low profile in the face of charges of elitism and misplaced accusations of intrusions on the property rights of old-timers, or even mine owners. To fulfill their mission they buy land, and to buy land you have to be able to develop relationships based on trust. They do not shy from the big policy battles, and they enter national and statewide debates on funding and legislation, but a Dog Town brawl having to do with acoustic and visual impacts originating on private property was a different matter altogether. But in the fight I saw coming, there was no room for collaboration. No trust. There was only *us* vs. *them.* Me vs. Charles. Ollie vs. Paul. Saving the mountain or tearing it down.

After thanking Katherine for agreeing to see me at all, I slunk out of The Nature Conservancy's office, chastened. Out of the nice, clean light of collaboration and conciliation and back into the dark fight. I missed the old me. But I was changed. I didn't know how to restore myself, rehabilitate my own sense of myself, unless it was through winning. My meeting with Katherine had opened my eyes to what my life would be like for the next several years.

Frantic now, sensing downward momentum, I decided to dig into my old bag of tricks. I was not completely without resources. In my former life I'd had some connections. I had gone to law school with a class of bright, aspiring attorneys who were now fanned out across the state in positions that gained them some authority. Growing up in Chapel Hill, I had been surrounded by talented kids who were now making things happen in careers ranging from medicine to politics. I started with my friend Josh Stein. I grew up with Josh, played soccer with him. I dated his sister in seventh grade. I always knew Josh was going to do great things with his ambition and his intelligence. Now he was working in the Washington office of North Carolina's recently elected junior senator, John Edwards. Edwards was known as a plaintiff's attorney and courtroom star in legal circles in the state but had not yet burst onto the national stage as he soon would with runs for the vice presidency and later the presidency.

After a little ice-breaking, the necessary explanation of why I had dropped out of the known world, had decided to live alone on a far mountain to conduct an experiment in simple living, Josh was ready to hear me out. I ran through the antics, if not fraud, of Paul Brown's company and the incompetence, if not negligence, of the state officials who had failed to protect the Appalachian Trail. Then I made my plea. "Josh, who should I call? I'm hitting dead ends. I'm getting killed. People run when they see me coming."

After assuring me that Senator Edwards would not be able to take a position on Paul's rock crusher, as the facts did not appear to have federal implications, Josh suggested I call Trip Van Noppen at the Southern Environmental Law Center. I wrote the name down on my growing list of contacts. Before thanking Josh for his help, I delivered a terse dissertation on the mine's potential impacts on the Appalachian Trail, which, as a National Scenic Trail, is about as federal as you can get. He thanked me for the gratuitous lecture and said he would see what he could do.

Finally, I had a place to start. The Southern Environmental Law Center's Carolinas office was right there in Chapel Hill, not two miles from where I was working that day. I decided I would drive over and see if I could find Mr. Van Noppen right away. I slipped some of Witt's pictures into a folder and headed out.

The Southern Environmental Law Center is the most prestigious public-interest law firm dealing with environmental issues in the South, and one of the premier conservation voices in the country. It was founded by Rick Middleton, a visionary attorney who left a promising career with an elite national conservation group to build from scratch a blue-ribbon outfit dedicated to saving the air and water of his benighted native region. He had some money to start with—his family included prominent figures in the steel industry in Alabama—but perhaps even he could not have predicted the attention and funding he would draw to his cause. Since its founding in 1986, the Southern Environmental Law Center had grown into a juggernaut employing fifty staff in three offices. I didn't know any of this yet. I also didn't know that Trip Van Noppen was the director of the Carolinas office and that getting in to see him unannounced was roughly equivalent to a young film student walking up to a certain address in Los Angeles and asking to speak to Mr. Spielberg. Trip was, I would learn, the busiest man I would ever know. When he was not in court, he was usually buried in preparations for mediations, drafting complaints or briefs, raising money to keep the group's attorneys on their cases. Or he was being interviewed by journalists tracking the progress of the dozens of filings and rulings and appeals that were stacked on his desk at any time. In the slivers of time between those responsibilities Trip was always on the telephone, building coalitions, lobbying for conservation legislation, providing information to regulators. All day long.

I stepped up to a hushed, immaculate reception area and announced that I was there to see Mr. Van Noppen. "It's an emergency," I said. I felt the need to explain myself further to the receptionist, who eyed me with an expression of skepticism. So I added this bit of exaggeration: "Senator Edwards's office sent me."

I found Trip a handsome man of fifty years. He projected the sanguine air of the outdoorsman, combined with the cautious intellectual disposition of the overworked attorney. Like me, he had the mountains in his blood. Linville Gorge, Harper's Creek, and Lost Cove, these wilderness settings were his backyard growing up, instilling in him a deep love for the outdoors in general, the Southern Appalachians in particular. He shook my hand with a vague wariness, as if he had confronted impassioned, aggrieved young men on emergency calls like mine many times. He seemed to be wondering why he had agreed to see me on no notice, with no appointment, and I feared my presence might earn the receptionist a reprimand for failing to keep this one at bay.

I knew I had to make my case from the jump or I would lose him, and I didn't care to endure another drubbing like the one I'd suffered at The Nature Conservancy's office. I started with my secret weapon. I laid Witt's pictures out on a large conference-room table and stood back. As I hoped, the sight of the sprawled timber, the orange openings in the forest, pained him.

"This is bad," he said. "Where are we?"

I helped orient him in the photographs. I showed him where Grandfather Mountain was in relation to the site, which way was south, and how the afternoon light shone on the excavated area. I showed him where I thought the boundaries of the pit would be. I described the beepers and the sound of the drills cutting into rock. Feeling the clock ticking, I raced ahead to tell him about my meeting with Charles Gardner. Trip seemed impressed that Ollie and Ashley had already covered so much ground. But what really snared his interest was when I relayed what Gardner said about the Appalachian Trail.

Trip repeated my words back to me. "He said he wouldn't have issued the permit if he had known how close it would be to the Appalachian Trail?"

"That's what he said," I swore. "I think those were his exact words. He said he couldn't rely on my report, but if what I said was true, he would not have issued the permit."

"How close is it? I can't really tell from the pictures." Trip leaned over to peer into one particularly arresting shot.

"I don't know. A mile, more or less, as the crow flies," I guessed. "But you can see all the way to the Smokies from there, seventy miles, so a single mile is pretty damn close."

"Did Gardner see these pictures?"

"No. I just got them FedExed to me. My neighbor is a nature photographer."

Trip circled back once again. "Charles Gardner said he wouldn't have issued the permit? In those words?"

I checked my memory before answering. "Yes. He said that."

"Do you think he would repeat it if we asked him again? Under oath?"

Trip said *we*. I liked that.

"I don't know. He didn't seem to be holding back. He just said it straight out. It was the first thing he said."

Trip drummed his fingers on the table. "For starters, the Appalachian Trail Conservancy must have been aware of this. Did they engage the state at all?"

"I don't know. They didn't think it would be visible from the Trail."

"And this picture is taken from the Trail?"

"Adjacent to the Trail. This one is from Big Yellow."

"It looks like they were wrong," Trip said, stating the obvious.

"They were wrong. I was just on Hump Mountain, yesterday. They were very wrong. But the Appalachian Trail Conservancy doesn't have any reason to listen to me. They've never heard of me."

I picked up one of the pictures and ran my finger down the long spine of the ridge. "This is the actual footpath of the Trail. And that's the mine site, over here."

Something was missing from my telling. Trip was trying to connect the dots.

"All this should have come out before the permit was issued. Are you saying that the Appalachian Trail Conservancy didn't contest this at the public hearings?"

So that was it. "There weren't any public hearings," I said flatly. All of a sudden I remembered how I felt in Gardner's office. The only witness to Gardner's remark about not issuing the permit was Tracy Davis. And Tracy worked for Gardner. Gardner had asked Tracy about the public hearings, then quickly dropped the topic.

Trip moved forward in his chair. "Say what?" He actually laughed.

"There were no public hearings."

"Why not?"

"I don't know."

Finally we reached the point in our meeting where Trip had to explain to me that the Southern Environmental Law Center has limited resources and limited staff, that they survive on grants and on private donations, and that they are only able to take cases that have the potential to set legal precedents. My story was certainly interesting, and Trip wanted to find out more about why no public hearings were held before the permit was issued. He wanted to know the exact distance between the Houston Ridge overlook on Hump Mountain and the quarry site. He wanted me to do the legwork and get back to him. But as for taking the case, he could make no promises.

Oh, and he wanted more pictures, but he wanted them taken from the Trail. What I had showed him was interesting but useless.

Our meeting was over, and Trip had to excuse himself. Not rudely, efficiently.

I just had one more question. "Would it be precedent-setting for Charles Gardner to admit he made a mistake and shut the mine down?" I asked, following Trip out the door. "You said you can only consider cases that might set legal precedents."

Trip stopped. Again, he laughed—at me, I guess. At my persistence and the sparks of fire he must have seen shooting out of my heart. I liked him more and more. He paused to choose his words carefully. "Yes, if that is what Gardner would do, it would set a precedent. You bet."

# Chapter 4

On Trip's advice I placed a call to Don Barger. I used the last pay phone in America, on the sidewalk just outside the Southern Environmental Law Center's offices. Don is the southeast regional director of the National Parks Conservation Association, the outfit founded in 1919 to protect the country's most magnificent public landscapes. Trained as an architect, Don had turned his attention away from the built environment to devote his life to conservation of the natural world. I was pleased when he came on the line promptly. I told him where the Putnam Mine was going in and scrambled to hold his attention while I ran through my long list of impacts.

He interrupted me, "Where did you say this is? Exactly where?"

"You see it from the Hump. Right on the edge of the Roan Highlands between Hump Mountain and Grandfather. Right next to the Appalachian Trail."

"Little Hump?"

"Big Hump. And Little Hump."

For a moment I thought the line had gone dead. Some telephonic shutdown, sunspots.

"Don? Mr. Barger?" I checked to see if I'd lost him.

"I'm here. You're talking about one of my favorite places in the world, Jay. I mean, I've made love on that mountain."

With this remark Don Barger became my new best friend. Here was a man who understood where I was coming from, the passion I felt for this place, the powerful tug. Here was a bona fide nature boy. He seemed to have an endless appetite for the story I told. He asked me to repeat what Charles Gardner had said, the part about not issuing the permit if he had known where the Trail was.

"That's an extraordinary admission," Don said.

"Precedent-setting?" I tried.

"Oh, sure it is. You better believe it."

I had the sense Don might be walking around while he talked to me. Pacing. Had I not been tethered to the pay phone, I, too, would have been pacing.

"Jay, what we have here is a permit that was never valid."

"But they're working right now," I corrected. "They have a permit in their hand, signed by Charles Gardner, and James Vance is welding the crusher hopper together, *right now,* trying to get it running. They're dropping timber and scalping the mountain. They cracked the foundation of this lady's house. Ollie Cox."

Don asked a few more questions. I told him about Trip's reaction.

"Do you think Charles Gardner will repeat what he said to you, about not issuing the permit?"

"I don't know."

Now Don took a moment to weigh his reply. "Could you ask him?"

"I guess I could."

Don instructed me to ask Charles Gardner to write a memo to his own file, to the effect that he did not have all the information he needed when he issued the permit, and that if he had known where the Appalachian Trail was when he was considering the application, he would not have issued it. "Tell him to write it to his file, and then file it. That way, if we have to sue the state, he won't have to testify to it and we won't have to rely on him living up to our high expectations of him. It will be in the file and can be admitted as an exhibit."

This was a lot of information. Did he say *sue the state?*

I was not surprised when Don asked me about the public hearings, but I was stunned when he followed that question with another. He wanted to know who had participated, what position the Department of the Interior had taken on the issue.

*The Department of the Interior.* Just hearing the name of the estimable agency caused my heart to leap in my chest. But Don was clearly missing what I was saying. This was not Washington, D.C.–caliber stuff, never mind the lecture I'd given to my friend in Senator Edwards's office about federal responsibilities. I knew with growing certainty that this was a small-time backroom deal cooked up by the county commissioners and Dear Ol' Dad and a guy known around Dog Town as Nasty. It was a sad story with an unlikely cast of good guys who lived in a cinder-block garage and seemed destined for a life of shaking earth and dust-filled lungs. But I didn't say any of that.

I told Don that there weren't any public hearings and that I didn't know what position the Department of the Interior had taken, if any, but that I would check. For the third time, I had run into the phantom Putnam Mine public hearings.

I did not drive home to the mountains that day, as planned. Instead I went to the undergraduate library on the campus of the University of North Carolina. The seventh floor of the undergraduate library is where I studied throughout college and law school. This was the floor where they shelved the Walker Percy novels, the Robert Penn Warren, and William Faulkner. At my familiar desk I poured through the copy I had made of Paul's permit application.

Under North Carolina law, an applicant seeking a mining permit must first notify *all owners of record of land adjoining* the proposed mining site of their right to seek a public hearing. The hearings provide adjoining landowners and neighbors to the site the opportunity to raise their concerns and make the agency aware of special circumstances that might lead to denial of the permit. Ollie had provided me with the tax maps for the area, and it didn't take but a minute for me to identify sixteen landowners whose property shared a boundary with Paul's permitted tract of land, the Putnam tract. The list included Ollie's cousin Philip Cook. Also the Belview Baptist Church. Jean and Wayne Barksdale and Gary Tolley and Bruce Zobel. These were some of the people who deserved, and were denied, the right to voice objections—or support— before Charles Gardner approved Paul's permit. Ollie's land, the site of the new house, met Paul's Charles Smith parcel, the haul road parcel, in the middle of 19E, the little two-lane highway that runs from Eliza-bethton, Tennessee, to Mars Hill in North Carolina. Did that make her an "adjoining landowner" in the meaning of the statute? I didn't know. I wrote a note to myself to ask Trip.

I spent the afternoon combing the permit application and the survey map of the Putnam Mine tract. I wrote notes on the sequence of events leading up to the issuance and filled page after page of a legal pad with questions I would later track down the answers to.

The most curious find of the afternoon was evidence of three peo-ple Paul *did* notify. Because they were attached to the permit applica-tion—as required—I now knew that Paul sent notice letters to Robert Putnam and to Charles Smith informing each of their rights to contest the permit and seek a public hearing. But why would they? Putnam owned the land where the quarry pit would be, all the way to the top of the mountain, and had entered a ninety-nine year-lease agreement with Paul that made Putnam a partner in the operation; and Smith had owned the twenty-five acres Paul bought at an inflated price for his haul road and access to Highway 19E. Paul had notified his best friends, his partners. In effect he had notified *himself* of his right to contest his own permit. Can you notify yourself? Must you?

In the case of the Putnam Mine, the only other notice letter went—as called for in the statute—to the county manager, to Don Baker, the glum functionary who had invited me to let my conscience be my guide at the meeting of the county commissioners. And it seemed Mr. Baker's conscience had guided him not to request a public hearing on behalf of the people of the county. Is that how this thing got done? Did Don Baker run this by Sam Laws, head of the commission and hauler of stone? And did Sam Laws weigh whether to ask for hearings so that the good folks in Cranberry Gap and Dog Town could raise their legitimate concerns? Did he ask Don Baker to do his duty and inform the state that he wanted a full slate of hearings given the potential impacts on the Appalachian Trail, a linear unit of the National Park system, which traversed the western side of the county? Or did Sam Laws, with gravel running through his veins, lean on Mr. Baker and ask him to bury the notice letter? Sam Laws surely had little interest in calling attention to Paul's crusher, attention that might draw yet another round of fire from another tough bunch living hard by the Tennessee line. Surely Laws had an interest in avoiding a repeat of what had happened at the Cranberry iron-mine site and again up in Sawdust Holler. And maybe that explained this sorry situation. Maybe the Appalachian Trail Conservancy had not taken a position because they did not have a clue what was coming. And maybe that was part of a plan.

I called Don Barger again that afternoon. He was stunned when I reported that Paul had not notified any of the adjoining landowners of their right to be heard, but that he had notified Robert Putnam.

Don howled. "Not even Vulcan pulls stuff like that!" He was referring to Vulcan Materials, the largest gravel and sand mining company in the world, a company known to be aggressive in pursuit of its permits. Don was elated. "If there weren't any public hearings, Jay, and if they didn't give notice to anybody but themselves, we've got a shot. We're going to get this sucker declared *null ab initio.* We're going to kill it."

"What does that mean? *Null ab—*" I was jotting this down furiously. "Spell it."

"It means 'void from the beginning.' Like it never existed. In other words, if you don't do the process right *before* you issue the permit, then the whole process gets thrown out. Your friend Mr. Brown messed this thing up so bad I think we've got a hook. He notified his own partner in the operation! That's really priceless. Who is this guy?"

I hung up from the conversation with Don and I called Witt. He was cheered by the news that I had made contact with a couple of conservation groups, and I waited on the line as he relayed some of my report to Beth. We all decided to meet for dinner in Southern Pines, halfway between Chapel Hill, where I was, and Hartsville, South Carolina, where they were, so Witt could give me some new pictures he had just developed, and so I could tell him more about Trip and Don and the latest adventures of Paul's crew up on Belview.

63

I had never met Witt's wife, but it seemed as if we were old friends. We now shared more than a common property boundary on the mountain; we were bound by our common foe: Paul. Within moments of taking our places in a booth in a restaurant by the side of the road, we were laughing and telling stories and hatching plans to take on Paul Brown and Nasty and anybody else who wanted to try us. Anybody sitting nearby would have taken us for cousins who had been too long apart.

The two new pictures Witt had with him were great, and I told him so.

"These will do for now," he said modestly. "More to come."

He had made me ten copies of each. We decided on a favorite, a jaw-dropping shot taken from the side of Little Hump, with the golden evening light illuminating the terrific scar in the lush flank of Belview Mountain. Witt said he would enlarge the shot and mount it on poster board for me. I told him to send copies to the Southern Environmental Law Center and the National Parks Conservation Association right away, and he wrote the addresses down in a professional-looking, black binder. My job was to deliver a cover letter and a copy of the photographs to every conservation group in the state and to the local media in the mountains. And to the Department of Commerce, which might find it alarming that western North Carolina was facing an unprecedented eyesore in one of the most photographed spots in a state that had long prided itself as the ultimate Variety Vacationland. *Where else?*

The Department of the Interior?

Hell, why not!

Beth couldn't sit still. "What can I do?" she said, offering to pitch in wherever help was needed. "This is getting exciting." And it was.

The next day there was another meeting of the Avery County commissioners. I couldn't make it home in time, as I had set up a meeting with a reporter from Raleigh's *News & Observer,* and now I wanted to photocopy the hundreds of pages of the Putnam Mine file at Charles Gardner's office, but Witt decided he would drive up for the meeting. He thought it would be useful for the commissioners to hear from someone other than Ollie or me. "That way they'll think there are more of us out there than there actually are," he reasoned. Witt would talk about how he was planning to build a house in the county—which would put sawyers and carpenters and electricians to work and add to the local tax base—and he would talk about how the mine might drive him and others away from considering the county a nice place to live. Witt was a natural optimist. "If this permit was issued illegally, maybe we could get the county to pull the plug on the building permit and save some face," he suggested. "Maybe they could deny the variance for the conveyor and revoke the building permit and avoid a legal mess. If Don's group gets involved and if there is interest from the National Park Service and the Department of the Interior, this could be very embarrassing for the county commissioners."

"I don't think the county is ashamed," I said, unable to keep from laughing at Witt's sunny take. "I think they back Paul one hundred percent. And I doubt Paul has gotten a county building permit in the last forty-eight hours, which is when Ashley last checked. Just wait until you meet Sam Laws. Oh, and one last thing: if you didn't already know it, the politicians in Avery County don't have a whole lot of interest in anything the federal government might have to say on, well, anything."

Beth was perplexed. "How can they build the crusher plant without a building permit?"

Witt shook his head. "She's got a lot to learn about the ways of the world."

"You're asking the wrong person," I said, taking up Beth's question. Now to Witt: "I think that's a good question for Commissioner Laws, though, maybe the central question, and I suggest you lead off with it. Go get 'em, champ."


Witt called me after the meeting.

"How'd it go?" I asked, expecting little.

"Sam Laws said I was a breath of fresh air."

"Well, that's something. So they're going to shut Paul down?"

Witt demurred. "I have to say I sort of doubt that."

———————

For the next week I went on a caffeine-and-honey-bun-fueled tear across the state. Everywhere I went, every office I stopped in, I left a copy of Witt's best picture of the mine site. When I was about to run out of copies, I called Witt and told him to overnight me another batch. My objective was to start a chain reaction of head-scratching. *How in the hell did this happen? Who the hell is Paul Brown?* A writer friend of mine taught me how to write a press release, and I tried out a couple of samples on her before putting together a press packet at a copy shop in Winston-Salem. Then I hit the newspaper offices in Greensboro, Durham, and Raleigh. I slept on friends' couches and changed clothes in rest areas and fast-food restaurants. I went to Hickory and on to Boone and Asheville, posting pictures on college campuses and in coffeehouses. I dropped in on conservation groups to inform them that a fight was brewing. I knocked on doors and dropped fact sheets on desks. When I met someone who would indulge me, I would regale them with my tale of the injustice being done to the people of Dog Town and Cranberry Gap and Little Horse Creek. I leaned heavily on Ollie's cracked foundation, the threat of inundation from walls of mud and rock, the outrage of sacrificing our scenic wonders on the altar of the mighty dollar. If people told me they knew a reporter or an environmental activist or a retired attorney who had through-hiked the Appalachian Trail, I wrote down the name and contact information and made plans to pay a visit. My journey took me to tackle shops and gear outfitters and the front porches of weary warriors in conservation battles. At each stop I left my phone number in case the person I had just met had ideas of how to help or money to invest in our cause. I wanted to get an entire community, an entire state, to understand the drama unfolding up in the far mountains. *Because of a bureaucratic mistake—or a fraud, take your pick—a mountain is being torn down, up in Avery County. Right next to the Appalachian Trail. Right now.* Finally, after five days on the road, after 1,180 miles and countless hours spent with a borrowed cell phone to my ear, I crept back up the mountain and fell into bed and slept for most of a day.

The honey-bun tour paid off. Our story made the front page of the second section of the *Charlotte Observer* on Saturday, February 26, 2000. N.C. TO REVIEW QUARRY IN VIEW OF FAMOUS TRAIL the headline blared. My hand shook as I read the piece over and over, standing at the paper box in Newland. The reporters had done their homework. They had interviewed Charles Gardner, and taking my suggestion, they had talked to Don Barger. *A permit for an Avery County gravel quarry, granted without a public hearing, may be modified to reduce its impact on the Appalachian Trail, a state official said Friday. The trail crosses scenic Hump Mountain, in the Roan Highlands, about 1.5 miles from the quarry, which is not yet open but already visible. Don Barger, regional director of the National Parks Conservation Association, called Hump Mountain a grassy bald that looks like an old haystack. This section of the Appalachian Trail is "one of the prettiest places in the southeastern United States," he said. "If you tried to create one of the worst places in the known universe to put that kind of operation, that would be the place," Barger said.*

No picture accompanied the piece, but other than that it was perfect. The *Charlotte Observer* is one of the two most widely circulated papers in North Carolina. Better still, the Associated Press picked up the piece and it ran in other papers around the state. I read aloud Don's quoted remark: "worst places in the known universe." We were on the map. By the time I got back to my house from town, my answering machine was blinking wildly, filled with *Attaboy*s and *Go get 'em*s from well-wishers far and wide.

I called Ollie on the phone.

"I hope to hell you're on a landline, Little Buddy," she said.

"Of course."

"Well, what have you pulled now? You're going to get us all shot." Yes, she had seen the paper. But Ollie couldn't hide her excitement. She was tickled by it. "Is all that for real?"

"All what?"

"I don't know. That paper, Don Barger from the National damn something or other."

"National Parks Conservation Association. It's for real, Ollie. I've got twenty new messages on my answering machine from people who want to help us."

She let it sink in before resuming the thread. "When are you coming home? You never know what Paul's got up his sleeve, and I don't want you to miss anything."

"I'm already back."

"Up on the mountain?"

"Yes."

"Hmm. I'm surprised you got back into Avery County without me a'knowing."

"You must be getting slack," I scolded.

"Aw! Not likely. I ain't slept for a week. If anybody goes up on the site, I make their picture."

"Ollie, you've got to sleep. We need you on the top of your game."

"Hunh," she remarked, a sort of universal get-off-my-back grunt. "I'm killed," she said, asserting her bona fides as a fighter. I heard her pull on her cigarette. "Just tell me this. What other surprises have you still yet got a'going? Tell me now, because my heart can't take any more thrills."

"You know that's classified, Ollie Ve."

"Well, I was just going to say, if we've got Paul back on his heels, now might be the time to drive the blade a little deeper. We can't let him catch his breath or we're done. I've already got one foot in the grave and the other's on a damn banana peel."

It was a stunning reel of metaphors, and I shook my head in amazement at my hero, Ollie Ve Cook Cox.


I hiked down to Witt's campsite and found him tending his morning cook fire. I handed him the paper from the day before and let him take it in. He shook his head in wonder.

"I guess they'll have to get in now," he said.

"Who?"

"The Appalachian Trail Conservancy."

"That's the plan," I said.

Unlike me, Witt was glad the *Observer* had not used the Little Hump photograph. He had better shots in mind. "I'll take one that will help us more," he said. He thought if he could get just the right photograph to demonstrate the impact the mine would have on the Trail, taken from Hump Mountain, we could use that to attract more press and possibly get the undivided attention of the Appalachian Trail hierarchy.

A couple of days later, Witt got the shot he wanted. He swung by my house to tell me about it.

He had waited for two hours, all the daylight he could spare between a meeting with a log peeler in Boone, and a work commitment back in South Carolina. He was sitting on the peak of Hump Mountain—the Big Hump—waiting for a hiker to come along while he had the good afternoon light hitting the scarred-up openings for the mine. He had the shot all set up, but no hikers. Most hikers cross the Humps in the morning when the light is behind Belview, right over the site. Most through-hikers spend the night at the Overmountain shelter, at the headwaters of Roaring Creek, and that puts them only a few miles from the summit when they wake up. They're usually long past it by noon. But all Witt needed was a single afternoon hiker to come along, just one, to give his shot the right perspective. He was about to quit when his luck changed. A fit specimen came hurrying up the Trail from behind him. Not only was this fellow walking in the right direction, north on the Trail, he was wearing a bright red Windbreaker. Perfect for showing a hiker in the foreground and how big the mine would be in relation to the scenery. Witt nodded at the subject as he steamed by. Once he had passed, Witt snapped a dozen shots. He thought surely one of them would work.

"When do I get to see it?" I pressed. Witt always seemed mildly surprised by the attention his pictures drew, but I was charged up by his confidence that this shot would be special, and I wanted to put it to immediate use.

"I'll develop it tomorrow when I get down to Hartsville and send you some copies."

"Can you overnight them to me? We can bundle the picture together with photocopies of the newspaper article."

"Sure."

"Lots of copies."

"How many?"

"I don't know, a hundred."

"You're the boss."

That night I set aside the leftover spaghetti I had planned on for my dinner and pulled a venison tenderloin out of the freezer to thaw. Witt said he could use a break from the grilled-cheese sandwiches he was living on down at his campsite. We sat up late into the night drinking beer, waiting for the meat to thaw, trying to figure out what to do next. Whom to contact, where to apply pressure. Paul was working hard to get the crusher running. But now we were working just as hard to stop him. Seeing our grievance appear in the fixed, tangible medium of newsprint was transformative. We were newsworthy. We were for real. We felt we had earned our tenderloin.

We were a month into our battle. I had put a couple of thousand miles on my truck streaking between the mountains and the middle of the state. In the week I spent on the road I also racked up an $830 cell phone bill on the borrowed cell phone. This was an astonishing sum for a man who was living on $500 a month. Something called "roaming charges" had done me in, a hazard for the neophyte cell phone user. During that month I had lost sleep and learned how to write press releases and gained a first-name acquaintance with some of the luminaries in the conservation world. So far, it was an awful lot of fun. The meetings, the creation of the press packets, the building of our case. It was exciting. Every morning I sprang from the bed, eager to tell our story and sway the persuadable. We weren't just letting it happen, we were taking the fight right to Paul. And to Charles Gardner. Of course I knew we were just getting started, and I was painfully aware that I was an amateur gunslinger. But the flurry of activity, for now anyway, served as a welcome distraction from our long odds. Was it productive? Would it prove the difference as we made our case to a wide audience? I could not know. At this stage we seemed to be building a credible case that a great wrong had been visited upon the Coxes and Cooks and the other folks in Dog Town. And upon the Appalachian Trail, too. Now we had a model for how to fight smart. Alert the press and feed them good stories. Poke the state agency in the eye until it's shamed into action. And make life miserable for Dear Ol' Dad.

Owing to her concerns regarding surveillance, Ollie preferred meeting face-to-face when possible, and she always welcomed my visits.

I found her outside, on her pouting porch. Smoking a cigarette. When she smoked, she pulled on it hard. Her eyes shut with the effort to draw something she needed out of the cured leaf. I wanted to show her the print of Witt's picture, which had arrived in the day's mail. She put out her cigarette and took a copy of the picture from me.

I ran through all the things that had happened in the last couple of days. The meeting with Charles, the meeting with Trip. She listened, rapt, as I told her about Don Barger and his latest idea. "He says that sometimes an agency will put modifications on a permit that will make it so expensive to comply with that the applicant just quits."

"Paul won't never quit," Ollie guaranteed.

"Maybe if it's about money, he will. Don's smart."

Ollie swooned at the mention of our favorite conservation warrior. "I sure like what he said in the paper. Did you put those pretty words in his mouth?"

"No, he thought them up all on his own."

"Then Mr. Don Barger must be smart."

"You'll like him," I said. "He said he wants to come and see the mine from the Trail. And he wants to see it from your house. I told him all about your foundation."

Ollie was impressed. When Ashley and Freddy arrived home, she made me repeat everything I'd said.

"We're taking Paul down," she gushed. Her glee was something I had not before seen. She hugged herself, as if to contain an emotion she felt rarely, one that she ought not give free rein.

Ashley, cynical Ashley, was eager to hear more, too. "Was that real when they said the *National* Parks Conservation Association? I read that in the paper and I couldn't believe it. I'm going to put that up on my wall."

"You take the Charlotte paper?" I asked, always prepared to believe everything.

"You can read it online and print it out, Mr. College Graduate. It's called the World Wide Web."

I had a lot to learn yet. Ashley promised to show me how to read the newspapers online. For free.

Freddy was not so sure about the intimations of progress. "Why, hell," he said, falling into a chair. "You won't get Charles to admit to a damn thing when he's on the stand. It's hard to roll over with all that dirty money stuffed in your pockets. You know that."

Just as with Paul, Freddy and the rest of Ollie's family assumed an instant, first-name familiarity with Charles Gardner. From this point forward he was simply Charles.

I brushed off Freddy's pessimism. He was just being contrary. I explained that Don had devised his strategy to take Charles out of the picture, how the memo to his own file would get Charles off the hook in a way. We would not have to rely on his testimony.

"And what makes you think he's going to write this memo to his file?"

"I don't know. I think he wants to fix this."

Freddy scoffed. "Only thing Charles wants to fix is his retirement fund."

Now I pulled a copy of Witt's picture out of the thick mailing envelope.

The Cox clan gathered around it.

Finally Freddy spoke. "Well, dayum!"

"That's what it looks like from up on the Trail." I nodded up the hill, to where the Trail lay. I knew that they had not seen it from up there—Ashley had explained to me that she was strictly an "indoor" person and had never been on the Appalachian Trail—but I had not fully appreciated the impact the shot would have on them.

Freddy had more to say. "I'd say them hikers is going to strip a gear."

"They'll raise hell all the way to Raleigh," Ollie said.

"Maybe all the way to Washington," I said. "The Appalachian Trail is managed as part of the National Park System. That's why Don is fired up."

"I'd say the Trail is about ruined," Ashley concluded. "Who the hell would hike ten feet to look at that?" She pointed at the timbered clearing.

Ollie instructed Freddy to get out some soft drinks, to celebrate Witt's new picture and our new best friend, Don Barger.

Curly came home. He listened intently as Ollie told him about Don's latest idea. He took a cursory look at Witt's photograph, then dumped a big bucket of cold reality in the middle of our party. "You can't whip Paul. That's all there is to it, Jay. He's too big. I'd say if we keep on, he's going to snap. We've got him aggravated, but Paul ain't going to take but so much off us. Son, I'm telling you, he's rough and it won't be too much longer before he quits barking and starts biting."

Ollie waved away Curly's talk. She had taken some new pictures of her own and wanted to show them to me. The south-facing window of the garage apartment afforded a perfect view over Paul's haul road. Ollie had taken stacks of pictures. She recorded the license tag of every visitor to the site, and she kept daily notes of suspicious comings and goings. Ashley was her willing accomplice. Ashley was learning from the master. Homeschooled, she could usually finish her schoolwork in a couple of hours, and that left the rest of the day for conspiring against Paul and Nasty. But everybody was in on the effort. Freddy rides motorcycles, big dirt bikes. At Ollie's request, he would race up Belview after the crew left, at night even, for recon. Ashley called this *special ops*. And Freddy had uncovered many violations of the Mining Act. His reports were full of rich detail about the catch basins, which were out of compliance with Division of Water Quality standards, and how Richard and Nasty were clearing tracks to get the drill in position. He could detail right where they were stockpiling old equipment, and he would ask leadingly, "Don't that qualify it as an illegal, unpermitted dump site?" If Paul's crew was cutting timber in a designated "undisturbed area," Freddy could tell me what day they'd done the felling. If Nasty was piling stumps, Freddy could roll out his copy of the mine map, draw a circle with his finger, and say, "Right here's where they're at." It was truly a family affair, with Ashley on the computer, Ollie manning the cameras, and Freddy scouting on the ground. Generally Curly laid low. As a county employee, his boss was Sam Laws, and that meant his job was on the line. Further, Curly was worried about Ashley's and Ollie's safety. Paul Brown's crew was a pretty rough bunch, was all he would usually say. *Son, them boys is rough.* And Curly feared if they knew they were being photographed, having their picture made while endeavoring to dodge the spirit and the letter of the Mining Act, they might make trouble. But I don't mean to suggest Curly was not wholly on the team, that he didn't want Paul gone as much as Ashley did, as much as any of us. He did. And Curly had big ears. He brought us all the talk from town. He reported on what the commissioners had up their sleeves. What they were saying in the office of Tommy Burleson, the county inspector, about building permits and variances and inspections. Curly was willing to try to help, he just didn't think, being honest, that we had any chance at all.

With all our scouting and research, our adversary was coming into clearer focus. Each visit with Ollie and her family shed new light for me, opened possible lines of attack against Clark Stone Company. At the top there was Paul. My brother's father-in-law told me that over in Watauga County, word was that Paul Brown would rather lose a limb than let go of a dollar. Paul would do anything for money. Everybody had something to say about Paul. He worked like a Turk, never took a day off. He pressed flesh. A former employee told me, "Paul don't like to let the bartenders get lonely." He put the lawmakers in Raleigh in liquor and women. Paul, lover of money, crusher of rock, and political force to be feared, was the head of the beast. Then there was his surveyor, Randy Carpenter. Ollie called Randy "the Bald Eagle" because he was thinning on top and because he had the gait of a big, awkward bird. Randy surveyed the proposed mine site and prepared the application. He was also an attorney, but we weren't sure if he handled Paul's personal legal affairs. Ollie didn't yet know what to make of Randy. "He's not the worst of them, but I don't trust him" was all she would say. Freddy was not so charitable, saying, "I'd say if he works for Paul, he's crooked as a broke dog leg." The crew on the site consisted of James Vance, the foreman, aka Nasty, and Richard Whitehead. Richard didn't have a nickname, so we just called him Richard. Curtis Hughes, "Trackhoe Daddy," came and went daily. Electricians tore up and down the mountain in shiny white trucks sporting a distinctive lightning-bolt logo on the doors, and the folks with the blasting company arrived regularly. A welder drove a black Dodge pickup. "The El Camino Kid" usually came to work late. If he came early, I usually got a call from Ollie. "The El Camino Kid was on the mountain at six thirty this morning. What do you make of that, Little Buddy?"

Then there was Tony to consider. Tony had a well-established violent streak. He would fight anybody. Ashley said he had once threatened to kill the entire family over a fight with Ashley's mother, and nobody doubted his resolve. He was often drunk or high on pills. He was Ashley's father, Ollie's brother, Freddy's uncle, and he started the fight I stepped into. He had led the charge, had buried Charles and the folks at the state in stacks of letters, and his family had rallied around him. But when he sold his house to Paul, swore his own self to silence with the drug-impaired stroke of an ink pen, Tony earned the withering dismissal of his daughter and the others. He now professed hatred for Paul, regretted the deal he had struck, but that was not enough for Ashley and Ollie. Tony was worse than Paul. He was a sellout. We would have to watch him at all times.

# Chapter 5

It happened so slowly I almost didn't recognize it. In all the racing around lining up allies, in all the angling and speculating and gearing up to fight, I was making myself ill. Even when it was fun, the constant uncertainty, the dread of the outcome, was exacting a toll. Effort began to anneal into anxiety. My sleep pattern was now so erratic that I began to loathe nightfall. I was unable to think about anything but the mine. I wasn't surprised when a routine checkup turned up elevated blood pressure. Not high, but "high normal." My doctor put me on a low-dose beta-blocker, but it made my fingers and toes cold, so I went off it. The doctor ordered an MRI, but I skipped it, not wanting to know what it would turn up. I had shooting pains down the back of my leg, a flare-up of an old basketball injury, and sitting became painful. As did standing and hiking. Some days I felt I was falling apart. The most obvious Paul-related distress was born out of the constant low rumble of construction equipment. The various noises made by the machinery took up residence in my brain and gnawed small holes in my head all day long on those occasions when I tried to reclaim my writing life, needed to concentrate, and then a phantom thrum lingered into the night when the Clark Stone crew could not possibly be working at the site. When they were working, when the bucket of the trackhoe hit rock, it went through me like a whistling arrow. I could hear it over conversation, over the radio, over the sound of my own footfalls as I hiked the woods or cast to trout in Big Horse Creek. I was struck by a sad realization: the only time I felt free from the racket coming from Belview was when I was mowing. The noise from the mower drowned out the sounds coming from the crusher site. This place that had been, all my life, a place of quiet remove from the outer world, a left-behind place of ancient ways, was now filled with more aggravating modern impacts than any other place I had ever lived.

I was also left to wonder over my own reaction. How could a backup beeper on a truck do this to a man, bring him low? I had never considered myself to be overly sensitive. Or weak. But then I had not always lived on the mountain, in the splendid isolation I now enjoyed, and perhaps I had grown too used to the perfect, the lovely.

I had lived in towns, then briefly in a city. Chapel Hill, where I grew up and went to college, was home to thirty thousand people. It has the sounds typical of a forested burg. Cars zipping through neighborhoods. A radio playing through an open window up the street, the drone of a leaf blower. Rarely, though, does that symphony of suburban sounds exceed the expectations reasonable to one living in such a place. But the noise emanating from the mine site shattered the expectation of birdsong and wind through trees and water seeping over rock. The constant clatter, clap, and jangle from the mine site destroyed the expectations of blessed, natural silence. Having borne witness, right out the windows of my home, on the ridges near and far, to a booming second-home and resort industry, having mourned the loss of my sense of utter wilderness solitude I'd known as a child in the summers, I found that the loss of *quiet* on top of that was maybe more than I could bear. Home was becoming my torment. I had a notion that maybe being sensitive to the destruction of Belview Mountain was called for, was the least I could do. If I could come to terms with that, with the dismantling of a mountain, with the daily churn of devastation out my door, then maybe I would become the kind of man who could accept anything, could give in until there was nothing left. And that seemed to me like dying.

In 1969, friends of my parents' were hiking a remote and uncommonly scenic portion of the Appalachian Trail when they became lost. They tramped through the woods and eventually came upon a couple camping on a primitive site on the east slope of Big Yellow Mountain. The couple told of their plan to sell off the mountain, a thousand acres of creeks and pastures and rich cove forest, for the princely sum of $42 an acre. That night, after relocating the Trail and eventually arriving home, those friends called my parents to tell of their adventure. Within days my sister, brother, and I were loaded into the station wagon with dogs and fly rods and rolls of film, heading for the top of the world to stake our claim to a piece of Appalachian wilderness paradise.

My parents bought into a land-holding corporation as shareholders in the new enterprise and secured a cabin site of nine acres on the edge of a pasture that fell away into dense forest. The cost of the land was $900. In later years my mother purchased more of the land adjoining ours to ensure its protection. A few others bought, including the friends of my parents', a few true believers in backwoods living. And who but a true believer, a genuine lover of mountain solitude, would pay such a hefty tab for raw land in the middle of nowhere? The road up our mountain was a treacherous one-lane gravel way that traced the route of an old game trail. There were no facilities, no improvements, no signs that this was in any way a sound investment. Electric lines were being run under a rural electrification program. There was no newspaper delivery, no place to buy food for miles around—no amenities of the kind most people were seeking in a holiday destination. But a few came. Including my own, six families bought land on Big Yellow between 1969 and 1973. These early-timers brought their horses with them, and the community was called Yellow Mountain Ranch. There were no fences. The horses simply roamed the mountain, mingled freely with the wild herd that thundered across the bald peaks of the Highlands of Roan.

Right away my parents decided to build a cabin next to the pasture, a summer place, a getaway from the university work that occupied them nine months of the year. They bought a pair of old farmhouses in Durham County to reclaim the wood. The farmhouses sat forlorn, condemned, consigned to a watery death by the coming of Jordan Lake, and the pair were had for $100. The houses were treasure troves of hand-hewn timbers from the 1800s, wide plank floors, and thick, pine doors. The two structures provided the bulk of the building materials for our cabin, down to the rock for the chimney. For much of a year we all, parents and children included, spent our free time stacking lumber and pulling nails and knocking mortar off old bricks, preparing all of it for transport to the mountain. Everything else was gotten around Big Yellow. In the 1970s mountain people were tearing out the thick chestnut planks their ancestors had built their houses of. The American chestnut was now virtually extinct, ravaged by a blight that killed nearly every member of its kind, but the rarity of the wood was of little concern to those who had grown up surrounded by more trees than could be counted, and it was a symbol of status to replace old, worn boards, what they could, with new wonder products: gypsum board and sheet paneling. Mountain people burned chestnut in their woodstoves. My parents put the word out in the valley that we would take what chestnut folks didn't want, and soon we had enough for the rest of the cabin.

The house was built by Lloyd Blair and the Taylor boys from up Little Horse Creek. Lloyd was a striking, tall mountain man with hands as strong as iron. Lloyd didn't read blueprints, had no use for such things, and so the house was built based on conversations he had with my parents while leaning on the hood of his truck or our car, and Lloyd's own sense of proportion. He incorporated the materials we fetched to the site as we delivered ever more old lumber, old bricks, old doors. Every weekend we traveled to the mountain to see what Lloyd had come up with. And it worked. The house became a decent pile of stout walls and rich, weathered wood. Features we considered novel, make-do, back in 1970 were, by the turn of a new century, prized in the local real estate market. *Old timbers! Rare rough-hewn chestnut paneling. Traditional dry-stack rockwork!* But marketability was not a consideration in a house you would never sell. This was just fine stuff to build a cabin with.

The first families to build on Yellow Mountain made up a hardy bunch. We carried most of our provisions with us when we came to the mountain for the summer months. We enlisted the help of a man who had lived his whole life on Birchfield Creek to plow a field, where we put in a communal garden to provide us with fresh produce. Most of the people in these high mountains had their own gardens to eat out of. What they didn't eat fresh, they canned for the winter. They would can anything. Jams and jellies, of course, and vegetables, pickles, and even meat. Sausage was water-bathed just as tomatoes were. They canned eggs. Admiring their enterprising use of the earth's bounty, we emulated them in every way we could.

The county forbade the sale of alcohol, so anybody inclined to take a store-bought drink of anything harder than Dr. Enuf, the local soft drink, had to drive across the Tennessee line to buy spirits. Luckily for my parents the first establishment on the Tennessee side was prepared for the flood of Tar Heels seeking Miller beer and Gallo wine. The place featured a drive-through window so the customer could keep right on trucking while making those nondiscretionary purchases of booze and fireworks. White lightning, the illegal local liquor, was more easily gotten on both sides of the state line, just one more thing stored on groaning shelves in glass jars.

As children, my brother and sister and I spent our summer days in the garden, or hiking. Picking wild strawberries in June, blackberries in early August, and wild huckleberries on the bald tops before we had to leave for school. We built tree forts and dammed creeks and stalked critters with BB guns. We played with the other children on the mountain and in the valley and got introduced to motorcycles and poker and bareback riding as forms of high entertainment. We introduced our mountain neighbors to darts and slingshots and frog-gigging. We wore overalls all day of every day, just like the mountain children, and by the end of the summer those overalls were soft as chamois.

We called our hikes wildflower walks, and anybody who could identify the spring ephemerals was dubbed one of us. Ours was an open society. If you were brave enough to drive the road, you were a welcome visitor. If you could tell stories or shoe horses or wield a fly rod, you could get fed, and if you could play a stringed instrument, you could count on a cold drink and a place to lay your head.

The people in the valley were our friends and our entertainment. We drove off the mountain to go to their gospel singings and street fairs and rodeos. They came up to hunt coons or gather branch lettuce and other herbs as their ancestors before them had. They taught us which roots were valuable, which had medicinal purposes, and which would kill you dead. We begged them to tell us stories, sometimes just so we could hear them talk in their magical singsong. We collected their colorful phrases and took them home with us. If you felt sick, you had a *swimmy* head. If a kid was filled with mischief, he was *just the awfullest mess.* Of a shy dog it might be said *he don't cater to strangers.* We all took to calling irises *irishes* and we said *flares* for *flowers,* and we forgot all about gray squirrels, for we were surrounded by *boomers,* the red squirrels that would eat your house down to the ground if you didn't continually chase them off the rafters under the eaves. The balm of Gilead tree became the *bamgidly* tree, and if we had a lot of something, we said we had a *right smart* of it. As in *we cut a right smart of firewood and stacked it.* When I was older, I learned that we were as much of a curiosity to our valley neighbors as they were to us. My family, along with the other first families, were called *original settlers* by our Buchanan neighbors at the mouth of Birchfield Creek, and we earned the high honor of being considered *stout.* "Son, a man's got to be stout to stay high up on that mountain," Ralph Buchanan would say, and that was some compliment. In those early days we formed relationships with Buchanans and Blairs and Thomases that will last after this generation passes.

When George Vanderbilt built the largest private home in the country, the Biltmore House outside Asheville, he had already begun to purchase nearly his entire viewshed, over 125,000 acres, which now comprises a district of Pisgah National Forest. Once the estate was completed, it must have been an astonishing site to stand on his terrace and gaze upon Mount Pisgah, part of his holding, and dozens of ridges and peaks, all his. But in the middle distance he could see several woodlots and farmsteads in the yonder valley. His eye offended, he went about buying out seventy landowners so that he might turn the visual clutter of the Bent Creek settlement back to forest. My family and our mountain neighbors were not able to buy all of the land on the mountain, or all that we beheld from its overlooks. A thousand acres seemed a gracious plenty, more than enough to ensure peace and quiet and provide a remove from the outside world. Indeed, to maintain our road and pay the land taxes, my parents and the other early settlers had to sell some of the tract to others who were willing to brave the ascent to enjoy the views and join our rarefied way of doing. Still, the first families were determined to avoid becoming a resort, a Sugar Mountain with its ski slopes and mushroom-shaped cabins, or another Beech Mountain, the seemingly LSD-inspired village to our north, with its bizarre "Land of Oz" tourist attraction and faux Tyrolean motif. The landholding corporation we formed was nonprofit, and a board was elected to ensure that the road was maintained. Almost immediately upon the completion of the first three houses on the mountain, there arose a sentiment, then a policy, against selling more land than was needed to be able to afford the road and its maintenance. Some of the things we loved the most could be lost in the sharing. Consequently what little land we sold was sold in large tracts, and eventually each tract was voluntarily deed-restricted against subdivision. In 1974 two fledgling conservation groups, Southern Appalachian Highlands Conservancy and The Nature Conservancy, combined forces to buy 395 acres, the entire top of Big Yellow Mountain, including its grassy bald summit, from the Averys, the cattle family that had owned it since the 1780s in a land grant from the king of England. In the 1990s my parents and their neighbors elected to sell 210 acres, the north end of our holding, to the US Forest Service as a buffer for the Appalachian Trail. That block of land runs from just past my house nearly to the bald opening on Little Hump Mountain and another nineteen thousand acres of publicly owned conservation lands.

It seemed that we were perfectly isolated, living in a time warp. When we looked out our windows to the south or north or picked wild berries in the meadow by the house, the scene we gazed upon looked much as it must have looked when the Cherokee camped here on hunting parties. Mature hardwood forest, some of it old-growth, virgin forest, stretched for miles in every direction. Looking east when I was a boy, I saw not a single building in the viewshed. And to the south the country was even wilder without a single home or road visible.

Our sense of perfect isolation changed in 1980 when a developer began construction of the mammoth Sugar Top condominium atop Sugar Mountain, seven miles to our east.

Sugar Top's size and its placement on the top of the mountain meant that it was visible from every other prominent peak in the area, from as far as fifty miles away. It was visible from the bald top of Big Yellow and from the Appalachian Trail. And from my living room. My family was disgusted by the imposition of Sugar Top, the excess and poor taste it seemed to exude. But at least we were not alone in our disgust. The outcry from leaders in the tourism industry and the conservation community was swift and fevered, and North Carolina's General Assembly quickly cobbled together its landmark Mountain Ridge Protection Act to preserve what was left of the prized scenery of our mountains. But something special had been lost. On Big Yellow Mountain we felt that the wilderness setting of Avery County had suddenly been breached by an unwelcome interloper from another time and place. Never mind that we were, ourselves, relative newcomers to Avery County. Or that we had made our own homes in woods that had been inaccessible to any but the most tenacious drive train, the most ambitious hiker, before our arrival. Though we had pushed a road, it was primitive, not much wider than a game trail. We had put up cabins, but they were simple, modest affairs. Frankly, we felt our simple lifestyle, our stubborn refusal to profit off the land, afforded us some insulation against charges of hypocrisy. In truth we thought we were better than the people who had violated Sugar Mountain, humbled the very horizon with their concrete pile. Sugar Top was forty-five minutes away by road, seven miles as the crow flies, but in those years after it was built our eyes worried it like a sore tooth that gets all the attention.

Since Sugar Top had gone up, not a single day had gone by that I did not gaze upon it and seethe over the greed that would make one man, or one corporate entity, impose a perverted vision on so many others. But it was not just Sugar Top. Sugar Top was just the beginning. Now developers were pouring into the mountains. Golfers wanted town houses, and stone and stucco mansions. They wanted recirculating-water features and hot tubs and clubhouses. They wanted crisp mountain air and rolling fairways. And views. Mostly, they wanted views. In the 1990s, with a booming economy and a red-hot stock market, every slope to the east of Big Yellow seemed to sprout roads and houses in the hungry search for "view properties." Unlike my neighbors, the developers of these communities seemed to have no interest in leaving a light footprint, in leaving the forest intact. They seemed bent on one thing: making money. Up went large houses on small lots, mansions hung off ridges, looming over the treetops. Mountain families were bought off and the old places torn down, or burned, to be replaced by gated resort communities patrolled by private security guards.

But all that activity was still *out there*. It was happening on the other side of the county. We could see some of it on clear days, and we encountered the traffic when we had to go to town, but we still had miles of forest buffering us from the worst impacts of modernity.

In 1992 I quit a job I had taken after law school. I was working for Waterstone's Booksellers, helping to establish the company in the United States. The job sent me to Boston and to Chicago, and I was offered a position opening the group's chain of airport bookstores, a job that would take me all over the world. But I did not want to go all over the world. From the time I was a boy I knew where I wanted to live. I wanted to live in the forests of the Southern mountains. I wanted to fish the Roan's creeks and drink from the spring on my family's property. I wasn't poor, wasn't married, no one was counting on me to provide or contribute, and so, that is what I did. As soon as I had enough money in the bank to survive on, I quit my job and headed for home. In effect, at the age of twenty-eight, I retired. I figured that while I was healthy enough, I would live a wild life. I would fish every creek in Avery and Mitchell Counties. I would heat my house with wood. I would hike out long ridges and dive into the lush woods in one of the last relatively untouched places in the eastern United States. I intended to live the good life while my joints were loose, my muscles firm. My real needs were few. I figured I could afford to write for a few years without going hungry, without depriving myself of the essentials: fishing line and flies, upkeep on my truck, food for the dogs. I would put myself on an austerity budget, a fixed income. I would cut my own hair. (This was harder than I imagined, and my first efforts were repaid with odd, sideways glances when I went down the mountain.) I would take cold showers with the lights out and cease at once buying new clothes and other nonessentials. In a couple of years, I figured I would have my own book appearing on the shelves of the world's bookstores. I imagined going off the mountain twice a month or so, to the post office, to collect royalty checks that would pour in from publishing companies happy to have me in their stable. I figured if I needed money in the future, if my writing career flopped, I would always have the option to clean up proper and get a job. I had a law degree I could turn to. I knew time would slow my ability to scramble up mountains and wade swift streams. Surely I would be able to secure employment in my middle years, after I had fulfilled my need to climb and swim and dive and cast to trout. I couldn't find anyone else making the same gamble, any fellow experimenters inverting the establishment progression from school to marriage to work to retirement, but it seemed perfectly reasonable to me when faced with the alternative, a job behind a desk, riding in airplanes in a suit and a tie.

A couple of years into my experiment in living, with little prospect of the publishing success I imagined—at least not on the timetable I had envisioned—my parents called the family together and announced that they were to divorce. In the division of property, my parents, and my mother's attorney, agreed that I should own the house on Big Yellow Mountain. It was too far from where either parent lived, and nobody else in the family had the energy to keep the old place up. I had been living there, improving it, making it my home, so there could be no doubting my commitment to keeping the place standing. Suddenly I was a homeowner. The deal was signed, sealed, and delivered. My heart was married then to this place, this mountain. As the union between my parents was ending, the mountain was my stay.

In a sense I was ruined for every other place, every other life I could imagine. To live like this, to live simply, in this place amid rock, seeping water, the dirt bursting forth with wild orchids and rare lilies and jewelweed and all the splendor of the natural world pressing into the daily routines, both wrecked me and made me. The mountain infused my days, mixing with my blood as I drank springwater that tasted of leaf litter and sunlight. As I worked and fished and moved through the woods with increasing assurance, the mountain left this man ill-suited for any other life, any other place. And that is a risky place to find oneself when the world closes in.

I'm not proud of this, but as Paul Brown began to take down Belview Mountain, I took some comfort knowing that I was not alone in my growing sense of doom. My neighbors, too, were becoming alarmed by this new threat emerging so close by. Our sense of tranquillity was under threat. The spring and summer after I first met Ollie, the backup beepers, the drilling, and the falling of trees became our constant companion on Big Yellow. We awoke every morning to the rumble of engines, the churning of cement mixers from across the Gap. When I led hikes for the conservancies, horrified looks came across the visitors' faces as I explained to them how much of Belview Mountain would come down. During the first phase of the permit, 46.82 acres of the mountain would be removed. That would take out the summit. The overburden, tens of thousands of tons, would be hauled off the site or pushed off the ridge into the low places. High benches of granite would be created by the blasts into the core of the mountain. While you could see the initial clearing from the nature preserve at the top of the mountain, I could not see it through the thick forest down below my house. Still it was always there, reminding me that there would never again be peace and quiet on the mountain. Not for the ninety-nine years of Paul's lease. Not unless we could stop it.

I developed a routine. When the racket got really bad, when I thought my head would burst with the incessant noise, I would get up from my desk and hike to the top of the mountain and over to the Appalachian Trail. There I would sit. I would punish myself by watching the crew work. From the Trail the trucks looked small as they zipped up and down the haul road. And the trackhoe looked like a toy as its operator plunged the shovel head deep into the earth, ripping out root balls and boulders and fresh brown dirt. Somehow, watching it briefly ameliorated the agony of hearing it. It was only one trackhoe after all. It sounded like an army of trackhoes but it wasn't. And there weren't a thousand Euclid dump trucks. There were only three. But then, as I sat longer, on land owned by the people of the United States of America, land acquired using taxpayer dollars to provide a wilderness walk from

Georgia to Maine, I would feel the bloom of anger feed itself and rise through my chest. Maybe that is what I sought. Maybe what I needed on those days was whole knowledge of why my anger was appropriate. I wanted to exist in a perfect sense of self-righteous outrage. Because I was right.

As that spring wound on, as the trees kept falling, a punishing reality was born in me: if Paul Brown succeeded in his effort to take down Belview Mountain, I would have no choice but to leave the mountain and the house I had spent my childhood summers in, the house I had turned into my homeplace. How could I write, how could I possibly concentrate with the white-hot anxiety building in me, taking its toll as the mountain came down in the phases detailed in the mining permit? How much of the mountain would disappear through the jaws of the primary crusher, get hauled away, over the term of the lease? Over my lifetime? I knew, or I suspected I knew, that my perfect state of fury—as satisfying as it sometimes felt—would ruin me.

But if I did decide to sell, to leave the home and land I loved, who would buy it? Who would buy a house situated so near to a clattering, groaning quarry? The views from the house, while no longer of undisturbed forest, were magnificent—Sugar Top excepted—and would remain so, even with the quarry running. By artful pruning, a buyer could maintain the views of surrounding mountains while blocking the view of the quarry pit indefinitely, especially since mined mountains grow shorter over time, while trees grow taller.

I won't say it wasn't tempting. By no design, without calculation or effort, the house had become valuable since we built it. Old wood with hand-pulled nails had become a high style over the thirty years it had stood. But the question remained: who would buy a house where it was impossible to open the windows, impossible to sit on the deck or work in the yard without the incessant reminder that the neighboring mountain was being pushed through metal heads of a rock crusher?

I would run through the scenarios. I would visualize calling my sister and brother and telling them I was selling the house we grew up in, the house we had all worked on with our own hands. *And why?* they would ask. Because I couldn't take the noise, the strain, I would reply. I could nearly hear their howls of protest. I imagined showing the home—reduced to mere real estate—to potential buyers. *That's the window we took out so Pokey the horse could be at the table for my brother's fourth birthday party. That's the beam where my pet raccoon attacked the mounted owl Mr. Robert shot by mistake. This is where the guests slept when we had Arthur Griffith's funeral in an April ice storm.* Of course I would show the house on weekends only, when the crusher might be silent. Even though the permit Charles issued allowed the crusher to run twenty-four hours a day, 365 days a year, surely the crew would not run it all the time, I reasoned. They would shut it down to go to church on Sunday, and for prayer meeting on Wednesday nights, at least, and probably take Christmas Day off, too. In Linville, Paul's operation had shut down on weekends, so that gave me hope and offered a potential selling point. *Surely it won't run all day, every day,* I might enthuse to hot prospects. Maybe a nice deaf couple would take a liking to the forest, the pasture. I figured I would have to accept a fraction of the pre-mine value of my home and land. Land values in western North Carolina—at least for desirable properties, "view properties," those not neighboring major industrial sites—had risen in a dizzying upward spiral and would certainly be out of my price range, so little would I recoup from the sale of my own house. And if I could find the money to move, where would I go? I could try the backside of Big Yellow. The backside of the mountain had always been even wilder and more remote than the east face. But now a developer from Florida was boasting of bringing a luxury bed-and-breakfast and resort cabins to the 450 acres he owned there. Could I try the valley? Beautiful land lay to the south along the Toe River. But nothing was safe. With no zoning in the mountain counties, I had no assurance that another neighbor might not decide to put in a truck yard or an asphalt plant in another location. Or a Walmart superstore. Unless I could afford to buy an entire valley, ridge to ridge—and surely I could not—how could I know that I would not leave the devil I knew for a devil I had not yet imagined?

I tortured myself by considering moving out of the mountains entirely. The rest of my family lived either in the middle of the state or at the coast. Could I live on the coast, in the heat, with every wooded parcel of land being razed and reshaped by the golfing pilgrims that arrived in droves? With the oyster beds silting up and the water quality falling into the "impaired" column due to overdevelopment and the explosion of industrial hog-farming down that way? Could I actually live there? Having lived this long at the pristine headwaters of a stream, where I ran a pipe straight from God's green earth to my faucet, could I ever live downstream again, where the water has passed through hundreds of septic systems and dozens of sewage-treatment plants before reaching the tap? I couldn't come up with a scenario I could bear. I was too wedded to this spot, this land, and these neighbors. Even these boomers, these manic red squirrels who were chewing on the tail ends of my rafters. That left only one option: fight like hell. Fight like you have everything to lose.

I called Charles Gardner on the phone at his office in Raleigh. He seemed perfectly willing to indulge me. But I didn't want to ask him about writing a memo to his file on the phone. Too easy for him to rebuff me. I wanted him to look at me while we spoke. I wanted to see his serious eyes, his worn face. But it was a Friday and there was no way I could get to the middle of the state before the end of his workday.

"Can I come out to your house this weekend?"

He paused, but only briefly. "That would be fine. Come out in the morning."

Charles had told me about his house on one of the many photocopying visits I paid to his office. We had, in an entirely unexpected way, come to enjoy each other's company. Charles was either bemused at or impressed with my passion, and I was appreciative that he made his files available to me—as required by law—without any unnecessary unpleasantness. By way of explaining that he understood my concerns as a homeowner, that he *felt my pain* in the argot of the day, he had told me about his concerns for his own peace of place. His house was out in the country, in a quiet part of Chatham County, which was still, for the time being, a rural green-belt left out of the bustle of the Raleigh–

Durham–Chapel Hill sprawl. The house, he said, was oriented to take advantage of the angle of the winter sun, enjoying positive passive solar heat gain. But now Chatham County was in the crosshairs of the big developers. Change was coming and Charles was having to acquaint himself with the new reality.

It was a sunny Saturday morning. I drove out of Chapel Hill and pulled onto ever-narrower roads, past farm ponds and cedar-post fences, and through piney woods that were marked here and there with survey tapes, signs of a major road-widening project.

Eventually I turned onto an unlined road, then an unpaved driveway, and parked next to a nifty but timeworn sports car. A convertible.

Charles came out to welcome me. "You made it."

"Having invited myself, I thought I should show."

It was slightly embarrassing. As many times as I had seen him on the sixth floor of the Archdale Building, I didn't really know Charles, but here we were, strangely conjoined, connected by events and interests, engaged in this knot of contention, this strange dance of pending litigation.

We went inside the house, and my head was flooded with a sense of well-being. As Charles had described, the floors were brick, the better for absorbing and retaining a winter day's heat when the angle of the sun was low. The views out into the piney forest were lovely with the sunlight slanting down to the rich earth.

"I baked you a loaf of bread," Charles said.

That was it! Fresh bread. The house smelled of yeast and egg and a warm oven.

"It's sort of a tradition on weekends. I bake bread," he said.

His wife was away, he explained. She taught college in Greensboro. They normally spent the weekend together, but on this weekend she was away and he was a bachelor. Charles headed into the kitchen. "I knew you were coming, so I baked you a loaf, too."

I didn't know what to say. It was an unexpected gesture. And I really like fresh-baked bread. I fell over myself thanking him.

I sat on the sofa, he on a chair. We talked for a while, about his family, about mine. It turned out we had a mutual friend in Chapel Hill, had attended the same oyster roast in years past. He told me about his travels in Guatemala. His eyes flickered. About growing up in rural Georgia. About his love for his adopted state.

Finally I told him why I had come.

"If you will write what you told me the first time I met you, that you would not have issued the permit if you had known where the Appalachian Trail was, that would help clarify the matter." I chose my words carefully. "If that's still what you believe." My heart was thudding in my chest and I could barely hear my own words for the blood chugging through my ears. I felt I needed to elaborate. "Don Barger, at the National Parks Conservation Association, recommended this to me." It was a cheeky move, the blatant dropping of a name, but I wanted to borrow the credibility of Don's organization and in that way tip Charles off that this was getting serious. I waited to see if he would lose his cool. I had just told him that in the event my group sued him and his agency, a memo in his file, stating his take on how he had failed to perform a critical step in permitting, how he had made a mistake, would help my side enormously.

His face betrayed no alarm.

"I think I can write a memo to the file," he said, utterly composed.

"I see," I said, trying not to telegraph my elation. "You can." I wasn't sure he understood what I was suggesting. There was nothing unethical about it, and I was certainly in no position to coerce, or threaten, even if that had been my wish. But it was a bold step to make the suggestion, and I was a little surprised it met with no resistance.

But Charles was not fazed. "I'll look into it. Of course I need to know a little bit more. But if when I learn more about it, I feel the same way, I'll write the memo. And I'll send you a copy, if you like."

"Of course. Please do."

This was going better than I dreamed. I imagined Don Barger awarding me a medal for effective advocacy, at a banquet, held, perhaps, at the National Parks Conservation Association's annual meeting. Possibly on the rim of the Grand Canyon, at El Tovar, say, the handsome old lodge, or some other suitably rustic-yet-posh venue. While I entertained myself with my reverie, Charles went to get a piece of paper, and a pen.

He had me write down my mailing address so he could send me a copy of the memo he would write. If he did write one, that is, after finding out a little bit more about the situation.

The rest of the meeting was awkward. Charles gave me the loaf of bread. He walked me out to my truck.

I was sliding behind the wheel when he stepped forward to speak. "Jay, I appreciate you coming out here. I've grown to like you and I respect what you're trying to do. I mean that."

I took a moment before speaking. I was touched by his kind words. "Charles, I didn't think we were going to get along. But I appreciate how you've handled me coming to your office. I know I come on strong. I've only got one speed, forward, all out. And I know I'm having trouble making clear sense. I can't sleep anymore." I paused to compose myself. "You've treated me well. But we've got to solve this problem. There's nothing personal about it. If the permit wasn't issued properly, we've got a chance to fix it. And we have to do that."

Charles smiled in a sad way and swung my door closed for me. I rolled down the window to shake his hand. "I don't doubt it," he said as I pulled away, my tires flicking rock up into my wheel wells.

After the meeting with Charles I went home to the mountain.

I sat on my deck with my neighbor Bill Lowndes and ran through all I had learned in my research, on my travels around the state. It was Bill and his wife, Kim, who had originally told my parents about land for sale on Big Yellow. From that day to this, Bill has devoted his efforts to protecting the mountains all around the Roan.

I told him about Don's idea for Charles, the memo to the file.

"We need a lawyer," Bill said in his even tone. "Right away."

"Okay," I said. "You're a lawyer."

"We need a lawyer who knows mining," Bill elaborated evenly, his manner. "And that's not me."

Meanwhile, Clark Stone Company was racing ahead putting their crusher together. Rigid trusses and hulking arms sprung from the long spine of the beast. Supports for the conveyor system. The trees kept falling as the opening for the equipment grew like a spreading sore. Nasty had laid down a black ribbon of crush-run from another quarry on the haul road, and Richard was seeding the slopes they had previously graded. The welding crew showed up at the entrance to the site every morning at seven o'clock and worked right up to dark. They hauled fuel, opened ditch lines, and drove rivets like they were running out of time. Did Paul have any hint that Ollie and I were working together? That I was talking to conservation groups about how we needed to move fast if we wanted to save Belview Mountain and the Appalachian Trail experience at Hump Mountain? I didn't know. Surely he had seen the article in the Charlotte paper. Perhaps he was onto us. Or maybe not. Maybe we were invisible to him, our concerns irrelevant.

Ollie figured Paul was outflanking us. It seemed that Richard and Nasty were speeding their pace, tearing up and down the road outside Ollie's window with a new sense of urgency. Arriving on the site earlier and staying later. Ollie told me everything that went on in daily reports that left me suspended between amusement and tremors. Every conversation began the same way: "Well, hello, my Little Buddy. Are you on a landline, because you ain't going to believe this?" Nasty had stayed on the mountain until midnight last night. Mountain Electric was stringing a powerline; then they weren't. Freddy had heard that Richard was pushing a track for the drill skidder right above Faye Williams's house on the north end of the Putnam tract. He would go up and see about it. The reports were stunning in their detail. Pumps were hauled onto the site at eight thirty in the morning by a guy driving a brand-spanking-new Ford two-ton with Tennessee tags. A lowboy went up with steel trusses on a rainy day, and they nearly broke an axle.

I reported all this to Bill as we sat on my deck. He grew serious. He did not think we could wait any longer on the Southern Environmental Law Center or on the Appalachian Trail Conservancy—or their boards of trustees—to decide what to do. We were going to have to act on our own.

A week later I drove the two hours down to Hickory to meet with Bill and a lawyer by the name of Forrest Ferrell. Forrest was a retired Superior Court judge, known in every courthouse in every county seat in the mountains. He came highly recommended in the area of statutory interpretation. Tall and good-looking, with silver hair and an incandescent smile, Forrest Ferrell was a lawyer's lawyer. But just when you think you know everything there is to know about golden-throated Southern attorneys in penny loafers and starched Brooks Brothers shirts, consider Forrest. Every summer Judge Ferrell slips out of his poplin finery, flicks on his answering machine, kisses his wife good-bye, and peels off for a two-week, high-speed tear on his Harley-Davidson motorcycle.

Hickory was built on furniture money. For generations, Henredon and Kincaid and Bernhardt and the other furniture giants have taken lumber from the Appalachian mountains down to Lenoir and Hickory and Morganton, where they turn raw lumber into dining-room tables and sofas and bedroom suites. Hickory is a once-affluent city facing an uncertain future as cheap imports from China and Indonesia capture an ever-larger piece of the American market and the local factories close their doors one by one, moving operations overseas with a wave from the politicians, who have wrought exactly what their donors wanted, if not their voters. Forrest's firm was housed in a tastefully renovated former public library on a tree-lined street of handsome houses that spoke of the town's luminous past. He ushered us into the bright conference room in the lower level of the firm's offices.

"Gentlemen," he began, "what brings you down from the higher elevations to consort with the foothills people?"

I told Forrest the story. I disgorged my file of photographs and documents. I introduced him to Charles Gardner, and Tony Cook and Trip Van Noppen. I unloaded on Dear Ol' Dad and Randy Carpenter and the county commissioners. Forrest nodded and jotted notes, occasionally raising an eyebrow when I veered toward unsubstantiated allegations and too much local color. He tilted back in his chair. Sometimes he took notes when I was only telling him background. I wanted him to write down the sexy parts, the greatest hits, the buyout of Tony, Ollie's cracked foundation. But I was not so bold as to suggest how he conduct his review of my review. He asked a few questions, pled for clarification a couple of times, but mostly he let me run. Occasionally he would pick up a photograph with a manicured hand and peer at it.

After a while he checked his watch. He leaned back in his chair and stretched. "Gentlemen, we're going to need to get the Heel Hound in on this thing."

"The Heel Hound?" Bill repeated, uncertain he had heard right.

"Ron Howell, the Heel Hound himself, oh, yes. He's a hoot. Just you wait."

The next morning I drove south on Highway 19E, to meet with Ron Howell, the aforementioned Heel Hound. Witt, Bill, and Forrest met me at the door of an unassuming brick building on the road going into Burnsville. I introduced Forrest to Witt, hailing him as our photographer and the less volatile half of the Jay and Witt show.

We stepped inside a cramped lobby, filled a space cluttered with a jumble of cast-off furniture and piled books. It looked as if a creek had jumped its banks and coursed through the place, rearranging all. A kindly receptionist apologized for "this darn mess" and told us we could go on back.

We navigated a hall filled with reams of paper and more piles of books. Dysfunctional fax machines and a photocopier. We squeezed into a small office, where we sat on orange vinyl sofas that looked as if they were cast-offs from a health clinic or a dormitory lobby. Soon enough, Ron Howell himself appeared. We all rose. Judge Howell stepped around file folders to land behind his desk, where he lumbered into his big swivel chair. He then reared back and, as suddenly, leaned all the way forward. He squinted hard to regard us. Had he not actually seen us until he was seated? "Judge Ferrell, is that you?" he queried, as if he were only venturing a guess.

Forrest bowed, rather elaborately and deferentially, to make greetings and introductions. "Everybody, this here is Ron Howell, the Heel Hound of the mountains. Once you've got Ron Howell on your scent, he'll nip you until you tire. He don't ever give up."

Ron seemed pleased at this summation of his qualifications. He shook hands all around and mumbled kindnesses and greetings. He asked us to be seated, and we sat.

Ron Howell was a country lawyer in the best sense. Like Forrest, he was a retired Superior Court judge. He came from a long line of mountain men. But he had traveled out of the mountains as a young man, sought education and betterment, and stood tall as one of the leading citizens in the small town of Burnsville. He had won his judgeship by penning a handwritten letter to every soul in Yancey County asking for his or his vote. He had a rumpled air about him, as if he had just been reading a Russian novel in a reclined position. He confessed his eyesight was poor and he didn't hear awfully well. Either that or he didn't care to hear all that was said. He was turned out on this day in a blue, three-piece suit, not fine, but clean. He had a watch fob dangling from what was, one could only assume, a pocket watch.

From where I sat, I could see behind Judge Howell's desk, and what I saw tickled me. I watched, transfixed, as he used his right foot to kick off his left shoe. He then repeated the maneuver with the other shoe. I watched as he slid his stocking feet into a pair of corduroy bedroom slippers, the kind men get from their grandchildren on Christmas morning.

"Now, Judge Ferrell," the slipper-footed judge said at great length, what business do you bring before me today? What have you?"

Forrest cracked up. "Well, Your Honor, we got us a mess over in Avery County."

Ron pushed his eyeglasses up on his nose. "Avery County, you say. The Gomorrah of the mountain counties." Now he tilted his head to see over the eyeglasses he had just repositioned. "I hope none of you fellers is related to the sheriff over there, or is running for sheriff, or has ever served as the sheriff of Avery. Assuming that you are not, and have not, well, then, you may proceed. You couldn't shock me. Go ahead and try."

With the mess going on over the allegations against Sheriff Richard Buchanan, stealing from prisoners and the rest, the SBI investigation, all that, we all enjoyed a good laugh over Ron's stipulation.

Forrest asked me to describe the conflict over the permit for the

Putnam Mine. "Tell him the good parts," he said. "His Honor can take it, I assure you of that."

I dove into my story. I lay heavily on the failure of Clark Stone to notify the adjoining landowners of their right to seek a public hearing, then veered to Ollie's latest brainstorm. Ollie was tracking down information on the haul road Nasty had built. She was certain that he had failed to secure a DOT Driveway Connecting Permit for it. She was also "one hundred percent lock-solid certain" that Clark Stone crews had burned down a house on the Charles Smith property without first obtaining a burn permit. I wasn't sure exactly how that was relevant, but it seemed to paint the crew as bad actors, so I liked it. I told him how the mine site was the dominant landscape feature for a hiker walking from Hump Mountain down toward Doll Flats on the Appalachian Trail. Judge Howell nodded and took off his glasses, rubbed his eyes. At one point he interrupted me, "Don't tarry, Counselor, for Judge Howell suffers with narcolepsy and you might loose him at any moment. Let's get to the part about Charles Gardner."

I was impressed. Did Ron Howell know Charles?

"Charles issued the permit," I said.

"Of that I've no doubt," Ron said, nodding.

I hurried along. Presently Howell said, "Let me ask you something, young man. I can't remember your name. I'm bad to forget things. How long did it take this permit to get itself issued?"

"I don't know. I'd have to check."

Not content to wait, Judge Howell motioned my way. "Give me those papers you've got there."

I handed him my file folders, which were in considerable disarray, one thing piled on top of another, random sheets seeking escape. But the retired judge knew what he was looking for. Once he'd extracted the permit application, he flipped through it with economy. He hummed and nodded and tapped his desk. "Seventy-four calendar days." He sat up higher. "And that might be a new world record."

Forrest smiled broadly at this feat, his taste in co-counsel plain for all to see.

We all sat in silence as Ron flipped through more of my papers. There was no telling what else he might turn up.

Finally, Forrest slapped his thighs. "Well?"

Judge Howell looked up, as if he had forgotten us. "Well, what?"

"You see a case here?"

Judge Howell put his face in his hands, as if he were washing it after a nap. It was a gesture of exhaustion. Surely we had interrupted some arduous task that had sapped much of his energy. When he took his hands away from his face, he spoke.

"What we have here, Judge Ferrell, gentlemen, interested parties, is a new world record in the heptathlon event of permit-issuing. This permit went through Charles Gardner's office like shit through a goose. I say we've got us a case. Somewhere in here we do." Judge Howell tapped on the stack of documents.

Forrest tossed out more details, then said, "Jay and Charles belong to the same baking club, Judge Howell. Jay goes down to see him for Sunday dinner, and Charles bakes him bread, so you can ask him about anything you want. He knows Charles quite well indeed."

I was made to tell about going out to Charles's house, out past Chapel Hill. About coming home without any memo to Charles's file but with a nice warm loaf of bread under my arm.

Ron laughed softly. He closed my file folder and patted it with a big, sun-stained hand. "Let me give you a piece of advice about Charles Gardner. All of you. And especially you, young man," he said, zeroing in on me. I nodded, awaited a searing remark, a home truth. "When you go to see Mr. Gardner, in his office, I suggest you back up when you quit his presence. You can't trust Director Gardner to do anything but fight for the miner. Watch your back or do otherwise at your peril."

For an hour I answered Ron's questions. I ran through the other issues that had arisen. Ollie and Ashley, the photographs they had taken. I started with the unreclaimed mine site at Linville. The Mining Act covers mining sites even after the mining has ceased. The law states that a miner abandoning a site, for whatever reason, must perform certain duties. The site must be left safe and *the final slopes in all excavations in soil, sand, gravel and other unconsolidated materials shall be at such an angle as to minimize the possibility of slides and be consistent with the future use of the land.* Of special concern was the collection of foul waters. *In no event shall any provision of this section be construed to allow small pools of water that are, or are likely to become, noxious, odious, or foul to collect or remain on the mined area.* Freddy and Ashley had gone over to Linville and taken pictures showing numerous violations of these reclamation provisions: standing *odious* water, inadequate fencing. They could find no sign of returning the property to its original contours for future use. I pulled out the pictures they had armed me with and laid them out on Ron's desk.

"What we have here," I declared, "is a serial bad actor."

Ron sat back and hummed a tune, "Wildwood Flower."

"What we have here is a failure to give notice to the adjoining landowners," he corrected gently, but at length, interrupting his tune, "and a failure to have public hearings in furtherance of the objectives of the Mining Act." He rapped on his desk with a closed fist. His voice then shot way up in his nasal passages as he said with great thrust and emphasis, "And you can't do that!"

Ron had represented adjoining landowners in mining cases before. He told us about a case involving Vulcan Materials, the same sand-and-gravel behemoth Don Barger had mentioned. Vulcan owns quarries all over the United States. Ron's case involved a quarry planned for a site alongside a major highway. "Vulcan filed a complete application in which they notified everybody, even people across a four-lane highway, even people they didn't have to notify. For all I know, they notified Judge Ferrell here. By the end they were inviting dogs and cats and winged creatures to submit public comments."

"Why would they do that?" Witt asked.

"The big companies, they don't fool around," Judge Howell said. "They might be bad neighbors and destroy everything you own with the blasting and the dust, but they don't fool around with notice and they don't flout the statute. Because, you see, public hearings never yield much in the way of impediments, rarely do they yield anything at all, save for the feel-good misunderstanding that one is being heard. But, woe be unto that man that skips this part of the process, for avoiding notice can be fatal to one's cause. It never has, er, stopped anybody from going in—not that I know of—though I'm not sure anyone has been so bold as to try avoiding this relatively toothless regulatory hurdle." Ron breathed deeply. Were we done? No. "And why is that, you ask? Because it's like original sin. And of course the fruit of a poison tree will kill you just as dead." He tapped on his own temple with a crooked finger. "I'd say that's your case. Notice to your friend there."

"Ollie Cox?" I asked, just to be sure.

"Ms. Cox. Indeed. She has been violated, if only in the constitutional sense. But that ought to be enough to get us in front of a judge. If we can find one that has read the constitution, that is."

Witt pulled out the most recent of his photographs and he played them out on Ron's desk. The wizened lawyer picked up each one and turned it this way and that, possibly in an effort to reduce the glare on the glossy finish.

He dropped them one by one and let them fall in an untidy heap, as if to discard such newfangled storytelling tools. When he was through them all, he made to speak, but not about the photographs. "Have you come to retain my services?" he said to me now, rather suddenly.

I looked to Forrest and Bill.

Bill said, "We have. If you're interested."

Ron couldn't help but smile. "The things Charles Gardner gets up to are of great interest to me. I like it better than the movies."

"What do we do next?" Bill asked.

Judge Howell seemed to have more important business to tend to for a moment. He took great care plucking a stray thread from the sleeve of his jacket. He then ceremoniously set it loose over the edge of his desk, letting it drift to the floor. That done, he looked at me over his glasses. "You say you've got these ladies living next to this proposed site. And you've got these hikers who may or may not be driven to the point of despair as their wilderness perambulations may be adversely affected by all this purported racket. But they have to meet with their boards of directors and conduct—what did you say?"

"Meetings?" I offered, sheepish for reasons I could not name.

"Meetings!" he repeated, smiling a wild smile. "Meetings and evaluations of ramifications. And in the meantime the mountain is coming

down, the soil is running into the creeks and killing the helpless speckled trout and the waterborne whatnots, the elktoe mussels."

"Yes, sir."

"Well, that brings me to my point. If you want to act, you need to
act fast. Yesterday is not too soon, because, hear this, if they turn that
crusher on, if they get it running for a single second, for a minute or an
afternoon, it will run flat out for the ninety-nine years of that lease. I
do not know the judge who will stop that thing if it's operational, and
I know all the judges you're likely to appear before." He paused. "Judge
Ferrell, do you agree with that assessment?"

Forrest nodded gravely. "I defer, as always to your reading of the
situation, Your Honor. If he turns that thing on, this matter is closed."

Ron nodded, pleased. "And you see the thing about this Mining
Act is this: once a man has a permit to quarry an acre, he might as well
have a permit to take down the entire range. There are some hurdles to
getting a permit. Not many, but some, but none at all for an expansion
of an existing permit. None atall."

Forrest frowned and shook his head at the folly of regulators who
were up against a statute such as this one.

Ron carried on, "And that brings me to the most important part of
my aforementioned point, a point which I have now been brought to,
which is the matter of my fee." We all leaned slightly forward. "I ask
you this," Howell said, turning his gaze toward me. "Are you, young
man, going to have to have a cake sale to pay my fees, which are not
inconsiderable? It sounds like a band of widows and orphans and boys
in short pants to me."

At this Forrest howled. We all took Forrest's lead, joined him in this
good laugh, including me, though I had no idea of where we would get
the money for a single lawyer, much less a pair, was not sure anything
funny at all was going on here. But it was done. With a robust shaking
of hands all around, the Dog Town bunch had officially retained the
services of Judge Forrest Ferrell and Judge Ronald Howell, the Heel
Hound of the mountains.

# Chapter 6

have thought a lot about mountains. Maybe it is because I had ancestors in the hills at the foot of these mountains in what was then, in the 1700s, called Rowan County, now Burke and Iredell, and I was born to it. Of course mountains have power for those born to prairie and vale, too. In nearly every culture, mountains are revered and held in esteem. They are the source of myth from Tibet to the Caucuses. The lofty elevations are where the spirits reside in the nine sacred mountains of China, and the indigenous people in the Andes still make pilgrimages into the mountains to convene with the spirit world. In Mexico there is a story about the great massif that lords over Mexico City. Popocatépetl is named for a warrior. When the warrior went away to war, the father of his true love told his daughter that her warrior had perished in battle, a lie, and she died of grief. Upon his return to his village, the warrior learned of his true love's death and, in despair, took his own life. Upon their bodies the snow piled and made the mountains that stand as sentinels over the city.

In the Blue Ridge we have our own myths. The Cherokee told stories of the mountains, of how they were formed by great spirits, of how the Long Man, the god of rivers, had his head in the upper reaches, where waters were born. How the streams carving the mountains into ridges are the blood of the Long Man. Just to the east of Big Yellow the Blue Ridge drops away to the foothills. This escarpment, this forested wall, is a land of waterfalls and sheer cliff faces. One of the prominent rock outcrops is called Blowing Rock. Here, a Cherokee maiden leaped to her death when her father refused to let her marry her true love. The wind blowing up the face of the rock, a constant force of nature to this day, is said to have lifted her back to the rock.

Big Yellow was a Cherokee hunting ground. The bald tops of the Roan feature gentle, rolling topography. Elk herds and bison grazed the openings, and the Cherokee came to pray and hunt.

But mountains, these mountains, have long held another allure, for they are also a source of money. For three hundred years now, European settlers have extracted wealth from the high ground in the Appalachians. They stripped the timber, dug for the minerals. Just to the north of the Roan, up the chain of mountains, are the coalfields of southwest Virginia. For generations, a mining industry bent on riches has torn into seams of coal to power the nation, leaving the slopes in ruin. Mica, feldspar, olivine, and gemstones, all have been pulled out of the risen earth with disregard for their other value, for their inspiration, their standing.

On a raw February day Ginna McGee and I went to meet Faye Williams. Ginna was a former law school classmate of mine. I had been telling her stories about Paul and Randy and Charles, and she had come to Big Yellow to learn more. After law school she worked with the Southern Environmental Law Center in their Atlanta office, and then for the Environmental Protection Agency. In one of the great romantic tales of modern regulatory history, she met her future husband when she was assigned work on a case brought by the US attorney, an enforcement action against a subsidiary of his family's company, in which they were alleged to have sold fertilizer augmented with toxic dust to Bangladesh. To accept his invitation for a date, she had to step out of the case because of the conflict of interest. Now they are happily married, with four children underfoot, and the company has become a model citizen.

Ollie had told me about Faye. She said Faye and her husband, Grady, lived even closer to the crusher jaws than she did. She said Faye was mad as hell at Paul. That was enough to start with.

In a driving rain Ginna and I inched up a narrow drive that followed the northern boundary of the Putnam tract. Faye stepped out of her tidy white farmhouse and waved us in. A diminutive redhead, smart and trim, she was bursting with bright humor and positive energy. As advertised, she was mad as hell. Her eyes danced as she showed us around her place. "Look right there," she said. We stood in the kitchen, looking out the window at the crusher jaw.

"When they turn that thing on, this old house will fall down." She used a finger to point out her common boundary with Paul. "Back here, his line runs right behind the house."

I unrolled Freddy's copy of the mine map and showed Ginna how the proposed site nearly wrapped around Faye's farm.

Faye had never seen an original, full-size copy of the mine map, the permitted area, and it made her more angry, seeing the lines laid out just so.

"My family, the Statons, have been in this house for seventy years," she said. "We used to own a lot of this mountain, way back, and this was my mama's house. I can't open my windows when they're working around the crusher. My house shakes just from the weight of the big shovel. When they pulled that first shot, to set the jaw, everything in my house moved. And they're not even crushing yet." Through her anger I could hear the strain, the anxiety, about the mine, about meeting with me. About what her life had become since Paul arrived.

Now she explained something Ollie had not told me. While Faye wanted Paul gone and was properly outraged that she was never given an opportunity to contest the permit before it was issued, her husband, Grady, had reservations. Grady was not home on this day. He ran a small business on the other side of the gap, selling flowers to florists.

"Grady doesn't like the crusher," Faye explained. "But he doesn't want to cause any trouble, that's just how he is." She stopped and thought before speaking. "But this is my house and my land. It's Staton land from way back."

I told her that we were seriously thinking about suing the State of North Carolina for failing to enforce the notice requirement that she and Ollie were due. I told her about Forrest and Ron.

"The State?" she asked, confused. "I want to sue Paul. I'd like to run him through a crusher for what he's done to my life. I'm scared all the time and I've never been the kind that scares easy."

"That's my instinct, too, suing Paul," I assured her. "It may be that Paul was behind the lack of hearings, maybe he put pressure on the county. It might have been a plan, a fraud, but that's hard to show. If you ask me, something happened there. But we can't find it. Our best chance now is to get the permit revoked so he can't go in."

"But he's already in."

Now Ginna spoke. "That's what makes this so hard."

Faye appreciated Ginna's plain speech. This was going to be tough.

"Tell me one thing," Faye said, addressing Ginna. "Have they ever revoked a mining permit before? I've never heard of that."

Being more familiar with case law in Georgia, Ginna didn't know, but I did. "No," I said. "That's why we may have to sue them. We have to get a judge to shut them down."

"What do I have to do?" Faye said, stiffening.

"Nothing." I wasn't sure what she meant.

She blushed. "I have some money, but not much." Faye explained that she worked in the library at Lees-McRae College, the small private school in Banner Elk. She was nearing retirement and had put aside some money to travel, to have a vacation.

She didn't have to say more. I understood part of her problem. "Is Grady worried about the money?"

"He says these things can drag on for years and years and eat all your retirement. He says you can spend all your money on lawyers and then you still might lose."

"He's right," Ginna said.

"I'll pay for it," I said somewhat impulsively, and as the words left my mouth, I regretted them. I didn't want to present myself as the kind who could bankroll efforts as large as this one was likely to be. It sounded arrogant. And it was untrue. I thought about my austerity budget, my little experiment in living. "I'll get the money. But we need your name on the lawsuit. You're an adjoining landowner and I'm not. I'll make you this deal. You will never have to pay one penny. That's a promise. And we'll sue somebody. If we don't sue Paul, we'll sue the State for issuing the permit." For a moment I was afraid I had wounded her pride. This was clearly a woman who prized her home and

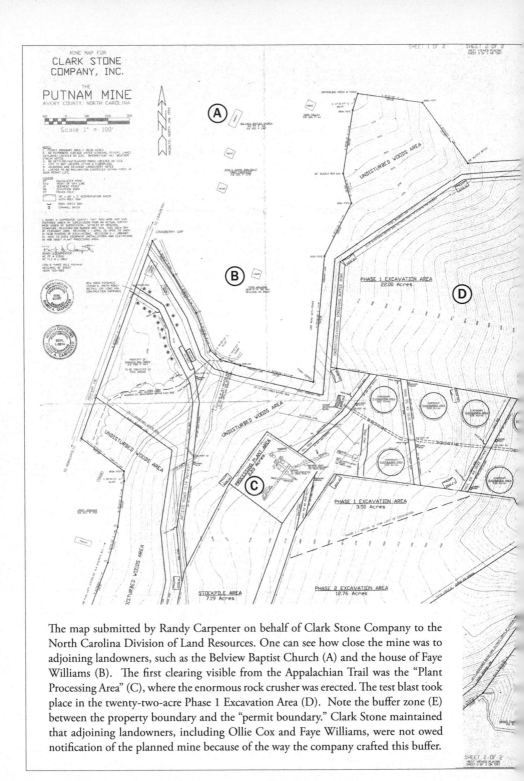

The map submitted by Randy Carpenter on behalf of Clark Stone Company to the North Carolina Division of Land Resources. One can see how close the mine was to adjoining landowners, such as the Belview Baptist Church (A) and the house of Faye Williams (B). The first clearing visible from the Appalachian Trail was the "Plant Processing Area" (C), where the enormous rock crusher was erected. The test blast took place in the twenty-two-acre Phase 1 Excavation Area (D). Note the buffer zone (E) between the property boundary and the "permit boundary." Clark Stone maintained that adjoining landowners, including Ollie Cox and Faye Williams, were not owed notification of the planned mine because of the way the company crafted this buffer.

her independence. I suspected she would rather pay her way if it was at all possible.

"You do the suing," she said. "I'll do whatever you tell me to do."

"You're sure?"

"I want him gone."


After we left Faye's house, Ginna suggested we drive up the haul road and look at the crusher. It was a Sunday and nobody was working. I had never been up to the site, had only seen it from across the gap. I had not been up on Belview, on Hartley Ridge, since I was a child, when we used to climb it in our 1946 Willys Jeep.

There were no signs forbidding trespass and no gate. Up we went. The morning's rain had stopped and a cool fog hovered over Belview. The haul road was huge, wide enough for enormous equipment to pass, tandem-axled Euclids, or Ukes, as Freddy called them, two abreast.

We took the big switchback just opposite Ollie's new house and came into the flat clearing I first saw from Witt's pasture back in the summer. My original estimation of the size seemed accurate enough. Four acres I guessed, an acre being roughly the size of a football field. Four football fields.

Piles of rusted trusses were half-buried in the soft earth. A guard-house built of T1-11 plywood sat high and at a slight angle, its paint somehow already peeling, its Plexiglas windows bowed. Huge hoppers sat on the bare ground. I was impressed with the sheer size of the equipment. Ginna wanted to walk around and examine the thing. But now I was getting anxious, wanting to leave before we got caught. I imagined Nasty pulling up and our having to explain what we were up to. Ginna prevailed and took off, banking long strides to get up under the main plant. It was compelling to walk around the structure. From Big Yellow the growing metal frame looked menacing enough, but almost toylike. An Erector set dwarfed by the massive forest around it. But from this side of the valley, it rose out of the earth as a futuristic behemoth come to eat whole mountains. I tried to imagine it coming to life, the cogs whirring, the conveyors conveying boulders the size of small cars into the hoppers, dumping the material into sorters, and the crushing heads grabbing and shattering the rock. Huge front-end loaders dipping into the hourglass-tidy piles of crushed stone, lifting it, pouring it into the teams of Ukes lined up to take it down to the scale house.

I left Belview with my head swirling. There was this issue of money. Paul's operation represented an enormous investment. He had money. The evidence of that was everywhere at the site. The sheer tonnage, the number of welded joints, spoke of thousands of hours of labor. Paul had money and had been sinking it into the side of the mountain in expectation of handsome returns. By comparison, I had little, only my nest egg, which would keep me so long as I didn't stray outside my strict budget each month. But Paul could bleed my accounts dry just by delaying matters, and I had no plan for replenishment. Not for the first time, I wondered how different things would be if I had a normal life, a job. Steady income. I had never sued anybody and I had no way of judging how much it might cost. Forrest's initial estimate of the legal fee ran to $30,000. But since that time, we had added Ron Howell to our team. We were going to have to pay both of them. And everybody in the legal field will tell you that you can take an initial fee estimate and multiply by four. At least. That would mean $120,000 for starters. That was to file a complaint and get into court and wade through the appeals process to a resolution. Hopefully the one we sought, but possibly not.

Reality hit pretty fast. Witt offered little encouragement when I asked him whether he thought we could get the Appalachian Trail Conservancy to help defray the costs. They had still not committed to take up the fight, much less contribute money. Friends allied with the other conservation organizations assured me that they either did not get involved in litigation, or that they did not have any money to devote to legal work. Don, at the National Parks Conservation Association, said he might be able to find $1,000, but certainly no more than that.

This is where most cases die: at the bank. Most claims, be they legitimate or frivolous, wither for lack of funding. Especially where industry is involved, with deep pockets, with legal-defense budgets, the ordinary citizen is normally bled out of the courtroom when the first bills come due.

Our best hope was going to be the Southern Environmental Law Center. As a nonprofit, they did not bill their clients. Instead they paid their attorneys out of funds raised from grants and individual donations. But so far, they were not acting as our attorney, and Forrest didn't think we could afford to wait for them to decide.

Bill Lowndes agreed with Forrest. We couldn't wait. Ron Howell's words rattled through my head: *If they turn that crusher on, if they get it running for a single second, for a minute or an afternoon, it will run flat out for the ninety-nine years of that lease.* Bill drafted a letter to each landowner on Big Yellow, and a few others in the community who had voiced opposition to the mine. The response was swift and startling. Within a week we had raised $20,000. I was overwhelmed. Forrest said we ought to form a not-for-profit unincorporated association of concerned citizens. "Okay," I said, "how do we do that?" Forrest chuckled. "You just say you are one, and then you are." So it came to pass; immediately upon learning what an Unincorporated Association of Concerned Citizens was, I became the chairman of one. Without time to think it through, Forrest and I settled on a supremely uncatchy name: The Unincorporated Association of Concerned Citizens to Protect Belview Mountain. The day we deposited the $20,000 in the bank, we put Forrest and Ron to work drafting our complaint. As Ashley said, we were now "in the lawsuing business."

From time to time I dropped in on Scott Nicholson at the *Mountain Times*. Scott was the first to tell me there was a story here, at the County Commission meeting. I delivered new pictures and I told him the latest from Cranberry Gap. Scott was an aspiring fiction writer and dissected what I told him with a novelist's eye. He ran a piece on March 2 under the headline STATE, NATIONAL PARKS GROUPS DEMAND PUBLIC HEARING ON MINE. The "national parks" group he referred to was Don's group. It was a thrill to read the headline. It came right out of one of my many press releases. I raced through the article. The best part was on the second page of the piece. Scott broke the news: our state attorney general, Mike Easley, who was now running for governor, mentioned us in a speech. *"The waters and mountains of western North Carolina belong to the people," said Easley in a statement issued from his office. "This mine will be operating near a particularly scenic and sensitive area. The public deserves to be heard about any potential threat to precious natural resources."*

Ollie called me, breathless. "What have you done now, Little Buddy? Are they going to lock Paul up? You're a troublemaker, worse than me. We're all going to end up at the bottom of the Toe River wearing cement bedroom slippers."

"You saw the article."

Ollie whistled high. "Did you, uh, catch the attorney general in a compromising position involving a farm animal? What made him say all that?"

"I didn't have anything to do with it," I said in all earnestness.

Here's what happened. A friend of mine, a kid I grew up with, was legal counsel to the attorney general, who was preparing to run for governor. Like everybody else I had ever met or heard of, I had sent Hampton Dellinger copies of Witt's pictures. I had sent him the press releases. That was all. And some weeks later it came out of the candidate's mouth. It was a huge break. Ollie was beside herself, thoroughly impressed and convinced, now more than ever, that I could do just about anything.


Even as the lawyers were busy drafting our complaint, I tried to get to Raleigh when I could, to remind Charles of our interest in the matter, and to needle the political class. I stalked the offices of the Southern Environmental Law Center, made myself available in case Trip had any news for me. By this time I had stopped writing my novel. I felt as if I were *in* a book. As if someone with a wicked sense of plot were writing my life, this case. Because I couldn't sleep, I busied myself raising antagonism to an art form. I worked the telephone and crafted press releases. When there wasn't any news, I rehashed old news, repackaged it, to see if it might grab the attention of some editor at some paper that had not covered us. I sought the attention of public officials, angled for invitations to receptions where I might meet people who could help us. I cultivated reporters and continued to court leaders in the state's conservation community. I reread with obsession the Mining Act of 1971. I studied accounts of successful, and unsuccessful, citizen battles.

I now regularly roamed the hallway outside Charles's office. Ostensibly I was there to pour through the growing Putnam Mine file. I was always greeted politely, without fail, by people we were about to sue. I usually popped into Tracy Davis's office to talk basketball or make some other small talk. Tracy went to NC State and pulled for the Wolfpack. I was a Tar Heel. We were natural, but genial, enemies when it came to sports, and perhaps in everything else as well, but Tracy was always pleasant, always willing to listen or to accommodate any request. I stopped by the secretary of the agency's office on a couple of occasions, just to let his staff know that we were coming, that we were not going away. That the secretary, Bill Holman, was a hero to me and to other conservationists across the state made it all the more painful that we were probably going to have to name him in the lawsuit.

After the meeting with Ron Howell, Forrest had asked me to get him a full-size copy of the mine map. Freddy had one but I couldn't give that one to the attorneys. Every mine in the state, all eight hundred, must have on file with the state an official map of the site. The maps are so huge that the Division of Land Resources doesn't own a copier large enough to duplicate them on-site. A citizen who wants a copy of a mine map is welcome to make his or her own copy, but it takes twenty-four eight-and-a-half-by-eleven-inch images and a lot of Scotch tape to get the entirety of the map laid out. I was wrestling the original mine map onto the photocopier one day when Charles happened by.

"I need to see your pictures," he said. "Do you have the good one, the one you told me about, with the hiker?"

"I don't have it with me," I said, taken aback at his request. "I've got a copy in the truck." I didn't quite know how to answer him. I had not showed Charles all of the pictures because I figured they might one day be admitted as evidence.

"I need to see what you've got." He helped me straighten out the map on the screen of the copier.

"I need to ask my lawyer." It was the first time I had told Charles that the Dog Town Bunch had retained counsel.

"That's smart, Jay," Charles said, not surprised. "Ask your lawyer."

"I'll call him when I get done with this."

"Why don't you get Witt and show me what you have. It doesn't have to be today. I want to know more about this. If your lawyer says it's okay, of course."

"Of course."

I went down to the lobby of the Archdale Building and called Forrest. I asked him if there was any reason I shouldn't talk to Charles, shouldn't show him the pictures.

"See what he wants," Forrest said. "You can talk to him and show him the pictures. Just don't leave any of the pictures with him."

Now I called Witt in South Carolina. He could come in the morning. He would work that afternoon making enlargements, and he and Beth would drive over and we would meet with Charles in the morning. My heart beat hard in my chest. The picture, the one with the hiker in it, and some others Witt had just shot were powerful. I knew that if Charles saw them, and if he was already thinking that the state should not have issued the permit, this might make up his mind. Maybe we could avoid filing the lawsuit. Was it possible we could save all the money involved in filing a complaint and save the mountain, too?

That seemed a long shot, but I was excited at this prospect. My mind filled with possibilities. I thought, maybe, just maybe, I could use this moment to convince Paul to write the memo to his file. That would lock the thing up, and Paul would see the hopelessness of trying to continue at the Putnam site. There might be more than one way to skin this cat, after all.

I stayed up most of the night, studying for our meeting. Deep in the blurry part of the early morning I was staring at the Appalachian Trail Conservancy's official website. A passage from their home page burned itself into my frontal lobe. The North Carolina Mining Act lists seven reasons for denying a mining permit. One in particular formed the basis for our grievance: *The Director of the Division may deny the permit if it will cause significant adverse effects on the purpose of a publicly owned park, forest or recreation area.* I had read this line a thousand times, dissected it, and usually I focused on the angle that the Appalachian Trail in the Roan Highlands is not only a publicly owned park, forest, *and* recreation area, surrounded by publicly owned forest and globally imperiled forest communities in the midst of a nationally significant natural-heritage area, it is also the most important kind of park, carrying the designation with the highest level of public interest: the Appalachian Trail is a national park, a unit of the National Park System, which is administered by the Department of the Interior. Just like Yellowstone and Yosemite, and Great Smoky Mountains National Park.

But now, at four o'clock in the morning, with my eyes desiccated from reading, I was struck by the word *purpose.* The word *purpose* appears both in the Mining Act, and in the welcoming passage on the Appalachian Trail Conservancy's home page. Under the heading "The Purpose of the Appalachian Trail," I read: *The Appalachian Trail experience represents the sum of opportunities that are available for those walking the Appalachian Trail to interact with the wild, scenic, pastoral, and natural elements of the environment of the Appalachian Trail, unfettered and unimpeded by competing sights and sounds and in as direct and intimate a manner as possible.* Purpose! Lawyers exult when statutory language dovetails with their client's interest. They delight at the repetition of key words, magic words. And here was such a word. *Purpose.* I was not a practicing attorney, I was just a dilettante, and I was half-crazy or, as a generous friend preferred to frame it, *intoxicated,* but right at that moment, tired as hell, strung out, I could see this case, *our* case, coming together.

A college town, Chapel Hill has a twenty-four-hour copy center, a relentlessly bright, humming shop devoted to duplicating course packs and dissertations and term papers all day and all night, every day of the year. At four thirty in the morning I was the only customer in the store, but machines were thrumming, pages slapping the ends of feeder trays. I photocopied the language from the statute, then printed out the Appalachian Trail's purpose statement. I then convinced the late-night skeleton crew, a lone kid with a collection of nose rings in his left nostril and a tattoo of Sylvester the Cat on his neck, to dry-mount my handiwork on foam boards. I even bought little cardboard stands for each presentation piece. If I was going to win this argument with Charles, I was going to win it with sharp advocacy skills and a solid grasp of the statute, all buttressed by professional-looking, litigation-caliber display materials. If this worked the way I hoped, we weren't going to need to go to court after all. I was going to present the plain language of the statute to Charles, and he was going to wince. He was going to call over to the attorney general's office, after notifying the secretary of the agency, and he was going to revoke the Putnam Mine permit.

Finally, with the sky now gray, I got into bed. I slept for an hour.

When the alarm went off, I sprang from the bed. I felt sick from lack of sleep. From nerves. From the nausea of hope. On the thirty-minute drive to Raleigh I pulled over twice, expecting to vomit. But nothing came. Possibly because I had not eaten anything since the day before.

I milled around in the dark, little lobby of the Archdale Building waiting for Witt. He and Beth were running late, but they arrived just in time for our meeting. Witt was wrestling with an armload of pictures. He, too, had dry-mounted his presentation pieces. Late at night, he had learned how to superimpose words on his pictures. Some had arrows pointing out the footpath of the Trail. Others included labels for all the notable peaks in the background. We picked the best of the lot, the ones that showed the cleared areas illuminated by warm afternoon light, the ones with the sharpest contrast between leafy forest and bared earth. And of course the one with the red-jacketed hiker. Beth was nervous for us and told us it was time to go up. Perhaps sensing that I was weak and dizzy and incapable of the simplest task, she seized the initiative and pushed the elevator button to summon the carriage. Witt and I got on the elevator and Beth wished us well. The doors closed and we were sucked upward, to the sixth floor. Beth went down to the coffee shop in the basement to wait on us.

---

We met Charles in the hallway. I introduced him to Witt and we headed into the big conference room, the same room I had sat in the first day I had come to Raleigh, the day I first pulled the permit. After a few awkward ice-breaking remarks, some throat-clearing, we launched into our presentation.

We started with Witt's pictures.

Witt laid out the photographs and described each. He talked about the perspective, the time of day, the light. I was grateful for his presentation, though it made me self-conscious. Unlike Witt, who is a professional photographer and a former forester, I did not possess quantifiable expertise in any area that might be relevant in our cause. I had always been able to talk my way through any sticky patch, befuddle any opponent with wit and the spoken word, but that was just a talent, a craft. Except for my law degree—the value of which was negated somewhat, or entirely, by my failure to retake and pass the bar exam—I lacked credentials.

Charles was grave throughout Witt's presentation. He nodded but asked few questions. He lifted each picture and regarded it. Witt took out a marker and pointed out the detail that appeared in each shot. From a distance of more than a mile, you could clearly see trucks and a track-hoe at the site. Witt traced what he thought was the property boundary of the Putnam tract for Charles. The permit boundary. I pointed out Faye Williams's house and barn, perfectly visible in the photos, taking pains to highlight how close her kitchen was to the primary crusher jaw.

Witt drew a circle on the first page of a new legal pad. Inside that he drew another circle.

"It looks to me like what happened is that Paul was trying to avoid giving notice by drawing a balloon around his mine site. It looks like he was saying that if you own a big piece of property and put a mine somewhere inside that balloon, you don't have to follow the Mining Act and notify any of the neighbors. But you can see here how close this is to Faye Williams. This is not a *setback* for operations. A setback doesn't relieve you of notifying the neighbors under the Mining Act. I think the Mining Act is trying to protect people like Faye when it says you have to notify her so she can contest the permit."

Charles did not respond. But I could see him thinking, his mind turning behind his stony exterior. He was either preparing his defense or he was trying to recall how this mess came to be, trying to light upon a strategy for either absolution or vindication.

I stared at Witt's sketch. That was it in a nutshell. Paul, or Randy as Paul's surveyor and engineer, thought that by pulling the permit boundary in fifty feet from the property line, they could avoid notifying any of the adjoining landowners. But this was horseshit. If a miner could pull his permit boundary in all the way around his property, why would any miner ever have to provide notice to the adjoining landowners? Every mine has a permit boundary. Under their theory the statute allowed the disenfranchisement of the public from *all* mine permit decisions so long as an engineer or surveyor drew a line inside the outer "permit" boundary. I stared at the mine map countless times, for countless hours, and I could not have described the wrongheaded dodge Paul and Randy had concocted with the economy Witt just had.

Charles moved the legal pad away. He wanted to move on to my presentation.

I set up the dry-mounted excerpt from the Mining Act, the line regarding the protection afforded to publicly owned parks, forests, and recreation areas. Charles was impatient at my pointing out to him language with which he was well familiar. He was not a schoolchild. So, then, right next to the language from the statute, I deployed the board with the "purpose" statement of the Appalachian Trail Conservancy. And I lit the wick of my little firecracker.

I read the purpose statement out loud, grateful that my voice didn't betray me.

Charles was fixed on the dry-mounted language. "That's very interesting." He smiled ruefully. "It appears there's a published statement of purpose that talks about sights and sounds. That's really very interesting, Jay. Who wrote it?"

"The Board of Managers of the Appalachian Trail Conservancy," I said as plainly as I could without coming off as a smart-ass. "They have a congressional mandate to protect the Trail. You're familiar with the Organic Act of 1916, which created the National Park Service?"

Charles was unnerved by this revelation, or perhaps by the combination punch Witt and I had delivered. He stroked his gray beard, his stony, sad face a near grimace. It was more reaction than I expected.

Witt followed up. "It seems pretty clear that this permit wasn't issued the same way other permits get issued. With no public hearings. It seems like the best thing to do is to put a hold on the permit and maybe start the process over. Do all the notification and have the hearings so it can be done right."

This was the right thing to say, but not what I wanted. I didn't want to start a new process. I wanted to end a process.

"Or you could revoke the permit," I said. "I don't think, technically, there ever was a permit, because of the failure to give notice."

For just that moment it seemed something remarkable was happening. Here we sat, Witt and I, citizens, albeit interested parties, sitting with Charles Gardner, the head of a division of an agency of the state government. We had made an amateurish but perfectly coherent presentation of facts. The state regulator with authority to correct the improper issuance of the permit was clearly listening to us, and it seemed for the moment that citizens could walk into state agencies and speak the truth and have state officials see the wisdom of the pleading and swing into action. And perhaps even take decisive action. Just like that. I was beginning to believe that this was really quite simple and straightforward. Maybe not even worth the nausea I had invested in it.

Now Charles surprised me. Us. "We don't revoke permits," he said flatly. His tone was not quite derisive, but nearly.

"What do you do, then?" asked Witt. He was very matter-of-fact but always has a sense of wonder and delight in his voice.

"We take in information, and, if it's necessary, we modify permits," Charles said. "We do this all the time. It's not unusual."

Was he kidding? This was not unusual? Were we to believe that the state regularly issues mining permits next to national parks without holding public hearings first? That the foundations of people's homes crack *all the time*?

"Modify them how?" Witt pressed.

I was unable to speak because I felt as if I had been sucker punched. *Not unusual?* Bullshit.

Charles appeared to be wrapping this up. "We work with the mine owner and we might limit the hours of operation. Or reduce the size of the permitted area. But we don't revoke permits."

Witt pressed his fingers into the desk. He slid one of his pictures back and forth. "But this permit was a mistake. You've said so yourself."

Charles was pushing the photos away, preparing to stand. He seemed to be tiring of us. Of our questions and our pictures and our statutory language. Now he stopped. "No. I never said that. I have never used that word." He looked at me. "Jay, you think this thing can just be fixed because you want it fixed. But it's not as easy as that. I could revoke the permit. The statute allows for it. But it would never work. The Mining Commission would never allow it. They would overturn it."

The Mining Commission. I had never heard of it.

Charles continued, delivering the punches in a flurry now. "What we do is, we require the applicant to bring the site into compliance with the Mining Act. That's the way it works."

When he was done, the air in the room was dead, the light flat.

My mind raced to something Don Barger had told me. He had told me about modifications. He had said that the agency might be able to impose modifications that are so onerous that a project no longer makes economic sense. I grabbed ahold of this hope. "Maybe you could modify it so that Paul can only crush for a single ten-year period, on the part of the tract least visible to the Trail."

Charles stiffened. I was reminded anew that we were, in the end, adversaries. "The first thing is, Jay, I need to see the site. I can't do anything until I have seen the site. I appreciate your photographs, Mr. Langstaff, but I can't really rely on them."

"Good," I said. "We don't want you to rely on us. When are you coming? Once you see it, you'll understand what we're talking about."

"Soon. I'll arrange it."

I invited Charles to use the Birchfield Creek Road access, as that provides the easiest walk to the affected section of the Trail.

"I'll probably go up in a helicopter," Charles said, dismissing my hospitality.

I was heartened a bit. Charles would fly to the Hump in a helicopter and land next to the Stan Murray plaque at Houston Ridge. He would gaze to the east. His hard eye would snag on the gaping scar in the side of Belview Mountain. And he would be horrified at what had been done under his signature.

My reverie was short-lived. As soon as Charles played out a line, he tugged it back.

Charles called our meeting to its end. "I'm sorry, Jay. I know you're disappointed. But that's the way it goes. Thanks for coming over today." He offered a helpless gesture of resignation and moved for the door. I had the sudden desire to adopt Charles's tone of voice and to tell him to shove it. *I'm sorry, Charles, I know you're disappointed, but you fucked up and now you're going to have to fix this or else Witt and I are going to have to kick your ass, Avery County–style.* Witt had driven three hours to make this meeting. And I had delayed my trip home. For this. Charles had invited us to make the presentation. But I didn't say anything ugly. I didn't level any threats. And I was not at all sure I could take Charles in a fight anyway. Instead of trying to kick his ass, I thanked him for giving us the opportunity to meet with him.

He had his back to me when I lobbed a final question: "I don't suppose you've written that memo to your file?"

I expected him to wheel around. To take this up. Maybe jump me. But he didn't. He just kept walking.

After the meeting, Witt and I rode the elevator down to meet Beth. Sick with nerves before the meeting, I now felt poisoned with frustration. Charles had set the terms of a new kind of battle. Revocation was not on the table. Shutting Paul down was out. This would now be a battle about how to modify a permit, how to allow a kinder, gentler dismantling of Belview Mountain over Paul's ninety-nine-year lease. *We don't revoke permits.* My mind crawled around the new terrain, tried to grasp the reality that Belview Mountain was coming down. I never felt worse in my life. To compound my personal loss, I had to imagine how I would tell Ollie and Ashley. How I would tell Faye that she would probably have to move? She would have to sell her homeplace. If she could find a buyer, that is. Surely she had much, or all, of her wealth tied up in her farm. If she could find a buyer, she would only recoup a fraction of its pre-mine value. Who would buy such a place? Maybe Paul, so he could burn it and chase the granite under her yard?

Witt felt the way I did. We had used all our powder, and we left the meeting in a worse position than when we went in.

After the meeting with Charles, the only thing the Dog Town Bunch had to hang on to, the only hope, was the lawsuit. Charles was clearly going to use the authority granted to him in the statute to choose the path of least resistance. Modification. He certainly wasn't going to write any memo to his file. As I turned this over in my mind, Charles Gardner, the enlightened state agent who offered me good faith in the form of an open door and an affable way, became my enemy. He had baked me bread, and now I felt like a sucker. Ron Howell's sucker, that was me. I recalled what Judge Howell had said, how a man ought to leave Charles's presence face-on, and I was now prepared to believe the worst. That Charles was a tool of the mining lobby. That he was a dogged foe of reason. Perhaps even a bought man.

That dim view certainly put me in good company in Cranberry Gap. Upon my return to the mountains, I slunk up the stairs to Ollie's. Told my tale. "Charles has his hand in every pocket in the state," Freddy said. "They all do. What did you expect?"

"There ain't no telling," said Ollie, "how much money he's got stuck away somewhere. In the trunk of his damn car."

Ashley figured state officials had off-shore accounts where they stashed their take. She imagined bank vaults in some banana republic bulging with dirty lucre.

Freddy figured that the bureaucrats from the regional offices collected payoffs from the mine operators, then kicked some of it to Charles. "Old Charles probably has a luxury yacht tied up somewhere."

Curly piled on. "Why sure he does. And I wouldn't be surprised if he's got a Learjet. All the big shots in Raleigh, they've all got Learjets and motorboats and convertible sports cars."

"They've all got houses in Florida," said Ashley. "Raleigh's nothing but a bunch of crooks."

I was not as cynical as that, and neither were they, but they did delight in trouncing my naive worldview. And what could I say? They had been right. Charles wasn't going to do what the statute clearly let him do. He was going to wriggle away from his responsibility, and Paul was going to get away with one of the least stealthy frauds in state history. He had drawn his mine map to slip through the permitting process with no notice to the adjoining landowners. At least that's how it looked to me now. Dear Ol' Dad had pulled one over on everybody, including the professionals down in Raleigh, and he was probably laughing himself to sleep over it every night.

So while I suffered, Ollie took the news in stride. I had to remind myself that she had been running into roadblocks for well over a year at this point. She was hardened where I was still green. Or maybe I had just failed to convey the true gravity of the situation. Maybe I had spared her a little of the worst of it. If I told her everything, expressed my own hopelessness, she might lose faith in the lawsuit, in the entire battle we were trying to get off the ground. And in me.

"My Little Buddy," Ollie said when I answered the phone one morning. "Are you on a landline? Because you ain't agoan believe this."

"Tell me," I said, not yet fully awake. "I believe everything."

"Well, you remember how I told you about when they bought Charles Smith's twenty-five acres, they was this old homeplace on it?"

"I remember. They burned it, right? Without a burn permit."

"Not only that. Did you know that there's a rule says you can't put any foreign objects—what do they call it, Ashley?"

I heard Ashley call out, "Unclean fill."

"Unclean fill," Ollie repeated. "Listen to this." Now she appeared to be reading. "Unclean fill makes it a *landfill,* and you've got to have a permit to operate a landfill. Even in Avery County. Well, that old house, that house was Damon and Willy Smith's house. They run that store that used to be in the garage down under the apartment, and I knowed Willy all my life. She was a fine person. And that house was old. You know what that means?"

"What?"

"That house was full of lead paint and who knows what all."

"It probably had asbestos siding," Ashley contributed. "It had those fake shingles."

"Where is it? Where was it?"

"Well, what they done was, Paul hired some boys. You might of knowed them, it was boys from around Dog Town, and Paul had them burn down Damon and Willy's old house. To the ground. But instead of hauling it off, you ain't agoan believe what they done."

"I probably won't. What did they do?"

"They buried it in the haul road. Right where I was showing you, right over there where they smothered that little creek. See, they had to build up a lot of dirt to make the haul road, and they just pushed all the rubble from that burned house into the roadbed. Ashley's been reading the law on it on the Internet."

"Unclean fill," I said out loud. It didn't sound overly pernicious.

Ollie thundered on, "Ashley found it in the regulations. Read it, Ashley." Ollie held up the phone and Ashley read to me.


I went down the mountain to Ollie's and we pored through the papers. I went again through the permit application and the papers I'd copied in Raleigh. In the meantime, Ashley had been developing another paper trail, the caper of the DOT Driveway Connecting Permit, and she ran it by me in its every sordid particular. Clark Stone Company received their DOT Driveway Connecting Permit on February 4, 2000. The permit specified that the driveway *must be constructed in accordance with the attached plans with corrections shown in red.* The applicant was directed to notify the county maintenance engineer *in advance of the date you plan to begin construction.* There was only one problem with that. Clark Stone had built their driveway the prior year. When they applied for their permit to construct it, they might have filled out the application at the crusher site and then driven down their eighty-foot-wide driveway onto Highway 19E to mail their driveway application to the state from the Dog Town Post Office. They had not only violated state regulations in building a haul road with unclean fill, they had also constructed their road with no connecting permit, making a mockery of the whole process. If there was an earlier permit we couldn't find it. We began to plot. If we could get Paul's haul road removed, then he couldn't reach the rock up on the ridge. And that might be as good as a revoked permit.

One door closed and another opened.

I called Forrest.


There was also the matter of the building permit from the county. That spring the physical plant, the beast, was taking shape. The hopper had been mounted on the primary crusher jaw, completing the head. It bristled in the sun, nearly ready to come alive. Clark Stone's crew was working full-out welding the secondary crushers at the end of the conveyor system. The problem was that they didn't have a building permit to do any of this. Tony had pressed the county on it before he changed sides, excoriating them for letting Paul work without first obtaining the necessary approvals. But when Tony switched sides, sold his house to Paul, some of those early leads had been abandoned.

Our county inspector, Tommy Burleson, is a local legend. At seven feet two inches Tommy is a mountain of a man. He was a natural basketball talent and went to college down in Raleigh, where he led NC State all the way to the national title in 1974. He also starred on the US Olympic team in 1972, the year the Russians upset the Americans in the most disputed basketball game in Olympic history. Nobody from Avery County has ever been more famous than Tommy. After a career in the NBA he came home, to Newland, and settled down to be a county commissioner and director of planning and building inspections.

Now, responding to some of the information we put before him, Tommy was calling a meeting to discuss the crusher. We turned out a small crowd on a Wednesday night and prepared to state our case. Tommy rolled out a nice, fresh copy of the mine map, and we pointed out what we thought were violations of the Mining Act and county ordinances. Paul's crew had felled a swath of trees straight up the mountain, right through what the mine map designated an "undisturbed area." This cleared swath was to be the route of the powerline that would deliver the electricity that would quicken the beast. Cutting trees, surely a disturbance in an "undisturbed area," appeared to be a clear violation of the terms of the permit. Possibly because of the land-clearing activities, the sediment traps on the haul road were failing to keep mud from washing into Little Horse Creek. Ashley presented photographs as evidence of this. Also, Clark Stone had pulled the shot to set the primary crusher jaw without having a seismograph on-site to record the impact. This violated the Mining Act *and* the terms and conditions of the mining permit, Ashley explained. Tommy listened intently. Ashley flooded him with information. Employing the tone of universal scorn she reserved for descriptions of Paul and Paul's crew, she brought to Tommy's attention the DOT Driveway Connecting Permit and the unclean fill in the haul road.

Tommy likes everybody and pretty much everybody likes Tommy. He has an easy manner. He nodded as we hurled accusations and tales of malfeasance. He whistled in response to our claim on the DOT Driveway Connecting Permit. "That's no good!" he exclaimed over the blasting accusation.

When Ashley was finished detailing how the dirt bank behind the new house was subsiding where Tony had let Paul borrow soil for the haul road, Tommy stunned us all. He scratched his head and leaned over on the table. "I think we ought to string a yellow tape around this place and look into what's gone on over there." He stroked his long, bony neck. "I don't see how we can let them work until we have some of this sorted out."

We were ecstatic. If Charles wouldn't act, we would just keep poking until we found someone who would. Now Tommy was the man of the hour. We slapped him on the back. He was pleased to be the bearer of good news, pleased to be amenable, a useful public servant.

We celebrated until the next morning. At seven o'clock Trackhoe Daddy went up on the mountain. We waited for somebody in a county vehicle to show up and give him a stern talking-to. But nobody arrived from the county that morning. No yellow tape was strung, and nobody looked into what had gone on over there. Paul's crew came and went unmolested. At will.

We called Tommy's office, but our calls went unanswered.

Then a few days later, a county inspector pulled up at the haul road entrance. Ollie called me. "Get ready," she said.

"What is it?"

"I don't know, but something ain't right over at heaven's gate." Ollie called around to some of her sources in town and got the scoop. She called me back. Jason Vance, a young inspector for the county, had been sent from Tommy's office. Ollie lowered her voice. "What he done, he went up there about, oh, I'd say ten thirty. I got pictures."

"Up on the mountain?"

"He went up for about, why, it had to be twenty minutes, and then he come back down."

"Then what?"

"About an hour later, down come Nasty. Then down come Trackhoe Daddy. They shut the new gate they put up and they left, toward Elk Park. And I missed the rest, but if I'm not badly mistaken, Tommy went up there after Jason did. That's what Jimmy Hicks told Freddy." Ollie paused to pull on a cigarette. "What do you make of that?"

"I don't know. We'll see."

"Do you think he shut them down?"

"Either that, or they went to lunch."

It took Ollie a while to learn what had transpired. Tommy had sent Jason Vance out to inspect the crusher on the building-permit issue. But Paul's crew ordered Jason off the site. That's what Ollie heard from friends of hers down at the courthouse. Presently, Randy Carpenter dashed off a letter to Tommy instructing him that if the county wanted to conduct an inspection of Paul Brown's business, Tommy would need to provide twenty-four hours' notice. Hearing of this letter, I went to Tommy's office and asked for a copy of it. Tommy made me a copy. He looked down at me and said, "Jay, I got nothing to hide."

The letter explained a lot about how local governments work: *Dear Mr. Burleson: I have been notified that on February 29, 2000, you visited the Putnam Mine area and ordered all workers and contractors of Clark Stone Co., to stop work, to leave the site, and not to return for sixty days! Is this so, and under what authority do you exercise this jurisdiction? May I remind you that Clark Stone Co., Inc. has been issued a Mine Permit and an Air Permit to Construct by the North Carolina Department of Environment and Natural Resources (DENR) covering the Putnam Mine.* Randy continued with a two-paragraph lecture on jurisdiction. His point was as clear as his grammar was bad. *Why I make such a point? It is because many workers within this county recognize and have a certain respect for you and your position and when you walk onto a job site and say jump, they jump, whether it is a lawful order or not. I am glad that you also brought to my attention in your letter of January 12th that part of the statute concerning failure to perform duties as contained in N.C.G.S. & 153–356. It is my opinion that your negligent act of walking on to Clark Stone Companies property and ordering workers to leave without due process, for, and notification is a willful failure to perform the duties required of you by law. It is for that reason that I respectfully request that you do not enter the Putnam Mine site unless you have first notified my office or Mr. Paul Brown's office and an escort is arranged for you, and further that you do not direct orders, oral or written, concerning any activities over which you do not have jurisdiction.*

Randy's twisted understanding of what constitutes negligence would be humorous if it weren't part of his chilling purpose. What could be the benefit of an inspection if the inspector was not free to inspect the site on his own terms? But the county rolled over. Jason Vance had left the site with instructions not to return. And that was that. The stop-work order appeared to vanish. There was no review of our claims from Tommy's office. And certainly no yellow tape strung across the road. After that tentative foray from the county's inspection department, nothing at all happened. The Avery County Inspections Department approved a building permit for the Putnam Mine on March 8, 2000, one week after the inspection department visited the site. For all intents and purposes we had run into a wall in the county. Everywhere we tried to turn, Paul's team had already been there, talking to a receptive audience, getting the matador defense and green lights to operate.

Faye called me. She had the new copy of the *Mountain Times.* Scott Nicholson had interviewed Charles. Knowing that I didn't get the papers, she read to me, *There's a lot of concern about the impact of noise and the sight from the trail, Gardner said in an interview Friday. "I'd say at this point it's likely we'll be talking with the owner about mitigation of some of the impact."* Faye stopped reading. "What does that mean?" she asked, her voice taking on a sharp edge. Though I didn't want to, I had to answer, "That means he wants to modify the permit, not revoke it." Faye was incensed. This is what she feared. She read on, *"I understand the concern that neighbors might have," said Gardner. He said the community didn't seem interested enough in the quarry to justify holding a public hearing on the matter.* At this Faye was unable to contain herself. "How do you show your interest if there's no public hearing?" she begged of Charles, who was fully two hundred miles away from Faye's house, well out of earshot. "Were we supposed to stand out in the yard and yell at a trackhoe?" I had to laugh. Faye collected herself, then said, "Well, I did that and it didn't do one bit of good. Not one bit."

I went to Raleigh that week with renewed purpose, having learned from his own lips—and now from the newspaper!—what Charles had in mind. I was copying documents from the files when Charles called me into his office. He seemed in good humor, though he retained with me his steady air of bureaucratic propriety. He told me he was going to Hump Mountain. The original plan was for him to fly in a helicopter, but that plan had fallen through. Possibly, I guessed, because North

Carolina was now experiencing the worst budget deficit in its history. I told Charles he was welcome to use the Big Yellow road access and that I'd walk him right to the summit of Hump Mountain. I explained that my years of leading hikes for the conservancies made me a reliable guide, but he declined my invitation. He would instead be driven up as close as possible to the bald section of Hump Mountain in a four-wheel-drive vehicle, then hike the last stretch. He would be led by State Trails staff in the Division of Parks and Recreation and the US Forest Service.

"Can I go?" I asked. "I mean, am I allowed to go?"

"It's public land, Jay. You can go if you want to. But you can't go with me. There might be insurance issues with you in a state vehicle."

"Just tell me when you're going and I'll meet you over there. I won't even talk to you, if you don't want me to. But I want to see you see it. Plus, I want to make sure you get to the right spot." I was aiming to steer Charles's visit. "The Stan Murray plaque. That's where you have to stand if you can't walk the whole section. I don't trust anybody but myself to take you to the right spot."

"I'll be traveling with folks from the State Trails program, Jay," he said a little dismissively. "We know where we're going."

"I especially don't trust the Trails staff," I replied.

Back in the summer, Witt had turned his attention to the State Trails folks as a potential ally when the Appalachian Trail Conservancy initially begged off. He had ended up talking to Dwayne Stutzman, who was in charge of the state's trails management program. Dwayne Stutzman had told Witt that the Putnam Mine was a done deal. Able only to see black and white, that was all I needed to hear out of that division to label them *unhelpful*. I could not bear the idea of Charles's seeing the mine from the Hump without my being there. I didn't want him to not be able to see it because of fog or low clouds or bad light, then claim the impacts were insignificant. In an irrational burst of self-regard I thought my mere presence would keep him honest. I also didn't want Dwayne Stutzman from State Trails, or Tommy Burleson from the county, or anyone else getting a private audience with Charles, filling his head with ideas that could worsen our position.

On the appointed day, I estimated Charles's driving time from Raleigh—five hours—figuring he would have gotten on the road first thing, then started walking from my house. It would take me about two hours, walking at a normal pace, to reach the summit. As compensation for my effort, the walk covered the most dazzling scenery in the eastern United States. For once, the weather was just right. A few high clouds, bright sunshine, and thirty-five degrees. I was about a mile into my walk when it struck me that Charles would probably not leave from his office; rather, he would leave from his home, which would cut down his drive time by forty-five minutes or so. Because I had gotten a little bit of a late start, I decided to run the second half of the route. I do not know how long the trip took me, but I'm sure I have never done it faster. When I arrived near the summit of Big Hump, I found a place out of the wind behind a low rock outcrop. Now the sky went slate gray and the temperature dropped into the twenties. I waited an hour, and the only people I saw were a couple of hikers. I waited another hour. I walked a stretch of Trail to keep warm. I ate my lunch. All told, I waited four hours, I guess, and still no Charles. I took a nap, curled up in the gold grass. Finally, it was getting dark, the sun was diving behind Roan Mountain, so I hiked home, cold and stiff. And pissed off.

Back at the house I called Charles and asked him what went wrong. "I was there, Charles. You weren't."

He was sheepish. After driving all the way from his home, more than two hundred miles, Charles met up with the good folks from the state. When they reached the US Forest Service gate on Big Horse Creek, the guide discovered that he had brought the wrong key. I was ready to believe this snafu was the work of Done-Deal Dwayne Stutzman. I had been driven to conspiracy theories and expected the worst. Rather than walk up the mountain from the gate or try the Big Yellow access, Charles had turned around and driven all the way back home, back to Chatham County.

"I will get there, Jay," Charles said. "I told you I would and I will."

"I'm trusting you, then."

The next week, he made another try. This time I drove around the base of the mountain and drove part of the way up Big Hump, up the old logging road that follows Little Horse Creek. That cut my hike down to an hour and a half or so. I stayed with the creek almost until breaking into the bald. I was waiting on top when Charles and his caravan of SUVs streamed out of the woods into the knee-deep grass.

A team of state and county officials piled out of one car. Charles. Richard Phelps from DENR. Tommy Burleson. Out of another came Randy Carpenter. James Vance. Morgan Sommerville, regional director of the Appalachian Trail Conservancy. Dwayne Stutzman. It was a hazy, cool day. The light was flat. Not the best light for viewing the impacts of the mine site, but not the worst either.

Everybody was on good behavior. Tommy and Randy were surprised to see me up there. Surprised maybe that anyone would, or could, hike it. I told them I'd left my car up in Little Horse Creek, and they seemed impressed that I knew the little-used logging road past the cemetery. They were on my home territory now, my side of the county.

After much orientation, all eyes turned to the quarry scar. Cameras came out. Dwayne Stutzman, whom I was prepared to despise, had a feature on his new camera that would record his voice as he shot pictures. He stood on the footpath and said, "I am standing on the footpath of the Appalachian Trail and I can see, with the naked eye, the windshields of vehicles at the site of the quarry. That's how close it is." I was astonished and pleased at his tone. All along, I had been trying to convince people that the site was perilously close to the Trail, that one mile or one and a half miles might as well be one hundred yards in a viewshed spanning sixty or seventy miles, and now, here was Dwayne Stutzman helping to build my case with his smart little camera. I lay back and let the others talk. We had to raise our voices over the lashing wind. When a member of the party made a mistake, misidentifying this peak or that, a valley or a riverbed, I offered gentle corrections, but mostly I just listened.

The team of officials wanted to conduct a sound test at the mine site, to run the backup beepers on the trackhoes and shovels to see if they could hear it.

They called over to the site on a cell phone and told someone on the ground to run the beepers. Nothing. We couldn't hear anything but the whistling wind. This round went to Randy.

In small groups we set off to walk the section of Trail most impacted by the quarry. Finally I was able to get Charles alone.

"What do you think?" I asked, staring straight ahead, not wanting to crush him with my gaze.

His eyes dove to his shoe tops before he spoke. "The area is not quite as untouched as I'd thought, Jay."

He pointed to a logging road up in Blevins Creek. Another near Buck Mountain. He noted the many Christmas-tree farms carved out of the forest at the lower elevations. "Tommy says the roads in Blevins Creek are going to become a development." Charles brightened at his own report. "And that," he said, pointing to a spot seven miles to our east, "is a problem."

Sugar Top.

My face burned. My gut turned over.

Sugar Top, the concrete carbuncle!

I pointed out the obvious. Blurted all my ammunition. "That's *seven miles* away, Charles, and The Sugar Cube takes about *four* acres of airspace. The Putnam mine is a *mile away,* or if we use your numbers, a mile and a half away, and you've approved a permit for *one hundred and fifty-one* acres. There's no comparison. Plus, as ugly as Sugar Top is, it doesn't make any noise."

Charles was unmoved. "It just makes the area less deserving of protection," he said coolly.

I tried my last volley. "With Sugar Top, they were too late. They let it happen and then passed a great law to make sure it never happens again. But we're not too late. We have a chance to avoid that here. Let's do it right this time so they won't be talking about your failure in twenty years."

As the meeting was wrapping up, Randy stepped away from the

group and spoke something into the ear of James Vance. He nodded at me, I thought he did, and James smiled. Randy then pulled out his cell phone and placed a call. Suddenly, I felt a sense of menace. Randy knew my car was parked up Little Horse Creek. In a remote holler. Whom was he calling? And what was Nasty smiling about?

Once the crowd piled into their SUVs for the ride down, I headed off on foot. When I was out of their sight, I pulled out my own cell phone, the one I had borrowed from my brother-in-law, which from the open bald picked up a decent signal from the new tower on Linville Mountain. I called Ollie. I told her briefly what had taken place, then asked to speak to Freddy.

"What're you into?" he said, the universal greeting around Dog Town.

I told him how Randy had given me a look that didn't sit right. How my truck was parked in an isolated bend in the old logging road up Little Horse Creek.

"Son, them boys is pretty rough," Freddy said. "You need to be careful." This was not reassuring.

I asked Freddy if he would drive up Little Horse Creek just to make sure nobody went up the logging road until I got down.

"Yeah, boy," he said. "You ain't got to worry. I'm on my way."

I hiked down through the hawthorn and blackberry thickets on the edge of the bald, then plunged into the dark holler, under towering maples. I nearly lost myself in the beauty of the walk, nearly forgot my anger. Was Charles preparing to use Sugar Top as a defense? As a justification to deliver the coup de grâce to the viewshed? When I got down to the creek crossing, there was Freddy in his chop top, blocking the way. He gave a little wave, and I walked down to thank him. Across his lap lay a Harrington and Richardson 12 gauge shotgun.

"Damn, Freddy. I didn't want you to shoot anybody."

"Well, hell, why come if you're not prepared to do something? This ain't a damn tea party."

He had a point and I was grateful.

I got in my truck and followed him to the house so I could brief Ashley and Ollie.

Ashley was on the computer, writing a term paper on allergies.

I told them about Tommy and Charles taking pictures. About the guy from State Trails who was marveling that the site was so near that he could see individual vehicles with the naked eye. *It's that close!* he'd said, practically pleased. I told them what Charles had said about Sugar Top. They were furious.

"Charles is a damn snake," Ashley said. "He's just trying to weasel out of it."


That night I called Charles at his house.

"I think you're full of shit," I said. "You saw what you wanted to see. I saw you taking pictures of Blevins Creek, hoping that the area was less than pristine. Preparing to document it. I guess that all goes into the file."

Charles chose his words with care. "Jay, since I left that place, I've thought of little else." My blood rose into my face, making my neck itch. "That is truly one of the most beautiful places I have ever stood. I really didn't know that there was a place like that anywhere in North Carolina."

I was floored. It was the same reaction I got when I led hikes for conservation groups, the same reaction I had several times a year when the light fell just so, when the clouds poured over the bald tops and the place turned to a dreamscape, even for a man well acquainted with splendor. Those who have never seen the Southern Appalachians from Hump Mountain have a hard time believing such a place exists. It had become the terrain of the fight for me, the theater of battle, but every once in a while I was reminded that it was also one of the most scenic spots in the nation.

Every time I thought I knew what Charles was thinking, I was wrong. I kept thinking I knew him. But I did not.

While I had him on the phone, I seized the opportunity to strengthen the case for revocation. "The permit needs to be revoked, Charles. No hiker will ever have the experience you had today if it's not revoked.

It's an embarrassment to the state. It's worse than Sugar Top because it's not only going to look like hell, it's going to make noise. A lot of noise, and for ninety-nine years. That mountain will come down while we're watching and listening to it."

He didn't answer me directly. "It'd be very nice to be able to decide these things based on your assurances, Jay. And on my impressions. But we have to follow a process. And that's what we're going to do."

# Chapter 7

Sometimes you make your own luck and sometimes it arrives with no warning.

On an overcast day in early March, I got a call from Scott Mason, a reporter with WRAL-TV, the CBS affiliate in Raleigh. Winner of three Edward R. Murrow Awards, Scott did some hard reporting—murders, apartment-complex fires—but he had also created a special niche doing human-interest stories. I once saw a story he did on a man in Chapel Hill who mows grass for clients despite having no arms. He did stories on hay fever and dunking booths and the state's roadside wildflower plantings. In one of his stories that gained national attention, a patient at a nursing home had passed away. But on the way to the embalming table a funny thing happened. The deceased came to, was in fact quite alive, raising hard questions about nursing-home care and mortuary services.

"I'd like to come up there and do a story on the mine," Scott Mason said. "I read a press release a while back and it sounds interesting."

I was surprised, figuring our story fell somewhere outside the yawning gap between murder and roadside wildflowers. But I didn't bother to ask why he wanted to do such a thing. "You want me to come down and get you and cook you some dinner?"

The next day Scott drove the five hours to Avery County with his cameraman, Jay Jennings. They got a late start, and by the time they arrived it was nearly two o'clock. I had planned a full day for them but we'd lost precious time. I wanted Scott to interview Ollie and Ashley. Most important, I wanted to get him up on the Trail to get shots of the mine site from the nation's premier linear national park.

Their van pulled to a stop next to my truck at the top of Little Horse Creek Road.

"How long will it take us to get up there and back to the van?" Scott asked, piling out. "To the Appalachian Trail and back?"

I thought on it. Then I lied. "Probably, forty-five minutes, an hour. Something like that."

He checked his watch. "We can probably do it then." The cameraman smiled with a sense of congenial doom. I suspected a history of many adventures out in the field for this pair.

We prepared to walk up the mountain. Heavy equipment spilled from the van. A hulking Panasonic DVCPRO 50 camera. A stout tripod. Microphones, cables, and an extra battery. Granola bars.

The camera weighed every bit of twenty-five pounds. Roughly what a cinder block weighs. The tripod pushed ten. Plus a sound-equipment bag had cables and extra tapes. All this had to get up on top of the mountain where we would film the site. I offered to carry the camera or the tripod, or both. Hell, I was dying to get these guys up the hill and would have given either a piggyback ride, but neither Scott nor Jay seemed willing to let me touch their bread and butter. The tripod alone ran over $1,000, and the camera was worth more than any car I had ever owned. I grabbed the bag with the cables and tapes.

"Let's move," Scott said.

I headed out and they fell in behind me. "We'll stick to the creek for a little while, then we'll climb the ridge," I said, projecting confidence. "We ought to be able to see it from there."

When I lead hikes for land trusts and conservation groups, I am usually the cautious one who encourages the group to go slowly and enjoy the country we are walking through. To stretch out. To drink lots of water. "This is not a race," I say when folks look winded, when their eyes start to wheel. I like to dispense facts on native flora and soil types and regional history as we go. But on this day I was goal-oriented. I was the rabbit, and this was a mad scamper up the hill. I figured if

I got out ahead, Scott and Jay would chase me, and we would eat up lots of ground in minimal time. I had told them forty-five minutes, but we were on what I figured was an hour-and-a-half walk. Each way. I feared that if they learned how far a walk this was, and how rugged, they would balk. And the walk was just the first hurdle. Once they had their pictures, they would still have to do the interviews, mix the sound, and send it all down Raleigh for the six o'clock news. The stakes were high. The story they would produce had the potential to be a huge break. Maybe our last break, our last chance to influence the agency before Charles decided how exactly to modify Paul's permit. I wanted the story to be perfect. Charles lived in the Raleigh television market. The attorney general and the governor, and all the decision-makers who would have a say, lived in the WRAL television market, including the judges who might one day hear the case. Getting these pictures on television in Raleigh might go some way in determining whether and how Paul could go in, how much damage he could do.

Up we went. About twenty minutes into the hike, Jay looked as if he might collapse under the weight of the tripod. The blood vessels in his forehead stood out like blue twine under the skin. I washed my face in the creek and suggested he do the same. "Are we almost there?" he asked. "You bet," I said. "We've gained a lot of elevation." The cold creek water revived him a little, and I took off again, nearly sprinting. I pointed up to a thin place in the tree canopy and said, "We're heading for that. See that opening?" I didn't wait for an answer. I crashed up the hill ahead of them.

After an hour, we were still in the woods.

Scott checked his watch. "I think we need to go back down. We can interview you down on the road, in front of the entrance to the mine."

I winced. "That's a bad idea. We've come a long way. You don't want to give up all this elevation gain, now. You don't want to waste it." I forged ahead, and to my astonishment they faced the mountain and followed.

At about three thirty we broke out onto the first open area. This was pastureland, not part of the Appalachian National Scenic Trail, though it was part of the federal land buffering the Trail. From here you couldn't see the mine site yet, not from this far down the slope. A risen stretch of woods blocked it. Unfortunately, what you could see from this spot was the top of the mountain we were climbing. An intimidating sight, the summit loomed high above us, like some distant kingdom of grass and granite. My team had no will for tackling it.

"No way, not possible," Scott said, sucking wind. "Let's shoot it here. We can get Grandfather Mountain in the background."

"All we've got to do," I enthused, "is get up on that broad place, there." I pointed up the hill, to a spot well below the summit. "The Trail makes a bend there. At that point we will be on the Appalachian Trail, and we'll be able to see the mine, I promise. It's only a little bit farther. You can't come all this way and miss seeing the mine from the Trail. This part is easy," I ensured, pleading. And still lying.

By now they were amused by me and seemed resigned to having been duped.

They hung their heads and followed. It took another twenty minutes, across a wide, grassy flat, then straight up a rocky cow path, but finally we were high enough that the quarry site was in view.

"This is it," Scott said. "We shoot here." For a moment I thought he meant to shoot me. With a gun.

Jay turned around, and as he did so, his face widened, as if a pair of shutters had been flung open in his mind. "Wow. That's going to make some good pictures. That's incredible." In an instant, all was forgiven. I had delivered them to a place of rare magnificence, and they knew it.

I named the peaks in the distance for them while they recovered their breathing, restored their vanity.

"When did we leave North Carolina?" Jay said. "It looks like Scotland. And Norway."

I was thrilled. The experience of being on the Hump, on the balds, never fails. First-time visitors search for words, for comparisons, to describe it. But words have a hard time of it. Scotland is probably the most oft-mentioned in comparison. But no peak in the entire British Isles is over four thousand feet, and from Hump Mountain one encounters a dozen peaks over five thousand feet, several over six thousand. I think I understand the Norway comparison, the velvety green, the orderly valleys, and lush, sheer slopes, yet the entirety of Norway would fit inside just the Virginia section of the Southern Appalachian Mountains, so vast is the chain. It is a wonder to behold.

But the reverie of the visitors was short-lived.

"And that?" Scott asked, appropriately horrified.

He gazed down the nose of the ridge and there is was. The object of our disaffection.

"That's the proposed Putnam Mine," I said simply, letting the sight itself tell the story. "The cleared area right now totals eleven acres, but they have a permit to take one hundred fifty-one."

Scott shook his head, and I saw what I believed was a wince streak across his face. Like every hiker who arrives on Hump Mountain, he had endured a terrific challenge to reach the high ground. The blood had slammed through his temples, his skin had flushed with the exertion. His thighs had turned to jelly. And the payoff was to behold not only the wondrous natural vista, but, in the same instant, the ham-handedness of man.


Scott and Jay set up their equipment, taped a voice-over, then Jay shot some B-roll, background pictures they could splice into the story. They interviewed me with the quarry looming just off my left shoulder, Grandfather Mountain behind that. They were wrapping it up when Witt appeared over the peak. He hurried down to us, and he got some still pictures of them filming the mine, and of us leaving Big Hump.

Of course Scott and Jay missed their deadline and the story did not make it on the air that night. But it ran the next night. My brother in Raleigh recorded it for me and overnighted a videotape up to the mountains. Luddite writers on austerity budgets do not have video recorders or DVD players, so I went to a neighbor's house, slipped the tape in, and peered into the screen as the storm of pixels took shape and became coherent images.

The report was fantastic. Better than I could have hoped for. It opened with Ollie's videotape of the blast Clark Stone pulled when they set the main crusher jaw into the face of the mountain. The shower of orange earth and granite dust was graphic and astonishing. Then we had a zoomed shot of the primary crusher jaw from the Trail. Scott's opening was fetching and dire: "The state agency charged with protecting the environment may have made a big mistake—one that already seems to be impacting the North Carolina mountains and the Appalachian Trail. The North Carolina Department of Environment and Natural Resources allowed a mining company to begin blasting a mountain in Avery County that is within sight of hikers and tourists. Homeowners are up in arms, the state's back is against the wall, and the mountain may be forever scarred."

There was a snippet of the interview with me. Jay Jennings had taken shots of me walking through the tall bald grass with the quarry right behind me. My claim that the mine equipment, the blasting, and the backup beepers would broadcast industrial sounds up to the Trail "like sound from a stage up to the balcony" was illustrated by the wide-angle shot that showed the whole of Belview below and behind me. Then Ollie appeared in a T-shirt and jeans. She looked bright with fresh anger. "It's a disgrace destroying a mountain," she said, her eyes fluttering. "It's all torn to pieces now." Then, suddenly, Paul himself, Dear Ol' Dad replaced Ollie in the frame. He was standing beside a busy road, with trucks roaring past him, the slipstream pulling at his thin hair. "I've got a lot of money invested in this operation," he complained, his skin dragging down his face. "I'm just hoping the problem will go away." Next, Scott interviewed Don Reuter, the spokesman for DENR, for Charles. With Scott nodding grimly, Reuter admitted that the state made a mistake in not considering all the information they should have. I sat up at this admission. Charles had been so careful in pointing out that he had never confessed to a mistake. And now Don Reuter, the official spokesman for the agency, had used the word in the most public of forums.

Best of all, Scott had tape of a conversation he recorded with Hugh Morton after he and Jay left the Hump. Morton is a conservation icon in North Carolina. His family has owned Grandfather Mountain for over a hundred years. It is the only privately owned International Biosphere in the world, boasting dozens of rare and endangered species of flora and fauna, including Paul's original nemesis, the Virginia big-eared bat. Mr. Morton looked into the camera and said it plainly: "From what I've been told, the mine will be a tremendous scar. All of us are obligated to save for future generations the best of what we have. From Grandfather Mountain we won't be able to see the first part of the mine, but if they start taking off the top of Belview Mountain, the visitors to Grandfather Mountain will be able to see it. I think there's better places they could put it."

After watching the tape a dozen times, I took it down to show it to Ollie and the rest of the Dog Town bunch. As the tape ran, they sat in silence. They fainted with embarrassment at the sight of themselves on television.

"I don't see how Charles can refuse to hold hearings now," Curly said. "I'd say you put him in a box."

"I'd say we're killed," Ollie concluded, cocking a hip, her blue eyes bright with this delightful mischief. "Dear Ol' Dad ain't gone like it."


As I hoped, the story put us on the map in Raleigh. There's no way to calculate the impact it has on a state official when the call comes that a reporter who wants to interview him or her for an exposé. The actual impact of a story landing, of its running for the two or three minutes of airtime, is hard to quantify, but the psychological impact of the press's inquiries, sniffing around the story, might hold the most lasting value.

In the days after the story ran, I started getting calls from newspaper reporters. Other environmental organizations called to see if our team could help them out with battles they were fighting, help them get some press for their causes. Another quarry, this one down in the piedmont, was seeking a permit along the banks of the Uwharrie River. Farther east a landfill project had turned the town of Holly Springs upside down, and asphalt and cement plants were unwelcome wherever their owners sought to put them. I listened to stories from neighbors to these operations and proposed operations, and I offered what little advice I could, but my hands were full with our battle, and I was not eager to commit a single ounce of energy elsewhere.

Within a week of the airing of the television piece on WRAL, Charles called for a series of public hearings to consider what action to take due to the escalating controversy over the Putnam Mine.

I called Forrest. "Is this good?" I had learned that I needed to check with the experts on even the most elementary, obvious matters. To do otherwise was to waste precious time and emotional capital.

Forrest scoffed at my naïveté. "Public *meetings* aren't in the statute. This is a patent diversion."

I offered gentle correction. "I think he used the word *hearings,* not *meetings.*"

Forrest shot back, "A *hearing* is what you have before issuance. Let's keep that straight. Anything along the lines of what Charles has planned is a *meeting,* not a *hearing,* and *meetings* are not in the statute."

Charles also proposed opening a period of public comment before and after the *meeting.* Forrest was unimpressed. "This is where they try to appear not to be arbitrary and capricious while being both," he said dismissively.

I went down to Raleigh to see Charles and to copy the latest entries to appear in the Putnam Mine file. My own document stash now consisted of well over a thousand pages, everything from Paul's lease agreement with Robert Putnam, to copies of Paul's DOT Driveway Connecting Permit, to the entire Mining Act of 1971, and Paul's original permit application. I had groaning file boxes in my truck, with tabs reading SAWDUST, LINVILLE VIOLATIONS, PERMIT APPLICATIONS, and dozens of others. There was barely enough room for the dogs anymore. Biscuit was beginning to lose heart.

I went down to the end of the hall to give Charles Witt's latest pictures. I laid them down on his desk and stood back awaiting a response.

The season was changing, and with the greening of the forest floor, the openings made around the crusher jaw stood out in bold relief.

Charles was in a good mood. He seemed amused by me on this particular day. He offered me a seat. "You've got a problem."

"I've got a lot of problems," I allowed. "Which one are you talking about?"

"I understand why you're so upset about this. You live right across the gap from it. And Witt, too. The problem is that Witt's pictures demonstrate clearly why he is upset about the impacts on the Appalachian Trail, why you are, but I have to say, I hear more from you and Witt about the impacts on the Trail than I hear from the Appalachian Trail people."

I protested reflexively, said that the Appalachian Trail community had not had a chance to comment, which was the whole problem with a lack of public hearings. Changing course, playing good cop and bad cop simultaneously, I commended him for putting a fine point on the problem, for recognizing his own failing, his failure to hold public hearings, which would have included the Appalachian Trail community *before* the issuance of the permit, when it might have done some good. But I was just treading water. I could not deny that his larger point was well-taken. Somehow Witt and I had become the voice for a national park that had little to say in its own defense.

I left Charles's office plotting our course. Patent diversion or not, we had to get a crowd to the courthouse for the public meetings. If Charles wanted to know what the Appalachian Trail community felt about the Putnam Mine, we were going to have to find out and make sure the message wasn't lost in subtlety or politesse.

With Charles's words, his challenge, firmly rooted in my mind, I dug furiously into the Internet. I found dozens of web-based forums for Appalachian Trail hikers. An entire cyber subculture was built around hiking and maintaining the nation's footpath. The community was divided into Through Hikers, Section Hikers, and Day Hikers. Through Hikers inhabit the upper rooms of this community. Their small club consists of those who have hiked, or are hiking, the entire route, all 2,134 miles, at one go. Section Hikers hike the entire trail, too, but in segments, over a number of years, while Day Hikers access short stretches of the Trail for recreational outings, walks in the woods. I learned that I am a mere Day Hiker, the lowest rung on the ladder, though I think I deserve some special recognition for repeat hikes. I learned that Through Hikers and the most serious-minded of the Section Hikers traditionally take nicknames, and some of these nicknames stick for life. I leaned about Trail Magic, the secret gifts of kindness that Day Hikers and neighbors to the Trail leave for Through Hikers: bottles of Gatorade placed in a stream at a crossing; Band-Aids hanging from a tree in a Ziploc bag. I learned that the Trail community was tackling issues such as cell phone use on the Trail. Many purists thought cell phones interrupted the entire purpose of using the wilderness corridor, made it too easy to keep one foot in the other world, the world of instant communication and news of the place the Trail was established to give a reprieve from, while others came down on the side of safety and a concession to the "real world." In one of the forums I came upon a heated exchange over the tactics of a Trail legend named Wingfoot, who seemed to be engaged in a number of Trail-protection fights. I then did a Google search for *Wingfoot* and was interested to see dozens of hits. After a little more digging I learned that Wingfoot was an author, provocateur, and tireless advocate for the Appalachian Trail. His guidebooks were lovingly referred to as bibles for hikers. A little more research and I learned that Wingfoot's off-trail name was Dan Bruce and that he lived in Hot Springs, North Carolina, about an hour from the Roan.

I logged off the computer, picked up the phone, and called directory assistance for Hot Springs. Given the obscurity of the place name, or the complications that arise from my accent or speech pattern when I speak to robots, the computerized voice on the line quickly yielded to a real live human being, and a nice young woman delivered the requested number. I dialed it, and after a single ring I was greeted by a busy voice.

"Wingfoot," the man said simply. It was pure Georgia, an officious, clipped drawl. I had the immediate sense of being one in a long line of callers to this man. "Go ahead."

"Mr. Bruce," I began, not quite comfortable using his Trail name.

I wasn't sure that Day Hikers have any right to employ Trail names, and besides, it seemed sort of silly. I started to tell him about Hump Mountain, the Roan Highlands, how the Appalachian Trail—

He interrupted to speed me on my way. He had work to do. "Did you say a gravel pit?"

"The largest open-surface mine in western North Carolina."

"Where?"

"Hump Mountain. Avery County."

"Highlands of Roan," he said, resorting to his preferred nomenclature.

"Yes, sir—"

"Did you say Little Hump?"

"Little Hump, too, but mostly from Big Hump. Hump Mountain."

He might have been typing as I spoke. Either that or he was working on something else as I tried to grab his attention.

I reiterated the location. "You walk right towards it from the summit, from the Stan Murray plaque at Houston Ridge all the way until you turn back to the north and head off the balds. WRAL just did a story on it, down in Raleigh."

There was silence for a moment. I wasn't sure the connection had not failed. Then he came on the line again. "What did Morgan say?" I had the distinct sense that he was rubbing his eyes, weary.

Morgan Sommerville was the regional representative of the Appalachian Trail Conservancy.

I explained what I had just learned from Witt, how the Appalachian Trail Conservancy, and Morgan Sommerville, had thought Paul was going to put the crusher in the old Cranberry iron mine, and how that site, while closer to the Trail, would not have been visible nor would the blasting and drilling be audible, because the activity would have been *under* the mountain. *Under* the Trail. Witt had learned all this after I first alerted him to what was going on over on Belview Mountain.

Bruce interrupted, "You didn't answer my question. What did Morgan say?" He was laughing now.

I told Dan Bruce about Witt calling Morgan and bringing the new site to his attention, and how Morgan had told Witt that the permit had already been issued, that nothing could be done. "Of course we will never know if the ATC would have attended the public hearings because there were no public hearings," I said. "It all comes back to notice." I hoped my wrap-up had been both comprehensive and sufficiently brief for the pressed man.

"Explain that."

"The beauty—from Mr. Brown's perspective—of failing to give notice is that he could begin his operation without anybody knowing about it. And now that he has expended money on it, it is almost impossible to dislodge him. Before work begins, when a project exists on paper alone, there's little lost if a permit is *denied*. But now that Paul has put in his roads and fixed his crusher to the mountain, he has sunk a million dollars, maybe more, in the project. And we're in the position of having to ask for a radical modification, or a revocation, which is a lot harder." Now Bruce wanted me to back up. I was grateful. It seemed I had gained his full attention. "What did the Appalachian Trail Conservancy say when you told them there was a 151-acre rock quarry going in next to Roan Highlands, which is the most scenic section of the Trail in the South?" He tossed in this editorial remark as if trying to anticipate and deride whatever my reply might be. "This is important."

"They said it to Witt, not to me. I think they said it was too late for them to get involved since the permit had already been issued."

"That's a typical bureaucratic response," Bruce declared, possibly pleased that I had confirmed his worst fear, ratified some low opinion.

Over the next hour I learned that Wingfoot is a veteran of battles both within and outside the Appalachian Trail Conservancy. He is considered a brilliant maverick by some, a pain in the ass by others. To many more, though, he is simply the voice of the Trail.

He told me about two other current events along the Trail. The purchase of the sixty-eight-hundred-acre Gulf Tract near Max Patch Mountain in North Carolina had engaged the Trail community and other user groups as never before. Further north, at the Saddleback Mountain, in Maine, a family was attempting to expand development of their ski resort with cabins and condominiums, and perhaps ski runs right across the footpath. Wingfoot explained his position on each issue, trying to win me to his view, even though I had no dog in either fight. In this he reminded me of myself. Always fighting. Always trying his case. I could tell he advocated his positions without rest. I liked that.

"Here's what we're going to do," he said.

*Here's what we're going to do!* With those words I fell into his thrall. I had been wanting to hear those words from everybody I had spoken to, as far back as the honey-bun tour. I stood up and leaned into the phone the way the hard of hearing will do. I didn't want to miss anything he might say. Wingfoot wanted me to identify for him who were the key decision-makers. "Where are the pressure points, and how do we reach them?" he asked. I told him a little bit about the power structure in Raleigh. Our attorney general was running to replace our popular governor, Jim Hunt, who was retiring after his fourth four-year term in office, though it was widely accepted that, but for term limits, Hunt could run every four years until his death and win reelection with ease. Roy Cooper was going to run for attorney general. "No," Wingfoot said, cutting through my dissertation. "Who is going to make the decision on how to modify the permit? Who is the guy? Who is the key?" I told him it all came down to Charles Gardner, but that perhaps the governor or the attorney general could provide cover for Charles as he made his decision.

"And how is Charles Gardner leaning?" Wingfoot pressed.

I told him that so far Charles was unimpressed with how strongly the Trail community felt about this issue. Beyond that, I couldn't say what he was thinking, except that he had taken revocation off the table. I explained that Charles was hard to read. I decided not to tell him about Charles's baking me a loaf of bread.

"And the Appalachian Trail Conservancy board hasn't put any pressure on Morgan?"

"Not that I know of. I don't know anybody on the board, so I would have no way of knowing that."

"Deafening silence!" Wingfoot declared.

I laughed along with him. This guy was a leader and I was ready to follow.

"It boils down to this, Jay. We need to shake up the decision-makers. And we might need to hurt some feelings."

I thought about that. If I had ever thought that the conservation community spoke with one voice, was a unified team of do-gooders that was going to come together and buoy our little band of fighters, row us over the seas, that vision was quickly being dispelled.

Wingfoot laid out his vision for me. "Listen, Jay, I like Morgan. Morgan is a nice guy. I like all of them. But these people are so used to collaborating and compromising that they might have forgotten what it feels like to win one. I consider it my job to light fires under their asses and keep them alert. It's good for them."

I was instructed to send Wingfoot the links to all the articles written about the Putnam Mine fight thus far. "Get me everything so I can read it." Next I was to get e-mail and postal addresses for the attorney general, the governor, and the head of the agency. "You do know the head of the agency, don't you?"

"Bill Holman," I said.

"Holman! He's a hiker, that's good. Used to be with the Sierra Club. A Through Hiker. And he let this happen?"

"It was permitted under his predecessor."

"Wow. Bill Holman is a damn good guy. That's got to help."

"I hope so."

"Get me Holman's address. But first, get me Charles Gardner's, before you do anything else. We're going to cover him up with paper. Charles Gardner is going to wish he never heard of Paul Brown and Belview Mountain."


In the Saddleback fight, Wingfoot had built letter-writing campaigns to convince the Interior Department and Maine's congressional delegation that they needed to be responsive to the user groups or suffer the political consequences. Now he thought we needed to do the same for the Putnam Mine case. But this time he wanted to harness the power of the Internet in a new way. And he thought we needed to do it right now.

"We need to shine a bright light on this thing," he said. "And if we lose, it won't be because we didn't try. We're going to kill ourselves trying. Okay?"

"Okay. That seems within reach."

Within a week, Wingfoot had crafted a program that would enable an Internet user to write a letter to each of the pressure points we had identified. These would not be form letters. He was building a website that would ask the writer to answer a series of questions. The responses to the questions would then be flushed into a letter format by a master computer in Hot Springs. Wingfoot would monitor the site around the clock as the responses came in to make sure the questions were prompting original and heartfelt replies. With no additional effort on the part of the letter writer, the letters would be sent to each and every public official Wingfoot prompted his computer to contact.

He seemed to have no off-button. He worked around the clock. He called in a few times a day, with updates and suggestions, and I was swept into the tide of his energy.

"These letters have to be real," he said on the phone on the day we built the site, "not duplicate postcards. They have to convey what the hiker really feels about having the best part of their Trail experience violated. I think I've got it to where we'll get some real original content."

I had avoided mentioning it, but seeing how much time he was committing, I had to raise it: "How much is this going to cost, Dan? I'm worried about how much time you're putting in." I knew from talking to him that he had just invested in state-of-the-art computer equipment that would make all this brilliant compiling and "flushing" possible. I feared getting a bill in the thousands of dollars.

Dan didn't say anything for a moment; a rare pause groaned wide. "I don't do this for money, Jay. I never will. I do this because I don't sleep real well when the Trail is at risk. We've got to stop this thing and it doesn't really matter what it costs."

That didn't really answer my question, but I was ready to leap.

---

We stayed on the phone for a couple of hours that night getting the questions, the prompts, just right. I had suggested that I could come to Hot Springs if that would help, I wanted to see this man, but Dan said he worked better alone, on the phone. So my ear got sore from holding the receiver to it. I could tell we had been on the phone for too long when I heard more than one train pass by Dan's place. The tracks of the Norfolk Southern went right by his home, and the lonesome train whistle gave mournful accompaniment to our work.

That night Dan e-mailed me our first draft.

*Have you ever hiked the AT in the Roan Highlands?*

The second question: *What was special about the experience of using that part of the AT?*

I read through the draft and pronounced it ready to go.

Well after midnight that night, we went online with the website. The public-comment phase of the "public meeting" was already open, and now we joined the fray with our campaign. Charles said he had not heard from the Trail community. Now he would either hear their voice loud and clear, or we would fail. I was exhausted and queasy with excitement. I imagined Dan flipping an enormous switch in his bunker in Hot Springs. The Norfolk Southern's train whistle wailed in the dark. And we were under way.

A visitor to Dan's website, www.trailplace.com, was met with this banner headline: NORTH CAROLINA AGENCY RECONSIDERING QUARRY NEXT TO HUMP MOUNTAIN. We chose that because it offered hope— hope that I only felt intermittently between bouts of abject despair and nagging doubt. We intended to draw the reader in with appropriate outrage combined with optimism that taking action might afford a desirable outcome. The user was directed to click on the banner to learn more. Clicking through brought up Witt's photograph with the yellow line showing our rough guess at the ultimate boundaries of the site. After an introductory paragraph detailing the history of the battle, the user was asked to answer the questions Dan and I had written. The site included a ticker, which told the visitor how many members of the community had submitted public comments so far. The first letter we got read as follows:

My name is Justin Gude, and I am from Gainesville, Florida. I first hiked a section of the Appalachian Trail in North Carolina in 1996, as a senior in high school. This was one of the places that fueled my interest and love for the outdoors, and I have been back at least ten times since then. The Appalachian Trail, especially in the southeast, has a special place in my heart, and I will continue to hike the trail until I can no longer walk at all.

Because North Carolina is so close to me, I have been on the NC AT many times, including in the Roan Highlands. I believe that the Roan Highlands are perhaps the best place to hike the AT, perhaps because of the sense of place that they provide. Nothing compares to being able to look out across an open mountain vista and understand that you are only a small part of it all. The AT provides one with a sort of fellowship with the natural world, and this is most evident in the high bald peaks in NC, Tennessee and Virginia.

The fact that the AT was overlooked in the permit process for the gravel pit on Belview Mountain is absurd to me. It is easy to see that an open gravel pit next to the AT is a conflict of interest. I have never met anyone who wanted to go hike the trail in order to watch humans dig up a mountain. Also of interest is the vast amount of noise and particulate pollution that the gravel pit would spew into the surrounding area. I think that it is safe to say that if the gravel pit were to be put there, I would never hike the AT in North Carolina again. Furthermore, I think that many people feel the same way, as the whole concept of the gravel pit is fulsome.

Please include my comments in the official record of public comments.

The letter from Justin Gude was everything we were hoping for. Impassioned yet polite. Well-informed, specific, and even eloquent. Justin Gude was a fresh voice and he nailed the issues. Of course if he was the only one to send an e-mail, other than the members of my family, and the folks in our Unincorporated Association of Concerned Citizens, then Charles might be able to brush off this singular cogent, heartfelt appeal. But Justin wasn't the only one to send an e-mail through the Trailplace website. Not hardly. In the first hour we had seven letters. I

was ecstatic. I couldn't walk away from the computer screen, even as my eyes were swelling shut and predawn delirium was dragging me down. I had been told that the most written public comments ever received from the agency concerning a mining permit was twelve. In the second hour of our campaign we added ten to our seven. And this while most people, in my time zone anyway, were fast asleep in their beds. Suddenly, as simply as that, we had announced ourselves as the most vocal protest in state mining history.

Wingfoot called first thing in the morning. "Jay, we're cooking, here. This is going fast."

I was cautiously optimistic. "Do you think they are landing at the agency? Do we know that they are?"

"I'm sure they are, but even if they aren't, even if they're blocking them, it doesn't matter. If we have to, we can print the replies out and hand-deliver them. My in-box receives a copy of each one here, and if we have to, I'll print every one of them out. But I don't think we'll have to. They're landing in Charles's computer right now. And the attorney general's. Like little darts."

Wingfoot said he would read all the letters that day and night and monitor the content to make sure the responses had what he called "integrity." He would not edit any of the letters, could not, but he could ask the questions in a slightly different way if we were getting nonsensical or ineffective replies. He would also have to watch to see if the site was being hacked by pro-mine forces. It all seemed like digital special-ops, which made it enormously fun. And it was working. I was watching the numbers roll. The next day I called my neighbors on the mountain and told them all to visit www.trailplace.com so they could watch the ticker roll as the number of responses kept going up. One neighbor told me she was going to buy her first computer just so she could track the progress online. By the time I was finished with my breakfast, we had forty-two letters entered into the public record.

While Wingfoot and I were counting the numbers, monitoring the letter-writing campaign, the board of trustees at the Southern Environ-

153

mental Law Center was meeting, reviewing possible cases to take on. In their internal review we were up against dozens of candidate cases, including another in a long string of hog-waste-disposal cases, and a Clean Air Act enforcement action in Alabama. These were big cases with powerful constituencies and precedent-setting potential. I could not guess how we would rate.

When Trip called me to tell me we had made the cut, I went down to Chapel Hill to meet with him. The deal was this. The Southern Environmental Law Center would take the case. They would draft briefs and issue public comments. The bad news was that we would have to share Trip with his other cases. To get the ball rolling, he was assigning our case to Dan Hirschman, an intern. In the meantime Trip was working on a big case involving water quality in Charleston harbor and had primary responsibility for the suite of hog-waste cases in the eastern part of the state, including a landmark case concerning the spraying of hog waste on fields after the massive flooding following Hurricane Floyd. North Carolina farms at the time were home to 10 million hogs, more than the human population of the state, but all this population was clustered in just a few counties between Raleigh and the coast. While we have determined that a civilized society must have fixed plumbing and waste-treatment facilities for human waste, there has been little regulatory guidance for how to deal with the massive amounts of solid waste and liquid waste leaving factory farms, most of which heads directly for the increasingly impaired rivers and ultimately the sounds, marshes, and the sea. Thinking about how to remedy this was only one of Trip's tasks. As the director of the Carolinas office for SELC he also had to manage personnel in a time of growth for the nonprofit firm, as well as keep up a busy schedule of outreach events to keep donors informed and engaged. With Forrest and the Heel Hound on board, already drafting our complaint, Trip may have calculated that we did not now merit his full-time attention, not yet anyway. Also, our case was still a dark horse. We were small when held up against the battle over Charleston harbor and endangered-species claims and defense of the Clean Air Act. Our prospects uncertain.

Dan Hirschman was fresh out of law school, good-natured, and instantly likable, with a gentle face. He was also, like everyone else at

SELC, overworked. A native of Gastonia, North Carolina, he left the state to get his law degree in Vermont, at one of the best environmental-law programs in the country. Now he was back, eager to cut his teeth on some rich material. As an intern his area of expertise was whatever Trip put on his desk. On my description alone, Ollie dubbed him Diaper Dan.

One of the beauties of our having an intern was that I felt emboldened to interrupt Dan at any time. I would never become comfortable interrupting Trip at his desk, but I soon learned I could sit in Dan's office and toss around ideas and strategies at some length. In no time we became friends, brothers-in-arms.

In the first week of March I found Dan deep into drafting SELC's public comments on the Roadless Area Rule. In 1999, the Clinton administration had proposed a rule designed to protect the last remaining wild areas in the United States from the Forest Service's appetite for building roads, felling timber, and permitting mines on public land. The rule would take areas that had never had roads, the most pristine of the pristine areas that had somehow dodged the saws and the drilling rigs, and protect them as they were. From Dan I learned that the US Forest Service maintained more miles of roads through the US backwoods than were in the entire network of interstate highways. I also learned that the agency often sells timber below cost and had a backlog of thousands of miles of roads that were in need of repair or rebuilding.

The natural question is why does the US Forest Service, an agency with management responsibility for 8 percent of the landmass in the continental United States, want to build more roads if it can't maintain the roads it already has? And why are there privately owned mines and private timber companies and ski resorts operating on publicly owned lands in the first place?

I had a lot to learn.

From inception, under the 1891 Forest Reserve Act, the nation's publicly owned forests have served multiple functions and those multiple functions have led to conflict. Part of this has to do with the very establishment of the US Forest Service as a division within the Department of Agriculture. At the turn of the last century, trees were seen as a crop, and one purpose of the agency was to ensure an ample supply of lumber for a growing nation. But by the second half of the century this mission seemed out of date. The vast majority, some 95 percent, of all timber felled in the United States comes from private lands. But the desire of private companies to have access to publicly owned timber on publicly owned land is intense. Private timber companies bid on timber contracts and cut trees, some of which end up being sold by the private companies in overseas markets. Why is the federal government giving away—sometimes at a loss—the natural resources of the nation? In short, politics. Forest policy has become the captive of the industries that use trees and drill for oil and natural gas. And, to a lesser extent, captive to the folks who build and maintain roads. In its more recent history the Forest Service has taken a broader view of its role as a steward of public lands. It has expanded its mission to protecting watersheds, and providing recreational opportunities. Even so the founding mission and the cultural history of the agency compels managers to field proposals to open public land to ever more new roads, private mine operations, private gas drillers, and private timber interests.

All this was relevant to our case because while the mine itself would be on private land, Hump Mountain, and the majority of the protected land in the Roan Highlands—the areas affected by the operation—are managed by the Forest Service and related agencies for recreational use and enjoyment.

I told Dan about the letter-writing campaign, and he immediately pulled up the Trailplace website on his computer.

We were up to 178 letters on the third day of the effort.

"Great!" Dan said with his trademark enthusiasm. "I'll e-mail this link to everybody I know."

Dan wanted to go over the files I had put together thus far, so he saved his current document, spun out of his chair, and we headed for the conference room. I started disgorging papers on the broad table.

I told him about what Forrest had said about the public meeting scheduled by Charles.

"Trip is going to let me go up for it," Dan said, clearly pleased.

"Forrest might be right, it might be window dressing. But he might be wrong, too. I've already started drafting our public comments."

I headed back to the mountains, pleased with the investment of Dan's time. Sure, Dan was young, but he was passionate and smart. Everything seemed to be falling into place in our assault on the powers that be. The public comments were pouring into the Trailplace website. And the public-meeting roster was coming along. Don Barger was going to send two of his staff from the National Parks Conservation Association. They were going to hike the Trail with a camera crew, then attend the meeting. The Tennessee Eastman Hiking and Canoeing Club, the club that monitors and repairs our section of Trail, would send representatives, as would the area conservation groups. But still, we were waiting to see what the Appalachian Trail Conservancy would do in its own defense.

The agony of that wait soon ended. My phone rang one afternoon, a week before the public meeting, and it was Dave Startzell, the executive director of the Appalachian Trail Conservancy. I wondered if Wingfoot's participation had spurred him to action. But if he was a reluctant warrior, he hid it well. Dave was excited about the prospect of the public meeting. I was thrilled to have him on the phone. If we could hold the attention of the Trail group, we would be playing in the big leagues. This in turn would keep SELC interested in a case that would require more investment with every day that passed. With the ATC on our side, the piece of our battle plan Charles had identified as our chief weakness would become our enduring strength. The Trail would be fighting for itself.

I found Dave Startzell to be unwavering in his support of the Trail and the Trail experience. He was also frank, terrifically bright, and somewhat irreverent. Clearly Morgan, as regional director, had been communicating with those at the highest levels of the organization because Startzell was well familiar with the current status of the case.

"Maybe Charles Gardner is trying to figure out how to revoke the permit," Startzell said.

"Maybe," I said. "Forrest is skeptical. Ron Howell is not even skeptical."

Startzell wanted to know the progress of the lawsuit, the complaint the Heel Hound and Forrest were drafting. I learned he and the Appalachian Trail Conservancy board were still weighing whether to join the case as plaintiffs. If they did, Startzell explained, his group would split all attorney fees with my group fifty-fifty. Every tense muscle in my body relaxed at hearing this. Startzell might not have known it, and I didn't tell him, but this cost-share arrangement might be enough to keep us in the case for years without fear of being bled dry. As we spoke, I began to understand anew the awkward position the Appalachian Trail Conservancy found itself in. A small, local group they had never heard of was seeking to sue the state in part for impacts the Putnam Mine would have on the national park that their group was authorized to create and maintain. They didn't know us and had to wonder whether we were competent to take on such a fight, or whether we would do more harm than good. But they also knew by now that we were right. That our little case was their best chance for protecting their own treasured stretch of the storied route.

I tried to reassure Dave Startzell that Southern Environmental Law Center had vetted us fully, and that he ought to be encouraged at the participation of the National Parks Conservation Association. Basically, I tried to puff up our group and assure him it wasn't just Ollie Cox, Jay and Witt, and a dog named Biscuit. As far as the draft complaint, I told him it was coming along in the able hands of retired Superior Court judge Ronald Howell. That Howell was known around here as the Heel Hound of the mountains, and that he had recently disappeared, had sequestered himself in the woods to draft in utter solitude.

The call ended with Startzell informing me that Morgan Sommerville would attend the public meeting. This was welcome news indeed. Morgan was well liked and respected among agency veterans, and as he was the face of the ATC, Charles would not be able to deny that his complaint about silence from the Trail had effectively been refuted. And Morgan knew what he was talking about. He had been to Hump Mountain.

But there was more good news, which Startzell saved for last. Pam Underhill from the US Department of the Interior would take time out of the Ranger Roundup, an annual get-together of Park Service and conservation officials from across the country, to deliver the official position of the federal government at the public meeting. I stared out the window, unable to fashion a response. The federal government had an official position on the Putnam Mine? *The Department of the Interior?* Not only that, Pam Underhill wanted to stay over for a day, hike Hump Mountain and see the damage for herself. Startzell asked if I might be available to hike the Trail with her, show her the mine site, and familiarize her with the terrain, both literally and figuratively. This was our biggest break yet. From the very first time I saw the scar on Belview Mountain from Hump Mountain I had believed that if we could get enough decision-makers to the Trail—or any decision-makers—to see the damage with their own eyes, we would have a chance to win. I quickly offered to find Ms. Underhill a place to stay and the offer was accepted. I imagined sitting up late into the night with an official from the National Park Service, drinking what? Whiskey? Tea? Pleading our case until she couldn't stand to hear another word of my argument. My imaginings all ended with her finally throwing up her hands and saying, "No more! The federal government will fix this!"

# Chapter 8

March 16. The day of the public meeting finally arrived. I drove up to the mountains from the middle of the state with my mother, who had taken keen interest in the case. My sister's family trailed us in a separate car. My mother owned the land next to mine, seven level acres of pasture, but had more than an economic interest or a sentimental attachment to the land. For her it was about right and wrong, and about good government versus crooked industry favoritism. And it was about knowing that her son was on the right side. She bent over a notepad drafting notes for the comments she would deliver to Charles. Meanwhile I was driving far too fast, trying to make good time while not killing us in a nasty brew of freezing rain and fog.

We pulled into Newland, the county seat, with an hour to spare. The entire valley was now glazed with a slick coat of ice. We were to meet Forrest and Ron at the Shady Lawn Motel—whose sign had for decades been a centerpiece on the main street of town, purporting cheerfully AIR-CONDITIONED BY NATURE!

The lawyers were already seated in the motel restaurant, and we joined them. Somehow Forrest had gotten word to the Heel Hound, up on the mountain where he was drafting, and here he was. After pushing my dinner around my plate, I headed over to the courthouse.

All the Cook-Carpenter-Cox clan were already there. Ashley had her video camera set up on a tripod, and the others had taken places in the front row. Faye was there with her mother, Jesse Staton, a fierce and upright woman, a fighter. They reported that it was now spitting snow on the other side of the county. This was not good. If it was snowing over in Elk Park, would that mean the folks coming from Elizabethton and Johnson City would turn back when they reached the state line? And if the word was out that it was snowing in Avery, might we lose our Asheville and Spruce Pine people, too? Surely nobody would drive all the way from Asheville or Boone in the teeth of a gathering storm. I stood at the top of the courthouse stairs and looked out the window over the dreary grass plaza in the center of town. I looked for cars pulling into the diagonal parking spaces ringing the winter-brown common, but none came. A couple of heavy-equipment operators were standing on the front apron of the courthouse, in the swirling snow.

I tried to explain my anxiety to Faye and her mother. If the Appalachian Trail folks failed to turn out in sufficient numbers, that would be reflected in Charles's public record. Not the weather report, I didn't guess, not the accumulation of ice on the powerlines, just a raw number of attendees that could be wielded against us. Joe DeLoach from Southern Appalachian Highlands Conservancy submitted written comments but I needed bodies. I hoped he would show up. I feared Charles would go back to Raleigh and write a note to the attorney general saying that the mine was of little public concern to the people of Avery County or members of the purported Trail community. Wingfoot was worried that the agency might be dismissive of the e-mails because so many of them were coming in from Kentucky, Colorado, Tennessee, and elsewhere, all over the country, and he and I both felt this meeting was important to establish that people around here, local Trail users and people in the local community, Dog Town and Cranberry Gap, felt abused by the lack of notice and nonexistent public hearings.

I needn't have worried about numbers. With five minutes to go before the scheduled start of the meeting, the people suddenly came pouring into our rickety, careworn courthouse. The old staircase rumbled and groaned. Dan Hirschman squeezed into the second row. Steve Perri from the Tennessee Eastman Hiking and Canoeing Club stood with a crowd in the back of the room. Morgan was there, too. By the time I made it to the front of the courthouse, Ollie had already been lobbying him.

Later, Ollie would allege that Morgan was wearing flip-flops—she liked to think of the AT folks as hippies—but I cannot confirm that, having been unable to see his feet—or anyone else's feet—in the crowd.

As Charles called the meeting to order, I scanned the room. Our side was ably represented. Hiking clubs from around the mountains had sent concerned members. My neighbors were all in seats or standing in the aisles. The other side was not without support. An old family friend who hauls gravel and pushes snow for the state was sitting near Paul. At the end of that row sat a kind old fellow who had replaced my hot-water heater on an icy Christmas Eve one year when I was a kid. I met a few hard gazes from other folks who either hauled rock or worked on roads or built houses, those whose livelihood depended on a cheap source of rock. There were also a lot of folks I didn't know, people from Boone, I guessed, folks who could go either way. Writers from the region's papers were poised to record the action.

Charles welcomed the packed house. "I know everybody here wishes they were somewhere else," he said, his voice checking with discomfort. "I especially want to apologize to the Appalachian Trail people." Our side seemed to swell while the opposition seemed to feint and then dig in. "The purpose of this meeting is to voice your concerns, whether you're opposed to the quarry or in favor of it. Your concerns and suggestions will be taken into account as we work with the permit holders to minimize adverse impacts as called for by the Mining Act."

*Minimize?* Ron Howell nodded at Forrest, his low opinion of Charles reaffirmed. Our side hadn't come here looking for ways to minimize the impacts. We were here to eliminate the impacts altogether.

Four men were on the dais with Charles: Tracy Davis, Mel Nevils, Jim Simons, and a guy I had never before seen. These gentlemen took inordinate care to spread papers out before themselves; they organized their ink pens as if a great deal depended upon their doing it just so. A couple of them looked wary, surveying the crowd with wide eyes. This could get ugly. Big Tommy Burleson loomed by the side exit with his radio on his hip. A deputy sheriff drifted in and out.

Randy Carpenter, the Bald Eagle, was the first speaker on the list.

And all hell tore loose. Randy calculated that playing to his base would be a winning formula. And he let it fly.

"Avery County is mining country!" He thrust his shoulders back and took off like the cock of the walk. "My ancestors came into these mountains in the 1700s, and everything they saw, they took it. They took the timber. They took the rock. That's just the way it was."

The assembled sat in stunned silence. Even Randy's allies were taken aback that he had come out so aggressively. A young girl sat in the front row with her hands folded in her lap. She brimmed with pride. Randy's daughter? Just an admirer? Certainly Randy had lit a fire with his words, with his attitude. But our side sensed a miscalculation, an opportunity. We lay in wait to see where it would go.

Randy meant to offend. He meant to become the hero of his constituency. He aimed to win the room by sheer force. Charles let him run, like a trout on a reel with a hundred yards of backing, and the gravel haulers were emboldened by what they heard. Soon they were whooping their delight as Randy swung with roundhouse punches. Charles, though, sat stock-still, with the occasional wince, as if he were absorbing blows.

Randy railed on. "There's no one here who isn't touched by gravel," he claimed in tones stentorian. "No one! So that we can have good roads, so that I can have that gravel parking lot in front of my house, so that I can protect the streams for all of us."

O Randy, redeemer of streams! The crowd seemed to rock, in anger and delight, and I watched in amusement as Randy became a parody of a country lawyer.

"The folks who live close to Putnam Mine," he broadcast, "they all knew! Why, me and James Vance, who works for Mr. Brown, we went to certain landowners right near the site. There's a whole strip of landowners down the Toe River Valley that wanted us to mine their land because they could see the dollars here."

His supporters whooped and shook the courthouse. Randy nearly wore out his rotator cuff congratulating himself. He couldn't contain himself. He was feeling it. So he stretched to one more inflammatory home truth. "Belview Mountain is a natural gravel pit. And you don't own it. We do."

Now the boos rained down. The place was electric with emotion coming from both sides of the aisle.

But Randy wasn't done. He took a quick tour of the front of the room. Now he stood right in front of Charles. With all eyes on him he made a quarter turn to level an attack at Ollie and Freddy. "I know some of the people around here, they have junk in their yards. Old car parts and rusted piles of stuff," he said damningly. "Now that's ugly to look at. But we don't think that's any of our business what their place looks like, if that's how they want to live. We came in here and we're going to improve this neighborhood. We're going to put people to work and run a clean operation people can be proud of!"

He had stepped over a line. Now Curly lunged forward. "You ort not to said that, Randy!" he spat. Ashley held out an arm to restrain Curly while hurling her own opinion of Randy's slight. The crowd tipped forward to see it all, and the building seemed to strain at the sill plates.

Now Tommy Burleson, with an economy of motion, lifted his radio to his mouth and spoke into it. Within seconds a pair of deputies appeared, just in case they were needed.

Randy was locked and loaded. Now he pulled the trigger. "Can you see Putnam Mine from the Appalachian Trail?" He let the question hang in the air for a moment. He had been watching movies. "Yes, you can. But you can see a lot of other things up there, too. You can see every vacation house on Yellow Mountain. Does that ruin the Appalachian Trail? No. And you can see the swinging-bridge tourist attraction on Grandfather Mountain. I never understood what was so environmental about that!"

There was a delicious drinking in of this comment. Randy Carpenter had just slandered the favorite tourist destination of every schoolkid in the state of North Carolina. The Mile High Swinging Bridge on Grandfather Mountain is one of the scenic, if old-school, wonders of the South. But Randy wasn't appealing to schoolkids. He was appealing to the old guard, the gravel-heads. The unreconstructed. He looked particularly pleased with himself now. He paused to let it all sink in, his own brilliant advocacy, the power of his words. Finally he resumed, growling like a tent preacher, "We're going to be here for a long time. This is not a five-year, tear-up-the-mountain job, in and out. This is a hundred-year, two-hundred-year mine. That's what this is all about."

I'm certain that Randy was trying to impress upon the assembly, and upon Charles, that Clark Stone was a legitimate business with staying power. Instead, he had succeeded in inflaming our supporters with a promise that the noise and damage to Belview Mountain, the communities of Dog Town and Cranberry Gap, and the Appalachian Trail would never end. Not in our lifetimes. Not in the lifetimes of our children. And he had done us one other favor. In driving home the point that you could see the Mile High Swinging Bridge from the Appalachian Trail, he had also succeeded in making graphic the point that you were going to be able to see the decapitated top of Belview Mountain from the Mile High Swinging Bridge. Forrest turned to me and did not need to wink.

After Randy sat down, to robust jeers and some violent applause, Ron Howell, the Heel Hound, stood to tell our side of the story. His method was to attack the process, the meeting itself.

He pushed his glasses around on his nose and leaned over his copy of the Mining Act. "Mr. Gardner, in all my looking through the Mining Act of 1971, I can find no mention of public meetings as part of any plan to modify a permit, or to revoke one. Nor to minimize impacts. You have brought us all here on a misadventure, for there is no status given to such a gathering. We are here, my clients and I, my co-counsel, in protest of this unauthorized"—here he stopped and searched for a word. The crowd leaned forward to hear what he might say—"*get-together,*" he finally said with bemusement, as if the very idea of holding a hearing after the fact was so preposterous as to warrant outrageous puzzlement. Now he restated his case. "Unauthorized *meeting.*" As he repeated his words he pounded softly on the podium. Now he leafed through the papers before him. "Hearings, Mr. Gardner. That is what we seek, that is what we are due. Just like in every other permitting decision, we are guaranteed due process *before* issuance of any permit. Not get-togethers, Mr. Gardner, *hearings.*" And that was all Ron said. He nodded at the podium, an act of deference, and took his seat. It was a fine performance, everything Randy's was not, and I was proud to be represented by one of the best. The opposition was clearly awed that the famous Judge Ronald Howell was there, speaking eloquently on behalf of Ollie Cox and Curly and the Dog Town Bunch. You could see their minds turning. *How in the hell did Ollie Ve Cox get Judge Ron Howell on her side?*

Next, my sister stood to make a direct plea to Charles. She explained that as the founder of a nonprofit organization working with under-privileged teenagers, to help them get into college, she dealt with a generation marked by cynicism. She explained that her students were natural skeptics, that they doubted the integrity of authority figures, all authority figures: teachers, parents, government officials. She described kids who thought the system was rigged against them at every turn. She then challenged Charles to prove to people like her students that government can own up to its mistakes, can work to protect the defense-less. "To be honest, Mr. Gardner, my students don't believe you'll do the right thing. They think that government officials are bought and paid for. That regulators in positions such as yours do the bidding of the rich and powerful. They believe money talks. I'm asking you to prove them wrong."

Standing ovations followed nearly every presentation, on both sides.

A powerful murmur swept the courtroom when Tony rose to speak. I glanced at Ashley. She looked as if she would rather have been under her seat than manning the video camera. Would rather be anywhere but here. Away at war, sleeping in a ditch, you name it. Her father struggled with his cane as he made his way into the aisle. We had heard he was now on permanent disability. He had wrecked his motorcycle, riding dirt trails with Freddy one day, and he had banged himself up pretty badly. A few days later he claimed he fell off a ladder at work, attributing his injuries to the fall. He threatened to sue his employer and applied for full disability. Of course his disability did not keep him from riding his Harley-Davidson up and down Highway 19E at all hours, tormenting Ashley and Ollie. In fact Ashley had driven across the state line, with a friend, to shoot video of her father working, quite ably, on the house he bought with Paul's fat check, hopping on and off of his motorcycle, lifting heavy objects, and she was preparing a package including the video to send to the Division of Social Services, the Social Security Administration, to demonstrate his fraud. Now he walked with a pronounced limp to the front of the courthouse.

He took his place at the podium and reared back, ready to let loose. Hoots rose from deep corners. Somebody called out, "Here we go!" Even Paul's team got a laugh out of Tony. Gomer.

Now he leaned over on his walking stick and looked right into Charles's eyes. "The Appalachian Trail," he snarled, "ain't nothing but a bunch of draft dodgers and rich kids and homo-sexshules."

Rather than drawing cheers from Paul's allies, Tony drew embarrassed snickers, and not for any love of draft dodgers or homosexuals. Tony was a pathetic figure. Someone cried that Tony was a sellout. That he was the one who put the fight on the map. "Now look at you!" a small voice barked.

Tony wheeled around to address the unseen accuser. "No, I ain't. I'm just a good businessman." He burst into a peal of laughter that was too loud in isolation. And that was it. Having said all he came to say, having entertained himself, he limped back to his seat, nursing his handicap.

Paul looked as if he'd been jabbed with a sharp stick, done no favors.

Speaker after speaker rose to tell Charles their story. His or her own impression of what had gone wrong here. My eleven-year-old niece took the podium to point out to Charles that every fifth-grader in the state knows where the Appalachian Trail is. "We take a class in North Carolina history, sir," she said, "and we learn all about the important places in the state." She asked Charles why schoolkids can locate the state's national parks on a map but state officials cannot. Somehow she managed to do this politely, without coming off as a smart aleck. The courthouse erupted, and Charles was gracious in receipt of the indictment.

My neighbor John Bledsoe is a lawyer in South Carolina. He and his wife own a home on the backside of Belview Mountain. Their garden is a wonderland of every flower that blooms, of viney bowers and simple architecture designed to take in the view of the creek that tumbles off the mountain. They feared that the blasting from the mine would ruin their springwater, rearrange the delicate subsurface fissures that allow underground water to rise and course down to the Toe River. John stalked behind the lectern, citing Charles for failing to hold public hearings before the permit was issued. "This is a sham process, Mr. Gardner. It's after the fact, and that makes no sense whatsoever if you really have in mind doing anything about this. You were supposed to have this hearing before the permit got issued, not afterwards. How were we supposed to raise our legitimate concerns about the project before it happened when we were given no notice whatsoever? We're down the road on this thing, now, and we ought to be talking about revoking this permit, or else you're wasting our time, and we're wasting yours. I read in the papers, you talking about *modifying* the permit. Tonight you said you'd like to *minimize* the impacts. Well, everybody knows, Mr. Gardner, that you can't minimize these impacts. Common sense says you can't hide a 151-acre hole when you're looking down on it from above, from up on the Appalachian Trail. We're smarter than that. Don't come up here and treat us like we don't have the sense we were born with."

John was good. Any client would want to have him plead his or her case. The effect of his remarks was momentous. For a brief spot of time the supporters and the opponents of Paul Brown's rock crusher met in the aisle, and you couldn't be sure that there would not be a small war.

When John sat down, applause and jeers still ringing, the boys behind him leaned forward and asked him if he'd like to step outside. "For what?" John asked. One of the boys made it plain: "To get your ass whupped." I didn't catch John's response, but whatever he said to them sent them back into their seats without any need for the swinging of fists.

Faye rose and gave a stem-winder on what it had been like to live next to Paul's operation. "The only people who received notification of what was coming in time to try to stop it were those who profited, either those who sold property to Mr. Brown or leased it to him," she said, "and if that doesn't violate the Mining Act, why do we have one? Nobody told us one thing about our rights to contest this before he moved right in. I feel like the state has really let us down. We need some protection from this kind of mine, and you failed us." She then presented Charles with her own written comments. "I don't know if you read these things or not. Nobody has listened to a word we've said yet."

Charles assured her he would read her comments and thanked her for them.

Tommy Carver, the dignified pastor of the Belview Mountain Baptist Church, which sits just under the crusher site, expressed his concern that the hill would collapse behind his church, inundating the cemetery. He also expressed his concern that Wednesday-evening and Sunday-morning services would be disturbed by the constant noise of drilling and crushing. "That's a twenty-four-hour permit, sir," he said politely. "And I just want to say that's got me worried."

Terry Buchanan, who lives in Dog Town, at the end of a long driveway marked with two cement eagles on pillars, took his turn at the microphone and seized the opportunity to express his wish that all the "tree huggers" in the courthouse sink in mud up to their radiators. "I'm all the time telling people, if you ain't got gravel, you ain't got no roads," he said summarily. "Without gravel, all you got is mud, and for all I care you can have it."

Steve Shoemaker addressed those who had raised the visual impacts. "If you don't like how it looks, you just need to walk faster," he sneered.

A man I did not know stood and approached the dais to address Charles. Somehow the crowd knew to settle down, to listen closely to him. When he reached the front of the courtroom, he pulled a photograph out of his shirt pocket and held it up for all to see. He explained that it was a picture of his daughter. In a shaking voice he told a story about taking his little girl up on top of Belview Mountain to pick Easter flowers, forsythia flowers, on Easter Sunday. He said it would be a shame for his daughter to grow up and have the mountain ruined when the law was not followed in the first place. "I know I'm being emotional, and not legal, or technical, but all we've got around here is places like this to go to. We can't afford anything better than this."

Pam Underhill was our star and champion, and our secret weapon. She was our cavalry and our nuclear option all rolled into one. She stood tall and lean, the spirit of the Trail itself. She possessed a silky voice and used language like a poet. She was, she said, here to deliver the official position of the US Department of the Interior and the National Park Service.

The room grew silent. Mouths literally fell open, and Charles appeared jolted to a new level of attention as she made to speak.

Pam Underhill asked graciously, but firmly, for Charles to consider her wish "on behalf of the people of the United States" that the permit be revoked so as to protect the values of the Appalachian Trail: "I would ask that you have the courage and the grace to rescind the permit, to renew the process, and to let it properly unfold." Our side was propelled into an ecstatic thrall of affirmation, but we did not stomp the floor and we did not rise to our feet. I was reminded of wise words Witt once spoke to me: "Once you've made the sale, stop selling."

I looked at Ollie and Ashley, who were, themselves, looking at each other. They appeared to be in shock. They had thought all along that Paul was the biggest thing in the mountains. The biggest business-man, the biggest threat, and the biggest single force of man. And they thought that he would roll them, roll Charles, because he had always won at everything. And they expected to lose because Ollie had lost at everything she ever tried. She had been stepped on, pushed around. But now, here was this exotic and powerful woman, who flew in from . . . from *where,* from the Pentagon? From the White House? She was standing right here in the Avery County Courthouse trumping Sam Laws and the despised county commissioners. Trumping the might of Tommy Burleson and Randy and all the rest. This here was the god-damn federal government riding in here to save some little dirt trail through the woods. Pam Underhill had come to stand side by side with Ollie Ve Cox, a mountain girl from Dog Town who sewed gloves for thirty years, whose grandfather had shot his own sister in the potato patch over a piece of land. It was hard to believe such a thing could happen to a person such as her.

The meeting lasted for two hours. But the time flew by. It was a culmination of pent-up stress for folks on both sides of the issue. If they had let everybody who had something to say speak, we would have been there all night long and into the morning. Dan Hirschman used his time well." He said, "The severe impact of the planned

150-acre-plus operation within the viewshed and soundscape of this extraordinary portion of the Appalachian Trail is of grave concern to the public and demands serious consideration by the state." Somebody actually marveled aloud, exclaiming, "Whoa!" over the sheer elegance of the argument. Dan continued, "A diligent or merely adequate review of the application should have readily revealed the proximity of the Putnam site to the Appalachian Trail. A cursory review of any topographic map or even a North Carolina road map would clearly indicate the location of the Appalachian Trail." Silence pressed in. Dan continued, taking up the cause of Ollie and Faye. "Individuals who are located a mere four hundred feet from the mine are surely the kind of interested parties contemplated by the Mining Act as being entitled to notice. The fact that the permit boundaries were uniformly drawn fifty feet inside the operator's property boundary to avoid having to notify neighbors must not preclude the right to notice for those parties contemplated under the statute. The only purpose for such boundaries is to circumvent the protective features of the Mining Act."

Faye and her mother led the long round of applause when Dan stepped down. Over the din I could hear Ollie explaining to Freddy, "That there is Diaper Dan and he's our lawyer!"

At the end of the meeting our side huddled, recounting what had gone well, and what had not. We knew blows had been landed by the other side. Joe Loven, the owner of the local cement company, had spoken in a perfectly reasonable way about how the county needed to create jobs in the mountains to keep young people from moving down to the cities. A Mr. Sizemore said he himself would lose his job if Paul was forced to shut down. At this, Mike Buchanan leapt to his feet to offer the man a job. "I'll put you on a dozer tomorrow, buddy, but we don't need this mine going in destroying Cranberry and Dog Town! You come see me tomorrow. I'll put you on a dozer, and I ain't fooling." This act of generosity won cheers all the way around the room.

All evening long I watched Charles. I felt sorry for him. He was a punching bag for both sides. Whatever action he took, he was going to make half the room unhappy. Lives and livelihoods would forever be altered depending on the decision he made. But I was also, in a strange way, in a way I could not explain, proud of him. He sat up there for two hours and took every blow.

Through it all, he gave away not a single clue, revealed nothing of his thinking. After the meeting was adjourned he shook hands, listened to more pleas, and thanked his hosts. I watched him still, amid the sea of folks milling around, slapping backs, recounting the action, as he sought out my niece, to commend her for her composure in making her point about our national parks.

The next morning I cooked grits and venison sausage and biscuits for Dan, Morgan, and Pam. They had stayed over after the meeting. Pam said she had always wanted to try grits, and she was polite about them. She ate her biscuit.

After breakfast, we headed out hiking, to help our guest from the Department of the Interior get a fix on how the Trail lay in relation to the quarry site. To this point she had relied on Morgan's description, on Witt's photographs, and on my highly biased narrative, which had been forwarded to her along a winding Internet trail. Now, suddenly, I was worried that, seeing the site, Pam might find the mine was too far away from the Trail to have the direct adverse effects I had alleged, or that she would have a hard time imagining the impacts once the cleared area expanded outward, metastasized, over the next one hundred years. Even if I could show the site to her, if the weather made that possible, I still could not turn it on for her, could not make her hear the drilling or experience a blast. So I was hopeful, but worried, my mind racing forward and back, unable to settle on whether this was a great day for the fight, or whether it would set us back. My fears were not unfounded. If Pam didn't see the threat posed by Paul's operation the way I had seen it, and the way Witt did, then her report could finish us. Had she seen worse than what I would show her? And if she had, she still might not put the weight of the federal government, the mighty Department of the Interior, behind our little fight.

I should have worried more about the weather. We headed out in a steady drizzle, but by the time we reached the top of Big Yellow, the temperature had dropped and we were in an ice fog. A knifelike wind blew the ice sideways, through us. Pam was wearing only a light sweater and a rain poncho. We all took turns offering her our jackets, but she assured us that she was impervious to foul weather. By the time we reached Bradley Gap, an hour on, we were caked in ice. The temperature was nineteen degrees. Knowing that we would see nothing but silver fog from the summit, and our own frozen eyelashes, we looped back toward the trailhead.

My guests were preparing to leave the mountain when the weather finally cleared. But it was too late. It would take us an hour and a half to get back over to Big Hump, then another hour and a half to get home and that would be if we were pushing hard. So Pam left without seeing the mine from the Trail. At least she hadn't seen anything to make her think that the impacts *weren't* adverse. I would have to comfort myself with that, and with the fact that her comments were already in the public record. Once again, we were thrust into a position where too few had a full understanding of what the hell we were talking about, why the stakes were so high, because too few people in positions of authority had actually seen it with their own eyes.


As we moved into April, then May, the days got longer, the sun warmer. The spring peepers were borned in the ponds and marshy places and moved into the forest. Out of the gray ground seeds stirred, new growth erupted, and every tree limb swelled at the buds. Salamanders respond to a magic trigger. A night will come with rain, and the temperature will hover above forty-five degrees, and in unison all the salamanders emerge from the rotting logs and the rocky dens and head for the damp places, the vernal pools and the bogs, to breed. If you happen to be outside on the night this happens, you are treated to one of the wondrous migrations in the natural world.

Upright members of the natural world stirred, too. Hikers packed tents and water bottles and little cookstoves and stepped out of their winter-musty dwellings. They began streaming into the area in ever-larger numbers to see the splendor, the carpets of fringed phacelia,

173

the squirrel corn, and Dutchman's-breeches. Bird-watchers took to the woods to note the arrival of the neotropical songbirds that had wintered in South America and in the islands. The first Through Hikers, those intent on completing the entire Trail from Georgia to Maine, began to reach the Roan just as its tattered hide was greening up.

In the time between the two "meetings" Charles scheduled, the public-comment period remained open. All the while our letter-writing campaign was pummeling the state with impassioned pleas from hikers across the land. The initial flood of comments ran into the hundreds. On our best day one hundred seventy newly minted letters landed. Mondays were the slow days, and on the slowest Monday I counted a mere thirty-four. But the stream never ran dry. Word spread, outrage, too, passion flared, and letters landed. Tracy Davis explained to me that each one, each individual letter, had to be entered into the official record. Each had to be opened, read, copied, and filed. If Tracy did nothing else during his workday, he could officially receive into the public record forty letters at most. He was badly behind and they just kept coming. This war was on.

My mood was reflected in the change of the seasons. I felt we had made a breakthrough at the first public meeting and with the campaign. We had drawn the Appalachian Trail establishment and even the federal government into our fight. We had hammered Charles with so many public comments, showered him with so many voices, that he could no longer deny that this was larger than just Jay and Witt. Still, it was becoming increasingly clear to me that gaining notoriety for the fight, garnering publicity, and the attention of the conservation community, while it felt good and was certainly better than the alternative, didn't fix much for Ollie and Ashley. In the lull that followed the public meeting, I was becoming more aware of the stress Ashley was under. And some of it had nothing to do with Paul's rock crusher.

Ollie would only tell me parts of the story. Tony had not just been a negligent parent. He had been violent. He had waved guns around, levelled threats that Ashley would never forget. And the conflict between brother and sister, father and daughter, seemed to escalate as we moved into the spring season.

One night before he vacated the house he sold to Paul, Tony crossed the road and demanded that Ashley follow him. He was fixing to move and said it was time she came on home. It was a strange request. Ashley had lived with Ollie and Curly for five years, and Tony never seemed to know, or care, where she was. When she refused to go with him, he threatened to take her across the road "by the hair of her head." When he moved for her, Freddy intervened and tried to get Tony out of the house. Tony had always been an oaf, a joke, a pain in the ass, and Ollie and Freddy could usually control him, could steer him out of trouble, and safely out of their orbit. But something in him snapped that night. Suddenly, he threw a looping punch in the direction of Freddy's face. The knobby Masonic ring on his finger caught the tight skin above Freddy's eye, and the blow sent Freddy sprawling on the floor. Blood came pouring down his face.

A gang-tackle ensued and Ashley shoved her father out of the apartment and down the stairs. The police were called, Ollie knew all the deputies, and charges were brought, for assault, for communicating threats, and, after that, for resisting arrest.

When the court date arrived, the judge, disgusted by Tony's conduct, offered him a deal. He and Nona, Ashley's mother, could relinquish custody of Ashley—to Ollie—in exchange for having the suite of charges dropped. With no apparent interest in defending himself, Tony agreed immediately to the deal. Nona thought on it for an instant longer, then she, too, ceded the custody of her daughter, her only child, to her sister-in-law. And walked away.

Ashley was pleased, but she was also hurt, confused. "I never thought I would be sold so cheap," she said after the hearing.

A restraining order was put into place making all contact between parents and child discretionary, meaning that Ashley could refuse to see her parents if that was what she wanted. And that is what she wanted. It was done.

At least outwardly, though, most of the troubles in the Cox household still revolved around Paul and the crusher. I began to notice that the mine fight was empowering for Ashley and Ollie. They would rather concentrate on getting Paul out of their lives than on the other myriad stressors pressing in on them. I could relate. The fight had become our constant companion, and I don't think any of us could have imagined what we would do with ourselves without it.

One day Ashley called me with the latest. "Did you get the *Mountain Times* today?"

"I haven't been down the mountain."

"Well, listen to this." She read to me, "'QUARRY LANDOWNER DEFENDS PROPERTY RIGHTS.'"

Ollie hollered out in the background, "He claims Witt used a telephoto lens! He says he wrote protections into the lease."

"Who?" I asked.

"Putnam," Ashley said.

"Robert Putnam?"

"Bingo."

Until now, we had not heard a word out of the owner of the leased land, Robert Putnam, the Putnam in the name that the agency assigned the quarry in its permit. Witt had called him, had tried to engage him, but it had taken Scott Nicholson to unmask the man behind the scenes.

"Read it to me," I said.

"Okay, here goes." Ashley commenced reading. *"'I did not enter into the lease with Clark Stone Company without first satisfying myself that this was the best economic use of the land, and for a purpose that would result in the contribution of a necessary material to the area's infrastructure and future growth—with no undue adverse or permanent effects on the land.'"*

Ollie couldn't contain herself from offering her own editorial remarks. "Huh? Removing a mountain is probably adverse and it's for damn sure permanent," she hooted.

Freddy savaged the author. "Putnam's one of them Florida millionaire people. What does he care about our infrastructure for? Let him worry about the infrastructure in Miami Beach."

Ashley piled on, "All Putnam wants is the almighty dollar. He's typical."

"Read!" I demanded.

"Okay. Listen to what he said. '*I have hiked portions of the AT for years, and personally believe it to be a great recreational resource. I have hiked over 6000 foot summits, through rhododendron gardens, past cow pastures, barns, apple orchards, cornfields, fishing ponds, fences, country roads, electric lines, and even country roads and near restaurants, where the trail crosses highways.*'" Ashley took a breath. "God, where hasn't he hiked? I mean he's got to be one of the most busiest hikers there ever was!"

"Ashley, if you're not going to—"

"Okay! I'll read. '*I must say, it never occurred to me that some might imply that legitimate economic activities were incompatible with usage of the AT, particularly when occurring at a substantial distance. It is surely a gross distortion to train a photographer's telephoto lens, or a TV station's telescopic camera, on a legitimate and permitted business some miles away from the trail and complain when the land is being put to a necessary and productive use in full compliance with the legal requirements.*'"

"Is that it?" I asked.

Ollie was apoplectic. She came on the line. "How the hell does he know what lens Witt used? That's grade-A, superpremium, two-dollar-and-fifty-cents-a-gallon bullshit."

Now Ashley took the phone back from her aunt. "There's more. Same article, I've got Dave Startzell's comments to DENR. You want to hear it?"

"Yes." I braced myself. We had been waiting to hear the official position of the Appalachian Trail Conservancy since Witt made his first approach the year before. Now the executive director was going on the record. It was one thing to hear it in person, in a private conversation on the telephone. It was quite another to see what official language the ATC would employ.

Ollie read: "'*As hikers descend from the summit of Hump Mountain to Elk*

*Park, North Carolina, they face directly toward the mine, which due to the open terrain, is fully visible along one mile of the descent, or for approximately 20 to 30 minutes at a normal hiking pace. Given the duration of visual exposure, and recognizing the fact that Hump Mountain is among the most prominent mountains in the Highlands of Roan—an area widely recognized as one of North Carolina's most spectacular scenic and outdoor recreation areas—we believe the visual impacts of the gravel quarry operations, particularly if they are expanded in scope, will significantly diminish the scenic quality of the area and detract from the outstanding recreational experience for many thousands of hikers and other visitors along the affected segment of the Appalachian Trail and the Roan Highlands.'"*

"Holy cow," I said, hearing the relief in my own voice. "Those are Dave Startzell's comments?" I wanted to consume these words. They were like honey. I begged Ollie to be honest. "Don't mess with me."

Ollie feigned indignation at the suggestion that she might have fabricated such important information. "I'm just reading what it says. What do you make of it?"

"It's huge. In every particular."

"I told Dallas you were going to like it. I said Jay's going to unleash some serious vocabulary when he hears this." Ashley and Ollie loved to discuss my vocabulary, which they found impressive beyond compare.

"It's perfect," I said. "Morgan had to have helped put that together. It's right out of the playbook."

"I don't believe anybody who wears flip-flops on a regular basis could have written that." Ollie was pleased, but she loved to needle Morgan. "You notice how they didn't say nothing about the poor old mountain people up here in Dog Town? All they care about is their little dirt walking path."

"I know you're joking, Ollie. That man, those people—," I sputtered to mount a defense of my new favorite conservationists.

"Aw, I'm just having fun with Morgan and them. Hell, I wouldn't know Dave Startzell if Scrappy bit him on the leg, but if I was to meet him, I'd give him a big ol' mountain kiss and thank him this way and that. You tell him if he ever wants to come by here, we'll set him a place at the table and I will personally cook him whatever he wants to eat."

"That's more like it," I said.

"Do you reckon he's a vegetarian?" Ollie asked, suddenly serious.

"I honestly don't have the faintest idea."

"Well, just let me know. I never cooked dinner for a vegetarian before."

# Chapter 9

The way Curly told it, "Paul come flying up here and slammed on his brakes, and, Lord, Jay, he jumped out of the car so fast, hit was still yet moving. He said, 'Curly! Your wife has done went and sued me!' And, Jay, he went to cussing the awfullest mess of four-letter swear words you ever heard. And I said, real calm, 'No, Paul, I don't b'lieve she sued you. I b'lieve what she done was—' And he cut me off. He said, 'Yes, she did! She's done gone and sued me!'"

Curly was amused by all this. "Lord, Jay. You ort to seed Paul. If you never seen hopping mad before, you ort to seed it. Paul was a-hoppin' up and down he-uz so mad." Freddy backed up this telling. "I'd say Paul lost a few blood vessels. He might need to go to one of those anger-management consultants. He looked about like one of those Tasmanian devils when he went off. He was turning up dust out there in the driveway. I was afraid he's going to drill a hole in the ground the way he spun around."

Ollie shook her head in wonder at all that was going on. "We're killed, now," she said, but she was only half-worried. She was also half-tickled. And she was purely disgusted that she had missed seeing Paul hopping mad. She would have liked to have witnessed it or even gotten a picture, but she had been in town when Paul came by.

Technically, Curly was right. Ollie didn't sue Paul.

Ron Howell had gone up into the deep woods, where he lived and worked. Except for his trip to the public meeting, nobody had seen him for a couple of weeks. That is how he worked. Alone, in seclusion, and at length, on the side of the mountain. I had thought of him many times, high on his hill in a rumpled suit of clothes, surveying the mountains between drafting sessions, then bent over a sweat-stained stack of unruly pages, his white hair in a mess. When he emerged from his hideout, descended the mountain, he had the Complaint for Declaratory and Injunctive Relief in his hands. Clark Stone was named as a defendant, right there along with Charles Gardner, as head of the Division of Land Resources, and Bill Holman, as the secretary of DENR. What Ollie and I did, as co-plaintiffs, along with our new best friends at NPCA and ATC, was sue the State of North Carolina.

Walking into the courthouse on a bright summer day with Forrest Ferrell and Ron Howell had been a special treat. Out came the receptionists from behind their desks. Lawyers gathered around us in the hallway. Forrest could remember the name of every clerk in every courthouse in the western part of the state. He could call up family illnesses and when babies had been born. He remembered dog bites and domestic disputes and who was on a diet. Ron blushed at the attention of his admirers.

Ollie was impressed at the attention her attorneys were getting.

We milled around for a while, while the clerk of court processed our paperwork. I had never sued anybody before so I was fascinated by the ease with which it happens. A couple of signatures, a stamp from the clerk, and that's it, you're suing. They don't teach you any of this in law school.

We were just finishing up the details when Faye pulled me aside. I could tell she was nervous, her eyes were darting around in their sockets.

"I can't sign it," she said.

Ollie had been worried for a while about Faye's commitment to the case, but I had dismissed the warnings. I had stood in Faye's kitchen and watched her shudder with anger.

"What is it?" I asked, hopeful I had misunderstood.

"Grady."

Grady. I had sat at her table. I had looked out her windows and seen how close she was to the main crusher jaw. I had met her mother, who was fierce in her condemnation of the county officials and of Paul. But I had never met Grady.

"I'm afraid of what will happen if I sign it. He'll be out the door." She was near to tears. I held on to her arm and her flesh was cold. I wanted to comfort her, but I was also thrown off. It wasn't clear to me what this would mean. Ollie stood against the wall down the hallway, glaring. We had just spent thousands of dollars having Ron write the complaint, and now, here, at the filing, Faye was telling us she was out.

I hurried over to Forrest. "Can we still file it if we lose Faye as a plaintiff?"

Forrest looked past me. "What's the matter with her? Do you think Paul got to her?"

"I don't think so. I don't know."

I put Forrest and Faye together and let them talk it over. Forrest was firm but Faye was visibly shaken now. After a terse appeal from Forrest, she shook her head and made her way out of the courthouse. Her name came off the complaint.

This was bad news. Faye's house was the one surrounded by the permitted area. Ollie's property, while technically *adjoining* within the meaning of the statute, lay across a two-lane road from the site. By virtue of sheer proximity, Faye's case was the more compelling. When you held up the mine map, you had to feel bad for the inhabitants of the little farmhouse represented by the faint blue line, the little box surrounded by the square-cornered carve-out representing the permitted area.

Had Paul bought Faye? Had he bought her house to silence her the way he had bought Tony's? Ollie would look into it. She would ask the register of deeds, and even if it wasn't filed yet, if there was a transfer of title, she would find it.

We lost Faye, but we were in. As Ollie said when Nub Taylor stamped the complaint, "We are now officially in it up to our necks. Lord help us." We swung the doors of the courthouse wide and took in the fresh air of the now-green grassy plaza on the town square. Ollie asked Forrest what our chances were. Forrest smiled and tilted his head to her. "Paul Brown's going to know he's been in a fight when this thing is over."

"Aw!" Ollie replied, employing the universal Appalachian exclamation. "I like that. Let him worry for a while. I'm worn-out of worrying trying to stand up that mountain."

On the front page of the July 27 *Mountain Times,* the two lead articles were about the dedication of the new hospital and the filing of our complaint. Few remembered anymore that Paul had had to move his operation out of Linville to make way for the new hospital, but the ironic juxtaposition on the front page was not lost on our team.

Even though I knew every word of the complaint, our Motion for Preliminary Injunction, I read the article to see which parts Scott Nicholson had pulled out. *"This action seeks to protect and affirm the rights of the Appalachian National Scenic Trail and the rights of the owners of the land adjoining the proposed mine site," says plaintiff's attorney Forrest Ferrell. "The agency has failed to guarantee the rights of the citizens to due process and has failed to protect our public parks. The agency has already admitted the operation will violate the Mining Act of 1971, but they have done nothing to correct the problem, and appear to have no interest in correcting it."*

We claimed among other things that Charles had admitted that he made his decision to issue the permit based on incomplete information. He must now revoke the permit, we maintained, because of this flaw.

We asked the court to find that *substantial and irreparable harm* was being done to a national park.

The *Avery Journal* also quoted liberally from the complaint: *Referring to the delay of more than three times the allotted 30 days in making the decision and continued work at the quarry in the interim, the suit says the plaintiffs have been "ultimately deluded by the defendant Gardner, who, with carefully crafted press releases ostensibly embracing plaintiff's claims, nevertheless shows a stubborn and utterly fixed intent to allow this mining operation to continue; that such action, in the face of irreparable harm to the environment, exceeds all bounds of reasonableness, and shows without doubt that any further petitions, motions or pleas to the DLR will be vain and futile.* This was pure

Ron Howell, undiluted Heel Hound. The language came down hard on Charles. It was thorough in its reproach, as legal writing must be, yet the lines flowed in a seamless eloquent skein to rise to the level of poetry.

We tried to settle into our new roles as contestants in a legal pageant, but once the complaint was filed we had to acquaint ourselves with that old directive tossed around legal circles: hurry up and wait. There was little for us to do but worry. So we worried, and we listened to the drilling on the mountain. Earlier in the summer, Paul had told Charles of his intention to start crushing. The Asheville Regional Office had signaled their intent to study the activity. Not stop it, but to observe and study it.

For two weeks, maybe three, the crew at the site drilled holes into the rock ridge where Paul planned to tear into the mountain in phase one of the operation. All day the drill bits screamed and whined, inching deeper into the mountain. From my house the drilling sounded like a vacuum cleaner running in a room at the far end of a hallway. Without ever stopping. I was pretty sure that I would go crazy if I had to listen to it for much longer, much less for ninety-nine years. The drilling was worse for my knowing what the holes were for. These were the holes that would be packed with dynamite in the first stage of this proposed exercise. This first stage of pulling down the mountain.

The blast was scheduled for July 12, but one week before that black date on the calendar, the mountains were hit with a brutal round of thunderstorms. Lightning struck. Literally. Four cows were killed on the Big Yellow Mountain bald, and Paul's Brown's primary crusher jaw took a direct hit. It lit up like a ball of fire. In no time at all the word was passed around the mountains. The crusher was out of commission. The damage was serious. The test blast would have to be moved to a future date.

Ollie called, breathless. "Now, Little Buddy, how in the hayull did you pull that one?"

I was, as ever, modest, replying, "Ollie, sometimes it's not what you know, but who you know."

Summer was hard upon us now, and while Charles's counsel in the attorney general's office drafted their reply to our complaint, and while Paul's lawyers huddled to plot strategy, and the crew at the site tried to fix what the bolt of lightning had wrought, we tried to get on with living. The dog days brought more thunderstorms, and the water stayed high so the fishing was fine in the evenings. This was the summer Ollie and her bunch moved across the road into the new house. They had finally gotten all their permits cleared from the county and had received their Certificate of Occupancy. They were no longer paying rent to Paul. Adding to the celebratory mood, Tony had finally moved, had lit out for Tennessee, to a spot fully twenty-two miles to the west.

We sat outside on the deck of Ollie's new house one evening, drinking from the tower of soft drinks she always had on hand. "I guess you don't have to be so nice to Paul anymore," I said, nodding across the road at the now vacant building they had quit.

Freddy shook his head and laughed. "How much meaner could we be? Didn't we just sue him?"

"No," Ollie corrected. "We wasn't never mean to Paul. It was just that boy from up on Yaller Mountain was mean to Paul."

I feigned surprise. "Me? What did I ever do? And we didn't sue Paul. We sued the state. How many times do I have to keep saying that?"

"I'd say you've about rurent his day," Ashley said, understating the current state of affairs.

"I don't know," Ollie sang. "Seems like you got something against Paul, and all he's trying to do is provide a cheap source of rock to the poor gravel haulers and road builders of Avery County. Why, don't you know he's just trying to create a few jobs for the hardworking folks around Dog Town?"

When we got into it like this, Curly usually stood off and listened to the foolish talk. Shook his head as if to say we had no idea of the gravity of the situation. But this evening he laughed right along with us. And we wondered if our way might be easing after all.

Ollie called me early of a morning, to use a local turn of phrase. "Well, my Lil' Buddy, wonders never cease."

"Now what?"

"Miss Janet Cantwell pulled up about thirty minutes ago in a big truck with state tags. And don't act like you didn't know it."

"I was asleep."

"Right. Sure you were."

Ollie said she wasn't sure which was more impressive, getting lightning to strike Paul's crusher, or getting Janet Cantwell from the Asheville office of DENR to visit the site. But this one wasn't even hard. I had called Cantwell the week before and told her that unclean fill was in Paul's haul road in violation of a state regulation. I said we had proof, and that we were prepared to go to the newspapers with what we had found. She professed to be outraged at the very mention of unclean fill and said she would get right on it as this sort of thing was not acceptable. "Not in North Carolina," she said. "Not in the least." After two years of howling about numerous violations by Tony and then Ollie, Janet Cantwell was on this day prowling the haul road, in the flesh.

I drove down the mountain to watch. Sure enough, there she was in her state vehicle. Ollie, Ashley, Freddie, and I sat in the window and drank 7UPs all morning, taking in the show.

Ollie and Freddy provided the commentary.

"Would you look at Captain Nasty? He looks like somebody burnt his biscuit gravy this morning."

"He's wondering what in the hell happened and how everything got turned upside down. He thought this thing was in the bag."

"He thought Dear Ol' Dad had this thing all straightened out."

"Yeah, but he never saw Janet Cantwell coming up 19E like a flying squirrel until it was too late."

We used the term *flying squirrel* to signify a surprise tactic or event. Sometimes we called Paul the Flying Squirrel because of the way he came over the ridge from the other side of the county to take us by surprise.

So now, on this morning, Janet Cantwell had swooped down on the scene like a most welcome surprise visitor. She was telling Nasty where to dig. She was looking for car parts, and the charred rubble of Damon and Willy Smith's old house. But by lunchtime Freddy was convinced James was leading Janet by the nose to the wrong spots. Not a single sample of unclean fill had been unearthed.

"Not there!" Freddy hollered, knowing we were out of earshot. "It's right up here, next to the road!"

After lunch the day turned gray and the rain came. Janet sat up on the hood of her truck under an umbrella while Nasty dipped dirt out of the haul road. By midafternoon, he hit a vein of black ashes. It was the remnants of the house. Janet hopped down to take a closer look. She directed Nasty to remove this material and load it in the back of a dump truck.

"My oh my," Ollie sang. "If I'm not badly mistaken, she's going to make them haul all of that burnt stuff out of here. I feel like Christmas morning."

By evening, the haul road was completely torn out in the search for more debris. They found some, a little, but not as much as we knew was in there. Freddy was beside himself, still not satisfied. If Janet had just crossed the road to ask, Freddy could have told her right where all that stuff was. A crankcase, an engine block. Asbestos siding. He got up and went over to the deck rail. "Look at that," he said, and I joined him, leaning over on the rail. He pointed to a spot right near the pavement. Three feet from the northbound lane of 19E.

"What?"

"Don't you see it?" He pointed harder. "It's a tailpipe from one of the cars they buried. You can see it from all the way over here! They're digging everywhere it ain't." Sure enough. The sun dropping to the west illuminated a chunk of metal. Once I could see that, my eye resolved other pieces. Right through the weeds you could see some of the car parts jutting out from the orangey soil. We could see it, but Janet could not, not from where she stood up on the road. So far, Nasty was doing a good job of keeping her distracted in a spot higher up the hill.

But still, I counted myself pleased. Responding to our call, the state had come to the site unannounced. Now the haul road was completely impassable, the middle of it was a hole now, a muddy abyss, from where Nasty had dug out the burnt remnants. That had been our mission all along in pressing the unclean-fill charge. We wanted the haul road torn out. Ashley even suggested that we should let Janet miss some of the debris so we could call her back in a few months if we needed to slow Paul down again. As it was, we figured we had set them back a week, or more, and after all, that was all we could do, buy time and hope for Paul to drop dead before they flipped that switch. We certainly couldn't count on a lightning strike to bail us out of every rough patch we encountered.

At the end of the day, Janet Cantwell delivered what looked like a lecture to Nasty. Then she got into her truck and went back to Asheville. Ollie called me in the morning.

"Is she back?" I asked.

"Nope."

"Wait a little while and call me back."

Around noon, Nasty hauled off the one truckload of contaminated soil. We didn't get a whole week out of the diversion, only a couple of days. But we felt vindicated. We had reported unclean fill, and by God, that's what they found. The haul-road repair cost Paul time and money. And good will.

While there were still auto parts and nearly an entire house still buried in other parts of the road, we never saw Janet Cantwell again.

Summer is usually a slow time in politics and community affairs. Even in the middle of our fight, the hottest days of the year settled around us and lulled us, making us forget that we'd ever had a winter or ever would again. I shed layers of clothes and took to the woods. I am drawn to shade and cold water, like a trout, and I spent long hours in the woods, fishing, swimming, staying lost. My sister's family came to the mountain for their summer visit. We read books and tramped in creeks and hiked the back side of the mountain. We slept in and worked a puzzle and renovated an old tree house for my niece and nephews. When we went to town, we loaded up on newspapers. It was a pleasure to read the papers and know that we would not be in them. The *Independent,* a free sheet out of Raleigh, reported that Beverly Perdue, a state lawmaker with gubernatorial ambitions, was introducing a bill to require school students to address teachers as *sir* and *ma'am.* She called her bill the Enhanced Character Education Bill.

The Asheville paper ran a story of more immediate concern to us in the mountains. The Southern pine beetle was tearing through the white pines in the mountains and the foothills. The pine beetle had never made it into the mountains before, but biologists thought climate change was increasing the breeding cycle, enabling an assault on the high-elevation trees. Whole hillsides of the massive pines turned brown and seemed to die overnight. The local paper was filled with ads for *The Music Man,* playing at Lees-McRae Summer Theater. Also, the Eighteenth Annual Gospel Singing Jubilee was coming up in Boone. Beech Mountain Elementary was named an ABC School of Excellence. Wilson Creek, a pristine ribbon of water flowing off the back side of Grandfather Mountain gained official designation as a Wild and Scenic River. Cass Ballenger, the congressman who had advocated for the designation, was an interesting case. With the Wild and Scenic designation he earned the admiration of conservationists across the state. At the same time, he was embroiled in a scandal over an old-fashioned cement Negro lawn jockey proudly displayed on his front yard in Hickory. His spirited defense of racist statuary made national news in a month with little competition for good stories. "It's a family heirloom," he said, gaining sympathizers and losing them in equal measure. Nascar legend Junior Johnson rolled into the county for the Hot Rod Classic Car Show, and all the press turned out. It is believed that Junior Johnson is the only person ever to receive a presidential pardon in person in the Oval Office. In 1986 Ronald Reagan gave Junior a full pardon for a moonshining conviction, helping secure the massive auto-sports—and illicit-liquor—vote for Republicans for a generation or more.

---

After a good break from the case, a summer vacation of sorts, we were jolted back to attention, like the first day of school. The repair to the primary jaw was complete, and on the first day of August we received word that the next day Clark Stone would pull their shot, ripping a hole in the face of Hartley Ridge. After this test blast they would turn on the crusher and run the rock from the blast through the primary and secondary jaws.

That night I slept little. After I quit the bed just before dawn, gave up trying to sleep, I set out for Hump Mountain by myself to wait for the blast. Witt was away on a job. I was on my own. Ollie would film the test from her front porch.

By the time I reached the summit of the mountain a cloud deck had settled hard on the mountain. I couldn't see the end of my own nose, much less Hartley Ridge. Nor could I see any sound engineers from the state. At about eleven in the morning, over on Belview Mountain, they pulled the shot. Even when I knew it was coming, it was astounding when it actually happened. It was a deep, rolling gather of sound. Percussive. And for a long moment it seemed to stun all things, grass, sky, a whole mountain.

I sat down at the Stan Murray plaque and tried to eat. But I didn't have any appetite. I felt sick all over.

After a while, they started up the crusher. There seemed some virtue in enduring the worst stuff they could throw, so I sat there and listened until they shut it off. Then I headed back down to Bradley Gap, and home.

I sent in my own report to Charles, and to the attorney general's office:

*Charles, I didn't see anybody else from the State, or from the acoustic engineering company on Big Hump, so I am filing my own report. The crusher running sounds like a ski boot being tumbled in a clothes dryer.*

That afternoon I went down to Ollie's. Freddy was working on one of his cars, a chop top, in the driveway. Rather than being despondent about the blast, he was animated by the footage they got. "Go on in there and see it. Ollie's about worn the picture off the tape looking at it. You ain't going to believe it."

Ashley ran the tape for me.

Just when my eye got used to the scene, the raw timbered-over slope of the mountain, *ba-booomb!*—a gush of red earth bloomed out of the mountain. It could be water squirting out of a tight passage, but it was liquefied earth. You could hear Ashley and the rest, hollering exclamations, as if the dirt were close enough to inundate them. It reminded me of the voices of astonished tornado-chasers who are about to be flattened.

Strangely, the day after the blast was quiet. The dogs rested on the deck without pacing. At first I couldn't pinpoint the difference. No drilling. That was it.

A week went by. Freddy went up on the mountain and reported that the material they sent through the crusher for the test wasn't rock.

"I'd say it was just hard mud they sent through."

I wanted some of it. "Can you go back up and get me some?"

"Why sure. I'll go up there tonight."

If it wasn't rock they crushed, not granite, but rather soft material, that could skew the acoustic tests, and the state might believe the impacts on the Trail would be less than they would actually be. It made sense to me though. If they were crushing rock, it wouldn't have sounded like a ski boot in a dryer. It would have sounded like, well, like granite boulders in a clothes dryer.

I e-mailed Dan and Trip and Forrest. Then I e-mailed Charles and Tracy and Jim Gulick with Freddy's assertion that the material crushed that day was shaley mud, not granite. I offered my humble suggestion that the test results were meaningless.

Dan learned that Charles had requested, and Clark Stone had agreed, not to mine while the test results were being compiled. But excepting the one quiet day following the test blast, there was no letup in the pace at the site. It wasn't crushing stone, but it was preparing to crush stone. The crew set about building a ramp to the scale house. Freddy's sources told him Paul's belief was that the more money he sank into the site, the less likely Charles was to revoke the permit. I e-mailed this report to

Jim Gulick at the attorney general's office and to Charles. It was a risk, antagonizing Jim and Charles. In the worst-case scenario, they could throw up their hands and admit that their handshake agreement with Clark Stone not to mine was just that, a gentleman's agreement carrying no weight of law—especially if there were no gentlemen involved on the Clark Stone side. But Ollie was growing desperate. We had to do something. All the evidence suggested we were going down. What did it matter at this point? I was swinging with wild punches. The county commissioners were meeting in closed session with Paul and Randy. The commissioners had adopted a "pro-mine" policy—by unanimous consent. When we challenged the action under an open-meetings theory, the county attorney cited attorney-client privilege.

August, it turned out, was also a critical month in Tony's effort to regain custody of Ashley. Despite the settlement of the charges against Tony, he was seeking to have a court reestablish his parental rights. Ashley and Ollie had filed a counterclaim to Tony's petition, an effort to have Ashley permanently emancipated. The hearing on this claim was scheduled, then rescheduled, then moved again. Ashley was now in constant anxiety over the matter. She was growing increasingly depressed over her struggle to get away from her father. Tony had filed a motion to ask the court to order a comprehensive psychiatric evaluation of his daughter, another worry for her. "He thinks I'm crazy," she said to me one afternoon, exasperated. "Hell, yes, I'm crazy. It happens to run in the family." The school year was starting up, and much to everybody's surprise, Ashley decided to reenroll in classes at Avery High rather than continue her homeschooling. Freddy wanted to follow her to school every day, was worried that Tony would find out she was in school and seek to approach her. He watched Ashley like a hawk, and we all feared what he would do if he caught Tony anywhere within striking range of her. We all feared an escalation beyond fists.

The day of our hearing snuck up on Ollie. We stood in front of the courthouse so she could smoke a cigarette. She looked ill, her eyes hollowed out. "With everything going on with that young-un, I've not had time to worry about Paul and Randy," she said. "I ain't scared, I'm just mad as hell, and I'm honest, I almost forgot to come to court today."

She was flustered, but she also professed to be angry with me. Angry that I had gotten her into this mess. "I never should have signed nothing," she said as we waited for Forrest. "That judge that's going to hear our case hangs everybody that sits in that chair. And now you've got me in his sights. You're a damn troublemaker."

"All you have to do is answer the questions," I reassured. "You're not on trial. You're a witness."

"Huh! That's easy for you to say. It's not your neck laid on the blocks."

"It's not going to be like that. It's just a chance for us to tell our side of the story. Remember, we're suing them. Nobody's neck is on any block."

Ollie was unconvinced. Her brushes with the law had not been as tidy as that. Now she was aggravated anew. "Why is it me going up there, anyway? You're the one who got this thing all stirred up."

"Making stuff up is not the way to go, Ollie. You and Ashley were giving Paul hell long before you met me," I needled her.

"I don't even know what to say. When I get nervous, I might say anything. You want me to use them ten-letter lawyer words you're always using?"

"I want you to talk like you always do."

Ashley couldn't resist: "God help us."

Ollie was nibbling her fingernail. "Maybe I'll be struck dumb," she threatened.

"No, that's your brother," I said. "You were born smart."

"Damn, I will get you for this, my Little Buddy."


Our witnesses would be Ollie, Witt, and Morgan, from the Appalachian Trail Conservancy. Faye had also agreed to appear. She still did not want her name on the filing, but she wanted to tell her story. I wondered if Grady knew she was missing work on this day to be at the courthouse.

We figured the state would call Charles to defend the process he followed in issuing the permit. Jim Gulick, as head of the environmental division in the attorney general's office, would serve as his counsel.

Clark Stone, as a named defendant in our Motion for Preliminary Injunction, would get to cross-examine witnesses and put on their own case. Their attorney, Harold Berry, from the white-shoe firm Hatch, Little & Bunn, had traveled five hours, from Raleigh, to advocate on behalf of Paul. Berry would call Randy Carpenter to tell their side.

At ten o'clock on the dot, the honorable Judge James U. Downs stepped from behind a door and took his seat at the high podium of the Avery County Courthouse, his robe settling around him. The judge tended to his desktop business before looking up at a full courtroom. First, he dismissed the crowd of potential jurors. They would not be needed on this day, but he thanked them for responding to his request to appear. He then shuffled through his docket. After briefly questioning the parties in the cases he was to hear, he determined that our case would take most of the day and cleared all other business from the afternoon schedule.

When we were called forward, the courthouse was empty except for the principals in our case.

Ron Howell spoke first, making the opening statement for the Citizens to Protect Belview and Miss Cox. "Your Honor, this has been going on and going on and going on. It's time to cool it. If this work keeps up like it has, these people won't have anything left to fight for."

Judge Downs was out of Macon County in the southwest corner of the state. Hard mountain country. I didn't know much about him.

Forrest told me that Downs owned property near the Appalachian Trail somewhere along the Tennessee line. It was hard to say whether this might hurt us or help us. If the Trail near his place was wooded, thick with vegetation, he might find our claim improbable. Knowing the Trail in the southwest corner of the state in no way prepared a man, even a fair, dispassionate man, to understand the glory of the Roan Highlands section of the Trail. I had come to believe that the only thing that really helped us was getting people to the Hump Mountain section of the Trail to see the damage firsthand. And that wasn't going to happen. We weren't going to get the judge and the court reporters, the stenographer and the deputies, up there. Instead we would sit in the big, old, drafty Avery County courtroom without even a single window to remind us of the mountain majesty we were seeking to protect.

When summoned, Ollie stepped forward to take the stand. She walked as if ordered to do so at gunpoint. After she was sworn in, she folded her hands in her lap and stared straight ahead. She set her jaw, and I feared she might remain just this way until the deputies hauled her from her perch. Forrest pulled out an enlargement of the mine map. He unfurled it for Judge Downs to illustrate where Ollie lived in relation to the mine. He asked Ollie to describe her dealings with Paul. She flew through her answer. "Paul is my landlord, or he was until we moved across the road. He told me over a year ago that he was going to go in and put a crusher on the other side of the mountain. And then, next thing we knew, there he was, on my side of the mountain. Right out my door."

Thankfully she got through her first remarks without resulting to swear words. I was proud of her. And relieved.

As the senior attorney in the environmental division of the attorney general's office, Jim Gulick represented the agency, Charles Gardner, Bill Holman, and the people of North Carolina—except for us, I suppose. A tightly coiled man with a blood-flushed face, he had the look of a second baseman, an old-school pinstripe look. My research told me he was a Scandinavian fiddle player, an academic, and an astute student of all he surveyed. On this day he was immaculately turned out in a dark suit and a shirt so white it seemed to glow at the cuffs. His job, as representative of the attorney general's office, was to defend Charles's issuance of the permit and the process he used to reach his decision. It fell to Gulick to cross-examine Ollie.

It was clear right away that he was aiming for Ollie to admit that she had knowledge, or *notice*, that Paul was coming to Belview Mountain.

I could see it unfolding in his questioning, and I hoped Ollie was not so thrown that she would fail to see what he was about. Then I saw her eyes go bright. And I felt sorry for lawyer Gulick, for he had never met Ollie, had never seen her at work. He had no idea what he was in for.

The Mining Act requires notice to adjoining landowners. That "notice" is supposed to be in the form of a return-receipt registered letter that goes into the permanent file in Charles's office. It informs the recipient that he or she has the right to request a public hearing at which he or she will have the opportunity to air any objection to the proposed project.

Often the objections raised by neighbors to mine sites are dust and truck noise. But Ollie had read the Mining Act and knew that dust and noise were not covered by the statute. Instead she stuck to notice in and of itself, stuck to it as if she had tar on her heels. I was in a knot but Ollie Ve was holding firm. Jim Gulick wasn't going to get her to say she had received notice just because Paul had said, over the hood of his truck one day, that he was moving his crusher somewhere up on the mountain.

"I was supposed to get a letter," Ollie said flatly. "I never got nothing from Paul."

Then she turned on the charm. "Randy, he works for Paul, he told everybody that the people in Cranberry Gap wanted Paul to come in here. He said they went up and down the road and everybody begged them to bring that crusher in here. He said people were fixing them hamburgers, trying to get the crusher on their land."

Jim asked that Ollie stick to answering the question, but she plowed on, undeterred.

"We never fixed nobody not one thing to eat. I didn't get any notice letter and Randy didn't get any hamburgers."

Judge Downs had to smile. Then he warned Ollie to answer the questions she was asked.

Ollie now fixed Jim Gulick with a cool glare in case he wanted to take off on any further adventures in his line of questioning. Any lawyer of Charles's, anybody on the side of Bill Beck, was no friend of Ollie's. She would treat Gulick the same as she would have treated the white-hot devil. Forrest leaned over to Ron and whispered something. I figured it was "Attagirl."

Forrest followed up with a last question, the softball pitch: "Mrs. Cox, did you receive notice from Clark Stone Company, by registered mail or in any other written form, about their intention to establish a 151-acre mine site on Belview Mountain, Mrs. Cox?"

"No, sir. No notice."

Next up, Forrest called Witt. Out came the photographs. Clark Stone's attorney objected.

"On what grounds?" asked Downs, pinning Harold Berry with a glance over his eyeglasses.

Harold Berry claimed the photographs were unreliable.

Downs overruled the objection. "I'd like to see them."

When it came time for Harold Berry to cross-examine Witt, Paul's attorney made a grave lawyer's mistake. He asked a question he did not know the answer to.

His goal was to impeach Witt as a neighbor to the site, to paint him as a self-interested and disgruntled party who, understandably, didn't want to live near, or look at, an open-pit mine.

"Mr. Langstaff," Berry began in a low voice, a surprising voice coming out of the slight man, "you live near the mine, do you not, Mr. Langstaff?"

"No, actually, I live in South Carolina." Witt didn't say it ugly, but it landed hard.

I knew at once that Randy had told Harold Berry that Witt was "one of those homeowners up there on Yellow Mountain."

Berry regrouped. "You have a house on Yellow Mountain, I mean. A vacation house, then."

"No. I live in Hartsville, South Carolina." I thought about Witt's tent. His getaway spot up on the mountain. His hammock strung between maples. "I do not have a house in Avery County."

Berry was flustered now. "Do you own land on Yellow Mountain?"

"I do."

Berry was relieved at this response, but he was shaken. Now he would have to second-guess everything Randy had told him. You could see his mind turning each question over before he asked it. He leafed through his papers. But when he pressed ahead, he only dug his hole deeper.

"Mr. Langstaff, these maps are confusing. Unless you have expertise in forestry, or surveying, you don't really have the expertise to determine where these lines are, and what the impacts will be, do you?"

Witt raised his eyebrows. "Well, my college degree is in forestry, and I have read surveys for the United States Forest Service in addition to being a professional photographer."

Ollie beamed as Harold Berry's face dissolved. He had wanted to call one of Witt's pictures into question. I saw where he was going. He was going to attack the picture upon which Witt had superimposed the yellow line. The shot had made it into the local papers, arousing much interest, and inflaming Paul and Randy. But from this point on Berry landed no blows. His confidence in whatever Randy had fed him was shattered. He raced through a few more questions and released the witness, but not before making his best point. "Your Honor," he said in his closing remarks, "the plaintiffs in this case are trying to convert a two-hundred-foot right-of-way for a Trail into a four- or six-mile-wide zoning jurisdiction to protect the view." In this way he raised the much reviled concept of land-use planning. If there's one thing mountain people despise, it is regulation of land use, and I was certain Harold Berry had done us considerable damage with his well-played assertion.

We spent all afternoon in the courtroom, hearing testimony, examining exhibits.

Late in the day, Jim Gulick rose to explain to the judge that the state was currently evaluating the status of the permit. That evaluation included a test blast, and an acoustic engineer's report. In so many words, the state asked the court to stay out of it. "Your Honor, the state's authority in this matter will be seriously compromised if the permit is suspended by the court and not by the department entrusted with that decision," Gulick said. "Even though this procedure may be cumbersome, the General Assembly has established it for just this type of situation."

Downs looked wholly unimpressed. "So you're just going to keep stringing Mr. Brown along and keep dragging him into courtrooms until you've come up with a resolution that suits your client, Mr. Gardner?" This comment stung all around. On the one hand, my group was in agreement with Paul that the state's process was arbitrary and capricious. We had said so in our complaint. The issuance of the permit was indefensible. But at the same time, it would do us no good for Paul to become a symbol of the common man being hounded by a faceless and inefficient bureaucracy, a victim.

Ron Howell called the drawing of the permit boundaries a "craftily disingenuous way of getting the permit through the DENR process," and for a while all parties focused on the mine map and the fifty-foot buffer and the failure to give notice to the adjoining landowners. "We allege the applicant basically gave notice to itself," Ron said, drawing a knowing nod from the bench.

At the end of the day, we made an important breakthrough. The judge asked the parties if all would agree that there would be no more activity at the mine until he, His Honor, issued a ruling. Clark Stone's attorney, muttering, but genial, agreed. Forrest and Ron both fell over the table accepting the terms of this impromptu, informal deal. We, of course, were thrilled at this spur-of-the-moment agreement. This was a rather amazing development. Normally it would take a separate hearing to have an injunction—a court-ordered halt—imposed. But Downs had just created his own injunction of sorts. He had simply concluded that it made no sense for Clark Stone to continue pouring money into a project that might be brought to a halt by some judge—maybe himself—at some point. Even Harold Berry had to agree it was hard to argue otherwise.

With all in agreement, Downs rocked back in his chair and said, "Thank you all for coming today. I will take this matter under advisement. Good afternoon." He rose, and in a cloud of black satin, disappeared from the courtroom, leaving a hush behind him.

I woke the next morning to . . . nothing. No chunky shudder of machinery gearing down. Biscuit was scratching, thumping her paw on the floor absentmindedly. But no vacuum cleaner at the end of the hall. No trackhoe and no backup beepers.

I think I made it all the way to noon. Finally I couldn't take it. I e-mailed Forrest. *How do you think he's going to rule?*

Forrest replied immediately. *Slowly, I hope.*

Yes, slowly. With the consent order in place, with all quiet at the site, time was now on our side.

I tapped out another message. *What's the longest he can wait to issue a ruling? Because I want to make sure to pray for the right thing.*

The reply came: *Judge Downs is under no obligation to rule on any timetable. So you may pray that he takes his own sweet time.*

I checked the e-mail all afternoon, but no ruling was forthcoming from Judge Downs. We had gotten in some licks and we had taken some. For now, though, we had won the most precious of all victories: cessation of the assault on Belview Mountain. A new status quo we could live with.


A week after the hearing, Ollie called.

"What you got?" I asked.

"They're dipping dirt."

"They can't," I said stupidly.

"Nasty is."

"You sure they're not maintaining the road? I think they're allowed to maintain the road. Under what Gulick said to Downs."

"Son, they're moving more than that. Nasty's dipping dirt. Should we tell the Weasel?"

"Who?"

"Harold Berry. I call him the Weasel. I'd like to show him who he's representing."

I had to laugh at Ollie's ability to define a whole character with a well-chosen sobriquet. She had a stiletto wit and a damn good eye. "Do you have pictures? Please tell me you have pictures."

"Freddy took the film to Elizabethton to get it developed, and I've got moving pictures, too."

I e-mailed Charles and Jim Gulick that we had videotape evidence of Clark Stone mining—*dipping dirt*—along with my unsolicited opinion that this constituted a violation of the consent order adopted by the parties before Judge Downs. Within an hour, Jim Gulick e-mailed me. This was unusual. Since we had filed the suit against his client, Gulick had never contacted me directly, and whenever I e-mailed him, he had asked me to please contact him only through my attorney, a request I ignored. But now Gulick was replying to me. I imagined him in a grand office down in Raleigh, his fine cotton shirt gleaming as he typed me a note. He asked me to send the videotape to Raleigh, today, if I didn't mind. I called Forrest.

Forrest was unimpressed. "What's their hurry?"

"I don't know. But Gulick wouldn't e-mail me unless this caught his attention."

"I don't want you to send it to them."

"Why not?"

"Because I don't want them having it in their files. I think they just want to see what we've got. I've become skeptical of all they say and do."

"Should I say no?"

Forrest had an idea. "Can you take it down there?"

"Sure."

"Do that. Take it down to Raleigh and show it to them and then take it home with you. That's the deal. They can see it, but I don't want them having it."

I e-mailed Gulick and we arranged it. The next day I drove down to Raleigh. On the drive down the mountain, into the hot middle of the state, I felt the familiar sick feeling I got whenever I neared Raleigh, and the Archdale Building.

I met Charles and Tracy and Gulick in the hallway of the fifth floor. A couple of other Division of Land Resources folks joined us, and we made our way into a conference room. Nobody felt like chatting. It wasn't basketball season, and nothing about the weather was remarkable, so by mutual consent we dispatched with the niceties. I slid the tape in its slot. A sea of floating green was born on the screen. Trees. Now we watched as Nasty rumbled up the haul road in the trackhoe. At one point he swung the massive shovel head and drove it into the soft soil. He raised the front end, swiveled, and dumped the load off the embankment.

"That's over near Faye Williams's," I said. "It may actually be *on* her property. They've been encroaching on her boundary from the beginning."

The tape ran about six minutes. We watched as James worked an area of exposed dirt, dipping it, swinging it, dumping it. When the tape ended in a bright dissolution of pixels, Charles sat still. Without turning to me he said, "Thank you for coming, Jay."

That was it. I had driven five hours—ten hours round-trip—to show six minutes of tape.

No one spoke as I ejected the cartridge from the player, slipped it into its paper sleeve, and made my exit.

*Chapter 10*

The second public meeting was scheduled for the end of August at the Avery County Courthouse. We were to consider a modification proposal crafted by Clark Stone. Randy had submitted to Charles his proposed mitigation measures. Now the public was invited to comment. In contrast to the first public meeting, weather was not a problem. It was hot and sunny all day. Our backers arrived in force, as did those supporting Paul.

This time Paul's team had refined their arguments. Terry Buchanan, the truck driver from Dog Town, set the tone with his aggressive attack on the conservation community. "I looked at them proposals," he sneered, "and I say if you'ns don't want to see the quarry, you can move the Appalachian Trail to one of them other mountains. But you better leave that quarry where it's at." His invitation barely drew a flicker of recognition from Charles.

Steve Perri, from the Tennessee Eastman Hiking and Canoeing Club, spoke eloquently in defense of the Trail, its current location, and the rule of law.

This time around Randy seemed to be in the mood to diffuse, rather than foster, tension. He launched a spirited defense of the value of rock crushing. He professed to have gotten the message from the first meeting. Referring to the heated suggestions from the speakers on our side, he replied, "We took all that to heart. And because of all the comments we got, we've agreed to be closed forty percent of the time. One hundred and twenty days out of the year. We're going to shut down on weekends. And on holidays. We're only going to run half days on Fridays. If it's a holiday in Virginia or Tennessee but not North Carolina, we're still going to close down. Out of respect. I would dare ask what business would shut down that had an economic impact on the county?" Randy also explained to a rapt audience other elements of his own landscape modification proposal. "The equipment would be painted 'warm gray' and the landscape plan would be altered to fit the lines, forms, and textures of the mountain. I'm not going to sit here and tell you we're going to be able to hide it, but all this is going to help."

Tony gave a repeat performance, complete with his greatest hits, minus the homosexuals. "I can tell you about the Appalachian Trail," he said, spitting volumes of saliva as he chucked words from his mouth. "Thirty-five years ago, it was nothing but draft dodgers, hippies, bums, and rogues. Now it's a place where idle boys go to hide and play. Tourists and hikers have rurent this place." I couldn't help it. I glanced at Paul. His head was in his hands.

Charles sat like a doomed soul, drinking it all in.

Dan Hirschman leaned into the lectern and went to work. He went straight for the relevant subject: the modification proposal. "With this minimal plan, Clark Stone has not shown a willingness to make a serious commitment to mitigation," he leveled. "This is a Band-aid on a bullet wound." And from there it just got better.

In the highlight of the hearing, a young and quite drunk firebrand stood to defend crushing rock as an inalienable right of a free people. He then veered quickly to address his own pet issue: four-wheeler access to Hump Mountain. "You people," he bugled, "have absolutely destroyed the Big Hump. We want to get up there on our four-wheelers and enjoy it, but the federal government has shut everybody out. I say what are you saving it for if a man can't get up on it. I hear all these people say they've been on Big Hump. Well, that's nothing but a lie. It's too steep to get up there unless you're in a truck or riding a four-wheeler. I bet nobody in this room has actually been up on Hump Mountain, and if you have, you was breaking the law."

The challenge was so baseless that the room was momentarily stilled. Embarrassed laughter escaped a few spectators.

Norma Forbes, a hero I did not yet know, rose—all fifty-nine inches of her—to address the claim. There she stood, fully possessed of the natural dignity that is the exclusive domain of the long-lived. "Young man," she said in a voice firm and true, "I'm eighty-one years old and I hiked it last month. If you can't make it on foot, then shame on you. You need to get more exercise."

Our side broke into rapturous applause, while the opposition felt compelled to give Ms. Forbes her due with shaking heads over the weakness of their case. Even the speaker himself was cowed by the pistol-sharp retort.

"Well, ma'am," he began, bowing slightly, "I ain't got no hat on my head, you can see that, but hats off to you if you actually done that. I'm impressed."

Two days after the hearing we got good news. As a result of the Putnam Mine case, the General Assembly had rewritten key provisions of the Mining Act. Legislators had solicited advice from the Southern Environmental Law Center, as well as from representatives of the mining community. The new language was finalized and the revisions were being signed into law. I called Ollie and told her she had rewritten the law. The revisions centered on the notice provisions in the original act. This victory alone was notable and worth the fight. But I knew it would be a bitter outcome if we ended up with an improved Mining Act and a destroyed Belview Mountain. Another Pyrrhic victory along the lines of Sugar Top and the Ridge Law. Having a hint of good news only made us hunger for more. We wanted a better mining act and a win on the merits.

Just after what Ron Howell called the second *get-together,* I got an e-mail from Bill Holman, the secretary of the agency.

> Jay,
> I have received about 1000 form emails on the Putnam Mine near the Appalachian Trail in Avery County. It is important for

DENR to receive and record public comments. However overloading my email makes it difficult for me to find emails from other folks. I'm also not able to guarantee that the emails sent to me will make it into the public record. Please send your comments to denr.putnammine@ncmail.net. I also respectfully ask if you plan a major email campaign to communicate with DENR, please contact us in advance so that we can set up an email address that will ensure your comments get into the record. I like the direct communication that email provides between me and members of the public. However, if this continues, I will have to get a private email address. Thanks.

I was delighted. When Charles told me that he had not heard from the Appalachian Trail community, I had sputtered to craft a defense to his claim. Now we had managed to antagonize not only Charles, but Charles's superior, the head of the agency.

Our e-mail campaign mirrored a pitched battle over the efficacy of public comment that was about to explode in the conservation world. The public hearing is a feature of every city-hall grassroots campaign, but the public hearing is actually a modern invention. In the environmental field, the right to a public hearing was created with passage of the National Environmental Policy Act (NEPA) of 1970. Under NEPA, agencies of the federal government must inform and consult with the public before setting policy that will affect the air, lands, and waters of the people. Often called the "look before you leap" process, it seems entirely logical to most. But ever since NEPA's passage, industry has strongly pushed to overturn it, to limit public input into decisions that industry feels are better made by industry.

One of the new fronts of the "public comment" battle is e-mail. As handwritten correspondence has been relegated to the dustbin of history, and the pace of modern life has made attendance at public gatherings a luxury for many, e-mail has become an efficient way for people to respond to solicitations for input into decisions that affect them. But after the turn of the new century and just as a few hot-button rules were coming under public scrutiny and a critical mass of concerned citizens were mastering the art of mobilizing public opinion using the latest technology, the new Bush administration aimed to make it harder for citizens to participate in rule-making. Take the example of the Roadless Areas Rule. In 1999 the Clinton administration began a three-year cataloging of areas in the United States that had escaped timbering, logging, and mining. Many of these areas fell within the boundaries of the National Forest system and Bureau of Land Management lands, lands, in other words, already owned by the public. Clinton's rule sought to set aside some 58 million of those acres as "Inventoried Roadless Areas." Some of these areas were already classified as wilderness areas, enjoying substantial protection, while others were at risk of industrial exploitation. Under the Roadless Areas Rule the most quiet, natural, undisturbed pockets of the country's public lands would be preserved in as near a state of natural perfection as we could attain in a modern world. To adopt the rule, the Clinton administration, and the US Forest Service, solicited public comment through a series of public hearings in compliance with NEPA. In a three-year public-comment period, the Department of Agriculture, the parent of the Forest Service, received over 1.5 million public comments on the Roadless Areas Rule. Six hundred hearings were conducted in town halls and library basements and courthouses across the country.

When George W. Bush became president in 2001, he immediately suspended all rules adopted by agencies in the Clinton administration, including the Roadless Areas Rule. No incoming administration had ever been so bold. Basically, the Bush Administration claimed that the Clinton administration was incapable of making valid rules because their political views made decisions by the people running federal agencies for the prior eight years arbitrary and capricious. All Clinton-era agency rules were suspect, in other words, just because they were Clinton-era agency rules. On the question of the Roadless Areas Rule, the Bush administration dismissed the public comments, saying, in part, that those comments were tainted because many were sent to the agency by groups using e-mailed form letters. The administration attacked the premise that a person who takes the time to send a form e-mail has an articulable opinion. Out went the 1.5 million comments received by the agency, and a new rule-making process was launched by the Forest Service, this time under the watchful eye of Bush appointees. Once again, advocacy groups invited their members to send public comments. They encouraged individual letters and implored attendance at public meetings. At the end of this new public-comment period, the Agency had received over 2.5 million new public comments, which were entered into the official record. The vast majority supported the Clinton Rule, but the Bush administration dismissed the public comments and junked the Roadless Areas Rule in its entirety. State governors would be invited to opt out of industrial development of the roadless landscapes within their borders, but industry would also have an opportunity to reopen old trails, declare them roads, and seek to open them—at public expense—to motorized traffic. It got worse. In keeping with the traditional way of doing business, timber and mineral rights would be sold, often at a loss to the public treasury, and the new roads, built at public expense, would ease the access to private plunder. So it went.

While the junking of the Roadless Areas Rule was a victory for the lobbyists who had fought against it, the business lobby was just getting started. The real objective was to eliminate the public from rule-making altogether. After a summer fire season that burned tens of thousands of acres of western forests, the Bush administration proposed a series of exemptions to NEPA. Basically, the administration launched an effort to rewrite NEPA in a way that would emasculate it. Forest "thinning" could be done on public lands without public comment under the new rule because of "fire emergency." Biologists who wanted to testify that burned forests regenerate themselves naturally when dead timber is allowed to decay at a natural pace were shut out from commenting on another set of exemptions drafted for "salvage" timbering. Drafts of legislation designed to weaken NEPA would impose mandatory time limits for public input. Opponents rightfully feared that this would incentivize "running out the clock" so that public input could, in effect, be removed from the rule-making process altogether.

What does federal public lands policy have to do with North Carolina's mining statute? Well, as with other states, North Carolina's environmental statutes, and administrative procedures, were written to mirror the federal process. The only reason North Carolina had a duty to give adjoining landowners a chance to comment in the first place was because it was settled federal policy to allow those who are affected by government decision-making to have a say in their own fate. It amounted to a constitutional right under the due-process clause of the Fourteenth Amendment because courts have held that people "similarly situated" must receive the same treatment. And states, including North Carolina, have realized that public-comment periods and public hearings are simply the fairest, most efficient way of ensuring this equal treatment under the law.

That afternoon I got another e-mail from Secretary Holman, this one a personal companion to the more official one I had already received: *Jay, if you can make the change to the website that's generating these emails or know who I can ask to change it, I'd sure appreciate it.*

I e-mailed Secretary Holman back: *I asked The Center for AT Studies to immediately change the address on their campaign. Sorry if it caused massive inconvenience before it was addressed.*

I detected a note of pleading in the Holman e-mail and it brought me no particular joy. An ardent conservationist, an accomplished regulator, an Appalachian Trail hiker, and a longtime member of the Southern Appalachian Highlands Conservancy, Bill Holman was a hero of mine. He was also a former executive director at the state's chapter of the Sierra Club, with a background in public advocacy. He was probably the purest conservationist who would ever rise to the top of the state's regulatory apparatus. There was always pressure to represent the business perspective at the agency, but he was there, right in the belly of the beast, doing his damnedest to steer the ship of state to rational policy, to cleaner water, and to healthier air. As head of the agency, we had no choice but to name him in our suit and steer our complaint his way. He had a job to do, as did we. It was nothing personal.

That night we hit 1,180 e-mails. Wingfoot scrambled to build another in-box to handle the volume.


The public-comment period officially ended the first week of September, yielding over thirty-six hundred public comments supporting the revocation of the mine permit. When I searched the official public record, I could find but a few public comments in favor of upholding the mine permit. Not even a dozen. But, again, as in federal rule-making, this was not a one-hiker-one-vote democracy. The agency would make its decision based upon many factors. And they would act, Charles would, with the full knowledge that the agency had already been sued once and would likely get sued again—either by my group, or by Paul, depending on the decision made. If Charles failed to act, if he let the permit stand, we would pursue our court case in Judge Downs's court with renewed vigor. If Charles modified the permit, we would sue, claiming that the decision was arbitrary and capricious. If Charles revoked the permit, we would be pleased, but Paul would sue, claiming the state, Charles, lacked the authority to take his permit.

Charles told me he would make his decision on September 6. On the night of the fifth, at 10:30 p.m., I called the agency's legal counsel, Dan McLawhorn. My intention was to leave a message on Dan's machine that he would hear just before he met with Charles that morning to announce his final decision. I knew the offices of the state would be shut, but I wanted the last voice Dan heard before his meeting to be mine. Much to my shock, McLawhorn picked up the phone. On the first ring.

"Dan, it's Jay. From the Putnam Mine case."

"I know who you are, Jay."

"What are you doing in your office this late? I was expecting to get your answering machine. I was going to plant subliminal revocation incantations in your head."

"We have a pretty important meeting tomorrow morning. You might have guessed that. I've still got some work to do in preparation."

"Charles told me. That's good, I guess."

I made my pitch, starting at the beginning. I told him about Ollie's foundation. About Paul's open disregard for the consent order. "Charles has an opportunity to avoid this going down in history as the worst mess DENR has ever made."

"I think Charles understands your Sugar Top analogy," Dan said.

My mind snapped back to an argument I had made the day Charles and I were on Hump Mountain. "This is worse than Sugar Top, Dan. And we can stop it."

Like everybody else in the state, Dan McLawhorn had a Sugar Top story. "I was up in the mountains, Jay, this was ten years ago, and I went to church on Sunday. And the preacher preached the entire sermon on Sugar Top, on greed and hubris. He called that condominium an abomination and an affront to God's intricate handiwork in crafting these mountains. And then he said something I'm reminded of every time I see that building. He said that condominium was like a finger stuck in the eye of the Lord."

I congratulated McLawhorn on a great story. I wasn't sure why he was telling it to me, though. Were we on the same page? In the same camp?

"That rock crusher would be the whole fist," I said. "Like a fist shoved in the gut of the Lord."

Dan liked my twist, but didn't make any promises.

"Charles can be the hero," I said. "And you, too."

"No," Dan said frankly, "there aren't going to be any heroes in the matter of the Putnam Mine."

After I hung up, I tossed that remark around in my mind. It could mean one of two things: it was either a honest assessment that either course Charles chose was going to be unsatisfactory to one or both of the sides, or it could mean that Charles was utterly fixed on the idea of letting Paul proceed with tearing down the mountain. If Charles was bent on that course, nothing now could stop him. Dan McLawhorn, and Charles's own counsel, Jim Gulick, could advise, could steer, but they couldn't make the decision. And I certainly couldn't.

The next day we had our answer. It came in the form of an e-mail from Forrest: *I just spoke with Jim Gulick who advised me that Charles Gardner has issued a Revocation of the Putnam Mine permit. I will send you the letter upon receipt of it from Mr. Gulick.*

I went out to the truck and drove faster than was safe down to my neighbor's house, where I could receive faxes. Sure enough, a fax was waiting for me on the floor of my neighbor's study. It was a copy of the letter Charles and sent to Paul Brown that very day notifying him that the state had revoked the permit for the Putnam Mine.

Charles had done the right thing. Why, I could not say.

We had won and Paul had lost. Then, as Ollie said, things got even more stranger than they already were.

By the end of business on that day, our case, which had been of interest to everybody in Dog Town and Cranberry Gap, and a few attorneys and politicians in Raleigh, became a sensation.

I searched the Internet, hungry for articles that landed on the AP wire. STATE REVOKES PERMIT FOR QUARRY NEAR APPALACHIAN TRAIL blared the headline in the *Asheville Citizen-Times.* In the article Charles provided the basis for the revocation: *"Substantial relevant evidence received and obtained by the department since the permit was issued has persuaded me that the mine site is plainly visible in good weather from an extended portion of the Appalachian Trail in the vicinity of Hump Mountain."*

The *Charlotte Observer* ran a big piece, too. *The state Division of Land Resources revoked the mining permit for an Avery County granite quarry Wednesday because it says the sights and sounds from the mine would spoil a section of the Appalachian Trail. It was the first time the state has revoked a permit for a reason other than operating violations.* I ran down the column looking for more highlights. *"I think that it always takes courage for someone to admit that they made a mistake,"* said *Trip Van Noppen, senior attorney for the Southern Environmental Law Center, which has worked with the Appa-*

*lachian Trail Conference and the National Parks Conservation Association in opposing the mine.*

I was delirious. The good news kept rolling in. My eyes raced around trying to devour whole paragraphs, entire print columns. Each article was more gratifying than the last as the full measure of what had happened began to sink in. *The state gave the mine operator, Clark Stone Co., six months to restore the site to a natural state. The company has 30 days to file an appeal. Don Hobart with the Attorney General's office predicts appeals could last years. . . . For that reason, the state will likely request a court order to prevent mining during the appeal," Hobart said.*

Over at the *Mountain Times,* Scott Nicholson had seized front-page real estate for his headline. His entry read like a dream. As if Dan Hirschman had written it. As if I had. *In a historic decision, the state has taken away the mining permit for a controversial rock quarry operation near Cranberry.* Nicholson included the best Charles quote of all: *"Visual effects and significant noise from the mining and crushing operation would thwart the purpose of a public park and violate the state Mining Act."* Visual and acoustic impacts both. "Good work!" I called out to nobody, to Biscuit, drawing a blank but eager stare. Nicholson had tried to get Paul's take, but Paul wasn't talking. *Paul Brown said he was surprised by the decision and referred all comments to his attorney Harold Berry.*

I hadn't found Forrest's take yet, or Ron Howell's, so I kept dialing up newspapers. In the *Burlington* (NC) *Times-News,* I found: *"I had no expectations but I was happily and pleasantly surprised," said Forrest Ferrell, a retired Superior Court judge who represented quarry opponents. "It's unusual when a department in effect reverses itself and revokes a permit, though we say the permit shouldn't have been issued to begin with."*

Somehow Jim Sparks over at the *Winston-Salem Journal* had gotten Paul to talk when Scott Nicholson could not. *"It's ridiculous," Brown said. "Them folks up there need that gravel. You can look off that trail and see things that are a lot worse than a quarry. It's frustrating. I've spent a lot of money and put hours and hours of my employees' time into that mine."*

By the end of the day, a producer at Charlotte's FOX News affiliate had contacted the Southern Environmental Law Center. They were preparing a story on the case. Their focus would be on the outrageous taking of a good man's hard-earned permit by a bunch of radical environmentalists.

The local television news got Paul talking, too. When asked if he might sue somebody over the revocation, Paul fumbled for a minute and looked at the ground. Finally, he said, "I don't know and I ain't gon say."

Ollie called. She nearly laughed herself silly over Paul's quote. "'I don't know, I'm not gon say!'" she hooted. "Why, that's the same as saying, 'I do know.' Ain't it?! Oh, Dear Ol' Dad, you do know, but you just ain't saying! I reckon you'll be a-suing me now if I ain't badly mistaken!"

# PART II

## THE CASE

*Chapter 11*

Winter claws at the ridges and valleys of the Appalachians, and it is slow to loosen its grip. Some nights the old pine and chestnut wood in my house seems to grow brittle in the frigid air, and there is a real fear during storms that the nails will pop and the whole affair will shatter like so much glass. In the coldest months I move into the loft above my kitchen to work and sleep tucked beneath the rafters because that is where all the heat in the house pools. With the sun low on the horizon I often wear sunglasses in the house, especially when it snows, because at this elevation it is like living in a dazzling snow-globe and my eyes water and burn with the glare. In late February the ice continues to accrue in the high elevations, and the snows drift onto the eastern and southern sides of the balds, driven off the tops by the lethal winds that come ransacking down from the north and northwest. The weak winter sun never climbs high enough to chase the dark from the valleys, and the hollers store cold air like dammed creeks hold water, and the ground shows no sign of living, of ever greening again. But by early March, the odd day reminds you of the southerly nature of the place. An icy morning turns into a warm afternoon on the ridges. The sun feels hot on the face. When the wind swings from the south, you can smell the piney woods of Georgia, the red clay of Alabama. The seeps and drainages are the first to green up, then the carpet of wildflowers seems to weave itself outward toward the ridges, then upward toward the summits. There comes a day when the fringed phacelia blankets the haggard ground like a jeweled throw, the little white parasols nodding in breezes. Trout lilies appear overnight, their speckled leaves firm and mottled with bronze and green, and it is hard to believe they make no noise so audacious is their arrival.

Some old-timers remember when the springtime slopes were still draped with a sea of creamy chestnut blossoms, when that great tree lorded over the forest. Felled by a blight in the years after the Great Depression, no chestnut trees stand anymore, though the stumps do sprout. No blossoms, just stumps and sprouts, and dead leaners reclining against other trees. Now the dogwoods with their wounds of Christ flowers are disappearing from Appalachia, too. A fungus from Asia attacks them in the cool, moist highlands, on the steep hillsides and the northern exposures. They are already gone from these places, the stream banks are bereft of their signature beauty. But the cherry trees still bloom, as does the shadbush, *sarvis* around here—as in *funeral sarvis*—announcing the ground is soft enough, finally, for burying the winter dead. The most astonishing values of green burst from the supple limbs of beeches and maples, and then, at last, the oaks. The mice pour out of their winter homes and dart into the fields seeking seeds, and the hawks come to see about that.

Through the long winter we knew that only half our work was done in our battle to stand up Belview Mountain. Paul filed an appeal of Charles's revocation of the permit on the thirtieth day of a thirty-day period. His appeal would be heard by an administrative law judge in a courtroom in Raleigh. And he could win. Our other worry was that any day Judge Downs could rule on our complaint in Avery County. His consent order, his handshake agreement with Paul's attorneys, was but a thin thread saving the mountain. If we won, we would beat long odds, and Paul's appeal would, perhaps, be moot. If we lost, we would have an appeals process available to us, but I feared we could not hold our little group together. The long winter had been hard on Ashley. Her health was bad, and she had threatened to drop out of school. Ollie was considering moving her family out of Avery County, to get away from Tony and a county that she saw as irredeemably crooked. And Faye was talking about retirement, about traveling far away from here. Grady was wanting to get out of the flower business, Faye said. The stress of not knowing how Judge Downs would rule was wearing her down. Not knowing if her home would make the perfect retirement spot, a place of dancing creeks and sunny garden rows, or a living hell of drilling dust and trembling granite.

The legal maze was difficult to follow. We had sued the state, knowing that it would not revoke Paul's permit because Charles had said he would not. But then in a stunning about-face, Charles had done the very thing he had vowed not to do. But, in revoking the permit, Charles had chosen a novel—and risky—theory to justify his action. The question turned on what constitutes a *violation of the act.* The question posed by Ron Howell was compelling: did Charles revoke the permit in good faith, because he knew that the Putnam Mine violated the spirit and letter of the statute, or had he deliberately sabotaged the Dog Town Bunch—and even his own agency—by choosing a dubious route to revocation? Having been fooled before, I no longer trusted myself, my own instincts. I turned the matter over in my mind a million times. I sat up late pouring over every utterance of Charles's that might shed light for me. I sought guidance from those who had worked with him before and from those who had tangled with him.

Here's what he did. Charles claimed that he had issued the permit properly. He then claimed that he had used his authority to revoke the permit properly, too. The only problem with the second part of the argument was that the statute is not clear on when and how the state can revoke a permit. The statute makes it clear that the state can *deny* a permit for any of seven reasons: if it is too close to a school or a hospital. If it is going to disturb a sensitive area of archaeological significance. If it will harm an endangered species. And most important from our perspective, *if the operation will have a significantly adverse effect on a publicly owned park, forest, or recreation area.* The statute contemplates that those seven criteria will be applied, given consideration, *before* a permit is issued. The public hearings and public comment period are when the state is supposed to learn of such potential impacts and factor such information into the decision of whether to issue a permit. But in our case, the state issued the permit without doing the proper analysis and without holding public hearings. Unfortunately, the statute does not provide a road map for fixing a mistake attributable to lack of knowledge or a flawed process. The statute assumes the state will follow the designated procedure in the first instance. In short, the statute only allowed Charles to revoke an existing permit if the mine operator *violated* the Mining Act. But the same statute is silent on the question of what constitutes a violation of the Mining Act, so Charles was left to fashion his own standard. In our case Charles's attorneys in the attorney general's office, and Charles himself, decided that violating one or more of the criteria for which the permit could have been *denied* was also a *violation of the act.* The logic sounds straightforward, but this is actually quite a reach. That is why, when we sued the state, we sought to make the state concede the following: *The permit was never valid because the state didn't hold hearings, and because it failed to hold hearings, it didn't have sufficient facts. Had it had held hearings and possessed the information it should have possessed, it would have denied the permit.* At that point it would be sensible for Charles to say, *Because of the deficiencies in the process, we are declaring that the permit was, and is, invalid.* Then the state could have paid Paul a settlement for his investment when he sued to dispute the finding.

Admittedly, it would come down to the judge's discretion—and perhaps whether the judge had a good night's sleep before crafting his ruling, along with any number of other variables beyond our control—to determine whether Charles's revocation would be upheld or overturned. If Paul challenged the revocation. If he sued.

Adding to the murky nature of the state's revocation was that we could not know if Charles really wanted the revocation to succeed. Ron Howell called this *sandbagging,* and he was certain this was Charles's diabolical method. Charles had told Witt and me that he would not revoke the permit because it would be pointless to do so, for the Mining Commission would never uphold a revocation. Ron suspected Charles was right on target when he predicted that the Mining Commission would rebuff an attempt at revocation. Further, Ron felt Charles had in fact guaranteed failure of the revocation by choosing an indefensible justification for his action. In Ron's view, Charles was bowing to pressure from the governor, and the attorney general, making nice, but he was also outsmarting them. In this line of reasoning Charles knew the process would get bogged down before the Mining Commission, and that he would then achieve the end he wanted: a public relations coup for public consumption accompanied by a modified permit that would let Clark Stone mine Belview Mountain in a slightly less onerous manner, but for all ninety-nine years of its lease with Putnam. I sat in the Heel Hound's office one afternoon mulling this over with His Eminence as he plucked and tuned his banjo. Without turning away from his tuning he said, "Why not issue a revocation if you're Charles Gardner? Why, you get the credit for trying to fix this embarrassing spectacle, but at the same time you keep the mining community happy because everybody knows your gesture is just that. A gesture! And then, when your career is over, there is a fat job waiting for you with a lobbying outfit where you can lobby for favors for the mining industry."

The other side of the case had pitfalls, too. In Clark Stone's view, once the permit was issued, and once the mine operator expended money relying on the permit, it could never be taken away. (Especially by the very people who issued it.) Even I would agree with this argument up to a point, but adopting this train of thought as state policy carries hazards. Such a directive might inadvertently invite fraud. All an operator would have to do is get up and running for a single second, or push a haul road and accrue some expense, and he would then have an inalienable right to continue. In a chronically underfunded agency that processes hundreds of permit applications for everything from hog-waste impoundments to asphalt plants, this might lead to some horrific errors that would then be enduring and unfixable. Which is, no doubt, the goal of many industry lobbyists. Nevertheless, no appellate court has held that the mere expenditure of money establishes a property right that alleviates the permitee of the need to comply with the language of the statute to obtain the permit in the first place. To me, it seemed fair that the state should be allowed to correct its mistake so long as it pays compensation for it. This penalty would certainly provide ample incentive to follow the statute more closely in the future, and it would guarantee an intensive review period *before* issuing permits. (This hypothetical leaves out, for the moment, the angle that I suspected all along, which is that Paul's permit application, with its failure to notify the adjoining landowners of their right to seek a public hearing of their objections, constituted either a willful fraud or gross negligence.) Paying Paul to save the mountain and the Appalachian Trail experience would mean, of course, that the taxpayers—you and I—would eat the cost of compensating him for his bad investment, his adventure in statutory misinterpretation if you choose the most generous take on what had happened. But the law goes even further. All states enjoy "sovereign immunity," which insulates them from liability in discretionary decision-making, even when they make mistakes. Even big, expensive mistakes. So the state had little incentive to offer Paul a single dime, except to save face. It's also worth noting that within DENR surely some agreed with our argument that Clark Stone had drafted their mine map to avoid public notice. Charles would not admit this, not to me, anyway, but in my heart I knew he had to feel duped. That meant Paul's best chance might be to sue the state and try to get the permit restored rather than to seek a settlement.

The Putnam Mine matter was, from a lawyer's perspective, a sexy case because both sides had a good argument to make. That's why Forrest was having so much fun. And why Dan and Trip were intellectually engaged. The dispute now involved matters of such complex statutory interpretation, matters of such great import and broad applicability to the environmental community, that Trip was increasingly taking on the role of lead attorney. He and Forrest and Ron now exchanged e-mails and faxes daily, and I watched as the case ripened into a cause célèbre.

While the work was serious, all three of the estimable attorneys appreciated that the case started by Ollie Ve Cox up in Dog Town was good damn fun, too. They got a hoot over the latest antics of Paul Brown and Captain Nasty, and I knew that they looked forward with relish to taking the depositions of Dear Ol' Dad and the Bald Eagle. One day I went to see the Heel Hound in his office. He was surprisingly alert for a lawyer famous for being afflicted with narcolepsy. He had his jacket off. He was working on a song for our case; he wrote a song for every case he took. His song for our case was "Rock of Belview," and it followed the tune of "Rock of Ages." The first line was *Rock of Belview, cleft for me . . . .* He sang through the first few lines, all he had crafted, and plucked along on his five-string. I laughed and clapped, tried to join in the more obvious rhymes. It was good medicine, singing and clapping, and welcome relief from the grind of the action.

The legal team took Paul's deposition on March 7, 2001. Affidavits were already filed, and answers to interrogatories, but now the attorneys would sit down in the room with Paul himself. The deposition is where you get your first crack at the witness for the opposition. We planned to ask Paul how much the mining equipment had cost, namely the Liebherr Litronic shovel, a yellow monster with a massive front-end bucket. Ollie called it the Big Dog. And why his company notified adjoining landowners at a borrow pit—a simple dirt mine—he sought to open in the adjoining county, but not at the Putnam site. Depositions can be instrumental in winning a case. One objective is to inform the witness, through the choice of questions, that their exposure in the courtroom might be quite uncomfortable, or even embarrassing. Good lawyers use the deposition to telegraph where the case is headed and to get inside the mind of the witness and the opposing counsel. I held out hope that Paul would crack under the pressure, or that he would at least give us some insight into what he might settle for. Was there a dollar figure that would make him walk away from his legal challenge to the revocation?

I was not allowed by the attorneys to attend the deposition. They were worried that Paul might be unnerved by my presence. I relied on Dan to give me a thorough review. Paul had a cold. I could imagine what that must have looked like. The skin hung loose on his gray face, and his shoulders slumped as if he had lost all hope. Paul looked whupped even when he was having a good day. Dan said Paul popped hard candies in his mouth throughout the deposition, making it hard for the stenographer, and the attorneys, to understand his words.

The first questions and answers were of a general nature. All of this was in the court record Dan sent me. Paul said James Vance found him the Putnam property. Paul said Charles told him the permit would be granted, so Paul went ahead and put in the road, spent the money to get ready to mine. Simple as that. According to Paul, Robert Putnam cut the timber. Paul was seventy-five years old in that year, 2001. Paul had signed an affidavit and now he reaffirmed what he had reported: that he'd spent $2.5 million in "reliance" on the permit. On land, surveys, and roadwork. Paul said he owned 50 percent of Clark Stone Company, while his four kids owned the other 50 percent. Paul claimed he had never met Robert Putnam. His foreman James Vance handled all such business.

Jim Gulick pressed the witness, gently, into expanding upon his answers. Paul plowed on, without enthusiasm. "I didn't even know there was an Appalachian Trail," he said. "Then I remember seeing that letter."

"The Intent to Revoke letter?"

"That's it."

Paul had a story he offered on his own, by way of explaining himself. "This month, fifty-nine years ago, I was seventeen and I went into the navy and stayed there for six years. And this—you know, this thing blowed me out of my mind."

"And you have said you think this was a mistake?"

"I don't think anybody made a mistake," Paul asserted. "I still don't think there was a mistake made. Three miles away from a trail that probably they don't even keep the grass—if there was many people walking on it, the grass would be beat down. If you go up there, the grass is not even beat down. The trail is about that wide." He indicated a couple of feet in width with his hands. "And the economy of the county over there, the people—the reason I got back into this thing is because the people over in Ashe—Avery County, said they needed rock and they needed some jobs. . . . All those—Johnson Motor Company, they closed down, making outboard motors. And the people over there is the ones that wanted me over there . . . . And like I said, you know, the thing is about that wide. It doesn't even have enough traffic on it to keep the grass out of it."

"The Appalachian Trail?"

"The Appalachian Trail."

When Gulick asked if Paul knew how popular the Appalachian Trail was, Paul seemed astonished that it might be popular at all. As far as Paul was concerned, maybe only two or three people used it a year.

Paul presented a box of receipts meant to demonstrate his expenses. "We broke it down and give a list of the items, too."

Jim spent a lot of time showing that many of the expenses couldn't have been based on the issuance of the permit because they came before the permit was issued.

In addition to restaurant receipts and receipts for flowers for a funeral for the wife of a former employee, and receipts for grass seed and straw and tires for trucks, there was one large number: $550,000 for the shovel, the Big Dog.

Paul said he had to borrow to pay for it. "Yessir. The shovel is sitting right over there doing nobody no good."

Paul said he had made a $100,000 down payment on the shovel, then given a note for the balance. When Gulick showed him evidence that Paul actually made an initial down payment of $50,000, Paul agreed that this was probably so.

Gulick asked a few more questions about the shovel, trying to focus on some solid evidence of expenditures, some numbers that might lead to a settlement proposal. Paul did little to move the ball on that, though. "I know I am making them payments. I do know that. But I know that I ain't got no—and I know that I don't have any—selling no rock and I know that I ain't got no money coming in."

When Gulick showed receipts indicating that Paul started making payments on the note on the shovel in 1998, a year before the permit was issued, Paul just shrugged his shoulders.

Paul felt Charles should have stopped him from buying the shovel if Charles was going to revoke the permit. "I felt that they would have told me, said, 'Hey, you better not buy that shovel. You better let it go because you don't need it. You're not going to be able to use it.' That's the only way I know how to do business, is to do it up-front."

Paul's frustration was clear. "I was waiting on a permit, and I was expecting a permit, and I was led to believe that I would have a permit."

"So you were counting on getting a permit?"

"Well, sure, because that is according to the law, as I understand it."

"Even before you applied for it?"

Paul nodded his assent. In answering these questions about the business of mining, it was as if Paul were speaking to a child who had little understanding of the way things work.

When it was Trip's turn to question Paul, the miner was slumped deep in his seat. Dan said he almost felt sorry for Paul. He crumpled the wrappers from his hard candies, and the reporter had to ask him to stop as the noise was amplified from the microphone on the table.

Trip asked Paul to recount how the revocation had progressed.

Paul seemed eager to answer. "I think there was a couple of good politicians in there that had more power than I had."

"Well, do you agree that it was a decision made by Mr. Gardner?"

"No, sir."

"Who—"

"Maybe Mr. Gardner might have made the decision, but he was influenced to make the decision."

"When you have referred to politicians having some influence over Charles Gardner, are you thinking of somebody in particular, some politician?"

"Not really."

"I mean, did you mean the governor, for example?"

"Well, I think he had a part in it, too."

"Did you speak to the governor about it?"

"Did I speak to the governor?"

"Yes."

"I tried to call him, but he never did call me back."

"Then what I want to know, if you will, is any specific facts, and specific things that anybody said or wrote, that you can point to that indicates that Mr. Gardner didn't make the decision here."

"Well, you know, I was thinking about that. I mean, I have been in politics, you know, for years and years, so I know how this thing works. I'm not a little baby. I wasn't born yesterday. Whenever people gets influenced, they—I know what happens. I just happened to be on the wrong side—well, I wasn't on the wrong side. I helped all of them. I just happened to be at the wrong—I guess at the wrong time. Well, why would Mr. Leutze and that other guy be down in Mr. Gardner's office and messing with Holman's secretaries and getting Holman's secretaries to start working with these other secretaries to try to get this permit revoked? I mean, what was the reason for that? In other words, they don't even know me. So anyway, there is a problem up on the Trail, so you know, how did it happen? I mean, you don't have to be smart to realize that."

"And you think other people than Charles Gardner made this decision?"

"I didn't say it was out of his hands. He just got wishy-washy. And like I said before, how many permits has been revoked? One. Somebody gave me a permit and I asked for a permit and I got the permit. I done everything legal. And now all of a sudden I am not legal no more. So what made me unlegal? I mean, I am a law-abiding citizen. I haven't done anything other than another person would have done."

When I finished reading the transcript, I felt a mixture of satisfaction and shame. I was glad that Paul acknowledged that his permit was basically cooked from the start, nearly preapproved without any review. His recollection was that he was told to apply for a permit so that he could get to work. That was how permitting in the state of North Carolina worked. Ask for a permit, await its delivery. But it was hard to take too much joy in this revelation of what I had suspected all along. Paul was an old man. He was either confused or was putting on a damn good performance. He seemed incapable of grasping the complexity of the argument being raised against the agency. In his eyes he was a good man trying to take down a mountain to provide crushed stone to the community, but he was being badgered by heel hounds and boys in short pants who wouldn't let him get to work.

*Chapter 12*

The first skirmish on the new front of our battle was a hearing before an administrative law judge. The state established an independent quasi-judicial administrative court system in 1985 to try to reduce the workload of the Superior Court, which had become hopelessly inefficient in the dispatching of justice. If unmeritorious cases could be dismissed in an administrative setting, that would save the state and the parties both time and money. Cases remaining unresolved at the end of this administrative process would still move into the traditional courts—with a record already established. Many elected judges decry the level of expertise of the "judges" that serve as gatekeepers and report spending considerable time cleaning up decisions that wander from the norms of judicial decision-making. As Forrest said, "The exhaustion of administrative remedies, is, well, exhausting." In our complaint in Avery County, before Judge Downs, we had skipped this step because we were alleging "irreparable harm" and managed to leapfrog into Superior Court. But now we were parties in Paul's effort to reverse Charles's revocation. We were, in a strange twist, defenders of Charles and of his authority. And in that matter we would have to mount our defense at square one.

Our team filed our motion to intervene in Paul's hearing before Administrative Law Judge Melissa Owens-Lassiter. We sought to appear at the hearing as *intervenors* supporting the state's authority to revoke the permit. Even though the state didn't revoke the permit the way we suggested, we were willing to back them up in their exercise of authority. What choice did we have? It was hoped that by appearing before the administrative law judge in the state's case, our group, along with the Appalachian Trail Conservancy and the National Parks Conservation Association, would bolster the chance for success. Also, as Ron Howell said, it might keep the state from going "wormy" on us. "From the time they wake up to the time they go to bed, they need watching," he said. "Especially Charles Gardner."

Ashley was frustrated. She wanted clarity and she wanted the "langering death" to end. "I don't understand all these hearings. I thought we sued Charles," she lamented one day, sitting in the living room of the new house, the boxes still unpacked. "When do we get to take him down? I want a jury and a hanging judge."

I tried to lay it out for her. The administrative law judge would not determine if we had "won the case"; rather, she would make a recommendation to the Mining Commission. The Mining Commission is a nine-member panel made up of three industry representatives, three conservation-community representatives, two Environmental Management Commission members, and one member who is the chairman of the North Carolina State University Minerals Research Laboratory Advisory Committee. The Mining Commission would receive the ruling of the ALJ, treat it as a recommendation, then make a Final Agency Decision. Whoever lost would then have the right to appeal in the Superior Court.

Ashley was wholly unimpressed: "That's going to take forever and cost a million dollars."

"Maybe a year to get to the Mining Commission," I said. "Then it can be appealed up from there. And the Southern Environmental Law Center will cover all the expenses except for Forrest and Ron. Trip works for free, donors pay his salary, so it doesn't matter to us how much it costs."

"And Paul can't work during that time?"

"He doesn't have a permit. It was revoked."

"Okay. You're sure he can't work?"

"As long as Judge Downs holds his fire, anyway."

"You're sure about that?"

"Of course I'm sure." I was pretty sure, anyway.

I was confident going into the preliminary hearing before the administrative law judge. This was Paul's first step in his appeal of the revocation. But this hearing would be down in Raleigh, and in spite of the local belief that Paul kept everybody in Raleigh *knee-deep in liquor and women,* I felt certain that in the state's capital, far from the local corruption of the county, Randy and Paul's antics would be seen for what they were: bush-league fraud. I drove the five hours to Raleigh and arrived at an empty hearing room. The lobbyist for the mining industry, Lucius Pullen, was standing in the corridor outside. With his head of dazzling white hair he cut a distinguished figure. He stuck out his hand and we met. "I'm Lucius Pullen." Then, much to my surprise, he spelled his first name: "L-U-C-I-U-S."

"Nice to meet you," I said, declining to spell my own name, simple as it is.

After some connecting of dots, that old Southern obsession—he knew my mother, thought she was "a lovely person," and he knew my brother, served on the vestry at his church, and so forth—Lucius explained that there had been an illness in the family of one of Paul's attorneys. The hearing would be rescheduled. I was disappointed. I was ready to rack up a win in a court of law, even if it wasn't a real court and the judge was not a real judge.

Lucius and I parted ways, with an unspoken mutual determination to remain cordial through what we both figured would be a protracted battle.

"See you at the hearing, young man," Lucius said. "Whenever it may be."

On the day of the rescheduled hearing, our troubles started before we could take our seats in the hearing room. The quasi-judge in the quasi-judicial procedure admitted our group and the conservation groups as intervenors, but she explicitly excluded the issue of *notice to the adjoining landowners* from being discussed. The whole reason we wanted to be in the case was to articulate the original sin: the lack of hearings that led to the blind issuance of the permit. We expected her questions to lead naturally to the big question, *Why didn't the state deny the permit in the first place, a right it clearly has in the statute?* The only way to answer that question was to explain that the state didn't have the information it needed to make that decision. Then to explain why that was the case.

At the outset of the preliminary hearing the questions made clear the tack the judge was taking. Rather than asking why there was no notice to the adjoining landowners of their right to a public hearing, she asked, "Why should the state have the authority to take away the permit that they themselves, the same officials, issued? Will basic fairness allow it?"

Uh-oh.

While she was pinning us with tough questions, she let Clark Stone's attorneys run through the dry recitation of how Paul applied for and was issued a permit, only to have it revoked. The attorney used a poster board with a time line spelled out in bold typeface that made it quite clear what had happened. With no mention of why.

Jim Gulick argued the state's contention that the state's General Assembly, in writing the statute, intended the agency, DENR, to have the broad authority to issue permits, to deny permits, and, in cases where the operator violates the act, to revoke permits.

At the end, the judge slapped shut her file folder, thanked all for appearing, and withdrew. All we could do was wait for her to rule. Given the tenor of the hearing, none of the lawyers on our side seemed especially eager to hear what she would say.

On April 19, an e-mail to all plaintiffs and plaintiff intervenors from Dan Hirschman ended the suspense: *Unfortunately, I have some bad news to report on the Putnam Mine front. Judge Lassiter has decided to grant Clark Stone's Motion for Summary Judgment. This means there will not be a full Office of Administrative Hearings hearing. The case will now go directly to the Mining Commission along with Judge Lassiter's recommended decision that the revocation is not valid.*

We had run into a legal buzz saw. Judge Owens-Lassiter held that the state had no authority to revoke a permit it had issued in a case like this. The ruling stated that Charles had missed his opportunity to deny the permit before issuance, and that revocation could not stand in for denial. While this was a rebuke of Charles, it let stand his error, just as Ron Howell suspected Charles wanted all along. In a final chilling act, the judge proffered her recommendation that Charles restore the permit to Paul.

When I had time to read and reflect on the ruling from Judge Owens-Lassiter, I ran through the seven stages of grief, alighting on each stage in turn. Denial. Anger. I spent long stretches of time on each stage, listing, wallowing, before wheeling on to the next. Denial was my favorite of these. We could comfort ourselves that Owens-Lassiter wasn't a real judge. Maybe she was even a partisan nut, but her ruling stood plain before us, oblivious to our fulminations.

The first arbiter to hear Paul's case had roundly rejected the state's argument that Charles had the authority to revoke Paul's permit. She ruled that there was no disputed interpretation of the law, and that State of North Carolina did not have the authority to correct its error. She found that Charles had clearly failed to exercise due diligence, and that if he had exercised such diligence, he "would have discovered that the Putnam mining site operated by the Petitioner was visible and audible from the Appalachian Trail." So, she slammed Charles for doing a bad job in missing the existence of the nearby national park, then ordered that the Appalachian Trail would have to live with the consequences of his failure. I read on:

*Given that there have been no changes in the permit application or the Putnam mine site, no discrepancies in Petitioner's preparation of the site, and Petitioner has made substantial expenditures in reliance on Respondent's issuance, it is now fundamentally unfair and inequitable to Petitioner, for Respondent to change its previous exercise of discretion because either its application procedure was flawed, or Respondent changed its mind after they issued the permit. Simply because Respondent made a mistake in judgment does not create an opportunity to re-evaluate the case now, nor does the legislature authorize it. To allow Respondent to reverse its discretionary decision of issuing a permit in good faith under this scenario would create unjust and appalling public policy.*

It was a punishing read. A masochist, I read it over and over. Took each word into my head and let it grind slowly at the ends of my nerves. *Appalling public policy.* Did she really write that, in defense of Paul and Randy and Captain Nasty? She did. And there was more.

*For the reasons stated above, the Respondent was without authority to revoke*

*Petitioner's Putnam Mine permit for the reasons stated in its Notice of Revocation, erred as a matter of law in its interpretation of the Mining Act, and failed to use proper procedure in its revocation process.*

*For the foregoing reasons, Petitioner has met its burden of proof, and is entitled to judgment as a matter of law.*

It was a thorough drubbing. *Summary Judgment for the Petitioner.* Her ruling put us—and the State of North Carolina—in a hole. The ruling would stand until a higher authority took it up, at which point it would either begin to anneal into the law of the land or come to an ignominious end.

At times like this, I found it comforting, necessary even, to drive to Chapel Hill to visit Trip. Trip was not given to wild swings in mood. He was solid and had seen everything at least once, most things twice. I found him both amused and dismayed over Owens-Lassiter's ruling. He ranked it "weak." He sat calmly and said he thought she was "flat wrong" in her reasoning.

This was good.

I submitted that bad rulings in lower courts could, sometimes, make good law in higher courts. I had learned that in law school. Trip allowed that the Lassiter ruling was bad enough that it might move a reasonable judge to clarify areas of the law that had given her the latitude to rule the way she did. In other words, he hoped that down the road we might appear before a judge who would take full delight in strengthening the law in this area, just so that policy opportunists such as Lassiter would be hamstrung by precedent. This line of reasoning was comforting for a moment. But I also knew, as Trip and I headed out for lunch, that we had entered perilous waters. This ruling was a blow. The less controversial parts of the recommendation went right to the heart of what the state hoped to win on: state authority to correct a mistake after the fact. We would have to lick wounds and reevaluate all aspects of our strategy. Suddenly, my mind swung to our other case, the case pending in Avery County. The ruling Judge Downs was sitting on in that case now loomed ever larger.

---

Sometimes when the fog rolls in on the mountains it stays for days. It seems to cling to the already damp slopes. The week after the ruling it was like that. On my way back up the mountain I picked up a heavy stack of newspapers. I wanted to lie on the sofa to stare at the fog. I wanted to swim in despair, to see our fate spelled out in newsprint and sear it into my brain. First I browsed the *Avery Journal* to see the local spin on the matter. The May 31 paper was the annual Heritage Edition, in which they used old typeface and ran old articles in their original format throughout the paper. One redolent piece was about the long-ago time when Elk Park was the hub for county activities. Next to that piece a column jumped from the page. It was reprinted from a 1931 edition and brought the news that western North Carolina was in the running for a national park. *A Forest Delegation will meet in Linville June 17 and 18 to determine its location. Three thousand officials and experts from all over the country will attend, and their choice will be governed by the contour of the land and the beauty of the forest and undergrowth. The park will be a preserve for all wildlife and will be stocked by the government with native animals and birds.* I tried to imagine three thousand people convening in the mountains for anything in 1931. Tent meetings didn't draw that many. And today, only Billy Graham or the Appalachian State football team could draw crowds measured in the thousands. This meeting was part of the process to select a site suitable for the first national park in the East. Highlands of Roan, I knew, finished the pageant as runner-up to the nearby Great Smokies. The Great Smoky Mountains National Park is now the nation's most visited national park, hosting double the annual visitors that make it to the Grand Canyon in a typical year. I moved on to the rest of the paper.

Tucked in with the old news throughout the Heritage Edition was the current news. On the front page, in the corner, a small piece caught my eye: BROWN WILL CONTINUE TO PUSH FOR MINE said the understated headline. I had never heard of the writer of the article, Marci Shore. Was she replacing somebody? *An administrative law judge ruled recently that a mining permit for Clark Stone Company in Cranberry be restored.*

*According to Brown, the halt in mining at Putnam is "only hurting the people of Avery County." Eighteen workers are currently laid off according to Brown, pending the final decision by the Mining Commission. Many of them have already used up the unemployment compensation available to them, he noted. "I couldn't afford to keep paying them," said Brown. He added that if the Mining Commission decides to permanently revoke his mining license, then he would consider seeking monetary compensation from a civil suit against the groups. "I've already put too much money into this to back down," said Brown.*

The article read like a warm, wet kiss blown in Paul's direction. We would have to start doing opposition research on this Marci Shore. I did not look forward to hearing from Ollie and Faye after they read the paper. They knew as well as I did that we were fighting this battle in the court of public opinion as well as in a court of law. Right now we were clearly struggling on both fronts. And it looked as if we might get sued by Paul Brown. On what grounds, I did not know.

Usually in May I am roaming the mountains with a fly rod. I am eating my lunch streamside and devouring the natural world in my mad, if small, race to live each moment in its fullness. I'm working my garden with my hands down deep in the warming soil. The mountains are electric green in May, and friends come to my place to fish and hike and gather ramps and branch lettuce. The wild leeks send up their velveteen leaves. I like to drizzle the branch lettuce with hot bacon grease, *kill it,* as my neighbors do. And the ramp leaves cook down the second they hit the skillet. I toss them in oil. The ramp bulb is so potent that mountain kids grow up believing that eating the bulbs raw will earn them a ticket home from school, as nobody can bear the smell of the plant passing through the skin of little boys and girls. This May I went through the paces of my spring routine. But there was no joy. There was only Judge Downs and the case and the not knowing. We worried, until, as Ollie said, we were worn-out of worrying.

I was trying to convince Ollie that her fear of hoboes was out of all proportion with the danger actually posed by hoboes, but I had my work cut out for me.

My brother-in-law was on the medical faculty at the University of North Carolina, and he had arranged to have a complete medical work-up done on Ashley. She couldn't get well. The infections in her kidneys never cleared up. The infections in her sinuses. Her immune system was "nonexistent" according to her own diagnosis.

Ollie and Curly would take her down on a Tuesday morning. Clay would meet them at the front door of the pediatric ward and usher them through the hospital for the battery of tests, during which time Ashley would no doubt teach the residents a fair bit about hemoglobin levels and white blood cell counts and the basic tenets of immunology. The Cox-Cook clan would spend the night at my mother's house, and then on Wednesday Ashley would undergo a second round of tests before they headed home.

It was all set. But now Ollie was stricken with this fear of hoboes.

"I was talking to this girl," she began, "and, son, she told me that Raleigh is wall-to-wall with hoboes and winos. She said the railroad tracks in Raleigh is covered up in drug pushers and fifty-cent drinking bars."

My first instinct was to mock this highly intelligent and capable woman. "I don't think we have hoboes anymore, Ollie. We stopped having hoboes in about 1940, I think. And if there are any hoboes, I'm pretty sure you can take them. They are notoriously weak and under-fed."

"Well, whatever you call them. Homeless vagrants. That's what this girl said."

"Well, I'm telling you you're not going to see a single hobo or homeless vagrant in Chapel Hill. Did you tell this girl you're not even going to Raleigh? Chapel Hill is a nice little town with lots of trees and pretty yards. Birds."

"Yeah, right!" Ollie crowed, certain I was making this up.

I realized I had no idea what associations Ollie had with Chapel Hill, or other places east of Boone. She had traveled some, with Curly when he used to do long-haul trucking. She had been to the Mexican border and even Philadelphia. ("I never took my hand off my pistol. Not once.") But her anxiety over Ashley's health, and the attendant lack of sleep that went with the anxiety, had combined with her natural suspicion of all things not mountain, not local, to leave her stricken.

To her credit Ollie faced down her fear of hoboes and the great unknown and went to Chapel Hill anyway. For Ashley. After two days of tests, every trick in the book, and more polysyllabic medical words than Ollie had ever heard before in her life, they came back with little to show. "Fatty liver," Ashley said. "We won't get the biopsy back for three weeks."

"What's fatty liver?"

Ollie weighed in. "There are more test results we're awaiting on. Some of the tests could take two weeks to run, but, no, they couldn't say right off what's giving her all these infections. I can't believe she came home with any blood in her body for how much they drew out of her." Ollie worked one hand into the other nervously.

I couldn't resist. "How many hoboes did you see?"

Ollie let her arms fall loose by her sides. "Little Buddy, I couldn't believe it. It was just like you said. People down there have yards and trees, and it's just as quiet and nice as you could hope for. And the people were some of the finest people I've ever saw. They treated us just like we were anybody else. And your mother, gosh, she's a lady. She treated me like I was the queen of England."

Ashley rolled her eyes. "Aunt Ollie wouldn't stop staring at all the black people at the hospital. I thought I was going to die of embarrassment. I thought she was going to ask this one nurse if she could touch her skin." Ashley paused for a moment. "We probably shouldn't go places."

# Chapter 13

Another summer, and the equipment sat silent. Nasty and Richard spent most of every day up on the mountain, doing what, we did not know. There was no drilling, no scraping of blades on rock. Ollie heard chain saws running, hammering, metal on metal, but the forest created a dense curtain her lenses could not broach, so she was left to guess at what the hell was going on.

"I need infrared," she said.

"Infrared what?" I asked.

"Infrared-sensitive lenses," Freddy volunteered.

"For what?"

"To see through the trees. It makes it so you can see the human body through walls and stuff like that. It senses the heat of the human body, but you could also see flying squirrels and coons with it. They use it in the military."

"Why does the military need to see flying squirrels and coons?" I just wanted to aggravate him. It was fun and he liked to aggravate me, so why not?

"They need it to see terrorists, Jay."

"I get it."

Freddy continued, "Did you see that show about that new bullet they got in the CIA?"

"I don't watch a lot of television," I said. "I like that farming show on public television out of South Carolina."

"Well, you ain't going to believe this, son, they got this new bullet and it's made of ice."

"How do you shoot it?"

"It don't use a combustion chamber because that would melt the ice. But the beauty of it is, you can lace it with poison and shoot it, and it penetrates and then it melts."

"I'm not sure why that's an advantage."

"It's untraceable. It melts."

"You're not in the CIA, are you, Freddy?"

"Son, I wish I could tell you."

"You better not say anything more. I don't want to compromise you."

"Bingo."

When I wasn't visiting with Ollie's family, I was probing the Appalachian Trail's history and the culture of the people who use it. More and more hikers were using the Internet to keep their families and friends apprised of their progress. A number of websites hosted these Trail journals. Entries were transferred from handwritten daily journals into web format when hikers passed near towns with public libraries. I read the journals, eagerly devouring the stories of hikers I would never meet. Always my heart beat as a hiker approached the Highlands of Roan and Hump Mountain. I wanted to see affirmation of my belief that this section of the Trail was special.

I learned more than I bargained for. While acclaim for the scenery of the seventeen miles of Trail that passes across the balds in the Roan is universal, the section of the Trail just off the Humps, down in the valley, is somewhat notorious. In the Internet forums hikers warn other members of their tribe that Elk Park is hostile territory. That hitching from the Trail into town, one is likely to get swerved at by trucks. That accepting a ride is risky. Day Hikers are warned that if parking along 19E, one risks break-ins or worse. An oft-reported story of a Day Hiker's car being set afire near a trailhead won't die, though no one can confirm its veracity. Even if some of the tales amounted to lore with questionable provenance, I was hurt to know that my own backyard was reputed to be inhospitable. Not entirely surprising, but hurtful all the same.

When I asked around the community, I found mixed sentiments regarding the Trail. Many people I talked to had never heard of the Appalachian Trail, which should not be surprising, I suppose, because the Trail is, by design, located in the remotest, least accessible parts of the country it passes through. Some had heard of it but had no idea it crossed Hump Mountain. I was reminded that many local people do not identify the region in which they live as Appalachia—home is simply this creek or that creek, this holler or more commonly "the mountain." So the *Appalachian* Trail is not a reference that signifies.

Locals who knew of the Trail and knew its course over Hump Mountain were divided into two camps: those who were proud that their neck of the woods merited a unit of the National Park System, and those who resented the Trail for the role it played in keeping four-wheelers off the balds. I had one young man of seventeen tell me all he wanted to do before he died was ride his four-wheeler on Big Hump. "Just once," he said with longing. "All I want is to run up that mountain and hit about thirty going across them grassy patches." I asked him if he had ever been on top of the Hump. He looked at me as if I had suffered brain damage. "You ain't serious. I ain't walking nowhere," he boasted. Our postmistress was another critic of the Trail: "What they done is steal that land from us mountain people. We used to go up on there and pick strawberries, every spring we did. But now we can't do that and they've rurent it."

"Why not?" I had picked strawberries and blackberries on the Hump many times.

"Why, it's the government!" she exclaimed, perhaps failing to recognize for just that moment that she was a federal employee. "The government won't graze it and the grass has rurent the strawberry picking. And besides that, you can't get up on there. It's impossible."

The consensus among the mountain people seemed to be that walking up Hump Mountain was as foolhardy as strapping on wings to try to fly up it. Which made me something of a strange character. Admired for my superhuman ability to climb hills using nothing but my own legs, but quite exotic all the same.

One local fellow who can outwalk me—and often does—is my friend and neighbor Ted Hoilman. He scoffed at the protestations of his mountain kin who were wedded to their four-wheelers and their trucks.

"We didn't never drive nowhere," he told me one day on top of Big Yellow. "I'm sixty-one years old and I don't have no driver license, and I don't need none." I had long known this to be true. Ted is one of my heroes and I have followed his exploits for years. That he does not drive just adds to the general wonderment that surrounds him.

When I moved to the mountain full-time, I spent long hours out in the yard, stirring up the dirt to plant my garden, mostly potatoes in that first year. Ted was one of my first visitors, stepping out of the woods to the edge of my garden so silently I did not hear him. I had not seen him since I was a boy, so he reintroduced himself with the local welcome that says you're all right: "I've not seed you since you was just little." We hit it off right away. Ted wanted to show me a patch of Gray's lilies I might not have seen. Wanted to make sure I knew that the ash trees on the bald had put out berries for the first time in seven years. We went over the health of each of his brothers, and of his wife and of his young-uns and grand-young-uns, one of whom had just been borned. He wanted to know if I went to church. Before I could answer that I was a lapsed Episcopalian, he said, tapping his chest, "Me, I'm like an Indian and don't need to go to any built church. The top of this mountain, that's my church." Tears swelled in his bright eyes as he spoke. As anyone who meets him soon learns, and as his brothers explain sweetly, Ted is awful easy to cry.

"People has got lazy," he says dismissively of his fellow man. "But not Ted." Ted often refers to himself in the third person, as if his own reality is so exceptional that he has to stand off from himself to regard his own features. "Ted gets up at three in the morning and leaves the house. I don't wake up Brenda and I don't look at the television. I just head up the hill. I walk up Whitaker Branch while you're still dreaming in the bed, Jay. And it don't take me long to get on top of the mountain. And then I walk my fences." Since the 1800s the Hoilman family has grazed cows on the top of Big Yellow Mountain, first for the Avery family, and now as part of the balds management program run by The Nature Conservancy and Southern Appalachian Highlands Conservancy.

In the absence of native large herbivores, elk and bison, cows have proven quite effective at keeping the treasured balds open. The current arrangement is good for all concerned. Ted gets a good deal on the lease, but he doesn't make any money at grazing. He does it to stay connected to the business his family has been in for generations. And it keeps him on the mountain, where he is at peace. The conservancies win because the bald in its open state is able to support dozens of rare, threatened, and endangered plant and animal species, species that are adapted to treeless balds and do not persist anywhere else.

After checking his fences, Ted usually peels off to see what he can see. He might march to Hump Mountain to see if the ginseng is up in a place he knows. Or he may wander over to Hampton Creek Cove on the Tennessee side to see a purple, fringed orchid he saw last year, or to drop in on his old buddy Denton Birchfield. Flowers, kinsmen, animal tracks, all are part of the daily wonder infusing Ted's life on the mountain, in the woods. Sometimes he walks down toward Roaring Creek to visit the place he wishes to be buried. Long after the sun comes up, he will still be walking. On many Sundays he comes to my house for his cup of coffee. "Your coffee ain't no good," he will say, busting with a grin, "but I can usually doctor it so it won't kill a man."

Ted loves the Appalachian Trail and The Nature Conservancy and the Southern Appalachian Highlands Conservancy. Ted is a true conservationist, though he might not choose that word to describe what moves him. He likes things the way they are, the way they have always been, and has nothing but contempt for the new things coming into the mountains.

Back in the 1970s when the land-trust movement was just beginning, when the conservancies were struggling for membership and funding as they watched the natural places of the region and the country fall into the hands of developers with real estate schemes, Ted determined that the only chance he had to keep his beloved stomping ground from falling to resort development lay with the conservation groups and the federal government. While his neighbors cussed the government as a faceless taxing authority, while they questioned the government's motives as Forest Service personnel from "off the mountain" came around, working to secure parklands and recreation areas, Ted celebrated that there was a force mightier than the slick real estate investors. Ted knew that one would shut him out, while the other would let him roam. He had heard how bad it had gotten over in Banner Elk, and around Linville. Hunters couldn't run their dogs over there anymore. The big developments hired private security guards to patrol the mansions filled with oil paintings and bronze statues of Rough Riders and who knew what all riches. On the other side of the county golf courses replaced the forests where medicinal plants once grew in abundance. The root hunting, for ginseng, for bloodroot and cohosh and ramps, was no good over there anymore. But Ted was not passive in his passion. Whenever he learned of a sensitive tract of land that might be for sale near Big Yellow or the Roan, he would contact "the Conservanty" in Asheville. This could mean either The Nature Conservancy or Southern Appalachian Highlands Conservancy. Once I had gained his trust, he began to come to me, too, with potential projects. He was kin to many of the people living in Roaring Creek and the other areas surrounding the balds and the Trail, and he was always on the lookout for opportunities to add protection to his personal back-of-beyond. He and I would stand on the bald and gaze out across the untouched lands to our south, over Spear Tops and Hawk Mountain, down the Toe River Valley to Big Bald and Mt. Mitchell, and Ted would talk of how we had to do more. How we had to keep the land the way it is. "For the young-uns and the grand-young-uns," he would say. "Otherwise they won't know nothing about God. They'll go out into the world and think that that's all there is. They'll go to places like Alabama. Or California."

I would assure him that the conservancies were working on it. We were raising money, talking with local families, trying to explain the difference between how nonprofits work and how the government works. We were trying to save the best of what was left in the Roan and beyond.

That would bring the tears. "If we don't protect it, it'll all be city. It'll all be Sugar Mountain."

Even though I never asked Ted his view on the Putnam Mine, if he wanted it shut down or wanted it to run, if he backed Paul, he and I talked around the issue, always leaving room for a difference of opinion. "Anything that makes noise in my church, well, I don't like that," he told me one day, looking down into the valley in the direction of Belview. But he was just as likely to tell me romantic tales of the mining days when he was a boy. His father was a miner. His father had mined mica, olivine, and feldspar. When he wasn't up on the mountain, Ted himself worked for Tarheel Mica, a processing plant that took locally mined mica and turned it into insulators for toaster ovens and hairdryers. The space shuttle even. The company is still running, though now it is more economical to import mica mined in India than to pull it out of these hills. "My daddy ran a boom arm that dropped miners down into the pits," he told me. Ted lamented the passing of those days. Those were hard days, he said, but that was good. Hard is good. "I've thought of building a boom arm in my yard," he told me one day. "Just because these young-uns ain't never seen one and all that history is lost. The ones coming up today don't know where anything comes from. Well, most of it, what's any good, comes out of the ground."

But if Ted was pro-mining by birth, he never held it against me. "I'll never tell you what to think, Jay, and don't you tell me. You are who you are." He would sling an arm around me. "And me," he'd say, tapping his chest, "I am what I am. And that's all they are to it."


Ollie didn't like it when I went away for long. "Where the hell have you been?" she said when I called on the phone one day.

"Fishing."

"Well, if it ain't Bill Dance," she said, unimpressed. "While you was off tormenting our fine-finned friends, everything has went to hell here. Trackhoe Daddy's been working double-time up on dirt mountain. I got it on tape, what I could see, but he keeps getting behind the trees. I only got a little."

"What's he doing?"

"I don't know. Putting in a road, or something. What are we going to do? That's what I want to know."

"I'm going to e-mail Jim Gulick."

She was unimpressed. "He won't do nothing about it. Gulick's on the dark side." She had not forgiven him for his cross-examination of her before Judge Downs.

"He might do something. It's all we've got."

"Well, then do it. The consent order ain't worth the damn ink they spilled on it, far as I can tell. Paul does exactly what he wants to do. Just like it's always been."

Every day now the crew was on the mountain. Freddy had gone up to do some scouting. It appeared they were clearing trees and slash, preparing to move the drill into position. The prospect of a resumption of drilling was enough to send Ollie skidding. She developed chronic headaches. Then an ulcer, and back pain. Ashley suspected Ollie had slipped a disk. "Somewhere in the lower lumbar," Ashley said. "Maybe L3 or L4 if I had to guess." But Ollie wouldn't see the doctor. She limped around the house, tender and weak. She did not have any health insurance. Between building the house and taking care of Ashley's medical problems, little money was floating around for anything else. Curly had insurance through a new job, with Asplundh, the vegetation-management giant, but to add Ollie to Curly's insurance would have cost $170 a week. I couldn't prescribe medicine for her, and I couldn't force her to see a doctor. She was too stubborn. I had had my own back problems, the summer before, and I gave her my leftover prescription for Flexeril, all three tablets. About all I could really do for Ollie was to stay on the case, to try to help her chase Paul off the mountain. So I e-mailed Jim Gulick about Curtis's activities. The state sent an inspector but determined that Paul's boys were not clearing drill tracks in preparation for mining. No, they were only getting firewood out, and gathering firewood didn't violate the consent order.

Ollie was furious. "Firewood!" she exclaimed when I told her. "What's he going to do, heat the whole southeastern United States of America this winter?" Curly was convinced that this inspection was more foot-shuffling from the Asheville Regional Office. I decided to try to prompt a proper investigation. I sent Gulick my report.

*The development of a new road continued yesterday. I stood on the Trail on Little Hump. You can actually hear the wheels creak on the trackhoe. I did not hike all the way to Hump Mountain but of course it would be louder and even more visible from that vantage point. It seems insane to let them continue to develop the site when this is damage which might require reclamation, and the cost of the work will likely be fashioned a "loss" should they sue for damages. It also seems, to me anyway, like contempt of a court order. . . .*

When Ollie, figuring she already knew, asked me what reply I'd received from Jim's office, I had to tell her the truth.

"Nothing yet."

"Crickets."

*Chapter 14*

It would be months before the Mining Commission would take up our appeal of the administrative law judge's recommendation to reverse the revocation. That gave us time to lick wounds, heal up, and then, probably, by all accounts, take another beating.

With the odds now stacked squarely against us, Don Barger thought we should be putting more energy into forcing some type of settlement. If Charles could modify the permit, Don suggested, and make it uneconomic for Paul to continue, then Paul might gladly take the money, rather than the fight. It sounded good, but we were just talking to ourselves. We couldn't force any action. We could only prod and lob suggestions in the general direction of the attorney general's office.

The suspense was nearly crippling to a plaintiff with no role in the preparations. We couldn't afford another loss, yet I was not in a position to improve our chances, even if I had known what to do. Trip explained the stakes to me one day in his office. "If the Mining Commission rules against us, which Forrest and Ron expect, we will no longer be on the same side as the state."

"Why not? Why can't we remain as intervenors?" I asked. "The state disagrees with the administrative law judge, don't they?"

Trip explained it. "Yes, the state feels like we do about the ALJ ruling. But the Mining Commission was set up in the statute to create final agency decisions, so the Mining Commission *is* the state. The state cannot very well disagree with the commission they established to police themselves."

After I left Trip's office, I went down the hallway for a meeting with Dan. He wanted to go over the mining commissioners, name by name, to try to get a handle on the task ahead.

We called out the name of each commissioner and, armed with little more than brief biographical sketches of each, tried to imagine how they would swing when presented with our case, and with the case Harold Berry—the Weasel—would present. No matter how we counted, it was easy to see how we could lose before the Mining Commission. And nearly impossible to see how we might snatch a win.

Meanwhile, Ollie and Ashley were watching Paul's momentum build every day right outside their window. Two septic tanks arrived on the site on May 4. Ollie had pictures. Paul's son Steve showed up at the site on May 7. A dozer came down the mountain, Nasty loaded it on a lowboy, and off it went. A gray van with state tags arrived and a heavyset man had a prayer meeting with Trackhoe Daddy. All this came to me in detailed e-mail reports from Ollie and Ashley. At least I couldn't see it from my house, didn't have it staring me in the face every minute. To punish myself, to keep up with the suffering of my co-plaintiffs, I kept a copy of Judge Lassiter's ruling on my desk. Self-flagellation seemed the least I could do in the face of what Ollie's family endured.

All that spring and summer it felt as if Paul was winning. He was preparing to go in. A drain field was dug for the septic at the scale house. Ditch work went forward down below the haul road. Jim Gulick, like Don, thought a buyout was a possibility, thought it was worth exploring, but Paul had not, so far, offered any numbers, any hard tally of his losses. The shoebox full of receipts he'd presented at his deposition was all the state had to go on. Ashley thought Don was wrong. Paul would never settle. After all, Judge Lassiter had handed Paul a powerful hand. Why would he settle now? Dan Hirschman, risking raising my wrath, voiced another option: a modification that would meet a "partial retention" standard under Forest Service guidelines and let Paul go in. Morgan, in a carefully worded reply to this suggestion, did my work for me. He didn't think it could work. Didn't think there was any way to meet partial retention.

Nobody, it seemed, wanted to take up my suggestion: find Paul in contempt of the consent order—for moving earth and putting in a septic system—and throw his sorry ass under the jail. I put it out there, but cleaned up the language, dolled it up before sending it around. The reply was quick in coming.

Jim Gulick conveyed his view of it in an e-mail to Dan Hirschman: *Charles thinks the recent activities do violate the consent order, but Charles is not going to take enforcement action because the activities in violation are not in view of the Appalachian Trail.*

I did not have the heart to tell Ollie and Faye that their concerns simply didn't have any traction with the agency and the office of the attorney general. That little dirt trail was all we had.


While we were ticking off the days to our hearing before the Mining Commission, our notice case before Judge Downs was proceeding on a parallel tract. In that case, the parties were ordered to appear for a mediated settlement conference. Mediation is a friendly forum where the parties meet with a mediator, rather than before a judge, in a final effort to resolve their dispute prior to further court activity. We were ordered to complete the mediation conference by the end of September. A long series of negotiations followed to find a mutually agreed-upon mediator, a suitable date and venue. Motions to Extend were filed, faxes crisscrossed the wires, expenses piled up for the parties, but finally we had a time, a place, and a mediator designated.


As a single man living out in the woods, I had the luxury of worrying all day—and most of the night—about the inner workings of Paul's mind and Charles's motivations. I had none of the distractions of family, no children requiring my attention, nor wife to fashion compromise with. Ollie was not so lucky. Her household was full of the struggles that arise when people live together. Ashley was now in a pitched battle against her parents. Her struggle to be emancipated from the custody of Tony and Nona was her best chance, she felt, at regaining her confidence and her peace of mind. The remedy she devised would not be easy. In effect Ashley sought to divorce her parents. She had seen a television story about a young person in Oklahoma who had successfully used a divorce theory to escape the grasp of his drug-dealing parents. In typical fashion, Ashley streaked past the ruminating stage and took herself down to the courthouse and filed a petition for removal. The prior court order rising out of the fight between Tony and Freddy, the dropping of assault charges in exchange for a relinquishing of custody, seemed too tenuous. What guarantee did she have that Tony would not show up again, on another night, with violence in mind? She was pleased at the prospect of being free, but what relief the process might afford came with a new set of challenges. Hearings on the docket. Testimony. The court-ordered psychiatric evaluation. To add to her troubles, her health was, if anything, worse now than it had been. Ashley was always sick, either with ear infections or kidney trouble or some kind of feminine troubles that Ollie alluded to but preferred not to spell out. Fatty liver. One of her new doctors had given her a new diagnosis: hyper IgE. "My immune system's shot," Ashley said simply when I asked her what that was. "My body can't fight anything, so I'm a sitting duck for infections. That's what my doctor says, but we want a second opinion."

I was not surprised when Ashley turned up in the hospital for emergency gallbladder surgery.

I rushed over to Boone to visit with the family. Ashley came through the surgery pretty well, but Ollie was worried about the potential exposure to things Ashley was surely allergic to.

Freddy was especially upset about the care Ashley was getting. The nurses weren't changing her dressings frequently enough. They weren't managing her medication properly.

After a long night in which Ashley was suffering with pain that the meds did little to address, the family Cox decided to break her out, AMA, "against medical advice," as they say around the nurses' station. Ollie undid Ashley's IV drips, and Freddy scooped her up and carried her down a back stairwell and loaded her in the van. They sped back to the mountain, and all felt better once she was home.

Ollie's health was still in decline, too. She was worn-out. She smoked all day and worried herself all night. About her brother Tony, about her ailing mother. About Paul. Her back was no better, her ulcer worse. But Ashley came first. If Ashley had a coughing fit, Ollie sat up with her. If Ashley had kidney pain, Ollie rushed her to the emergency room, stayed through the night. She walked with a hitch in her gait now, from the back pain, but she brushed that off. Her own discomfort was nothing compared to what Ashley was enduring.

On a stifling-hot summer morning, a team of us set out for the summit of Hump Mountain. The task was to engage the talents of landscape architect Dave Hill. The state had hired Hill to propose visual mitigation measures in the now seemingly likely event that Paul won the case before the Mining Commission and the permit was restored. Charles's office was allegedly planning to use this visual analysis as a way to prove that a modification of the permit, and of the site, could protect the Appalachian Trail from the significant adverse effects of the quarry. The tour on this day included Charles, Randy, Morgan, Dwayne Stutzman from State Trails, Steve Perri of the Tennessee Eastman Hiking and Canoeing Club, Linda Randolph from the Forest Service, Dave Hill, and myself. We set out driving up the south flank of Hump Mountain. But we didn't get far before the trucks spun out in the hard dust. Two of the vehicles made it, but we had to ditch a pair in the middle of the logging road. Half of us would walk up. With every minute the sun rose higher and beat down with ever more force. After an hour and a half, we were all on top. The deskbound were still trying to catch their breath from the climb when I overheard a snippet of talk from Dave Hill. He was talking to Morgan. "If the question is, can this meet partial retention under USFS standards, the question has to be changed. Clearly it cannot. There is no good way to mitigate that," he said, nodding at the site sprawled out below us. My heart leapt. These were magic words. *No good way to mitigate that.*

We all gathered at the summit and set off to walk the affected section of Trail. I fell in with Charles and Dave Hill. I became aware of Charles's slight limp, his bad knee, and fought the impulse to worry over it. Dave Hill was trying, once again, to get a handle on his task. "So, Charles, what you want is for me to show you how you go from three acres, which is the current disturbed area for the pit, that timbered area, up to twenty-two acres, or forty-six acres, phase one, without damaging the viewshed any more?"

I don't know why I thought it was appropriate for me to do this, but I leaned in and cut Charles off before he could answer. By now Charles was used to my zealous advocacy, so he did not flinch. "No, Mr. Hill," I said. "What we're trying to do is get from three acres down to zero acres. There is, right now, no permit for the Putnam Mine. Charles revoked it, and the miner has to reclaim the site until some final decision says otherwise. That's where it stands right now."

Charles reared back, then said, "That's right, Dave. Jay's right. We've revoked the permit and we hope to have that upheld, but if we don't, if we lose, we want to know our options for modification."

Dave Hill nodded and made a note of this. Charles continued, raising an arm to indicate the scene before us, the torn-up mountain, "I'm glad to see the vegetative cover grows back as quickly as it does." I detected a note of true relief. We looked over the excavation area. Indeed, in the past year the cleared circle had come back in blackberries. Locust would be next, then maples and ash and beech. The test-blast area was now far more dominant visually than the timbered clearing for the quarry ever was. The disturbance to the surface at the test-blast site was still raw and spoke of the violent explosion the state had invited. There was not a blade of grass or a blackberry cane in that area. Just a ragged orange hole of exposed soil and shale.

On the way down, I clung to Linda Randolph, of the Forest Service. I wanted to see if I could gain some insight into the thinking of the federal agency. What she said shocked me. She told me that Randy told her—on top of the mountain—that Paul would go away under the right circumstances.

"Could you say that again?" I begged. "What circumstances?"

She indulged and delighted me. "Mr. Carpenter, he said Paul doesn't want to fight anymore. He said the number would be in the neighborhood of three million dollars."

My heart was coming out of my chest. This was the first solid indication of a settlement offer. I flew while everyone else walked. Not that I had $3 million or knew anybody that did.

"Is that all he said? Did he say anything else?"

"He said that if they just clear-cut the entire mountain for timber, the scar wouldn't be so noticeable. He said it stands out more now because of the contrast between the cleared area and the forested area."

That was our Randy.

Now our posse went over to the site itself. We leaned against trucks below the pit area. Morgan asked Randy how Paul had picked the site, how he selected the west face of Belview for the primary pit location.

Randy looked at Morgan dismissively and said, "Paul just knows where the rock is." Randy then explained, somewhat wearily, how this thing works: "What we do is we follow a seam of rock. If we're finding good rock and the seam goes on off into the trees, we go get it. It doesn't matter if it's in the woods. We're not necessarily going to stick to where the map says we're going to go if the rock takes us somewhere else." This was a pretty reckless thing to say in front of Charles. I was pleased at the open boast, Randy's stubborn resolve to ignore the rule of law, his notion that he could craft his own personal Mining Act and permit boundaries.

The conversation turned to the color of the rock. Charles kept saying the rock would be "weathered." He made it sound like a feature prized in the marketplace. *The weathered look is the latest trend in the quarry industry.* I was not sure what *weathered* meant in exposed granite, but Charles clearly meant to indicate that it would not be bright, or arresting, and therefore neither *significant* nor especially *adverse* when viewed from the Trail. The landscape architects picked up sample rocks and turned them over. Randy handed them a piece of gray rock for a color analysis. Dave

Hill stepped in to say that they would hit a lot of limestone-colored rock, tan rock, as well. And quartz, which isn't just visible, but sparkles like diamonds. Hill wished for winter views of the site, and I pulled out some of Witt's winter shots. "These are great," he enthused. Thus encouraged, I kept pulling out photos, handing them all over. Randy looked as if the transmission had just dropped out of his truck.

Next we toured the plant area. It was exciting to see the machinery at my leisure. This time I was able to take it all in without the nagging fear of being shot. The footprint of the plant sat on nearly an acre, in the middle of a clearing that had grown to eight acres. Or roughly eight football fields. This was the clearing I first saw from Witt's place. The conveyers took in an area hundreds of feet long. From a small room on stilts, a raised booth with Plexiglas windows, an operator would run the machinery. Off to the side of the plant proper stood old trucks. Twisted trusses lay around, pieces nobody could find a use for. Mangled drums and truck parts. Massive rusted hoppers. As before.

We walked through the crushing process, followed the sequence a chunk of granite would take on its way from mountain to market. After being blasted out of the mountain and loaded into Euclid trucks, the boulders would be dumped into a hopper and sent through the primary jaw. Next, Nasty and a couple of other guys would transport the broken chunks, now about the size of microwave ovens, in those same Euclids, to this place, here. On this side, they would feed the rock into another huge hopper. The rock would then tumble down an embankment where a shaker would feed it onto a long conveyer. The conveyer would transport the rock across the face of the slope and down to the main plant. The plant consisted of a pair of cones and a series of sorting screens, lifts, and conveyers. The cones were large metal cylinders, each with a steel head about the size of a boxing glove. These heads rumbled around the cylinders and crushed the rock from microwave-oven size down to riprap size, and then, finally, gravel size, crush run. The material was then washed and poured into tidy heaps of clean bond at a stockpile area where customers in dump trucks would pull up, and the bond would be loaded and weighed.

The equipment was old and, to be charitable, a pile of elaborate disinte-grating junk. Only it wasn't worthless junk. It was worth a million dol-lars or more. Steve Perri was awed by it. Out of earshot of the others he asked, "This is what Clark Stone was doing without a building permit?"

I nodded. "They were welding this stuff together."

It had grown outward and upward since I'd visited the site with Ginna. The conveyors were all finished, linking the works from one end of the clearing to the other. After the state informed Paul that his permit was being reviewed, this is what Nasty and Richard had sped the work on. Their thinking was that if they sunk enough concrete into the ground, welded enough joints, if they sunk enough money, the state would balk at stopping them. And it looked as if they were right. Judge Owens-Lassiter explicitly cited the level of investment in the site as a reason to reverse the revocation. We didn't have access to Paul's books, but we did know, just from watching, that the crew had erected nearly half the plant equipment, expended enormous sums assembling it, *after* Charles informed Paul that he intended to revoke the permit. Now, under any negotiated settlement, any modified plan, they would want to leave this plant equipment right here, mostly because it would be hard—and terrifically expensive—to move it. There was no disputing that.

Next we walked around the conveyor system, with its brittle metal steps and rusted handrails, and dozens of rusted rollers for the belts to run across. The belts were frayed and faded. Steve Perri wondered if any laws applied to the equipment itself. "This looks like it would kill anybody who gets near it. Can this thing actually run?"

Now Morgan had a good idea. He asked Randy if he wouldn't mind turning it on.

"Turn what on?" Randy tried with his dull tone to glide away from Morgan. He was playing dumb.

"The crusher, the conveyors. Could you turn it on? I'd like to hear what it sounds like."

Now Randy looked panic-stricken. He turned to Nasty.

Nasty bailed him out. "It ain't ready to run. Hit'ud take us a while to get it ready."

Like Morgan, I wanted to hear how bad it sounded. But Nasty insisted it would take a lot of preparation to run it, on the order of days. This may have been true. I had no way of knowing. Freddy would probably know. He knew everything else having to do with engines and machines.

"It's got to be very loud," Steve Perri said.

"No, it ain't loud," Nasty corrected. "It makes a steady sound when it's going good." Perhaps he could tell we were skeptical. "It don't bother me at all, is all I'm saying, and when we get hit tuned up, she'll run all day long, flat out, so I'm just saying I'd knowed if hit was loud 'cause I've hyeared it."

I didn't like his choice of tense. I meant to ensure that this thing would never get tuned up, would never run smoothly or otherwise.


The meeting was over and we broke. Randy was getting into his Jeep Cherokee when I noticed a sticker on his bumper. I ♥ PADDLING. I figured it couldn't hurt to try to find common ground with him.

"Are you a paddler?" I asked, nodding at the bumper sticker.

"Yeah. Are you?" he asked without looking at me.

"Not kayaks. I've paddled a lot of the rivers down in the eastern part of the state. Canoes."

"I've run all of them, all the white water." He was cocky as hell.

"What's the best?" I stroked his considerable ego, humbled myself before him.

"The Nolichucky, hands down. The rest are dam-release."

"The water's pretty cold on tailwater streams," I said agreeably. "I fish."

"Well, there's that, the cold, but there's just nothing better than a river running free."

I had run the Nolichucky myself and I tossed that out. It was fantastic, being borne down the rushing river through the gorge past cliffs dripping with moss and ferns, spiked with white cedar. I was in complete agreement as far as the value of fishing, or paddling, a river that flows unimpeded, without the intervention of man.

We were getting somewhere here, so I pressed ahead. "Randy, the thing is, about the Nolichucky, it reminds me of the Appalachian Trail. I think that to me at least the impacts on the Trail with the mine working would be like building a bunch of houses in the Nolichucky Gorge. Or think of a factory that you would see for a mile of paddling where now there are only trees and rock."

Randy was not getting me. He turned his attention away.

I took one more stab. "I think it would be like putting a dam on the river."

He was making to leave, and now he stopped. "That would never happen," he said flatly. "The Nolichucky's all natural. It's protected." He didn't have it right, not exactly. But it is surrounded for much of its length by National Forest, and I took his general point.

*Bingo!* I wanted to shout. *That's it exactly.* But he was already pulling away.

# Chapter 15

Forrest called me. The state had come out with its mitigation proposal. It was easy to tell when Forrest was bearing good news. He opened with "Wake up, Jay, Mr. By-God Lawyer Man!" He was laughing.

"What's so funny?"

"Well, your buddy Charles Gardner has got this tiger by the tail and he can't figure out how to let go without getting hisself chawed up."

"What did he do?"

"He's just received the visual analysis put out by his own people, and . . . hold on." I could imagine Forrest leafing through pages of a briefing book. "I've got to read you this thing."

"What does it say?"

"It says . . ." He continued to search. Then he found it. "I kid you not, Lawyer Jay, two of the proposed mitigation measures in the state-commissioned visual evaluations are, brace yourself, number one, move the Appalachian Trail to another location." He paused and chortled. "Well," he said plainly, summarily, "we ain't doing that." I tried to join him in his revelry, but I was frankly in a minor state of shock. "And, number two, *reforest* the bald tops of the mountains to reduce visibility of the mine." I met his levity with silence. He felt the need to elaborate. "I'm not making this up."

"I'm not breathing, Forrest."

"I'm reading it. You think I could make that up? *Move* the Appalachian Trail? I'm reading it."

"It doesn't say that," I said a couple of times, a quiet mantra.

"Listen, it's a hoot."

"A hoot?!" I protested. "Explain that. If you and I get accused of launching an effort that results in moving the Appalachian Trail off the balds in the Roan . . ." I was stuttering, searching for words. "Do you have any idea how much time and money went into putting the Appalachian Trail right where it is?"

"No, no, listen," Forrest said, cutting me off gently, perhaps realizing I was in a delicate state. "We could not have asked for much better. In other words, what this little report is saying is, these impacts are so bad, so difficult to mitigate, and so unlikely to fit within the meaning of the statute, that you'd either have to move the Appalachian Trail or completely alter the terrain by planting a new forest between the mine and the Trail. Neither of those things is going to happen, Counselor. I think our point is amply made."

I had not thought of it that way. "You may be right. I hope so. Because either you're right and we're heroes, or the good folks running the United States Forest Service and the Department of the Interior are going to think this is a super idea, and they're going to try to pick up and move my favorite national park out of harm's way. In which case we might as well move to Argentina, because we're screwed."

I went walking to absorb what I had just been told. Everything is clearer, better understood, in the woods. I considered fishing, but a stiff wind was blowing and wind is the enemy of the fly caster. I set out for Big Horse Creek anyway, without a rod. Water helps. Biscuit and Maggie tore out on the logging road to catch up to me. Biscuit stayed right on my heel while Maggie ranged out ahead to make sure every whistle-pig and boomer knew exactly whom it was they were dealing with. I turned over the new information Forrest had shared. He was probably right. The proposals were so far-out, so unlikely to meet the approval of anyone at the state level, that maybe we had been done a favor by the landscape architects. But just hearing it said, knowing that it was in fixed, tangible media, *move the Appalachian Trail,* had given me what my mountain neighbors called the swimmy head. Morgan was going to have more than the swimmy head. Morgan might require medical intervention. I was scared to know what Wingfoot might do when he got wind of the proposals. When I got back to the house, I had an e-mail from Forrest.

*Jay, I see little impediment to implementing the mitigation proposal. All one needs to do is get the Congress to fund additional acquisition for the new Trail route. And no problem reforesting the Humps. That would only require forty or so years, a couple of million dollars and discovery of a nature-defying breed of tree. Despite evidence to the contrary, perhaps the balds were originally forested? Maybe the Overmountain Men deforested the balds for firewood when they convened for their march to Kings Mountain in 1780.*

I replied, *While we're at it, moving National Parks around to avoid embarrassments, do you think anybody would mind if we moved Great Smoky Mountains National Park to Kentucky? Right now it's too close to Dollywood. Or maybe we could give up on protecting the Trail experience altogether and move the Trail to Charlotte. That would give hikers much better access to chicken wings and smoothies.*

Forrest: *Jay, You must take into consideration the significant adverse impact the Trail would have on Charlotte, what with all those hippy back-packers walking through town. Do you want it to look like Hot Springs?*

As the summary of the mitigation proposal circulated through our group, everyone wanted in on this joke. I got an e-mail from Faye: *Jay, I will be away next week. If they move the Appalachian Trail while I'm gone, please leave me a note so I will know where they put it.*


The court-ordered mediation was scheduled for September 24 in Boone. Our mediator was Phil Ginn, a well-liked Boone lawyer and former Superior Court judge. I called Ollie to see if she knew anything about him. To my surprise she didn't know much.

"I'd say Paul knows him," she said.

"Think so?"

"Boone is not that big, and Paul is the biggest thing in Boone, so I'd say Paul's already bought him. Basically, I'd say we're killed."

After a lot of e-mailing back and forth, our team—Trip, Dan, Don,

Morgan, and I—decided to hike the Appalachian Trail across Hump Mountain the day before the mediation. Finally, weather permitting, Trip would see the quarry opening from Hump Mountain firsthand. Don, too. Dan had made a trip up over the summer and was the only member of the legal team to have seen it.

A couple of days before the mediation we got the formal documents with the proposed visual-mitigation measures from Hill Studio. I flipped through the stiff, expensive pages. What I saw was slick and professional and perfectly terrifying. The report considered five measures: *1. Alter the areas of proposed land use within the quarry. 2. Reduce the Phase 1 quarry area. 3. Relocation of the Appalachian Trail. 4. A considered process of rock extraction and planting. 5. Planting and camouflage measures.* Hill Studio recommended adopting all five of these measures in what they termed "a holistic approach."

Multicolored topographic maps with overlays showed where the most intense visual impacts would be as viewed from the Trail. A color code indicated intensity of exposure: red for high exposure, high intensity, all the way down to white, for not visible, out of view. The map made plain exactly what we believed: that of all the places on God's green earth Paul could have set up shop, with respect to the experience of a hiker using the nation's premier footpath, none could be worse than right where he landed. The map showed the proposed pit area as bright crimson, signifying highest visual intensity of impact from the Appalachian Trail. A few pages on, the proposal included computer-generated visuals of how the mine site might appear in the future as seen from the Trail. The proposals were bizarre: benches with troughs mined out in between. Vegetative screens forty feet wide, with irrigation systems intended to keep the plant life from drying out and dying. Page 16 offered a projection of what the quarry pit would look like with no modification strategies in place, then pages 17 and 18 illustrated the same view with modification strategies in place. The proposal amounted to a future of elaborate dirt and rock terraces carved into the mountainside. Bali came to mind.

By far the most alarming suggestion was illustrated on page 10 of the report. Here was the odious scheme for moving the Trail. In bloodless language the Hill team expressed it this way: *The idea of moving the Appalachian Trail is proposed to alter the cinematic experience of the hiker, and momentarily redirect views toward less-impacted parts of the landscape.*

We would carry the maps and landscape analysis with us on our hike. We would prepare for how to respond to each proposal in the mediation.

Trip called the day prior to the hike with bad news. He was not happy to have to convey it. The premediation hike was on, but . . .

"What is it? Just tell me. I can take it," I lied. I thought that perhaps by adopting a light tone, I could tailor this news. I was not at all sure I could take it, but I had no choice but to listen.

"Jay, we're going to look at it, the site from the Trail at Hump Mountain, and all the analysis and proposals," Trip began, and it seemed innocuous enough so far. "And if we see a way to modify the permit, if it looks possible, and if it's something Clark Stone would agree to, I will have to recommend that Morgan's group take it. It might be possible to get a modification that they can live with." Trip paused and his words settled in me, settled like gravel dust in the gills of a trout. There was more. "And there's a chance there is a modification proposal they can live with that you and Ollie can't."

These last words landed like big, looping gut punches.

I hung up the phone and headed out the door. I crashed into the woods. Biscuit turned back. I wasn't much company. I did not expect this. I was disappointed, then angry. Ollie, Faye, and I, Ashley and Freddy and Forrest and Ron, the Dog Town Bunch, had brought the fight this far. We had raised the money, filed the complaint. Put ourselves on the line. While the Southern Environmental Law Center was waiting for its board to meet and discuss the merits of the case, Paul Brown was ripping into the mountain and we were scrambling to get into court to stop him. The Appalachian Trail Conservancy was late joining the fight, too. Our fight. And now they might back a modification proposal that would pull the rug out from under the entire effort. Suddenly, I had a notion to call Wingfoot. He had warned me, right from the start, that the Appalachian Trail hierarchy might not have the stomach to fight this to the end. He had gone to war with them as an ally, and he had pushed against them as a foe. He had warned me, and he had told me that if they went wobbly, went soft, that he would step in as a plaintiff. I hiked to the top of the mountain. Calling Wingfoot would be like setting off a small nuclear device in the conservation community.

Against my nature, I decided to wait. To hold fire for now. I decided to roll the dice with Morgan and Don. I had this idea that when Trip saw the quarry opening from Hump Mountain, with Morgan and Don standing there, that Trip would see it the way I saw it. He would see that modification was not workable. That there was no way to hide the mistake that had been made, no way to hide a 151-acre open-pit mine from the Appalachian Trail on Hump Mountain, at Houston Ridge.

I felt sick all that night. When I woke up, I felt as if a dark curtain had been dropped across my face. Anxiety whistled through my chest. I felt like throwing up.

The next day was foggy, then hazy, with a good chance of afternoon thunderstorms. I couldn't eat. My clear head told me that if we failed to see the mine because of weather, we were going to lose. We would go into the mediation with a bias toward modification. I turned over the options. What kind of modification? No crushing on Sundays and holidays? No drilling at night? Maybe painting the conveyor tower moss green? Moving the Trail? It all struck me as absurd, a betrayal of the fight we had been waging. A betrayal of Ollie and of Faye. A betrayal of the thousands of hikers who had flooded the agency with their objections to the permit. After all of this, moving the Trail was on the table! My mind raced forward to all the possibilities, the so-called options, but always returned to this worst-case scenario, moving the Trail.

The team arrived for our hike and I struggled to keep my spirits up, to be a decent host. But part of me looked at my team sideways now. Suddenly they were not heroes to me, they were just regular fellows, good guys of course, but good guys doing their jobs. My darker angels howled that I was letting them off easy. They were weak! They were settlers and appeasers, *modifiers. Trail-movers!*

We set out walking. When we got up on top of the mountain, the weather was heavy and the sky serious. From the summit of Big Yellow we could see the mine through a cloak of damp haze, but barely. Seen this way, in this light from this vantage point, the quarry openings did not seem especially vast or dramatic, neither terribly significant nor especially adverse. We set out for the Hump. After thirty minutes we broke out into the open bald at Little Hump. And here came the sun to burn off the haze.

We could see the site clearly from Little Hump, where the Yellow Mountain Trail joins the Appalachian Trail. This was a good start. But, as I reiterated to anyone still listening, this was not the spot from which to measure the impacts. Still, I gave a little speech on how this was the first view of the quarry for the northbound Trail hiker. I wanted to emphasize that this view was the reward for climbing out of the woods on this side of Yellow Mountain Gap, that this view, this orientation, which put the quarry right in the notch between Houston Ridge and the east-facing slope of Big Yellow, framed, perfectly, the astonishing vista of Grandfather Mountain, one of the most dramatic scenes in all of Appalachia. I pressed my conviction that this first glimpse of the mine site set the stage for the impairment to the viewshed that would be reinforced numerous times as the hiker proceeded eastward, or northward, on the Trail, *toward Maine,* culminating at the summit of Hump Mountain, where the entire quarry site became visible and utterly dominated the experience of being on top of the mountain. My audience listened attentively. They were, in their own estimation, the converted. But I was not going to leave anything unsaid on this day. The stakes were too high, and modification was still on the table. When I was done, Trip said a few words. And Morgan. We all agreed that the plant area and the cleared area, the pit site, presented an ugly scar from Little Hump Mountain, but that if this had been the sole exposure to the site, we would have had no case to begin with. "It's bad," Trip said, "but it's probably too far away to build a case around."

"Come with me," I beckoned.

We carried on, over the grassy, mounded top of Little Hump, then down the rocky east face, into Bradley Gap. As we began the final campaign up the narrow spine of Hump Mountain, Big Hump as it is sometimes called, the blood in my head started to drum. This was it. They could laugh me out of here. All along, everyone in the fight from the Appalachian Trail angle had relied—at least initially—upon my word and Witt's pictures. Since becoming involved, Morgan had viewed the site a couple of times and told the tale admirably, and the Appalachian Trail Conservancy community had responded to his estimation of the damage by joining the case as co-plaintiffs. But the larger group, the public at large, and the Trailplace community were spurred to action based on Witt's pictures and the text I wrote with Wingfoot. The Southern Environmental Law Center and the National Parks Conservation Association had come all this way relying on Morgan, Witt, and Jay. Our credibility, my credibility, and the future of our case were now on the line.

At least the weather was, for once, cooperating. The sky was high and blue, with massive thunderheads hanging off to our east, dammed against the Blue Ridge, but standing off, giving us a classic summer afternoon.

We crested the last rise and there it was before us. The big, snaking scar tracking up Hartley Ridge this side of Bud Phillips's tree fields on Belview Mountain. The gouged-out hole at the test-blast site. The trucks and shovels winking in the watery sunshine.

I stared straight ahead, and for once I held my tongue. I gazed east and south, at countless acres of Appalachian wildlands, and for the only time I can recall, the mountains were dead to me. They were just props, presentation pieces establishing context in what I hoped would be our case. I awaited the verdict in a nervous trance.

Don spoke first. "You've got to be kidding." He emitted an involuntary snort that was neither laugh nor cough.

For just an instant my temperature spiked. His exclamation could mean one of two things. It could mean the impacts were appalling, horrific, or it could mean he was baffled that he had come all this way when the damage was so insignificant, so far away.

He quickly elaborated, allayed my worst fear. "It's worse than I thought," he said, flooded with the realization of what he beheld. "You have got to be kidding!"

Trip suppressed his own grimace. Then he spoke. But he didn't speak the way lawyers speak, with qualifications and stilted persuasion. He spoke as if he were on a hike with his buddies. "Ain't no way you can't hide that." My trance broke. I now turned to watch Trip as he took it in. I could see his mind churning, his eyes darting at the landscape laid before us, gathering information.

Now we were all seeing the same thing, and the walls between boss and intern, attorney and client, were dissolved. I wanted to grab Dan and shout, *They see it! They see it!*

The thousand feelings I'd had upon staring at this mess were echoed in rapid-fire.

Don could not get enough of the sight before him. "The pictures don't do it justice. The Trail couldn't face it more directly." He raised his hands to create a viewfinder framing a shot that took in the quarry site and the Trail. "Damn!" he shouted as he panned through the landscape with his crude tool.

Suddenly I revisited a thought I'd had on occasion: that Paul had done us a favor. He, or maybe it was Randy, had situated the pit nearly perfectly for building a case against it. Not only was it adjacent to a treeless bald, on the nearest facing ridge, which was rare in itself as the balds of the Southern Appalachians are rare as Lord God birds, but the quarry was sited right at the low end of one of the only *straight* sections of the Appalachian Trail. What were the chances of that? The Trail has only one or two bald, treeless, high-elevation, straight stretches and if you drew a line along the path from the summit, from the point where Houston Ridge intersects the Trail, and carried that line out, to where the ridge fell away into forest, that line would land right in the middle of the pit area, which is what the human eye did. It was as if the place-ment were intentional, designed to ignite head-scratching, fury. And litigation.

Dan pulled out the maps from his knapsack. We talked about the various modification proposals, brushed each off. We were teammates, again, and these guys were our starters, our moneymakers. Right there, on the ragged granite boulders at the summit of Hump Mountain, we tore into planning our defense. There had been some talk of moving the quarry pit lower on the hill, even closer to Faye's little farm. Closer to Ollie's. Randy had wondered if such a repositioning might not move the pit out of the viewshed from the Trail. I was against the proposal on principle, and looking at it from here, one clearly saw that a lower pit would not afford any real protection for the Trail. Plus, Paul thought the best rock was up high on Belview. At the top. Now Don and Trip took off walking the ridge, to replicate the experience of the typical northbound hiker. We all followed, walking that nearly straight line toward the pit. I read aloud from page 10 of the landscape plan. *The idea of moving the Appalachian Trail is proposed to alter the cinematic experience of the hiker, and momentarily redirect views toward less-impacted parts of the landscape.* This was the elephant in the room: relocation of the Appalachian Trail. We walked off the proposal. We were experts after all, the very owners of this public resource. And now Morgan rejected the proposal. Roundly. We all agreed that even a slight adjustment of the Trail off the ridgeline to the north would derogate the value of the trail experience, sacrificing the views of Grandfather and Linville Gorge and Mt. Mitchell. Replacing 360-degree views with 180-degree views would reduce the experience by half, if one were confined to cold numbers.

Just like that, we were united. We had been tested, our bond had been, and now it was like steel.

As younger men working for the Tennessee nonprofit Save Our Cumberland Mountains, Trip and Don had cut their teeth, laid the groundwork for their present careers. Now they were leaders, veterans of the conservation wars, and they had an efficient language for setting up opposition arguments, then knocking them down. Now, as we stared off into the distances, they compared the stage of this fight to others they had been in. They were full of battle plans and strategies.

I was content to let it flow, the talk, the plans. It was music. I loved everybody. The earth was shifting under my feet as we walked back home. The mountains were restored to their splendor, the summer light illuminating the folds and setting the grasses ablaze. I was not going to be alone on this ever again. If we won, there would be a lot of winners. And if we lost, I would just be one of a multitude who would feel it intensely. This, in some ways, was all I had wanted for a long time. There was no more talk of modification on the way back to Big Yellow. There was talk of digging in. Of standing our ground. Of getting into court—a real court—if that was what it was going to take.

The following morning I picked up Ollie and Faye and we drove to

Boone. Ollie wore what looked like new tennis shoes. They were spotless. The rainy, cool morning couldn't dent my mood. I was excited. It could all end today. Our position was clear and left little room for discussion. Perhaps seeing our united front, Paul would move to settle with the state. The state could offer a buyout. Charles would not have to admit an error in permitting, and Paul could be covered for his investment. Or Paul could dig in. He had his own reason to be confident. He had whipped us pretty good before the administrative law judge. He had in his pocket a solid reversal stating that Charles did not have the authority to revoke his permit. Would he overreach? Or was he ready to put Belview Mountain in his rearview mirror?

The mediation was held in a sterile hotel conference room across a parking lot from a shopping center. The hallway was crowded with the cast of characters who had become part of the scenery of my life: Charles, Mel Nevils, Jim Simons. Jim Gulick, Forrest, Ron, Ollie, Faye, Trip, Morgan, Don. Dan. Paul. A young attorney from Raleigh named A. Bartlett White was representing Paul on this day. No sign of Harold Berry, the Weasel.

We sat around a large table under a bank of fluorescent lights, awaiting instructions from Judge Ginn.

Ollie passed me a note. *Where's the Bald Eagle?*

It was curious. No Randy.

Judge Ginn asked each participant to introduce himself or herself. Faye spoke clearly, without any reticence. "I'm Faye Williams and I am the closest neighbor to the crusher. I had a constitutional right to a public hearing before this permit was issued. It's not fair and I think it breaks the law." She couldn't have said it better if the Heel Hound had written it out. When it was Paul's turn, he said, "My name is Paul Brown and I own Clark Stone Company. And I think this whole thing is ridiculous."

For the first part of the session it seemed as if a buyout were going to happen. Lawyer White said, "My client is at the end of his rope. He has had it."

Paul spoke for himself, ignoring his counsel's suggestion that he remain silent. "I ain't never done nothing wrong. I ain't a criminal. All I want is my money." As self-congratulation, this was pretty faint praise.

Most of the morning we spent divided into two groups, in two separate rooms, while Judge Ginn trotted back and forth between the rooms, offering threads of hope coming from the opposition. Clark Stone found the proposed modifications in the visual analysis impossible to meet. The thin strips of vegetation between the quarried pits would die. Not enough water was on the mountain to keep strips of forest alive if left perched on forty-foot-wide rocky benches. And digging behind these vegetated strips would be too dangerous. The benches would be unstable and might fall in on the workers. As Ginn outlined Paul's objection to the modification proposal, this fear of death from the unorthodox pit design, Ollie scratched me a note. *Poor Trackhoe Daddy!*

The next time Ginn came to us, he surprised us with his report and a question. Could Jim Gulick come up with a number if settlement was on the table? Had the state had time to go through the evidence Paul had presented to the state? The evidence of Paul's investment?

Here Jim Gulick gave us some insight into his working relationship with Paul. "Clark Stone Company has presented a shoebox with receipts in it. It has been difficult for us to ascertain Mr. Brown's level of investment."

Ollie slapped me on the leg. The shoebox! We had heard about Paul's accounting method from Dan, from the deposition. I dared a glance her way. She would not look at me, staring straight ahead, lest looking to her right, even for a second, would reveal us for what we were, schoolkids escaping the wrath of the teacher. We were to learn that Paul had had difficulty coming up with proof of his investment in the Putnam Mine. A note in the shoebox showed the lease payments for the Big Dog, the big shovel. We had learned this, too, in the deposition. There were receipts for flowers bought for a receptionist. Some restaurant receipts. Payroll records from the Linville quarry. But, as Paul would say, "I asked the girl that works for me to put together everything I have in that thing, and put it in a shoebox, and this is all she come up with."

After a recess, and some friendly banter in the hallway, it became clear that Paul was trying Judge Ginn's patience. Just before the break for lunch, the mediator reported to us the following: "Mr. Brown's lawyers are having a hard time with their client." He laughed softly. "Mr. Brown has dug in."

And that was it, for we, too, had dug in. Morgan answered a couple of questions from Ginn, making it clear that Morgan saw no room for compromise. We were not going to consider moving the Appalachian Trail, so there would be no deal on this day.

After the mediation failure, we all gathered in the hallway and made small talk with the opposition and the folks from the state office. I shook Paul's hand and we commiserated over how difficult it was to get anything done in this world without lawyers involved. He said, "Son, mine's bleeding me dry. I hope yours ain't as high." I wanted to tell him that mine were free, mostly, but I decided not to antagonize him. Ollie, Faye, and I went to get a sandwich. We sat on the side of Highway 105 in a cool rain. But the rain couldn't touch us. We were elated. Morgan hadn't folded; he had taken a firm stance and stuck with it, while Paul was left flailing for a solution. Settlement was still on the table, and it appeared Paul could be bought, if only he could show his investment, demonstrate to the state his "losses." The restaurant where we ate was just downhill from Vulcan Materials' Boone Quarry. Every time a gravel truck passed, which was every few minutes, the bridge over the Watauga River thrummed and a raft of cold wind bore down on us, lifting napkins and blowing the wet grass, reminding us of all that was at stake.

With settlement talks at a standstill, and the Mining Commission hearing fast approaching, I peppered Dan and Trip with my own oral-argument suggestions. Which way to go? Should we make Charles out to be a hero, a selfless public servant who took a bold risk in standing up to the industry he regulates by revoking the permit? The commission was, after all, a creation of the state, of the agency, so tying Charles's heroism to their own role in this might be winning. We could laud Charles as that rare public official who admitted a mistake and now must be allowed to fix it. *Why, Charles Gardner is restoring the faith the public puts in their leaders!* we might say, although we might have to sedate Ron Howell if we chose to go that route. I wondered if we could make the commissioners see that siding with Paul would be tantamount to cutting Charles off at the knees; it would eviscerate the agency—of which the commission was technically a part. Next, I thought we ought to stress the unique pickle we had here. All along we had heard that the state feared revoking this permit because it might set a precedent that sloppily issued permits were open to challenge and reversal. The attorney general's office envisioned adjoining landowners lining up crying foul on quarries and landfills from the mountains to the sea. I had come to suspect that the agency had issued more than one permit with little scrutiny. The last thing the state wanted was to admit its incompetence in a way that invited years of challenges to its exercise of discretion in other locations. But so far, revoking this permit had not set off a chain of challenges to other quarry permits. Why? Because no other quarry anywhere in the state was located so near to a popular national park.

I was full of ideas. The frustrated attorney in me came out. I urged Trip to say *national park* as many times as possible. *You might say, "Most people have no idea that the Appalachian Trail is a national park, just like Yosemite. Just like Yellowstone National Park and Grand Canyon National Park."*

Trip is famous for his pretrial preparation. As our case proceeded, I was reminded over and over by members of the legal community that our little group had secured the services of the best attorney working on environmental issues in the South. Trip was admired far and wide for his wisdom, his temperament, and his encyclopedic knowledge of the law. But he also possessed an intangible quality that made judges, arbiters, even opponents, like him. His reputation and his skill made him an ideal advocate, and he certainly didn't need any prodding from me to perform at the highest level, but I was unable to sit on the sidelines. My suggestions might have been presumptuous and possibly an unwelcome distraction. But I was done with worrying too much about how I was perceived. The state was losing this case, losing the defense of the revocation. Judge Owens-Lassiter had struck a blow that had left us staggered. If the settlement talks failed and we then lost before the Mining Commission, nothing would stop Paul from turning on the drills, packing the blast holes, and starting to bring the mountain down. I would not be able to forgive myself if I left any stone unturned, so I worked. Not with Trip, he didn't have time for that, but on a parallel track. And I tried to make myself useful. The alternative was to go slowly out of my mind.

Dan and I sat down in his office one final time to go over each mining commissioner to see what we could puzzle out. Whom could we count on to back the revocation and who was a gravel-head? Our first count had us losing 6–3. This was a stark realization, too stark, so we counted again. Then again. We evaluated each commissioner, then we redid our tally. Then we took them out of order, just to stay fresh. But any way we cut it, the result came out the same. A 6–3 loss seemed the likely outcome. Of course a loss of this magnitude would fulfill Charles's prophecy. *I can revoke the permit, Jay, but the Mining Commission will never stand for it. They'll block it.* His words rang in my ears.

Trip made his own notes on each commissioner before the hearing. He ran down a sheet of the names and jotted remarks, prompts to himself. Beside each name, he added his guess at his or her vote. For Leo Greene, he jotted *engineer, from Wilson, NC. Likely to vote no.* For John Bratton: *Wake Stone Pres. Outstanding citizen. Speculate will vote no.* Trip's count had us losing 5–4, not accounting for any absences on the day of the hearing. Forrest did not traffic in predictions. But Ron did. "We're going to lose," he told me. "Which is what Charles wants. Charles doesn't want to win, and when he loses, they'll turn on that crusher the next day. That's what Charles wants and that's what he'll get." Once again, we faced a day of reckoning. Coming off the loss before the administrative law judge, if we lost before the Mining Commission, we would be out of heart. I feared our team—having just come together as never before—would break apart. It would be enormously difficult to raise any more money to pay Forrest and Ron, for one. Also, if we lost, we would lose our partnership with the state, with Jim Gulick and with Charles, such as it was. We would once again be adverse to the state, to the Division of Land Resources and the office of the attorney general. Ollie would bear it. She had already told me she and Curly were making their plans assuming we would lose. Curly had applied for a job with a trucking outfit down in Kernersville, three hours to the east. The job came with generous benefits, which would help them with Ashley's medical bills. Freddy had heard a rumor that Paul might come around and wave some hush money their way, the way he did with Tony. I told Ollie that if Paul did that, if he made an offer to buy them out, they should take it. Ashley's health was fragile. And her father was agitating, seeming to want another confrontation. He had taken to driving back and forth in front of their house on his motorcycle. He called the house over and over, trying to spark a fight with Ollie, or with Freddy. Leaving Dog Town might be the best thing for them.

I drove down the mountain to attend the hearing in Raleigh. By the time I hit Chapel Hill, we already had bad news. We learned that one of Trip's *likely yes* votes, and one of Dan's *solid yes* votes, would not attend the hearing. Word was Commissioner Turner was on a sailing trip. A sailing trip! I was furious at Ryan Turner, whom I had never even heard of before this started. But all of this had become personal, these names and faces who would decide our fate. *Who the hell goes on a sailing trip when they ought to be sitting in a dingy hearing room waging a losing effort to protect a little dirt path!* Witt asked rhetorically. That put us down 5–3 by Trip's count, 6–2 by Dan's. I felt as if I were driving into the teeth of a storm. Or worse, presenting myself for a public flogging. I had the swimmy head real bad.

I met Trip, Dan, and Forrest in front of the Archdale Building. Trip huddled briefly with Forrest and Jim Gulick, then we all went inside. I'd grown to hate this building with increasing passion. I hated its dull modern shape. Its unadorned facade and lack of windows. Its gummy smell and the sticky feel of the sealed bricks in the dark lobby.

The hearing room stood at the end of the long, narrow hall on the ground level. The room was, if anything, more dispiriting than the lobby. Stained carpet, stained ceiling, a timeworn map of the state hanging off-center on the near wall. The far wall sported the portraits of each head of the agency. The earliest of these were oil paintings, while the latest, of Wayne McDevitt and Bill Holman, were photographs that looked like the shots they do at the local fire stations for their fund-raisers. The colors a bit too bright. The background an exercise in studied fakery.

Paul arrived. He looked the way I felt. He looked as if he had been dead for a while. For a week. The skin on his face was chalky and sagged for the floor. He had his hands stuck down in his pockets like a sore kid.

Lucius Pullen, the lobbyist for the mining industry, stepped through the throng of reporters and members of the conservation community to shake my hand. He was in a fine mood. Said he had just discovered that my brother's wife was expecting another child and wanted to make sure there were no hard feelings over all this legal mess. I assured him that I did not harbor any ill feelings over where the case had taken us, and then Mr. Pullen, L-U-C-I-U-S, and I made our polite retreats. All the lawyers greeted each other. Charles took his seat. He nodded at me, and I at him. I was done trying to figure him out.

The commissioners took their places.

So there they were. Regular sorts. Sitting in big swivel chairs. Leo Greene. And John Bratton, the president of Wake Stone Company. Somehow it was comforting to see them in their seats. I thought they would be bigger. They looked ordinary. Two seats were vacant, our sailing commissioner's, and that of Howard Nye, one of Trip's *likely no* votes, a welcome counterbalance to the absence of one of our yes votes. Now here came Ben Robinson. I had done a little research on Commissioner Robinson. He hailed from Spruce Pine, not twenty miles from Dog Town. He worked in the mining industry, and there was every reason to believe that he knew Paul. He entered the hearing room last, and all eyes watched as his stooped figure traversed the stained carpet, dragging a little wheeled cart with his very breath, a tank of oxygen, trailing him. Had a life in mining done this to him? A life spent inhaling clouds of rock dust? It was too late for me to find out the answer to the question. Maybe he had been a smoker.

The hearing room was packed. Lobbyists from the environmental community and their counterparts in the mining community were out in force. Activists, miners, and curious downtown attorneys clogged the aisles, eager to see Trip argue the weighty matter. Many of the Division of Land Resources staff took seats. Reporters from the state's largest-circulation papers readied their pens.

Hugh Franklin, the chair of the commission, brought the assembly to order, and the first words out of his mouth gave us reason to hope. "Today we are here to weigh the interests of an individual, a businessman, against the public's interest, the national interest."

This was the most beneficial framing of the issue we could have hoped for. All along we had tried to stress that Paul's interests shouldn't be favored over Ollie's. That Nasty's job was not more important than Faye's ability to remain in her home. That Paul's right to make a dollar per ton of crush run should not supersede the investment the US taxpayers had made in the Appalachian National Scenic Trail. Now Trip would not have to labor so mightily to make the point. The chair of the commission had just done it eloquently.

First up, the state would make its case. Jim Gulick argued for Charles's authority to issue, deny, and revoke permits. The commissioners interrupted him a time or two, but mostly Jim gave an unimpeded if dry presentation of the process the state followed in issuing, and then revoking, mining permit 06-09.

Now it was Trip's turn. He was swimming hard against the tide, but he explained that this permit would never have been issued if Ollie and Faye had gotten notice of their rights to a public hearing before the permit went through. I was surprised. Notice had been the centerpiece of Ron's complaint before the Southern Environmental Law Center became the lead attorney for the intervenors, but Ron felt, and I did, that Trip preferred the environmental angle, the "significant adverse effects on the purpose" of the Trail argument, but now Trip was channeling the complaint. Paul's side objected heartily. After all, the administrative law judge had explicitly excluded discussion of our notice issue. But the commissioners weren't judges, they were political appointees, and the rules of civil procedure did not apply in the same way they would in a courtroom. The commissioners were as interested as any layperson would be in how this thing got issued in the first place. So just as easily as the administrative law judge had barred us from raising notice, the members of the Mining Commission allowed us to bring it in.

Trip raced ahead, integrating a couple of my favorite arguments into his. The uniqueness of the situation. The lauding of Charles for the difficult decision he had made.

A. Bartlett White then rose to argue for Paul. He had barely uttered a syllable before one of the commissioners asked for a clarification, an explanation. Commissioner George Autry, the newest commissioner, and the youngest, said, "You're not suggesting that once the horse leaves the barn the state is powerless to correct an error, are you? And everybody has to live with the results of that error?" He questioned the core premise of the administrative law judge's ruling against us.

Commissioner Autry was a friend of mine from childhood. Our fathers were hunting buddies and our mothers were friends and companions. When his name appeared on a list of potential additions to the Mining Commission, I was pleased but I kept my mouth shut. I didn't want to put him in an awkward position should he end up on the commission, nor did I want him to have to forgo an opportunity to serve by sharing with him all the details of the matter. I knew that Paul had friends on the commission, business associates, even, so I wasn't concerned that any lines were being crossed on my end. All commissioners have an opportunity to recuse themselves if they feel they cannot make a decision based solely upon the merits.

A. Bartlett White looked flummoxed. Suddenly, the cocksure attorney was replaced by a defensive, plodding advocate.

But the commissioners were hard on Trip, too. Hugh Franklin asked Trip why the commission ought to listen to arguments that a prior judge said were not relevant or, worse, excluded. Trip labored to explain that it was our position that Judge Owens-Lassiter was in error when she excluded our notice claim, and that the commission ought not be bound by her faulty theorizing. Neither side seemed to sway the panel or be able to piece together a winning narrative.

Then a break came our way. In prefacing a remark, Commissioner Leo Greene signaled his intention to uphold Charles: "I know where I'm going on this." I looked at Dan as he hung on the commissioner's words. "Of course the state has the authority to do what it did," he said, as a mere aside, "but I just want to clear up a thing or two. . . ."

His preface, his toss-away aside, had the force of a persuasive tidal wave.

Dan was furiously scribbling in his notepad. Leo Greene, one of the commissioners Dan and I thought would certainly swing to Paul, and one of Trip's no votes, had signaled that he was going to uphold Charles, uphold the revocation. Suddenly we were only losing 4–3.

By a voice vote that went around the horseshoe table, the Mining Commission reversed Melissa Owens-Lassiter's ruling and upheld Charles's revocation of the Putnam Mine permit. And it wasn't even close. We won by a vote of 6–1. The only commissioner we lost was Ben Robinson, who dropped the mouthpiece on his breathing apparatus to cast the lone dissenting vote.

Following the vote, our team streamed out the narrow brick hallway, out into bright sunshine. Trip received his applause and our adulation with laudable equanimity. Lucius Pullen clasped me on the shoulder and predicted we would meet again. All the well-wishers and environmental-community insiders crowded around us to bask in the glow coming off Trip. He leaned over to me and balled his fist. "I should have taken the bet," he said. From day one, Ron had felt we would lose before the Mining Commission. He'd even offered odds on it, would have bet against us. As much as I hated to admit it, I had been convinced, too. But Trip had seen a way to victory. His notes, his projected votes, were recorded so that he might prepare in the face of insurmountable odds. But he had suspected all along that he could turn Bratton. Could build on Franklin's likely yes vote. That he and Jim Gulick, converging from two vantage points, could. And now Trip wished he'd taken Ron's bet.

Just like that the tables had turned again. The justice of our case, the righteousness of our cause, became so clear again. *Of course the state has the authority to correct its mistakes. It would be madness to make a national park suffer the consequences of a bureaucratic mistake—or a fraud scheme—out in a far corner of the state.*

Now Paul would have to weigh whether he wanted to spend enormous sums of money fighting this in the courts from a defensive crouch.

Because now he was losing. The more I walked this new ground, the better it felt. Paul and his legal team would have an uphill climb if they opted to appeal the loss to the Superior Court. The state's hand had been strengthened exponentially by the Mining Commission ruling. Charles's authority to revoke the permit had been upheld, and that revocation meant we would all remain on the same team for the duration of the case. Paul would have his high-priced attorneys, A. Bartlett White, Harold Berry, and his powerful Raleigh law firm, but we had the state's lawyers on our side, the Department of Justice, sitting alongside Trip and Forrest and the Heel Hound of the Mountains. An unconventional dream team, but not one you would trade.

The win had other important implications. I would now be able to raise additional funds to pay off some debts to Forrest and Ron without further impoverishing myself. Everybody wants to back the winner. It would be hard to overstate the importance of what had taken place on this day in the dingy hearing room on the ground floor of the Archdale Building. The Southern Environmental Law Center now had their precedent-setting case. The state had successfully revoked a permit with the intervening support from Trip's firm. The agency had flexed its authority to correct a mistake. That was good news without qualification. But the stakes were now raised. Our little fight was now a big deal with the potential to become a landmark case, for if a court down the road reversed this ruling and stripped the state of its authority so powerfully ratified by its own commission on this day, it would turn the law on its head, and not just in the area of environmental protection, but across a broad range of issues. Big cases have the potential to make good law or bad. For this reason Trip was now more eager than ever to go into court on our behalf and argue for the state's broad authority and its duty to correct mistakes that it makes—even or especially after expenditures have been made in reliance on a permitting decision.

I called Ollie and told her the news. I made her vow that we would now cease referring to the *Putnam Mine* and henceforth speak only of the *once-proposed site,* because, all of a sudden, there was no Putnam Mine.

# Chapter 16

E-mail from Ashley:

> Jay, You need to get your ass back to the mountain!! Things are NOT good. Paul, James and Richard have been squirrel hunting. A rock tester was up there yesterday (this is confirmed) taking rock samples. James and Richard are drilling all over the side of the mountain and didn't come off until after dark last night. The gate at Sawdust has been opened all week. Ashley

On October 19, Paul Brown informed Jim Gulick and Charles that he would appeal the Mining Commission decision to the Wake County Superior Court, and that Clark Stone Company intended to explore prospects for quarrying on the backside of the mountain, out of view of the Appalachian Trail.

Foolishly I had held out hope that Paul would seek the easier route and pursue a settlement. Once again I had underestimated Paul's staying power, his stubborn resolve to crush rock, while Ollie had read him right.

I drove to Chapel Hill to have lunch with Trip. Trip didn't put much stock in the noises about moving the operations to the backside of the mountain. He thought that even if Paul found rock and moved the pit to the backside, he would still want to crush the stone on the front, where they had installed all their equipment.

"But," I protested, "that would leave almost all of the acoustic impacts on the front side. And that would still be significant and adverse."

"Maybe," Trip said. "You would move the drilling and the blasting to the back, so those two impacts would be cured."

"I hope you're just playing devil's advocate."

"I'm being a lawyer."

If Paul moved the pit to the backside of the mountain and was permitted to leave all the crushing operation on the front, hovering outside Faye's windows, and looming high above Ollie's, and facing directly at the Trail, then Paul would have won. He would save himself hundreds of thousands of dollars and still be operating just about where he set out to. He would have won his game of chicken, his dare, the gambit to install as much of his equipment as fast as he could. Losers would include the Appalachian Trail, Ollie, and Faye. And me.

I had a lot of questions for Trip. "Would they need a new permit, or would this be a modification of the old permit?"

"There is no old permit. The revocation was upheld."

"Right. Why would Charles issue them a new permit for the back side after all of this? At what point does an operation, an operator, become poison?"

I found I could not eat when talking about the case. Trip spoke between bites of his lunch. "Remember Charles is an industry guy. Ron Howell has that right. Charles is geared to keep those folks happy. I'm not sure what convinced him to revoke the permit, the videotape maybe, or the politics in Raleigh, or maybe he really saw the operation as a violation of the act. It's hard to say. It's just out of character for DENR to do what they did, and my guess is that he would still like to find a way to appease the mining industry." It was never encouraging to see Trip as mystified as I was.

"Lucius Pullen," I said, pretty sure that I had nailed it.

"I'm sure he's hearing from Lucius Pullen and Vulcan Materials and Martin Marietta. That's the crowd he usually bakes bread for."

"Nice one."

Trip smiled. He was always smiling.

"But we would still have a case," I pressed. "We would allege that the impacts on the Trail from the primary crusher jaw violate the act. The noise. The clearing for the physical plant alone is—well, you know how big it is."

"Charles gets to decide what violates the act," Trip said evenly. "The Mining Commission strengthened his hand." Trip finished his sandwich.

I tried to think of things besides Paul to discuss. "What do you think Morgan would say about crushing on the front?"

"I don't know. Morgan would want to do some analysis from the Trail, I'm sure."

"*Analysis?* You can be the one to tell Ollie that."

"It wouldn't solve all of Ollie's problems," Trip said frankly.

"And the noise impacts would still ruin the experience of being on the Trail. Right now there is *no* noise. Any industrial noise is going to be significant."

"You've convinced me, Counselor."

"I know. I just like to hear people say they're convinced. I don't know why. Say it one more time."

"It would still be significant."

Now we had this to worry about. The same mine in a different configuration. In our favor was that moving the pit to the back side would require a new permit. Under the new, improved Mining Act, Clark Stone would have to notify a slew of adjoining landowners. This time there would be public hearings *before* any permit was issued. The state was not likely to make that mistake ever again. I felt pretty sure we could drum up a noisy group to fight any plan Paul could propose. And there was this: Paul might encounter a whole new universe of vocal opposition to any new plan. My initial analysis satisfied me that moving the site to the back side of Belview would point it directly at Grandfather Mountain, one of the most visited scenic areas in the South. That would pit Paul against Hugh Morton, owner of Grandfather Mountain and one of the most beloved figures in the state, and against the tens of thousands of tourists who take in the views from Morton's swinging bridge attraction.

Even without the Grandfather Mountain defense, our side would have ammunition in a new permit review. Charles was on the record deferring to Pam Underhill, and he would be compelled to rely heavily on the Appalachian Trail Conservancy's position on visual and acoustic impacts from the Trail side. Also in our favor, Paul was now a lightning rod for controversy. We, the scrappy Dog Town Bunch, had sharpened our messaging, developed some public-relations skills. We had made public Paul's citation for Mining Without a Permit. Word was now out about the debacle up Cranberry Creek, the road Paul's crew pushed up the streambed of a designated trout stream. Everyone in the community now knew he and Randy had lost the Putnam Mine permit for violations of the act, earning membership in an exclusive club. If Clark Stone was not now considered a "bad actor," who was?

But the other fallout from the commission ruling was something I had not counted on. As Trip explained, the Mining Commission hearing had strengthened Charles's hand enormously. His credibility with the body established to perform oversight was at a new high. That meant that if he wanted to issue a permit for the back side—after a couple of public hearings—he did not need to fear any internal division. He had been anointed Charles the Unarbitrary. Charles the Uncapricious. The Fair One.

Because of the threat of the new permit application, our celebration over the Mining Commission ruling was short-lived. After a week or so of patting ourselves on the back, we returned to a war footing. We were going to court on Paul's appeal, and we were still in the lawsuing business. We had tasted victory, and now we wanted nothing less than ratification of everything we had been fighting for.

While I was worrying about the new proposal to mine the back side of the mountain, the Appalachian Trail Conservancy's board was adopting a new policy. Morgan sent it to me in an e-mail. In relevant part, the new policy read, *ATC seeks to avoid, minimize, or eliminate the visual and aural impacts upon those [previously listed] resources caused by developments within the A.T. corridor and on adjacent lands in the vicinity of the corridor and will support any and all measures to do so.*

Our case had lit a fire in the venerable old body. This move, this new language, was not only the right thing to do, it spoke of the tenuous position of the Trail at the dawn of a new century. The original vision of the founders, the very idea of a wilderness walk in the woods so near to the busy cities of the eastern seaboard, was imperiled as the lands the Trail traversed were "discovered" by resort developers. Big land companies had figured it out: by following the route of the Appalachian Trail, or the Blue Ridge Parkway, or by hugging the boundaries of Yellowstone, they could parlay the goodwill of these national treasures into marketing gold. The very things that made the Trail experience special—the views, the quiet remove from civilization—were suddenly prized in a second-home real estate market that placed a premium on those values. The collision was inevitable, and with its updated policy statement the Trail Conservancy seemed to be putting itself on a new, more aggressive footing to face the challenge. I was pleased that our case had played a part in the evolution of attitude, served as a wake-up call, if you will, for the managers of the Trail, but I was sobered knowing that the clashes were likely to be painful, and unending.

One morning Ollie called, woke me up. She is an early riser. "Get down here."

"What. Why?"

"We got us a dead squirrel."

"Is it Paul or is it Nasty?" I guessed, figuring I was likely to be close. Paul was in his midseventies.

"No, sleepyhead. It's a damn flying squirrel. You got to come see this thing, and I ain't a-jokin'."

I threw on my clothes and tore down the mountain. Pulled up at Ollie's. "Let's see it."

Ollie took me under the house, where she had tossed the lifeless critter off the deck.

"What do you make of it?" she asked.

"Where did it come from?"

"Zeka dragged it in."

282

Zeka the cat.

I bent over and lifted a front paw of the decedent to reveal a web of skin running between its abdomen and its "wrist." This was the "wing" that allowed the squirrel to glide through the air, or "fly." Western North Carolina has two types of flying squirrel. The common southern, and the Carolina northern. The common southern is, well, more common, able to live in forests throughout the South. The Carolina northern flying squirrel lives only in the Southern Appalachians, and only at high elevation, where spruce-fir or hemlock forest meets northern hardwoods. With only eight known populations in the state, the gliding rodent earned in 1985 a place on the federal Endangered Species List. Did Zeka climb up onto the mountain to a red-spruce grove and bring this little fellow home? Or did it wander down toward the bright lights of Cranberry Gap and get jumped by a valleywise feline?

I didn't have to tell Ollie that if there were Carolina northern flying squirrels on Belview Mountain, Paul was finished. Was it possible that after meeting the Virginia big-eared bat head-on in the Cranberry iron mine, Paul had once again encroached on the habitat of a listed species?

"What are we going to do?" Ashley asked from up on the deck where she had remained. Ashley was not happy. "If it's endangered, is the federal government going to take my cats to Guantánamo Bay? I say we bury it."

"They are not going to take the cats," I said with authority ungrounded in any knowledge. It seemed an important time to lend assurance even if I had to fake it.

"All I'm saying," Ashley assured me, "is if the federal government takes my cats into custody, I'm going to blame you. Understand?"

"You've made yourself clear."

"Well," Ollie said, "what the hell are we going to do with the poor little feller?"

From inside his shop, Freddy hollered either a menu selection or a suggestion: "Stew!"

I tried to convey gravity. "We're going to call a biologist at the state and find out which guy this is. Common or northern. This is pretty important."

"I mean, what are we going to do with the body?" Ollie said.

Ashley had an idea that seemed sensible. "Let's put him in the freezer."

I held up my hands to end the discussion. "Let's do this. I'm going to take some measurements, some notes, and I'm going to call a biologist. And then I'm going to step out of this conversation. And when I leave, you're going to do whatever you want to do with the body. The evidence. But I suggest that we drop this as a topic of conversation. You are not going to tell me what you do with the squirrel. Because none of us wants to go to jail. Right? Everyone needs to have plausible deniability."

I made my calls, located the appropriate expert at the Wildlife Resources Commission. I took notes and did a quick examination. I measured the rear foot and I checked the base of the ventral hairs, those on the belly. I did not measure the baculum, the penis bone. I confess I did not know how to tell if there was a penis bone, and given that the other tests seemed conclusive, I rested my case. Even if we were at the low end of the elevation models for occurrence of *Glaucomys sabrinus,* by information and belief what the cat dragged in on this day was an endangered Carolina northern flying squirrel. I suspected that if we needed to enlist the sacrificial mammal in our fight to rid ourselves of Paul and his crusher, if it ever came to that, our furry friend might be available to make a cameo appearance. Not that I knew that to be true.

I was snowed in one day that winter, sitting at the window, watching the tiny flakes swirl around, when the phone rang.

"I'm Ken Hubbard," said the man on the line. "I've got big trouble over here on the north side of Beech Mountain, and I've heard you are the one who can help me."

Owing to the press the case had attracted, my name was now appearing on lists of environmental fund-raisers and strategists. I had been contacted about stopping a landfill in Holly Springs and about raising money to fight an asphalt plant. Another quarry issue was brewing in the Piedmont, and a medical-waste incinerator near Chapel Hill was spewing mercury into the fair Carolina skies, far in excess of its permitted levels. My e-mail in-box was frequented with more crimes against nature than a man could possibly turn his attention to.

"Tell me your story," I said.

Mr. Hubbard's problem was windmills. Big windmills.

The Tennessee Valley Authority is the nation's largest producer of power. The TVA, as it is called, was established in the 1930s to extend the wonder of electrification and guide economic development throughout the vast middle part of the Tennessee country and into Alabama, Mississippi, and Kentucky and small slivers of western North Carolina. It enjoys quasi-agency authority. From its inception, the TVA seized farmland and entire towns throughout the Tennessee Valley, using the power of eminent domain. It dammed rivers, flooding productive farmland for hydroelectric power, and built coal-fired power plants to extend affordable electricity throughout a poor, rural part of the country. In the 1940s and 1950s the TVA supplied the power needed for the enrichment of uranium, at the Oak Ridge National Laboratory, as part of the effort to build the first generation of nuclear weapons. Despite the fact that the TVA was set up to improve the lives of the forgotten people of the poorest part of the country, the heavy-handed land-condemnation drive earned the agency the enduring enmity of many. The very name, the initials, have become shorthand for all-powerful governmental intrusion in Appalachia. Fiercely independent mountain people cuss the mighty agency freely and often, while environmentalists decry its woeful record of Clean Air Act violations and the wholesale alteration of vast river systems. Now the TVA was proposing a wind farm on a large tract of land along the Tennessee–North Carolina border, a tentative venture into the nascent sector of alternative energy generation. Their study proposal envisioned fourteen thirty-six-story-tall windmills strung along a prominent—and windy—ridgeline. Kenneth Hubbard wanted to stop them before they dug a spade of dirt.

"On what grounds?" I asked.

"First, I should say I live right at the base of the mountain and it will ruin my view. That's for one thing." But that was just one of his objections. Areas of high winds often correlate with flyways. Hubbard could cite statistics of bird mortality at other wind installations from New Hampshire to California. "They are like blenders in the sky," he said.

"I doubt the TVA will find that compelling." I sounded more like a hardened cynic than I actually was. I'd attempted to channel Trip's calm demeanor, Forrest's wry take, but it had come out wrong.

"Well, the real reason I'm calling you is because I think the project will harm the views from the Appalachian Trail. I've read about some of the work you've done protecting the Trail."

Now he had my attention.

I found myself in an awkward position. I have always been fascinated by alternative energy. Solar, wind, wave power. Micro hydro. Geothermal. Wind power was booming in Europe. It provides relatively clean energy and is renewable without ongoing resource extraction, without emissions of greenhouse gases. But I understood Hubbard's point. The windmills alter the landscape and are visible for miles. Introducing them into pristine backcountry is usually cited by locals and conservationists as an unwelcome industrialization of the landscape.

"I want to know if the Appalachian Trail Conservancy will fight it," Hubbard said.

I had to laugh. "I assure you I don't know. I can't speak for the ATC, much as I'd like to. How close will the windmills be to the Trail?"

"Close. I don't know. I'll have to find out."

"Next question: who owns the land the windmills are going on?"

I imagined Mr. Hubbard thumbing through a notebook. "A guy named Paul Brown," he finally said. "Out of Zionville."

"Are you making this up?"

"No, sir. Do you know him?"

Paul.

It turned out Paul owned substantial acreage on the Tennessee–North Carolina line, including a long ridge on Stone Mountain.

A public hearing on the matter was to be held. I had a conflict so I couldn't go, which is just as well. I didn't relish the prospect of having Paul think that I was out to get him, that I was following his every move and bucking him at every turn. I sent Mr. Hubbard to Morgan.

Morgan was interested, but did not share with me what position he might propose to the board.

The Appalachian Trail Conservancy did take a position on the Stone Mountain wind farm. They stated their preference that the TVA wind project go forward adjacent to an already-existing wind project, near Oak Ridge, far to the southwest of Stone Mountain. But they weren't going to go to war on this. They registered their concern over strobe lights and expressed their hope that the blades be as nonreflective as possible. But, to be honest, the impacts on the Trail were not significant, even if they were adverse. Morgan determined that the project would be eleven miles from the Trail. That would hurt the case Hubbard would try to make. More important, there was no Tennessee statute guiding the opposition. Assuming the windmills didn't explode every couple of weeks or emit high whining noises all day, every day, or fragment critical habitat for rare, threatened, or endangered species, I did not find the opposition argument compelling. Of course it is all so subjective. If I were in Kenneth Hubbard's shoes, I'm sure my attention would have been fixed on each and every negative aspect of the proposal. And if I was losing sleep over my viewshed, and the industrialization of my beloved landscape, I might spend time in the library researching similar fights in other parts of the country, looking for precedents. But from where I stood, I could claim to be neutral, and I guess that's what I was trying to give to Hubbard: a plain assessment of how a conservation-minded fellow from outside that particular holler would look upon his crusade. I wished for him a strong stomach and a fat wallet. And the endurance of Job.

## Chapter 17

Finally, one day Paul called Morgan, ending our speculation about what Paul had up his sleeve. He wanted to move the Putnam Mine to the back side of the mountain. Charles had told Paul that he should invite Morgan and the Appalachian Trail Conservancy to vet any proposal before submitting a permit application to Charles's office. Now Paul had his new plan ready.

Upon receiving the news, I sat stunned. All it took was a phone call from Paul to Morgan? For a couple of seconds the blood raced hard through my head, my thoughts shot around inside my mind. Why had I never picked up the phone and called Paul and asked him to move the mine? I stared at the clock on my desk for a long spell, wondering if I was witness to the moment everything changed. *Move the mine?*

It seemed a significant turn, but I was no longer so easily fooled as I once was. Two years of wrestling with Paul and Charles had made me wiser. Morgan was still on the phone, still talking, and I snapped back to attention. Morgan reported that Paul mentioned "the operation." What did that mean? Was Paul serious about moving the crusher jaw to the back side, too? The primary crusher jaw, the secondary jaw, or both? Or neither? *The operation* could mean any subset of the whole. I would have to reread the statute. Perhaps the crushing plant did not need a mining permit. Forrest was doubtful the offer was anything other than a diversion. He suggested that Paul might apply for a permit for the quarry pit, then refuse to move the primary crusher. And if Paul wanted to leave the main plant where it was, would the state let him? Forrest warned we would trust Paul at our peril. And we were still watching Charles's office, and Charles, for clues and signs that he was going sideways on us.

I called Ollie to see if she had heard anything about this. I didn't want to upset her, or her household. They were still recovering from Ashley's latest round of medical tests, still awaiting results, and were strung out.

I told Ollie all I knew about Paul's proposal. But I couldn't engage her interest. She was tired of Paul. Tired of the crusher, and possibly of me. She ended the conversation saying, "Paul's going to do whatever the hell he wants so it don't really matter what I say."

I called Faye looking for a more substantive response.

"Paul has come up with a plan to move the operation to the back side of the mountain," I reported. "Charles has told him he will have to get the okay from Morgan, from the Appalachian Trail Conservancy, before submitting any new plan."

"I don't believe him," Faye said flatly.

"I hear you."

Then Faye took a moment to think through her reply. "Is this good?" I could hear the strain in her voice. The stubborn refusal to trust good news.

"It could be good, though we are all smart enough to distrust any-thing Paul proposes. I'm not sure if he wants to use the Putnam tract or the Charles Smith tract down by the highway to set up his scales or if he can go back up through Sawdust. Ollie said she saw some trusses stacked back in Sawdust. If Putnam is smart, he will tell Paul to get off his land altogether. . . . We'll see. I'll keep you posted."

I picked up a fly rod, my seven-and-a-half-foot small-stream rod and headed for Big Horse Creek. It was a warm day for December, fifty degrees, and I wanted to collect my thoughts in the stream. Maggie ran up ahead, while Biscuit settled into my pace just behind me. I ran every-thing over in my mind. What did *the back side* mean? Was there enough "back side," enough rock, back there to let Paul recoup his investment? I walked the old logging road, the High Falls Road, dodging stones and weaving through what was left of nettle stalks, and a horrible thought struck me. What if Paul wanted to swing the pit around so that it faced away from the Appalachian Trail but faced the Yellow Mountain bald? Would a new pit be visible from Grassy Ridge? How angry would the conservation community be if our work succeeded only in shifting the impacts to other beloved high-elevation sites? The last thing I wanted was to have my name attached to an effort that spoiled the view from somebody else's sacred ground. I stared out at Belview Mountain over Houston Ridge, visible through the bare trees from where I stood. I thought there might be a way Paul could site it, down low, facing north, where it would be hard to see from anywhere but Beech Mountain. The developers who owned Beech Mountain seemed to care little for protecting anything, even their own mountain. They had covered its slopes with condominiums and Swiss-themed chalets. The creeks coming off the mountain were degraded by poor planning and overbuilding. I had a slightly diabolical thought. Would a quarry facing Beech Mountain slow the pace of development there? Would it spoil the market for view properties? We had heard a new development was coming, a Florida real estate baron promised to bring the "Miami Beach lifestyle" to the south-facing slope of Beech Mountain. I did not like this trait in myself, this capacity to crave revenge for conservation misdeeds. But why should Beech Mountain get off so easy after despoiling that proud mountain, after carving it up into hundreds of half-acre parcels in the headlong chase for return on investment? But it was hard to puzzle the new plan out without knowing exactly what Paul would seek to do. It was a waste of energy guessing. And wishing others ill was, I liked to think, beneath me. I reached Big Horse Creek and began casting flies into the small, cold pools. Soon the rush of water, the constant fall of the bold stream, drowned out all thoughts of Paul and the primary crusher jaw and the Miami Beach luxury lifestyle. I cast to trout, high-sticking to keep my line free. Dabbled my fly on the edge of the froth at the head of each pool, and cast again.

Christmas came, and this year my stocking was full. Ashley called and insisted I stop by the house before going down to Durham to spend the holiday with my family. We sat on the big sofa and drank soft drinks, and then, unable to contain her excitement, Ashley told me to close my eyes. She placed an enormous box in my lap. I opened my eyes and unwrapped one of the most remarkable gifts I have ever received. A microwave oven.

It had been months since I had told a story on myself, a story that led to this gift. I knew it instantly. I had asked my friend Fred Davis, an old-timer, for his recipes for preparing ramps and branch lettuce, the wild greens of springtime. With great relish he had rolled out his recipe for "kilt lettuce," with strips of bacon laid over the tops of the tender greens. I followed each step in my mind as he spoke. Then, he shattered my image of an old-time, classic recipe unfolding in my own kitchen: "Then you put it in the microwave and run it for about forty seconds."

"The microwave?!" I didn't have a microwave. I'd explained I had no interest in such modern conveniences, such contraptions! But here was old Mr. Davis, with a white beard down to the bib on his overalls, invoking the modern wonder oven as part of his family recipe. I had told the story to Ashley and Ollie to make fun of my preposterous wilderness sojourn and my high opinion of the purity of my undertaking. Now they had bought me my own microwave oven.

Ollie grinned and clasped her hands. "You know we love you, Jay." Her eyes glimmered with tears that did not fall, her expression frank.

My neighbors up on the mountain had a gift for me, too. Explaining that they had no way to repay me for the man-hours I had put in on the case, for the investment I had made in time, work, and travel, they had all chipped in and bought me a satellite dish for my television. With two years of programming paid in advance. Since arriving on the mountain I had watched basketball games and public broadcasting on an old Zenith with rabbit ears sticking out its top. The picture was poor and it was impossible to regulate the volume so I usually just muted it. I was torn about this generous gift, for it represented not only friendship and generosity, but also the invasion of twenty-first-century technology into my old wooden house. Bright television pictures, dozens of channels filled with mostly inane programs, didn't exactly fit my vision of the simple life, my experiment in living. But I relented. Partly because I was raised better than to refuse a kindness. And partly because I was curious about what it would be like to have all those channels. It was fantastic. The picture coming on the screen was so clear. So vivid! Soon I found that the programming package my neighbors ordered got me four—*four!*—public broadcasting stations. I could watch *Austin City Limits* and *Mountain Stage* back-to-back-to-back on Saturday nights. I could catch *This Old House* every afternoon at four o'clock and on Tuesday nights I could catch *Making It Grow,* the farm and gardening show coming out of the Clemson University Agricultural Extension Service. The show was even better now that I could see and hear it. And the sports programming was a feast, endless games, endless talk about games. Then more games. Maybe television wasn't so bad after all.

It was spring before the site visit to evaluate Paul's new plan was scheduled. The wires had gone silent, according to Ollie; none of her sources had any clue what Dear Ol' Dad and Nasty were planning. Freddy had been to the east side on his motorcycle, had found dozens of test holes with powder piles next to them, but that was it. All we could do was show up and be prepared for whatever they threw at us.

The Saturday of the visit was warm and the sun was high when we met at Paul's gate. I looked across the road. Ollie was in the window with her binoculars and her camera. Freddy was out in the yard poking around his cars. In addition to the regular cast of characters—Morgan, Steve Perri of the Tennessee Eastman Hiking and Canoeing Club, Nasty, and me—a guy I had not met before, Steve Parrot, came from the state geologist's office. He explained he was also a part-time fly-fishing guide, and this encouraged me that he might be open-minded. Conservation-minded. A like-minded fellow.

Another participant stepped into the haul road from behind a truck. Bill Beck from the Asheville Regional Office. I knew Ollie was beside herself, tied in knots. I refrained from stealing a glance her way. Ollie could not stand the sight of Bill Beck, considered him to be the devil's own sideman, and now here I was, her Little Buddy, and I was shaking his hand, shooting the breeze.

As we set out, I was funneled toward the big, black Dodge truck. Suddenly everybody scattered into other vehicles, or into the bed of the Dodge. I saw I had no option and climbed into the cab. With Captain Nasty himself. I had never fully processed how big James was. His jacket barely contained him. His hands were massive, grease-stained paws, and the steering wheel looked like a toy in his grip. When I had arrived at the gate that morning, I had shaken his hand. When a mountain man is glad to see you, you'll know it. He will shake your hand with great vigor and usually grab you higher up on the arm as well, with the free hand. But James's hand was dead in mine. He was unenthusiastic about all of this, about me. But he was not of bad humor. He was just a big, quiet guy whose job was on the line.

We set off on a primitive road, crawling up over big rocks and tree roots, sweeping south across the slope of the mountain. James and I avoided talking about the crusher. We talked instead about hunting. I grew up hunting birds, an annual opening-day dove hunt, then waterfowl, geese and ducks, in the winter with my father. James seemed to think this was one of the stranger things he had ever heard. "Ducks?" he said, incredulous. Besides turkey hunting, and grouse for the upland enthusiast, there isn't any bird hunting in the mountains. "You hunt deer?" I asked.

"Naw," he replied. I wasn't sure whether this was credible. The mountain people I know are happy to tell you what they think you want to hear when it comes to deer hunting. That means almost all profess, to me anyway, that they don't hunt deer. Even members of deer clubs

293

lament to me the violence of hunting and hunters because they expect that I, as a hiker, as a land conservationist, oppose hunting, especially deer hunting. This always amuses me. It always shocks them when I say that I actually wish we had a more robust population of hunters to advocate for traditional land uses. I always draw surprised stares when I talk about my favorite ways to prepare venison. I pulled all that out with James, until, finally, he allowed that he liked squirrel hunting.

Suddenly he changed the topic. "You know, it don't make no difference to me, any of this. That side, the back side, or this side. It's all the same dime to me. I just show up and work. To be honest, I don't care whur it's at."

I asked him about Paul. "What does he do with all that money?"

The question surprised James. "Paul? He don't do nothing. He works."

"If it was me, and I had all that money, I'd have a place at the beach, and a boat, and I'd fish down there when I wasn't fishing up here. I'd go fishing all the time, all over the place. Out West. I'd buy a ranch in Montana."

"Paul ain't like that," James said, nearly amused at the idea of Paul going to the beach. "Paul owns a golf course, but he don't play golf. He don't never take a day off. He likes making money, but he don't like to turn loose of it."

I remembered again the words of my brother's father-in-law: *Paul Brown would sooner lose a limb than let go of a dollar.*

I asked James about the house on Beech Mountain. It was a famous story around Avery County. Paul's accountant asked him one day what he wanted to do about his house up on Beech Mountain: keep it, sell it, rent it out? Paul replied that he didn't own a house on Beech Mountain. The accountant dug around in his briefcase and presented the deed, showing Paul that he did, in fact, own a valuable house high atop Beech Mountain. I told James the story and asked if he could confirm it.

James shrugged. "Paul owns so much, he don't know everything he has got. I'd say he's probably got a lot of things like that. Me, I don't suffer with that problem. I can keep up with all I got."

"Me, too."

The truck climbed over the rocks and tree roots and fallen branches and carried us across the broad flank of Hartley Ridge. Here the mountain seemed to be all rock and little soil and I tried to see if I could see Yellow Mountain in the side-view mirror. If the crusher was moved to this side, the Appalachian Trail might be shielded somewhat, but I would probably still hear the operation every minute of every day from my house. If anything, the crusher would be louder from here. But James kept right on driving. This was not the spot, not part of the new plan. I would be lying if I said I wasn't relieved. The road swung hard up the hill now and took us back to the east. Then north. Now the ground flattened out and we came into the big Christmas-tree fields that drape Belview like a chenille cloak. We rumbled through the low end of the first field, then James pulled up to a halt. "This is where the jaw would go. Right in here."

We all piled out of the vehicles.

I didn't say anything, not yet, but this would be a great spot for the crusher jaw. The summit of Hartley Ridge blocked the views of both the Appalachian Trail and the Yellow Mountain bald, while the summit of Belview blocked the view from Grandfather Mountain. I searched for, but could not see, Grassy Ridge.

"Where would you take the rock from?" Morgan asked.

"I'll show you." James took off walking. North.

North and downhill. Down into a deep cove we went, toward the headwaters of Cranberry Creek. James thought this draw had a lot of rock, going all the way down the Sawdust Holler. Our party hiked down a logging road, and James led us to a spot he wanted us to see. He showed us some of his drill holes. Piles of rock dust and slaggy mud marked each drill hole. Morgan had survey tape and a GPS unit, and we walked the grade, making sure that we stayed well below the viewshed of the Appalachian Trail. But James wasn't happy with that. "We need to go up a little higher on the hill," he hollered after Morgan. "There's good rock up there." He tried to get us to flag a line higher up the slope, but Morgan stood firm. "Let's mark off the line we wouldn't contest, a real safe line, then we can talk about whether that would work." James shrugged and we carried on. All morning we tramped through the beautiful woods, through drifts of spring beauties, clumps of ramps. The leaves were just budding out, so we had a clear line of sight up to the Hump. "One month later, with the leaves on, and we might have flagged this way up the hill," Morgan said. "We wouldn't have been able to see the contour of Hump Mountain." I was suddenly struck by the importance of what we were doing on this sunny day.

I walked for a while with Steve Parrot and Bill Beck. We came into a boggy boulder field filled with mosses and sedums and many varieties of ferns. False hellebore thrust up from the leaf litter like green torpedoes. Soon the cohosh would send up long stems to nod in the breeze.

"There's a lot of rock in here," I said.

"Yes," Beck agreed. "But they can't take any of this. All this area would have to be taken out of a permit. There's too much water in here."

"Does James know that?"

Beck looked at me as if I had missed an important memo. "It's impossible to tell the Clark Stone people anything." The frustration in his voice was obvious.

"Mr. Brown is a character." I wanted to deflect from my desire to hear Beck say more and, in that way, encourage him to say more. It worked.

Beck wanted to spell it out. "Anybody else would do some research on a piece of land before sinking a million dollars into it. They would drill dozens of holes, a hundred feet deep, throughout the permit area, at least to see how much life the mine has in it. These guys have just scratched around back here. There's no way to tell if this is a good site or not doing that kind of study. Mr. Brown has his own way of doing things, all right. Let's just say it like that."

"Randy says Paul knows where the rock is," I said, trolling.

Now Steve Parrot joined the conversation. "There is a lot of rock in here, but it's not very good. I mean there is some of the best rock in the state within ten miles of here. In every direction, great rock, but this material is marginal. They had very good rock in Linville."

"Marginal?"

"There's better rock."

So this fight was not even over great rock. All this effort and energy and money was going into a fight over marginal rock.

Once we had gathered all the data we needed, we reconvened by the trucks.

James laid it out. "Like I've told Jay, I don't care one way or the other. It don't matter to me. Mr. Brown asked me to look for rock back here and I done it. Right down there, where that truck is at, that would be the jaw. Then we would take that broke-up rock around and put it through the secondary crusher."

Silence. I glanced at Morgan to see his reaction. We had not understood this part of it. Clark Stone would like to continue to process the rock on the front side of Belview Mountain, after all. Primary jaw on the back, secondary crusher on the front. All the rest on the front, too. Just as Trip had predicted.

Morgan said that the Appalachian Trail Conservancy would have a hard time agreeing to that. I thought back to Ollie's first impression of Morgan at the first public meeting. She swore he was wearing flip-flops. She had read him as soft, a hippie. But here he was, sticking to his position as if he had tar on his heels.

James shrugged. "Like I said, you boys can do what turns you on. It don't make no difference to me."

We ate our picnic lunch in the grassy pasture, thinking about the scenarios James laid out, but trying to keep it light. All on best behavior. From where we spread out on the grass, we were looking up at the Hump. I saw three hikers coming along the Trail, coming down off the top, heading for the big bend that would take them down to Doll Flats and then into Tennessee. I pointed them out. Morgan squinted and searched for them. "Oh, yeah," he said upon seeing them. "Is it two or three?"

"I see three," I said. "No, maybe it's two."

"Wait, now I see the third."

James and Beck looked at us as if we were talking gibberish. Or making something up.

"What are you looking at?"

"Hikers. There, on the Trail." I pointed toward the Hump. We were now about two and a half miles from the Trail. In silhouette the hikers stood out against the hazy blue sky.

James leaned forward. "You-uns can really see all that way?"

Morgan pulled out his binoculars and offered them to James, to Beck. Morgan did not need to speak, the point was amply made. *You may need these to see all that way, while Jay and I do not.* James took the binoculars and peered up at the Hump through the lenses.

He scanned the horizon. "I'm dogged!" he said, seeing the hikers with his own eyes now. "There they're at." He handed the binoculars off to Beck.

It seemed a moment that ratified our contention that we hikers are preternatural creatures, seers. That our senses are heightened, and if taken as we are found, we deserve deference when it comes to evaluating threats to the natural world. Our argument that the quarry pit would have to remain below a certain line because of the impacts it would have on the hikers was strengthened by our feats of visual acuity. James shook his head in wonder. For all he now knew, these hiker types were capable of nearly about anything. I imagined him reporting this to Paul. *Them hiker boys can see stuff with the naked eye that ain't even hardly there.*

We were wrapping up, packing up our lunch leftovers, when Beck shared a golden nugget of information. "I think Charles would like to wrap this thing up before July."

"July? Why then?" I asked.

"Because Charles is going to retire in July."

I went over to report the events of the day to Ollie, Ashley, and Freddy. They were cool to me, as if by talking with Beck, by shaking his hand, I was soiled. As if I'd switched sides. Finally, when I told them about Charles leaving, Ollie lightened up.

"Retired, or fired? Did you get Charles strung up?"

Ollie still clung to her notion that I could hire and fire state employees, possessed the power to direct judges to rule at my pleasure, if only I would apply myself.

Freddy was more interested in Beck. "What in the world were you saying to Beck? Don't you know he shares genetic material with the hell spawn? Did he put any spell on you?"

"Not that I noticed. But I guess I would be the last to know."

Freddy said, "Now you know, Jay, if he gets close enough to you, he can pull your beating heart out of your chest. Like they done on Indiana Jones. You didn't let him get within range, did you? I don't know which one is worse, Beck or Paul."

Ashley looked up from her computer, upon which she was doing her homework. She cocked her head as if seriously considering Freddy's contest. "It's a tie, I'd say. Tough to pick a winner in that one."

For the next couple of days our team huddled to consider what we might confront in the form of a new proposal from Clark Stone. Crushing on the front side. The pit climbing up the hill on the back side. And then, eventually, over the summit? Would they propose that? Surely they would not. And they wouldn't have to. The problem with the Mining Act is that once an operator has a permit to mine, extending the boundaries can happen at any time, with no additional public hearings. If Clark Stone left most of their equipment on the front side, this plan could be a Trojan horse that would have them back around the front side within years. With both jaws running full out.

We decided we would have to oppose any proposal that left any equipment on the west face of the mountain. Luckily, Morgan and I were in perfect agreement on this latest development, so I didn't need to agitate for my position. We now felt poised for a victory in the courtroom. We were sitting on a huge triumph before the Mining Commission, and we were heading into the appeals process with the wind at our backs. It had been four years since Paul had left Linville, four years since he had made a nickel crushing rock. We suspected he must surely be growing weary of paying his lawyers while his machines sat idle, sinking into the rich soil of their own weight, rusting in the mountain air. According to his deposition, Paul had spent somewhere in the neighborhood of $2.5 million on an operation that sat silent. In the meantime, he was making monthly payments on a $550,000 shovel, in addition to the lease payments to Putnam. Surely, if our side could press hard against Paul's backup plan, his last gasp, we could convince him that it was time for him to settle into a quiet retirement.

I suspected that Paul now wanted to crush rock only to save face. He was in his twilight years, and rich as Croesus. What else could it be? He couldn't be worried about his retirement plan. We knew from going through the documents he'd presented in discovery that the Linville quarry brought in $120,000 a year or so. Out of that, Paul paid his few full-time employees. He paid himself $50,000 a year, a trifling amount for a man of his wealth. At that rate, it would take ten or more years to make back the money he had already sunk in the unforgiving mountain. Could he live for ten more years?

That night I sent an e-mail to Morgan and to Dave Startzell: *Folks, I would hate to compromise on any of our shared values for a "marginal" quarry just so that Paul Brown can say he "won" and Charles can breathe a sigh of relief at his retirement party. If I were the Appalachian Trail Conservancy and Paul submitted a permit for the "new" quarry we are now discussing I would respond this way: Based on soundscape impacts alone: magnitude, frequency and duration—and here I'd quote from the ATC Policy—by information and belief, we find that the yet-to-be-proposed proposal has had and will in the future have significant adverse effects on the purpose of a publicly owned park, forest or recreation area, in this case the Appalachian National Scenic Trail in the vicinity of Hump Mountain. (Just in case anyone wondered how I feel about it.) We find that these impacts cannot be sufficiently mitigated—especially not by Clark Stone Company.*

*If DENR asks my view, which I grant you is not likely, that is what I will tell them.*

*Chapter 18*

Upon Charles's retirement to the mountains around Asheville, Jim Simons, a veteran of the Division of Land Resources, was named to replace him as director of the division. It just didn't feel right. I was used to pushing against Charles. We had been antagonists to be sure, but we had also been partners. I had relied upon our special relationship to gain access to information. I had begged his goodwill when I needed to be heard. I had put my trust in him, and I had doubted him, and I had railed against the very uttering of his name. And now he was gone. I didn't know where to push anymore. And I guess I missed him.

Throughout the summer, the lawyers prepared to appear in Paul's appeal of the Mining Commission ruling against him. This kept the lawyers busy, but I had little to do. Partly because the case had introduced me to many figures in the conservation community, I was becoming more interested in their work, the great issues of the day. I volunteered my time with the Southern Appalachian Highlands Conservancy, helping evaluate tracts of land for protection. I tracked elections more closely and followed battles in the General Assembly.

For over two years, little had distracted me from Paul's doings, from the daily goings-on at the site. I had read and reread every brief, every filing, every motion entered by every party in every venue taking up the case. But now, I had time to consider what was going on beyond Dog Town. Some of the issues of the day were depressingly familiar. The

North Carolina Pesticide Board was floating a plan to weaken rules for aerial spraying. They wanted the flexibility to spray pesticides closer to schools and homes. Current law allowed spraying within a hundred feet of an occupied residence, but industry lobbyists wanted to reduce that buffer. Scientists and environmental advocates maintained that this would put children and pets in danger of neurological damage, increase the risk of poisoning people's gardens and their drinking water.

One of our mountain congressmen was a staunch and proud opponent of the conservation community. Charles Taylor embraced his own derogatory nickname, Chainsaw Charlie, and now he was trying to slip money into the federal budget to build a thirty-seven-mile-long road through the most remote part of the Great Smoky Mountains National Park. The road would cost $590 million, cross 137 streams, and dead-end at a cemetery marooned in an inner pocket of the park, the last vestige of lives left behind when the federal government relocated whole communities to realize the dream of a vast wilderness park. Congressman Taylor, a multimillionaire banker and timberman, was pressing the National Park Service to declare that the road plan would cause no impairment to the park and park values. The plan would clearly punch a hole in the most extensive unroaded stretch of wilderness in the eastern United States. And incidentally, it would enrich the gravel haulers and road builders of Swain County, powerful constituents of the congressman. Strange days indeed.

Some of the news was good. In July of that year, North Carolina passed landmark legislation aimed at cleaning up the state's air. The Clean Smokestacks Bill was that rare proposal that gained support from both political parties, and even industry leaders. I had followed progress of the bill closely, as did many in the mountains. The mountains are especially vulnerable to foul air emanating from the Tennessee Valley and the sprawling suburbs of Atlanta and Charlotte, where regional planning usually means building ever wider roads to bring in ever more cars, ever more tailpipes. Relative to other regions, the South is still booming, and that means more people, and more coal-fired power plants to meet their demands for electricity to power refrigerators and computers and television sets.

In 1950 visitors to the Blue Ridge Parkway could see a hundred miles on a typical summer day. But now, in the first years of the new century, the mountain peaks of the Southern Appalachians are often bathed in a toxic stew of pollutants. Great Smoky Mountains National Park routinely issues public health warnings on particularly smoggy days. And the views? Some days the range of visibility is reduced to single digits. Seven miles. It is now routinely celebrated as the most polluted park in the entire country. Nitrous oxide levels at Clingmans Dome sometimes exceed readings in downtown Los Angeles. So Clean Smokestacks legislation was welcome news.

When the bill passed, I drove down to Raleigh to attend a celebration held in honor of the signers of the bill. The room was full of conservation-minded legislators as well as representatives of all the environmental groups in the state. DENR had played a central supporting role in the passage of the bill, so the event promised to be a happy hunting ground for arm-twisting on Putnam Mine.

I was unprepared for the warm reception I received. Now that the Dog Town Bunch had won before the Mining Commission, with the revocation upheld, we were embraced. I was. Everybody loves a winner. It was a kick. Suddenly I was not a wild-eyed agitator, coming out of the woods to hector and berate. Now I was rated an effective advocate, milling around with those I had long admired. People I had never met congratulated me and asked questions about where the case was headed.

It was tempting to bask, just for a moment, to wallow in this parade of backslaps and congratulations. But I was wired differently now. I was working. In only minutes I spotted Jim Gulick. I grabbed a couple of grapes and some heavy hors d'oeuvres and headed for him. Cornered him. As was his habit, he was turned out in an immaculate suit. Gulick expected a new application to arrive from Paul for the back side of the mountain, but he didn't know when that might be. I told him I was surprised that during the current budget crisis the state was spending so much time and money helping Paul find rock to crush, but Gulick wouldn't engage me. We just stood there, eating cubes of cheese with dumb smiles on our faces.

I learned the hearing date for our case in Superior Court from Ashley rather than from the lawyers. She called to tell me that Paul told a friend of Curly's that the date was set for late October. I told her I didn't believe anything until I heard it from Trip and Forrest, and that she shouldn't either. As if on cue, within the hour, I got the call. The hearing was set for the third week of October.

I called Ashley to tell her the date. She was tickled when I confirmed all she had heard. "So the old rumor mill around here isn't exactly bullshit, huh?"

"Ashley," I admonished, "your language is getting worse and worse. Did you forget that they're listening? And, no, I'm not on a landline."

This was a taunt.

She snorted at the implication. "Let me get this straight. You're telling me about government surveillance? Don't forget who taught you everything you know."

Within days we got our judicial assignment. We would appear before Judge Stafford Bullock. I called Forrest to get his opinion of Bullock's style, his judicial temperament.

"We could do worse," he said without elaboration.

"I'll take that."


By haranguing Trip and Ron and Forrest, and all my lawyer friends in the middle of the state, I was able to draw up a profile of what we could expect from Judge Bullock. The picture was mixed. He was a Democrat, which would ordinarily mean he did not have outright hostility toward taxpayer owned institutions, public parks, public lands. That seemed good. He was African-American, which didn't present any obvious fodder for speculation. A lawyer friend in Raleigh sized Bullock up this way: "He picks a winner before he hears the facts and lets the lawyers write his opinions." Of course in our case, if he sided with us, I would not have any problem with this method. The thought of Trip writing our opinion suited me just fine.

Instead of reading Bullock's other rulings, trying to dig into his record, I began to distance myself from the work Trip and Forrest would undertake in preparation for the hearing. I guess, like Ollie, I was worn-out of worrying. That we were sitting on a win from the Mining Commission might have explained my disinterest in the case as the summer unfurled. In any event, I reverted to my nature, my habit: I did my errands and grocery shopping on Monday mornings. I wrote on Monday afternoons, then all day Tuesday and all day Wednesday. Thursdays I reserved for reading, fishing, and hiking. On Fridays I worked in the morning and read in the afternoon. On the weekend, I usually had company in, which often involved either hiking or fishing, or ideally both. I imported much of my entertainment. Between my family and friends, my house was usually the scene of weekend fun until the winter set in. The few dates I had had over the summer had fizzled into disinterest. I was still happiest when I was on my own, when I was in the woods with no schedule. I spent whole days exploring the vast wilderness on the east flank of Grandfather Mountain. I got myself lost in the Green River gorge, coming as close to dying on a trout stream as I ever had, or hopefully ever will. I wore a new footpath along a route through the Dan Holler, to the headwaters of Big Horse Creek. This is what I liked, or needed. Nowhere to be and nobody particularly interested in what I'd found or seen or endured.

The fall came on quickly, with a sudden successions of cool nights. The forests turned dry and took on their yellows and bloodreds, blazed away in the sunny afternoons. The leaf people arrived in their long sedans to cruise the Blue Ridge Parkway and the back roads for a glimpse of real Appalachia. The apple orchards pressed juice for cider, and the roadside stands were busy selling honey and homemade jam from the summer bounty. I pulled my own small potato crop and froze the last of my blueberry harvest. Like the leaves, the speckled trout turn vivid colors in the fall, deep orange on the diaphanous, white-tipped fins, caramel-brown and bright red dots down the side. I sought them just to marvel that such a thing can exist in this world.

The day before our hearing in Judge Bullock's courtroom, I walked out along the edge of the meadow by the house and collected buckeyes for everybody on the legal team. The ground was littered with the big brown seeds. A buckeye brings good luck. Over time a good buckeye, one that brings good results, gets rubbed black. My grandfather, a proper businessman, carried one in his pocket his entire adult life. He died before I was born, but I loved to think of him meeting with regulators or borrowers or at his leisure in downtown Asheville or on the train between the mountains and Florida, in his snappy suits, with the coal-black buckeye tucked in his pocket. I gathered a handful of nice ones. Thus girded against misfortune, I loaded Biscuit and Maggie in the truck and headed down the mountain for Raleigh.

My spirits were better than they had been the last time I drove down for a hearing, for the Mining Commission. Now we had that ruling in hand. On the drive down, I reviewed the things we now had in our favor. We had the revocation. We had the consent order, loose though it was, from Judge Downs. We had lost before the administrative law judge, but she wasn't even a real judge. And besides, she had been overruled by the Mining Commission. The Mining Commission is the agency, I argued to myself, and they shellacked Paul 6–1. It would be strange indeed for a Superior Court judge to rule that the agency misinterpreted its own authority, I posited. Surely the universe wasn't so wicked as to undo all the good that had flowed our way. Paul's plan for the back side had not materialized. Mention of it had ceased back in the summer. Also in our favor, we had free lawyers working hard, while Paul's attorneys had their long arms deep in his pockets. Added to that, Dear Ol' Dad wasn't getting any younger. That year he turned seventy-seven. How long would he continue to care enough about crushing rock to press the matter? All in all, I liked our chances.

The hearing day was cold and raw, spitting rain from a tossed, gray sky. In the elevator going up to the sixth-floor courtroom, I ran into a

District Court judge I went to law school with. I told her briefly what our case was. "Who'd you get?" she asked, reducing speculation about the disposition of the matter to this single nub.

"Bullock," I said.

"Bullock?" She rolled her eyes.

"What? I heard he doesn't read briefs."

"There's that," she said simply without embellishment. "You better hope he likes you."

Now I was nervous. I felt the jitters roll through my gut, an old companion.

The hearing was held in a nondescript, overly bright courtroom that felt like a community-college classroom. Our team huddled toward the back of the room as Trip and Forrest went over who would speak first. They then broke and sought the margins of the space, refreshed their minds, ran through their arguments. When the clock struck the hour, I passed out the buckeyes and everybody took one with good humor. Even Jim Gulick.

Outside the plate-glass windows, a storm blew up. Between the buckeyes and the foul weather, the portents seemed to be waging war over us and our fate.

With no fanfare, Judge Bullock strode into the courtroom and took his place in a swivel chair at the front of the room. The old-school charm of the Avery County Courthouse was replaced by the sanitary efficiency and expedience of Raleigh. And we were under way.

At the opening of the hearing, the judge leaned forward in his chair to better regard us. "Now who can tell me what brings us here today?" he said easily. This was his cordial way of announcing that he had not a clue about the matter before him. I had been warned, so I cannot say I was surprised by the way the hearing started, but I soon became alarmed. Not only was Judge Bullock unaware of the identity of the parties in the case, or any of the issues, he also didn't seem to know what the Mining Act of 1971 was. Or what the Appalachian Trail was. Or the National Park Service.

As Trip was clearing his throat, beginning to explain what the National Park Service is, the judge suddenly interrupted, taking charge of the proceedings. He asked quite simply, "How did we get into this mess?"

Okay, I thought, maybe Judge Bullock won't be so bad. I liked the word *mess* and I liked the manner in which he posed the question. I was all for boiling this down. There is something to be said for plain dealing, after all, for brass tacks. The answer to Bullock's question was the meat of our case, and I settled in, eager to watch Trip seize the moment and run. The simple facts, the answer to Bullock's question, favored us. Trip began to explain that the question could be answered easily, that we were here on this day, appearing before His Honor, because the state had not held public hearings before they issued the permit for the Putnam Mine. And that there had been no hearings because there had been no notice to the adjoining landowners, and—

Paul's lawyer, A. Bartlett White, leaped from his chair, startling Bullock. White hurled an impassioned objection, citing the opinion of the administrative law judge that *notice* must be excluded.

Trip tried valiantly to plow ahead, to connect the dots for Bullock, to answer his question, but much to our dismay, Bullock pulled back.

Trip explained that the only way he could answer the judge's astute question was to explain that there was "no *notice* to the adj—"

Now Bullock objected. He bore down. "We're not going to hear anything that the administrative law judge said for us not to hear, Counselor. Now carry on, without taking us down that road. Objection sustained."

"So, shall I not answer your question, Your Honor? It was your question." No answer was forthcoming from the bench, just a disinterested stare.

This of course made no sense at all. Bullock asked how we got in this fix, but then he would not let our answer be recorded. And what relevance did the ALJ ruling have? It had been overruled by the Mining Commission. In its every particular.

A. Bartlett White was on his game this day. He was young, smart, and dressed in the habit of the recent graduate, with the easy manner of the entitled. I sized him up as a fraternity boy. I had seen him in the parking deck, getting out of his fashionably disheveled sports utility vehicle, and had noted his DUCKS UNLIMITED sticker. Something about all this was overly studied. In court, he used charts and enlargements, a time line, to make his case that Paul was being jerked around by the state, tossed into an arbitrary and capricious tide ruled by a political moon. "This is the day the state told Mr. Brown to start mining," he said, pointing to the date on one chart. "And then on this day, the state, the very same agency that granted the permit, revoked it and told my client they were shutting him down." I tried to scoff silently, but noticeably, when A. Bartlett White stretched facts or simplified matters to the point of parody. It's a trick I cannot say I mastered, scoffing while not being in contempt of court. I lack repose when faced with bullshit.

The hearing lasted two hours—two hours of frustration, and an utter loss of confidence in the judicial system. The hearing was adjourned with no decision from the bench. We would await a ruling, which would come whenever the judge so said.

Trip, Forrest, and I headed for a restaurant.

"What's he going to do?" Trip asked Forrest as we braced ourselves against the wind.

"I don't make predictions, not generally," Forrest said disingenuously, "but he's going to punt."

"Punt?" I asked.

"He doesn't want any part of this," Forrest said. "He's going to send it back to the ALJ and make her hear the notice claim. Otherwise there's a broken link in the case. The narrative makes no sense unless you understand why the state erred."

"What does that mean for us?" I asked.

"It means the thing kicks around for another two years. It goes down to the ALJ, then works its way back up. Maybe somewhere in there Judge Downs rules for us."

"That's good, then," I said, leading my witness. "Time is on our side." I waited for an *amen*.

Forrest nodded. "Time is on our side." But he didn't go out of his way to inspire confidence. "Heck, I'm just guessing."

*Chapter 19*

checked my e-mail a dozen times a day. Sometimes more. Sometimes I would check for new messages, then click to a local weather site, then immediately click back to my in-box. Sometimes on my dial-up Internet connection it would take six or seven minutes to open my mailbox. I now had thousands of stored e-mails connected to the case. I would click IN-BOX, then go outside to feed the dogs. Come back in and brush my teeth. I would return to the screen to see if any new messages had appeared. Then I would refresh the page in case an e-mail had slipped into the box while the pixels on the monitor were resolving. I was looking for signs of hope. A ruling. A message in a bottle. My eyes darted around my in-box looking for one of two names: Trip Van Noppen, Forrest Ferrell. When I saw a link to either name, a bolt of blood would race up my neck. Good news sent me reeling, high, bouncing off the walls. Bad news left me stunned, unable to eat.

I had six new e-mails in my mailbox on the morning of December 15, a light haul.

I opened the first one. It was from Ashley. She'd earned an A on her paper on antibiotics. I had proofread if for her and was pleased at her success.

The last of the six e-mails was from Forrest. It reported that Judge Bullock had reinstated the ruling of the administrative law judge, reversing the decision of the Mining Commission.

Judge Bullock ordered the permit restored to Clark Stone. To Paul. And to Randy and Captain Nasty and the rest of that crew. To Trackhoe Daddy and the El Camino Kid.

I punished myself, read the news all over again. This time, a court of law, not a mediator or an administrative hearing officer or a commission, ruled that the state was barred from revoking the Putnam Mine permit. Now came an e-mail from Trip. He reported it in plain language. The judge had not punted the matter back to the ALJ after all. He had upheld her judgment.

The rest of the morning was spent stumbling like a punch-drunk fighter from one blow to the next. Calls and e-mails from the larger team took me down.

It didn't help that Judge Bullock was clearly a fool. *He had never even heard of the Appalachian Trail,* I told myself. But it didn't matter. It was no comfort now.

It was left to me to deliver the news to my team. Chicken, I did it in an e-mail at the end of the day.

> Folks,
> Sorry to report unpleasant news. Judge Bullock called the attorneys yesterday to report that he will rule against us and for Clark Stone. He will overturn the Mining Commission and reinstate the decision of the Administrative Law Judge. To quote Jim Gulick, the state's attorney: "This is disappointing, but this is also why we have appellate courts." The state will file an appeal of Judge Bullock's order immediately upon its release and we will all head now for the NC Court of Appeals. The COA will assign a three judge panel to hear our case in Raleigh. It will likely take several months for the appeal to be heard and then more months before a ruling is issued. The loser at the COA can appeal to the NC Supreme Court. I'll also remind you that we have our case pending in Avery County on the "notice" issue. If we do not win before the Court of Appeals, or before the Supreme Court, we will go back to that case and proceed through the appellate process on that claim. Jay

Soon condolences from well-wishers poured in. Some of our supporters were despondent, others frustrated. Most were supportive of me and Ollie and Ashley and rallied to keep our spirits up. A few, the doom-sayers, chipped in with *I told you so.* They were the skeptics who didn't believe it was worth fighting battles with long odds in the first place. And there was no denying it, our odds were now long indeed. After all, a mining permit had never been revoked for violations of the act before. Maybe this was why. Maybe the act simply didn't make room for it, or maybe the economic might of the construction industry was too great. Maybe judges were just another joist in the power structure, part of the way things work, and we had just been strung along. The skeptics took every opportunity to point out certain home truths; first among these, money talks. They also offered the unhelpful bromide that *you can't fight city hall* or, in this case, the county commissioners—especially when the county commissioners are in the gravel-hauling business, the progress-of-man business. I had heard it all before. I even agreed with the evidence supporting the naysayers. I wasn't stupid. But something in me wouldn't let me rest, wouldn't let me stand for the status quo, not this time. Ollie was part of it. I wanted to win for her and for Ashley. I wanted Paul to be brought to the knees by the plain injustice of what he had pulled. I wanted to see Randy spanked for his cockiness, his smart-ass sass. But I wanted to win for myself, too. I wanted to stay in my home and I wanted quiet. I wanted to win at something.

The alternative was now staring us in the face, though. Losing would have devastating consequences. It would upend my life and the lives of many on the mountain, many in the valley, all around Dog Town. As I tried to walk this off, the other stakes flooded over me. The Appalachian Trail experience, that hard-to-quantify wilderness experience, was at risk now as never before in the Roan Highlands. The Southern Appalachian Highlands Conservancy and The Nature Conservancy and the Appalachian Trail community had sought to protect the Roan Highlands for nearly forty years. Now the Putnam Mine was going to ruin the experience of walking the eastern balds. Was it going to kill endangered plants on Roan Mountain, impact the *Lilium grayi* and the rock gnome lichen? Would it damage the native strain of *Salvelinus fontinalis* in Elk Holler Creek? No, not directly. Was it going to undermine the decades of successful land protection in the area? Not entirely. But it was going to mock the purpose of the work on the eastern edge of the Roan. It was going to alter the Trail experience radically. Northbound hikers swept up in two days of magnificent bald walks would leave the Roan with a stunning and lasting reminder that even the most wondrous places are accorded little value in this world we live in. That the idea of a remove from civilization, even in the remotest corners of the land, is so much folly.

The status of state law, the ability of the agencies to protect the environment from the headlong push of industry, would be thrown into limbo by the ruling. I was reminded as never before that a whole community was depending on our winning this case. I felt this in my abdomen, like blows from a sledgehammer. I felt it as a crushing weight on my chest. I felt at times I would come apart with sheer nausea. Now I had to go see Ollie.

Ollie had not been well. She thought it was a return of the ulcer, but she wouldn't go to the doctor to find out for sure what it was. Money was part of it, but also an old mountain reluctance to rely on modern medicine. Ollie was aggressive when it came to seeking medical intervention on behalf of Ashley, but for herself, she was not unlike many of her mountain neighbors, not unlike other members of her family I had known. Medicine that didn't come from a family member who knew how to cure ailments was frowned upon. Doctors, those with too much training, who had often come from away, were suspicious characters deploying strange methods from far off. Now, with the new hospital replacing the old, the resplendent lobby, the fancy architecture, modern medicine seemed to many to be something only appropriate for the rich, for those living in the gated communities on the other side of the county. Mountain people professed discomfort, intimidation, when they beheld this new hospital. As for money, I could give Ollie the money for one appointment, or for a small surgery, if that was what was needed. I could even raise money from those who had come to know and love her through the mine fight, I figured. But it didn't matter. She would not have let me, so I didn't ask. She was not going to go to any doctor.

I found her out on the porch, smoking.

"Bullock killed us," I said.

"Hunh?"

"Bullock. He's ruling for Paul, restoring the permit. I just sent Ashley an e-mail."

Ollie let it sink in, then immediately busied herself with her cigarette. Peeled some paper from the filter. "I'm not one bit surprised. Paul has put everybody down in Raleigh knee-deep in liquor and women. I'd rather have fought him up here. He's got everybody bought off in Raleigh. I told you that."

The idea of Paul and Judge Bullock swinging a deal in an alley in Raleigh brought a ray of light to my dark mood. Ollie had always maintained that Paul's influence spanned the state, from the coast in the east, all the way to the Tennessee line in the west. She repeated the common belief around Dog Town. The politics of her claim were interesting. No Democrat had ever held office in my county, not in my lifetime. This was Republican country, out of step with the eastern North Carolina Democrat machine that had run the state since Reconstruction. Did Paul have friends in high places in Raleigh among the establishment Democrats? I didn't have any idea. He did make a large donation to Jim Sasser, a Tennessee Democrat. I found that in an online database of campaign contributions, but that could have just been part of the politics of road-building. I had asked around, had done some research, but I couldn't find his stamp on anything east of Boone.

"What do we do now?" Ollie asked coolly. I had to remind myself that Ollie expected to lose. She had told me, more than once, that she had never won at anything, was born to lose.

"Trip says we appeal this to the Court of Appeals. He says it's our turn because he says this case is on a seesaw. We're down now, but maybe we're on the way up."

"Can he crush?" Ollie asked, referring to Paul. "I guess he'll want to start the drills tomorrow and get to crushing."

"The appeals process could take two years. The consent order is still in place so he can't crush. He can't drill."

"Two years? I can't take another day."

"The time frame is our best hope, Ollie. If we can drag this out, if it takes two years, Paul may quit."

"I've done told you, Paul ain't quitting. He come up here to bury me." Ollie winced as a streak of pain ran through her. She shifted positions to ease what she described as a stabbing sensation.

"We still have that order in Judge Downs's court. Paul can't crush."

"Are you sure? I thought Bullock said Charles has to give the permit back. Ain't that what he sued for?"

"I'm sure," I lied. "He can't crush." I thought I knew, but I didn't really know. Judge Bullock's ruling was sweeping. I did not know if it superseded the action in Judge Downs's court. Bullock's ruling might also cause Downs to go ahead and rescind his consent order. That was the sleeping giant, that order, casually consented to in the Avery County Courthouse.

Now Ollie smiled. Or, I should say, a smile escaped her. "Don't you just know Paul would stomp me if he could. You know he'd like to ring my bony neck. And yours, too, Little Buddy."

"I'd pay to see that tussle, you and Paul in the cage. To the death." I had learned this kind of talk from Freddy. When I was a child, the only television station people in the valleys in Avery County could get was out of Charlotte, or, depending on which side of a rise they lived on, maybe Channel 5 from Johnson City, Tennessee. And I had neighbors who only bought a television so they could watch professional wrestling, or *wrasslin'* as they called it. Even the old-timers who read nothing but the Bible for their leisure liked to look at the Nature Boy—Ric Flair—and Freight Train Jones.

"Oh, I could go a few rounds with him, but you can't kill the devil, Lawyer Jay. I thought I done taught you that."

Ashley was upset about the result, but not as badly as I thought. Or if she was, she didn't tell me. Freddy saw in the ruling confirmation of his belief that Charles had sandbagged us. He felt vindicated. But he didn't dwell on it. He had plenty else to worry about. He had wrecked his motorcycle over the weekend, breaking his collarbone. "Son," he said, marveling over what had happened to him, "I hit that dip and flew over the handlebars, and I don't know how I didn't break my neck. It's a mystery." He hadn't had the shoulder set and had no interest in following any doctor's orders. He just hugged his arm to his chest. He would wait for it to heal itself.

When I left Ollie's, I went across the road to talk to Faye. She, too, was philosophical. "I don't guess you've really won anything in Raleigh unless you win in the Supreme Court," she said calmly. "I don't think this thing will ever end."

Ashley took her college entrance exams and prepared her applications. Her English score would gain her admittance to any school she would apply to, and her math score would likely place her out of freshman math. She decided against applying to Duke and the University of North Carolina, though she would stand a good chance at admission to either. Her marks were good and some schools actively sought students from Appalachia to help meet self-imposed diversity quotas, a twist that delighted her. "God, we're right up there with the Eskimos and the Japanese!" In spite of the opportunity to attend a topflight university, Ashley thought she should stay closer to home, to look after Ollie, she said, so she focused on East Tennessee State, which has a fine veterinary medicine program, and Appalachian State, where she liked the look of the department of social work.

I was honored when she asked to use me as her emergency medical contact on her college applications.

"Well," she explained, "I had to have a contact down on the paper for registration, and I thought since none of my family is worth a damn and I don't really know that much about Uncle Curly's family, and I don't want Aunt Ollie worrying, I'd put you, if you don't care?"

"No problem. Furthermore, I feel I now have every right—a duty, even—to instruct you on matters of diet and exercise. I have a lot to say as far as your intake of orange juice and the minerals and vitamins essential to the growth and development of a young person such as yourself."

"Are you trying to make me get medieval on you? Because I will."

I feigned fright, just as I was supposed to.

I was getting better at absorbing blows myself. The acute agony of Bullock's ruling subsided within a day or two. I knew I had plenty of time ahead for anxiety and sleeplessness as we neared the Court of Appeals hearing. After a brief period of mourning, I dived back into my life, back into the fight.

Digging through the record, we discovered that Clark Stone had handed us a gem. In the hearing with Judge Bullock, A. Bartlett White had entered into evidence a memo from Secretary Holman, the head of the DENR, addressed to the governor. The memo was in response to the governor's directive to get maximum protection for the Appalachian Trail. White wanted to introduce the memo to demonstrate that the agency at one point preferred modification to revocation before taking a politically expedient—but improvident in his view—turn to revocation.

Now Bill Holman's memo was, in its entirety, part of the record, including this nugget in the second paragraph: "Practically speaking, public notice was circumvented." Here we had Charles's superior informing the governor that either Paul had defrauded the state, or that the state had been negligent in applying the notice provision.

I sat in Ron Howell's office, amid the stacks of briefs and pleadings and billing records, seeking his advice on what to do with this language.

"It would be far easier," he said, peering over his glasses, "for them to stipulate our case rather than have them encourage us to hit them over the head with their own incompetence—which they cannot get Gardner to acknowledge."

"Can this hurt them?" I asked.

"Depends on the judge. Everything, young man, depends on the judge."

"I thought it depended on the law."

"The law is what the judge says it is. The law is what the judge had for breakfast. It's what side of the bed he woke up on."

"That's inspiring."

"The law is not made by judges, young man. Results come from the appeals process. Of course not everybody can afford to get to the appeals process. That's a shortcoming of the system."

The "find" in the memo was a nice twist. But we also had setbacks in our effort to climb out of the hole Bullock had put us in. Our worst fear was confirmed. The consent order adopted before Judge Downs was not as tight as we thought after all. Ollie was hearing the talk around Dog Town and Cranberry Gap that Paul was going in. I asked Trip to assure her that Paul was stuck in the mud, but Trip, tossing it around in his mind, was not sure anything could stop him.

All around town the Clark Stone crowd was crowing about their win before Bullock. It seemed the next logical step for them was to start working and see what the state would do about it. After all, they had worked right through the county's stop-work order with no action taken against them. Forrest and Ron tried to think of a way to reenforce Downs's order, but they feared approaching Downs would alert him to Bullock's ruling and might trigger him to rule against us. And that would be a catastrophe. The state, worried about the same outcome, decided to seek a stay of Judge Bullock's order. The stakes were high. If they failed, Paul would almost certainly go in and tear apart the mountain while we were waiting for the Court of Appeals to hear our case. Ron's fear that the crusher, once running, would run every day, for ninety-nine years, seemed prescient, all too real a possibility. As Wingfoot said, "It's easy to steer a speeding car, but it's awful hard to stop it."

Meanwhile, Jim Gulick and Jennie Mau, the attorney for the Mining Commission, poured through Bullock's ruling and drafted the Assignments of Error, a point-by-point list of forty-seven mistakes made by Judge Bullock. This catalog of errors by Bullock—or by whoever had written Bullock's ruling—would constitute the basis of our request to stay the order and, also, ultimately form the backbone of the case we would file in the Court of Appeals.

The effort to obtain a stay of the order was a long shot. It meant asking Bullock to stay, or suspend, his own order until the Court of

Appeals could hear the appeal. The points our motion made were sound and logical: *the state must have the authority, established in a long line of cases, to correct its errors.* And so on.

On the day Jim Gulick sought the stay, Bullock appeared not to recall having heard the Putnam Mine case. Again, he seemed uncertain of what this Appalachian Trail was, and Jim Gulick had to lead him through the entire record again. Having heard our argument fresh now, Bullock ruled quickly. He refused to stay his order.

Now, with a sense of desperation growing in our ranks, we had to think fast. Our options were limited. We couldn't understand why Paul had not tested the consent order issued by Judge Downs. By now we feared it was toothless. Digging into the arcana at the fringe of the art of advocacy, Forrest thought we should ask the Court of Appeals for a rare writ of supersedeas. Forrest thought this desperation move was our only shot at stopping Paul from seeking to dissolve the consent order and start crushing before the Court of Appeals could schedule us. "And I don't have to tell you what it means if he turns that thing on," he reminded Jim Gulick.

No, he didn't have to tell Jim. Or me.

I tried to brace Ollie.

"A writ of what? Why can't you people just use regular words?"

"A writ of supersedeas. We're basically going to ask the Court of Appeals to invalidate Judge Bullock's ruling, to supersede it, even before they hear our appeal."

"Why would they do that?" Ollie asked in a level tone. She then hollered at Curly and Freddy that Forrest had "cooked something up and Dear Ol' Dad ain't agon like it!"

"It's a long shot," I said, trying to temper any optimism that might be born. "It's a last-gasp sort of measure."

"Why are we trying it, then?"

"Because it's an emergency," I said, answering her question.

"You think we'll get it?"

"I have no idea. The Court of Appeals judges are grown-ups. This is where the laws get made. These judges will have heard of the Appalachian Trail. I promise."

"Well, hell, it's been an emergency around here since the first day Paul rolled up."

"It's more of an emergency now. This thing is not going right."

"Tell me this. How do you get a writ of supersedeas, anyway? Who do you have to pay off?"

"You don't pay off anybody. You have to allege that the thing you're fighting over is going to be made moot, made pointless, if the court doesn't protect you from it."

"What does Forrest say?"

"Forrest says it . . . He says they almost never rule for you on it. It's unusual to even ask for it, and some of the judges may have never been asked to rule on a writ of supersedeas. But we don't really have much choice."

"I always knew we were unusual," Ollie said. "Especially you."


Witt was now a couple of months into building his cabin. The footers had been poured, and the log walls had been raised. He was camping on the mountain, in a pop-up trailer. On cold nights, I offered him a bed downstairs at my house. He paid me in wine. To be honest, I thought Witt had lost his mind. I spent a lot my energy trying to figure out where I was going to move if the mine went in, but here Witt was sinking considerable money, and a lot of his heart, into a new cabin. True, he had altered the location of the site just in case we lost and Paul went in. Instead of the cleared area with the sweeping view to the east, he had decided to put the cabin on a level spot farther down the slope. His new site afforded small views of the valley to the south. This scenic spot took in the sweep of his pasture and the low mountains rising above Squirrel Creek. Witt's thinking on house-siting had undergone a metamorphosis. "I don't need a big view from my house," he now said. "I can walk up the hill and have a pretty view, but maybe it would be better if none of the new houses coming into the mountains stood out so much." His relocation plan was born of an effort to shield himself from looking at the ruin of Belview Mountain, but it had settled into a gentler worldview.

I walked down the pasture fence to tell Witt the news about the writ of supersedeas.

After I finished painting the convoluted picture for him, airing the long odds, he said, "I still say I'd rather be us than Paul." He was smiling.

"Explain that," I said, wishing I had more of his optimism. "Paul is sitting pretty good right now, with Bullock's ruling propping him up. And we're—"

"Look at it this way," Witt said, warming to his notion, "we've got the whole machinery of the state geared up seeking emergency rulings. We've got the attorney general and the National Park Service hanging on the outcome. Do you think they're going to lose? We've got the best lawyers in the state fighting this thing for us, and for the most part we don't have to pay for it. We're paying half of a half. Now Paul, he's over there paying his lawyers, and facing this juggernaut. His permit was revoked. He's still paying on that shovel. He's still paying on his lease, but he hasn't been able to take one rock out of the dirt. That's the mountain he's got to climb. If we've got it bad, he's got it worse."

I appreciated Witt's take, even if it was an oversimplification, a sunny take on the large forces I figured were churning in Paul's favor.

I went fishing. The uncertainty of the outcome of the writ was gnawing at my inner organs, and long ago, as a teenager, I had discovered that insinuating myself deep in the natural world, deep in the woods, next to water, settled me. For four glorious days, I was out of range of television. No news. No Internet and no e-mail. Far from Paul and the crusher and the courts of law. Just fishing a big river. The Nantahala.

To fish for trout is to engage in a purposeful removal from the outside world. It is a statement I make to myself that there is still good left in us, for we have left some places alone, some places where a man can fish in peace. Not many, but some. Many stream miles we have already ruined, impaired with runoff and even effluent. We have built blacktop roads right to the edge of many of our fragile trout waters. Trout need clean, cold water to survive. When rain falls on hot blacktop, it heats the rainwater, which then sheets into the streams carrying oil and tar and other chemical by-products of the automobile culture. Water temperatures are rising throughout the Appalachians, and water quality is in decline. Every year we lose more and more miles of trout habitat in the South, to widening roads, to houses built to the water's edge, to industry that seeks to crowd the banks with parking lots. To acid rain. Even fertilized yards, which cause damaging runoff loaded with nitrogen. But still, in some places—mostly on public land, national-forest land, in the national parks, and a few state parks, and on a few large private holdings, trout clubs—it is possible to get lost in the casting, lost in the splendor of streams unmarred. Over four days I spent my time tying tight knots, casting flies to wary trout in clear pools. Floating dry flies through riffles, dragging bead-head nymphs through deep runs. In this kind of fishing, catching fish is good, and I caught my share, but it is not necessary. Rather it is pleasure enough to be standing in waist-deep water, climbing over boulders, sneaking up on pools. These efforts gain importance with repetition. A man can test his own patience, his own attention span and level of concentration. His ability to tie knots well.

I felt restored by my time away from the case, from the antagonism that needled me. On the fourth day of my trip I came out of the river in an April snow squall. I was streaking down a mountain, down through Winding Stair Gap, when I saw a beaten-down fellow walking with his dog on the side of the road. Both had snow piling up on top of them, the man on his head and shoulders, the dog across his crooked back. As I neared the forlorn pair, the man stuck out a thumb. I pulled over to offer him a ride into town. I had just crossed the Appalachian Trail at Wallace Gap, and as my passengers approached, trudging up the road to the truck, I registered the telltale signs. The backpack. The worn boots. This was a Through Hiker. He loaded his little dog into the back of my truck, where she joined Biscuit and Maggie, then settled into the passenger seat by my side. He stared straight ahead.

"Where you going?"

"Where you going?" he shot back wearily.

"Asheville."

"Okay," he said without affect. "I know somebody in Asheville."

I swung back into the road, into the driving snow.

After an appropriate pause, I inquired further. We were fifty miles from Asheville and I figured we could make the drive go by quickly by shooting the breeze.

"You hiking far?" I broke the ice, or tried to.

"I was."

"You doing the North Carolina section or more than that?"

"I don't know. I was going to do the whole thing. But . . ." His voice trailed off.

"What's your name?"

"Bonzo. It's a Trail name."

He told me he was quitting. After two of years of preparation, two years of getting in shape and saving his money, working long days hanging Sheetrock, which was good money, getting his gear together, he was stepping off the trail after 108 miles.

Sheetrock. I thought about Tony Cook's protestation that the Trail was a refuge for rich boys.

But Turbo couldn't let go. Not quite. "I might go back," he said softly. "I don't know what I'm going to do. I really don't." He fell silent and I let him drift into his thoughts. "I need to get my head right."

It had rained or snowed every day for a week. He was sick. His dog was sick.

"I don't know if I've got what I need to get it done," he said finally, picking up the thread. I caught sight of his eyes. He stared out the windshield, seeing miles fly by, miles that until moments ago had yielded only to the relentless act of placing one foot in front of another.

I offered him a Diet Coke. A Pop-tart. He waved both off.

Suddenly he wanted to talk about it. He had hiked the Trail before. "I hiked it ten years ago, a Through Hike. It changed my life."

"How so?"

He warmed to his subject a little. "I was an asshole before I hiked the Appalachian Trail. I didn't know what I was doing. And walking that Trail changed me. It changed my life. And now that I'm a different person—I'm not an asshole anymore—I wanted to do it again because when I think about who I was back then, I don't think that guy, the other me, had any idea what an amazing thing he was doing. Now I know more. I want to hike it as the person I am now."

I told him about my experience with the Trail. About growing up next to it. About the fight over the Putnam Mine. He had heard about it. About us. Through Hikers were discussing the Putnam Mine case in the trail shelters at night. They were hungry for information about the case. He was disgusted about the carelessness of the state in issuing the permit, but he wasn't surprised. He felt the Trail was under constant assault from the forces of the modern world. He was angry with Paul Brown over his greed. He wanted me to know how special the Roan Mountain section of the Trail is to Through Hikers.

Of course he had only heard my side of the story, and the take of the hikers he had been walking with. I wondered if he could be swayed to Paul's side, would have been, if A. Bartlett White had picked him up, rather than me. But I doubted it.

Because of the snow, the trip to Asheville took us nearly three hours. As we were pulling into the clutter on the edge of the city, I asked him where I should take him. "Hotel," he said. "Okay," I replied. I took him to a couple of hotels off Tunnel Road until we found one that would let the dog stay. After he checked in, he offered to pay me for the ride, pulling out a wad of wet $20 bills. I thanked him, waved off the offer.

I was leaving, walking out the door, when he called to me. "Can I show you something?"

I stopped and nodded. "Sure. Show me something."

Right there in the lobby of the hotel, he pulled his shirt up over his head and turned around. It took my eye a moment to sort out what I was looking at. There, covering the greater part of his back, was an enormous tattoo in green and black ink, of most of the eastern seaboard of the United States. Through the states, an inky skein representing the entire course of the Appalachian Trail made its way, from Maine at the upper right shoulder to Georgia somewhere near the kidney. As quickly as he lifted it, he pulled his shirt back down over his skinny ribs, called his dog, and headed to his room.

I was staying with a friend in Asheville. After recounting the fishing trip, and catching up on her news, I told her I had to answer the call of my addiction and check my e-mail. She logged me into her computer. And there it was, the news I had been waiting for, the matter I had been trying to escape. The North Carolina Court of Appeals had granted our writ-of-supersedeas petition! Within moments, after dancing around my friend's computer, I whipped out a press release, slanted our way, of course, and sent it to all the newspapers. This is how the piece appeared in the *Avery Post*:

## NC Court of Appeals Grants Motion
## to Keep Mine Shut

The North Carolina Court of Appeals on April 9 granted the State of North Carolina's Petition for Writ of Supersedeas, once again keeping the controversial Putnam Mine in Avery County shut. The order supersedes a prior order by a Superior Court judge which instructed the Division of Land Resources to restore the mining permit it had revoked two years ago. In December, Superior Court judge Stafford Bullock had directed the Division of Land Resources to allow Clark Stone Company to continue development of its potential quarry site, which sits off Highway 19-E near Hump Mountain. The state Attorney General's office immediately moved to appeal the decision to a higher court. While the case is on appeal, the Attorney General's office petitioned the Court of Appeals to keep the mine shut while the matter proceeds through the courts. On March 26, the Court of Appeals granted a Temporary Stay of Judge Bullock's order. On April 9, the Court of Appeals granted the state's petition for Writ of Supersedeas, which will keep the mine shut until the case makes its way up through the appeals process. "We are very pleased the Court of Appeals decided to keep the mine shut," said Jay Leutze, chairman of the Concerned Citizens to Protect

Belview Mountain. "Judge Bullock's order was filled with error and would do serious harm. We felt certain a higher court would stop it, but you never know what the courts will do. This stay of the order will protect the adjoining landowners whose homes would be destroyed if the mine were allowed to operate and will continue to shield the Appalachian Trail from significant adverse effects." The state of North Carolina is explicitly charged with protecting the Appalachian Trail in the NC Appalachian Trail Systems Act, and the state Mining Act charges the director of the Division of Land Resources with protecting homes, hospitals, publicly owned parks, forests and recreation areas. The Appalachian Trail is a National Park. The appeal of Judge Bullock's order is pending and will be heard at sometime in the future. "I'm not surprised this has taken years to work out," said Leutze. "There are important legal principles and a National Park, as well as people's homes and property values at stake on one side, and a very wealthy mine operator on the other, so we expected this one to go at least to the Court of Appeals and possibly to the Supreme Court." Among those who have called for the revocation of the mine permit are (Democrat) Senator John Edwards, (Democrat) Governor Mike Easley, the National Parks Conservation Association, the Appalachian Trail Conference and the United States Department of the Interior.

Bertie Burleson ran the piece in the *Avery Post* as I had written it, with two modifications: she inserted the word *Democrat* in front of the governor's title and in front of the senator's. Bertie was not too fond of Democrats and could not suppress her bias on this point. *Who but a Democrat would care more about hikers than miners?* Fair enough. It was my press release, but it was her paper.

The summer came and with it long, humid days and predictable evening thundershowers. The woods turned dark with leaf and vine. Ashley graduated from high school. With honors. A special commencement ceremony is held in Hickory each year for all the homeschooled students in the region, and I was honored when Ashley asked me to attend. After the ceremony, complete with pomp and circumstance, and the tossing of caps, I took Ashley and Ollie to a steak restaurant, my treat. I was careful about buying things for them. The generosity they responded with was often disproportionate and overwhelming. I thought about the microwave oven they had given me the year before. We had a nice dinner, and while we were enjoying our dessert, Ashley began laughing.

"What's so funny?" I asked.

"I just think it's kind of funny that I only did like a year and a half of classes and now I'm an honors graduate."

"Explain yourself," I demanded.

"I didn't have nearly enough credits. At least I don't think I did. I took all the finals, but I didn't take all the classes. It was too boring, so I would just sign up for the final exam and make an A on it."


I put in a small garden. Potatoes, spinach, lettuces. Tomatoes, which were doomed to suffer on chilly nights. I built a grape arbor, using locust posts I cut in the woods. Witt, who had begun developing his garden long before he started building his house, had a great crop of greens and lettuces. His asparagus was doing well in its second year in the ground. He enjoyed the distinction of being the only gardener on the mountain who had coaxed raspberries into production.

Witt's house was dried in now. The maples he'd cut at the original house site had been finished into paneling and flooring, and all was drying out in preparation for installation. He had dug a pond and would soon stock it with trout.

Ollie was feeling better. Curly had switched jobs two times in the last year and seemed restless. Freddy was buying and rehabilitating motorcycles, and his chop-top business kept him busy. One day Ollie convinced the reluctant artist to show me his latest work. We went downstairs into the garage, dodging grinding wheels and welding tools and air tanks. In the back of the garage was a 1956 Chevrolet. Freddy had already shortened it—for why would you leave a car the same length, or height, it was when it came out of the factory?—but he had something else he wanted me to see. We had to make it all the way around the back. We stepped around oilcans and air-compressor hoses. What I saw there was quite a sight. Freddy had molded, out of Bondo, a pair of hands and a face, which appeared to be pressing out of the trunk. His brilliant job had made the metal appear as giving as spandex. The molded face looked alarmed, appeared to be shouting, *Get me out of here!*

I asked the obvious question: "What does it mean?"

Freddy did not mind the question but was amused that I would suggest that any of his work had meaning. "It doesn't mean anything," he said plainly. "It's just what I do."

# Chapter 20

Since Paul Brown had come into my life, I had nearly grown used to the constant upheaval, the cycles of winning and losing. The case was the sore tooth I worried with my tongue, the ball and chain I dragged scudding behind me wherever I went. In the back of my mind, even when it felt as if we had won a battle, I was smart enough to know that we would in all likelihood lose the war. Not because we didn't have a good case, a plausible argument with solid statutory interpretation backing it up, we did, but because the legal terrain and the cultural terrain favors business over nature, the tangible, the measurable, over the experiential.

The grand American experiment is a lesson in building a country, in stripping a land and turning it into taxable assets. Subdivision of large tracts of land into small tracts of land. Digging for money. Selling, getting, and spending. Selling again. The so-called progress of man requires nothing so much as it requires roads to transport goods to market. It requires rock to level places out, to smooth the way of the consumable to willing consumers. Leaving a place alone? Letting it be because it is lovely, natural, or simply because it functions in a coherent and perfect way? There is no market for that. No profit to show, no quarterly result to report.

So I thought we would lose. That doesn't mean I was always in despair, for the fight itself had compensations. To fight was to feel alive. There were no dull moments while fighting. I barely slept anymore, and that itself seemed a sign of life. As the case wound on, I started to

wonder what it would be like for the fight to end. I was not sure I would know myself without it.

But one day I woke up to a new reality. I had let myself go. I looked around me and concluded the fight had robbed me of some self-respect. I had given up the essentials of decent living. The most obvious manifestation of this ceding to the case was that I had stopped maintaining things. My body was weak from bending over a keyboard trying to manage the lawyers, raise the money, and move the ship of state. I still hiked more miles a week than most people I knew, and I fished my way to some modicum of mental health. But I was losing the bandy-legged strength I had always relied on to take me up steep slopes and across swift currents. My eyesight was still sharp as a boy's, but my blood pressure was pushing the "high-normal" range, more that of a middle-aged man. When I looked around my house, with my still excellent eyesight, I saw that I had stopped keeping it up. Maybe because I secretly expected to lose the case, I had stopped making improvements to the house. What did it matter? Things that needed fixing I had turned away from. A gutter hung from two lone fasteners on the back of the house. Manic red squirrels had eaten the fascia board behind the gutter, and I had done nothing about it. Water had gotten behind the mortar on the chimney, and the freeze-thaw cycle had popped the material out of the carefully laid joints. A long bead of caulk had come lose from a window frame and hung down along the siding, a skein of rubber drool. I have always loved working with my hands, have loved carpentry, wood, but I had not let myself invest in the place. Things that were time-consuming and expensive, things that were unconnected to the case, had simply been left to ruin slowly in the mountain air.

The most immediate concern was the back corner of the house. It was rotting. And sinking. I do not know what drove me to do what I had avoided for over two years, but one day I picked up a pry bar and started pulling the corner of the house down. There was no turning back.

Now my brother, my brother-in-law, and I spent three long weekends ripping rotten cedar out, down to the studs, down to the hand-hewn-timber corner-post. Once we revealed the interior section of the wall, we could see what had happened. A groundhog had burrowed

under the crawl space, taken to chewing all the wood he could reach, seeking salt where the block met the sill and the subflooring, and that had let water wick into the joists. The floor was collapsing, held together by little more than the forces of stasis and habit.

The repair was both time-consuming and expensive. I rallied to it like a new love. Suddenly, it was the most important thing in my day. That it was unconnected to the case gave it therapeutic value. Where the case made me anxious, the physical labor of righting my house made me tired at night. I began to sleep.

First we jacked up what was left of the wall and replaced rotted studs with fresh material sistered to the old. Next we removed the glass from the decaying windowsills and replaced all with new clear cedar. Tearing out soft, damp wood and replacing it felt good. As we worked, I thought what many men have thought at one time or another: I would like a life like this. I would like to work with wood. Drive nails. See progress at the end of every day. After the project was done, a fine job, too, I moved on to other projects. Deck work. I rehung a door. I replaced some glass windowpanes that had lost their argon seals. I cut up downed trees back in the deep woods and made tidy stacks of wood to split for the fireplace.

I felt good about the work around the house, but slowly I slid into my annual autumn doldrums. With another winter looming after the promise of fall splendor, my mood sank. I looked at the carpentry project on the back corner, the clean lines, the finish detail, and could not imagine where I had got the energy to do it. When the temperatures fell into the single digits a couple of nights in a row and the first snow flurries spun in the air, the mountain froze up and felt like what it was, a solid hump of granite. The days were short and I stayed in. Winter would mean cold days, too cold for tying flies on delicate tippets, too cold for landing fish, or repairing gutters, so I leaned my rods against the wall and closed my toolbox. I shaved less, contented myself to live in the sort of bachelor filth that accumulates around men when they stop letting women come around. But as the seasons turned, and the holidays neared, somehow, as if by magic, my mind dodged the blues that often bedeviled me as the days grew short. It was as if my weary soul understood what my mind had not yet processed: the end was in sight. Only two courts were left in the state's defense of the revocation: the Court of Appeals and the Supreme Court. So it would end. It might take another year, possibly two, but the range of possibilities was narrowing. Either we would win a reversal of Bullock's ruling in the Court of Appeals and Paul would appeal that to the Supreme Court, or Paul would have Bullock's ruling upheld in the Court of Appeals and we would be the appellant.

And I couldn't do a damn thing about either of those outcomes. I was reduced to spectator. Sure, I felt the amount of stress I invested could help steer the outcome, just as I felt that the sheer force of my will helped lead the Tar Heel basketball team to their many victories, but really it was all in the hands of the lawyers now. The arguments were set, the briefs filed. The performances before the judges would matter, the mood of the bench, what the jurists ate for breakfast, all that, but I had the feeling that we were on a predestined journey, now. The train had left the station and was chugging across the land headed for home. We just didn't know whether we would reach the station to a celebratory reception or jump the track and careen off the side of the mountain.

Girded with realism, fatalism, I determined that I was going to live my life. They say if you want a job done, ask a busy man. I made myself busy. Sure enough, my capacity to do more, to travel farther, to experience more, seemed to feed more of the same. I sought trout water I had never fished, weather be damned. I arranged camping trips with friends. My brother-in-law and I paddled the rivers of the piedmont as if on a mission to see each one. I asked friends to set me up on dates. I had taken up the guitar that summer and now worked on chord changes and fingerpicking patterns as if I were going to take a test on it. I resumed an earlier interest, acrylic painting, and in typical manic fashion I filled my house with dozens of canvases, most depicting my crude take on a perfected state of nature.

It is a testament to both the size of my state and its array of wonders that in nearly four decades of traveling, fishing, and exploring I had only scratched the surface of places I wanted to go. I had only stepped foot in

Great Smoky Mountains National Park one time, for heaven's sake. So that year, the third year of the case, I decided to identify and visit ten of the natural wonders of the state I had somehow failed to see. I wrote them down on a sheet of paper: Shining Rock Wilderness, Snowbird Creek, Table Rock Mountain, Portsmouth Island, Max Patch, Looking Glass Rock, Stone Mountain, the Black River, Panthertown Valley, and the Uwharrie River. There were more, but that provided a good start. In that year alone, I made it to seven of my ten, camping, hiking, and fishing my way across the land.

In another fit of ambition, I reclaimed the yard of my grandmother's old house, two hours from my own. This is where my mother grew up, where she spent her summers, picking berries and hiking through tunnels of rhododendron along little creeks. The area had changed since then. It was a popular area with retirees. Silly stores on Main Street sold potpourri and scented candles, which retired Floridians and Ohioans seem to have a peculiar affection for. But the little town had charm, too. And young people were moving there. There were new restaurants and a new grocery store specializing in organic produce and free-range meats. It was different from the mountains I lived in, but it was still mountains. I had loved visiting my grandmother there. I had stood behind her, watching over her shoulder, as she ground apples, skin and all, through a mill, to make from early-June apples her famous pink applesauce. Now I worked to reset stones from the old paths leading to the door and the front patio. I dug out laurels and rhododendron that were crowding in on the place and transplanted them in ordered clusters on the edge of the yard. I dug new beds and put in perennials and herbs.

I could almost see myself living in that old frame house with its screened porch and feathery hemlocks. Its ancient Frigidaire and claw-foot bathtub. If Paul went in, if he won, this old house of my mother's family, this small town, presented itself to me as a reasonable backup plan. I investigated the cost of installing insulation in the walls, putting in a heating system to make the house livable in the winter months.

Partly because of my new escape plan, the investment of energy I put into the old homeplace that year, I was growing into the idea that it might be my last on Big Yellow. I even let myself consider again the inconceivable. I thought about selling the house. I revisited the reasons to sell, and the reason to hang on. My finances were in tatters. I had spent freely on the case. I hadn't bought a pair of shoes in a couple of years, I took showers in the dark to save on electricity. I had raised the deductible on my health insurance plan and dropped all but liability coverage on the truck. I had not seen the dentist since law school, but I thought nothing of running off a hundred pamphlets or poster-size charts to advocate for our case at speaking engagements. At root, the discussion of whether to sell the house always came down to money and love. If I did sell, what would it bring? Not much if the crusher was running. I know I wouldn't pay anything for a place like that. Not $10,000. Not $1,000. And if I couldn't sell my house for any money, then my options for moving, for fixing up my grandmother's house, would be limited. For a brief time I even considered selling the house right away, before the Court of Appeals hearing, while all was quiet, while our petition held Paul in abeyance. But I would surely have to disclose to the Realtor, to any prospective buyer, that just through the tree line, just on the other side of the gap, a quarry might be operating for the next ninety-nine years, shattering the peace of the place. I think I entertained such notions just to punish myself. I had become so used to mental anguish when it came to consideration of my sense of place. I guess I sought it as the familiar, my station.

Every year on the mountain we have a fall festival party. An Oktober-fest. The party is always held on the second Saturday of the month in the home of somebody on the mountain. It rotates year to year. Every-body brings something, and we have a big supper of nominally German foods: sausages, sauerkrauts, stews. When I was a child, no children were allowed on the mountain during the Oktoberfest weekend. Our parents would drink to excess and play cards, and we didn't know what all else. Now that I was grown, the party was a far more civilized affair. My neighbors often left the party at nine o'clock, to watch a DVD, to read a book, or simply to go to sleep. At the early Oktoberfest parties, mountain men would arrive and pull instruments out of trucks, along with liquor bottles and sometimes knives and guns. Men woke up under bushes, there was a fistfight that was often remembered. But those days were long gone. Our crowd was now more sophisticated, and we often looked over our shoulders at our own parties as if to say, *We're having some fun, aren't we?* Oktoberfest seemed that way to me, with a certain going through of the motions. But it was a tradition, part of the terrain, and so I went.

The weather is usually splendid in the middle of October, with the leaves at the peak of their color and the skies still warm with what is left of summer. This night was no exception. At our party fifty or so guests packed around a fireplace, drinking beer and scotch and reveling in the gentle air, the glory of an Appalachian evening. I was enjoying talking to one of my friends from the valley when a neighbor summoned me to cross the room.

"Jay," she said, "I've got somebody I want you to meet. He's upstairs. He's a judge and I want you to tell him about the mine."

"What kind of judge?" I asked.

"I don't know. He's big. He hears murder cases, everything. We told him all about the mine. We went hiking today, to Little Hump, and he seemed really interested in hearing about it. And I told him you know more about it than I do. I want you to meet him." She took my hand and we wove through the throng, up the stairs. "Come on."

"What did he say about the mine?" I asked as we neared the living room.

"He, well, he's a conservative," she said apologetically. She was clearly a little embarrassed to be host to a *conservative,* or embarrassed anyway to confess this to me, knowing my opinion of the political parties and my conservation bona fides. What a strange time this was, when "conservatives" seemed to have less interest in conservation, preservation of the natural world than "liberals."

"What did he say?"

"He said these mines have to go somewhere."

"You said he's conservative. Is he a Republican?"

She nodded. "I think so."

I find few things more stimulating than to ply my limited legal skills on a conversationalist who is inclined to disagree with me. This may be the trait that led friends and family throughout my childhood to utter, *That boy ought to be a lawyer.* My pulse quickened as I followed my friend across the party. I was going to try our case before a Republican judge with a stated bias toward Paul's position, and I was going to see if I could turn him. For the sheer sport of it. I took a long pull on the beer in my hand.

John Tyson was a big guy. He wore a roomy coat of smooth suede. We found him standing by the upstairs fireplace.

Blair, my neighbor, introduced us. "John, here's the one I told you about. I want Jay to tell you about the mine. Jay, John is a judge."

Judge Tyson handed me a business card, which I pocketed. I did not read it, but by now I had an idea what it said.

"Tell me about this mine," he said. "Blair said you've been following it pretty closely."

I dove into the case. I briefed His Honor on how Paul had tried to go into the old Cranberry Mine, but had run afoul of the Virginia big-eared bat. Then how Paul's crew pushed a haul road right up the delicate streambed of Cranberry Creek at the Sawdust site. I have found plenty of Republicans who are pro-business, and wary of environmentalists, but who are properly horrified at the wholesale destruction of trout habitat and want to see water quality regulations enforced. I wanted to see which type of Republican this was. I shared with Judge Tyson my view that Paul was a serial bad actor. This was great fun.

When Trip, Ron, and Forrest were advocating our position in hearings, in courtrooms, I could only sit still and pray they would train their argument on the issues I found relevant and particularly damning—in a word, winning. But now, on this pleasant night, standing by the fireplace drinking pale ale, I was the lead attorney. Employing litigation skills I had learned from the masters, I remained polite at all times. I had learned that was essential. I spoke with economy and precision. I tried a dose of humor but did not linger for confirmation. I struggled mightily to contain my love of bombast.

Now to frame the heart of the matter. I outlined how Paul drew his mine map in contravention of the Mining Act. How that mine map, the very permit application, shut out the adjoining landowners from their right to a public hearing. I held up one hand to demonstrate the 151-acre proposed site. I then used the index finger on my other hand as a pointer, to trace how the permit boundary was pulled in fifty feet around every bend and contour, every fingertip, which, in effect, subverted the intention of the law. "Brown claims this trick relieved him of his duty to give notice to the adjoining landowners, notice of their right to seek a public hearing of their objections," I said. Republican orthodoxy claims a "strict constructionist" posture on statutory interpretation so I appealed to this viewpoint. I quoted with fluency the statutory language. Then I turned to policy. I explained how the issuance of the permit was bad for the Appalachian Trail, a national park; bad for the adjoining landowners, who would lose their homes; and bad for the industry, which had already suffered a black eye due to Paul's avoidance of notice.

"It seems like the state should have denied the permit," the judge said.

I affirmed the wisdom of His Honor in nailing the critical point of this whole ugly affair. "And they would have," I said, pressing this, the central nugget of our notice case. *Hammer home the best points, leave the surplusage,* I told myself. "If there had been notice, there would have been public hearings, and the permit would have been denied before Paul spent the first dime. The failure to notify the adjoining landowners of their right to contest it was the original sin, and everything else is the fruit of a poison tree."

"But now Mr. Brown has his permit." Tyson stated the obvious. His words landed like an anvil.

"Actually, it was revoked by the agency."

"Under what authority?" Tyson said, his eyebrows lifting. "If the agency issued it, do they have authority to then turn around and revoke it?"

Now I spoke gently with myself, to create space between my argumentative nature and my better self: *Always do what you might to stroke the considerable ego of the judge.* "That's a good question. I think they do have the authority to revoke. The Mining Act of 1971 says the permit may be revoked if the operator violates the Mining Act. The attorney general's office felt that the very operation of the quarry, as designed, violates the act. And the Mining Commission agreed."

"Why? On what basis?"

"Because it will violate one of the criterion for which it could have denied the permit."

"Which it failed to do."

"Right. It's a mess." *Admit the obvious. And move on.* "We, my group, we wanted the state to revoke the permit because it was *never* valid. We maintain that it was *never* valid because of the failure to give notice of the right to have a public hearing. Original sin. But the state didn't want to admit it screwed up issuing the permit." *Disparaging public officials is generally popular with all Republicans, and even some Democrats.* "The agency wanted to say they issued it properly, and that they then revoked it properly. See, the statute is badly written," I summarized. Here I tested a limit with the judge: "It was badly written, in my opinion, because like most statutes the regulated industry was doing the drafting of the law that is supposed to police them."

"Don't you think it should be hard to revoke a permit?" Tyson asked the amateur advocate.

"Not really. No. These guys, like Paul, they get away with a lot. He's had more violations than you can count. Blasting without a seismograph on site. Burning houses with toxic paint without a burn permit, which violates Division of Air Quality standards. He built his haul road without a DOT Driveway Connecting Permit. He hired some boys to bury the burned rubble in the haul road, which is a violation of Division of Water Quality regulations. He built the crusher, the plant, without a county building permit. And for all those violations, this series of violations, he got slaps on the wrist. The fines were nothing to him. I think that erodes the public trust. And Paul is still kicking. Now, from what I've heard, I don't think Vulcan would pull all that stuff. Or Martin Marietta. The big companies. But I'd have to ask people who live next door to their operations to be confident of that."

"So where does this thing stand now?" Tyson asked, taking a bite of a sausage he had been holding since we started.

I ran through where we'd been. The ALJ. The Mining Commission. Judge Bullock. I told him we had our writ of supersedeas, which I loved saying. It sounded impressive and incontrovertible. "Now we're headed for the Court of Appeals."

At this point, Judge Tyson's face flushed bright and his big eyes swelled slightly, but noticeably, in their sockets. "You've come a long way." Now he found reason to excuse himself. "Good luck with it, Jay." He patted me on the shoulder and headed for the other side of the room.

Moments later, I reached into my pocket and withdrew the business card he had handed me. It confirmed what I suspected. John Tyson was a judge on the North Carolina Court of Appeals. My head was still spinning when I met his wife at the buffet. There is no dress code for the Oktoberfest party, but most folks are dressed in casual hiking gear gone-to-town. Canvas duck pants and hiking shoes work. A few like to dress up. Bolo ties. Denim skirts and shearling vests. The lone exception this evening was Mrs. John Tyson. She was turned out in a snappy navy jacket with large gold buttons. She sported what my parents used to call a "hairdo."

"John is a wonderful judge," she said as we browsed the heavy appetizers. "He's the only member of the Court of Appeals who has any business experience. He's the only one who brings that business perspective to the bench."

"That certainly is an important perspective," I said, reminding myself that at a party one should stick to small talk and pleasantries. What I wanted to say is that the entire system that runs our country, and most other countries, is *the business perspective,* and if the courts are a periodic check on that, representing the folks who sometimes get left behind, or crushed by sheer force of *the business perspective,* maybe that's not such a bad thing. But I didn't say that. Instead I remarked on how confusing it was to have so many different kinds of mustard on the table.

So with no intent, but with all my vigor, I had just tainted Judge Tyson. I had spent fifteen minutes advocating and embellishing the state's position, and the position of the Unincorporated Association of Concerned Citizens to Protect Belview Mountain, before a judge who could potentially hear the matter in the second-highest court in the land. Mrs. Tyson was still talking, about her child, and a school team, a trip they were taking, something, but my mind was in overdrive. If Tyson was assigned to our Appeals panel—and we did not yet have an assignment, so it was possible—he might feel compelled to recuse himself from hearing our case. He might have to step down. Which could be a good thing if he was indeed inclined to see the matter from the businessman's point of view. A very good thing. We wanted judges who could put themselves in the position of a hiker on the Appalachian Trail, appreciate a hiker's perspective with high expectations of peace and quiet and expansive views of a natural landscape. And we wanted a judge who could easily imagine being a middle-class homeowner in Appalachia, having his or her home rendered unlivable by the shaking of the earth, the torrents of mud and rubble coursing down the mountain—the inevitable result when the business perspective collides with steep mountain terrain.

Judges do not have to recuse themselves even when tainted at cocktail parties. Their duty is to recuse themselves only if they do not think they can be impartial. It's totally discretionary. And maybe Tyson could still be impartial. Rather than tainting a judge, steering him to recusal, maybe I had stirred up a hornet's nest. Maybe John Tyson was a business-minded judge who would now go into our case having heard our side only, and that would cause him to be even harder on us. Now he had plenty of time to chew on, and perhaps rebut, some of my argument. So it could help, or it could hurt. At the least, tainting Judge Tyson was bad form. And I figured Trip was going to be angry with me. So I decided not to tell him. Not yet.

The Court of Appeals works this way. The fifteen members of the bench are elected in ostensibly nonpartisan elections, and vacancies are filled by the sitting governor. In 2003 the court took up seventeen hundred cases, everything from motor-vehicle violations to public-corruption cases. Everything short of death-penalty cases. Each case coming before the court is heard by a three-judge panel. When I asked lawyer friends of mine who determines the makeup of each panel, the responses were vague and unhelpful. It turns out nobody knows how the assignments get made. Or if they know, it's like a fraternity handshake or a secret password. *I could tell you, but then I'd have to kill you.* Some speculate that a Byzantine rotation system is in place. But for all we know the judges are drawn from a hat. Or darts are thrown at a board of names.

Within days of my tainting Judge Tyson, we got our assignment. Trip sent me a note: *We have Judges Wynn, McGee, and Tyson. Kind of a mixed panel in terms of their likely leanings in this case. No way to predict how it will go other than to say I doubt we'll get Tyson's vote and McGee is in a re-election campaign so may be sensitive to angering both business interests and environmental groups. A ruling is likely 90 days or so after the argument. Trip.*

I read it over. Judge Linda McGee. Judge James Wynn. Judge John Tyson. My stomach clenched in a knot.

Of course we drew Tyson. Seeing the assignment, I knew right away I was going to have to tell Trip what I had done, what had happened at the party. Would he and Forrest find this to be a desperate ambush? Probably. *But I wasn't 100 percent sure who he was until I looked at his card!* What were the chances of meeting a judge you might appear before in the home of a member of the plaintiff group at a faux-German–Appalachian harvest-festival party up at the head of Big Horse Creek? At a home within two miles of the Appalachian Trail with a bird's-eye view of the subject of the dispute on a mountain in the back of beyond? My chief fear was that Tyson would think that I had tainted him on purpose. Such a move could anger a judge, and the last thing you want is to appear before an impartial but angry judge. What Judge Tyson could not know is that I was by now half-insane. He could not know that I had tried the Putnam Mine case before hundreds of people I had met over the last three years. That I had tried the case in front of every member of my family countless times, including my six-year-old nephew. I had argued it before the checkout girl at the grocery store, old law-school classmates, and the assistant secretary of commerce. I had assailed my neighbors with the irrefutable facts, I had piled data and facts and figures on my best friends, and on unsuspecting dates, and on an old girlfriend at my twentieth high school reunion. I had won every appeal in appearances before Biscuit and Maggie. I had looked into the mirror and tried to sell my own self on my arguments. With mixed results.

I called Trip.

"Trip, I might have tainted Judge Tyson."

My confession drew silence, for longer than was comfortable, then this:

"Tell me what happened."

I told him all about the party.

To my relief, he was not angry.

I peddled my story. I shared with Trip Mrs. Tyson's worldview in order to shed light on whom exactly we were dealing with.

Now Trip was laughing. "On this particular issue, vested rights and Paul Brown's so-called property right in his permit, John Tyson is the worst judge we could have on our panel." I listened intently, thanking my stars and the Lord, disbelieving my dumb luck. I could see Trip in his glassed-in office, leaning back in his chair, smiling over this unlikely turn. "How in the world does stuff like this keep happening to you?"

"Honestly, Trip, I was just drinking a beer, and—"

"Do you still have his business card?"

"Yes."

"Well," Trip said at length, "I guess Judge Tyson should count his blessings that lightning didn't strike him."

"Never entered my mind. I wouldn't do that."

Now Trip made my day. "Jay, if Tyson will recuse himself, it will turn the case. I could be a nice break."

He did not add, *Good work,* but I could tell he was pleased.

Trip, Forrest, Ron, and Jim Gulick would have to decide whether to ask the judge to remove himself from the case. There were pros and cons. Questioning Tyson's impartiality could backfire. Tyson could decline to recuse himself and come into the courtroom with wounded pride, or a burr under his saddle. Also, my arguments, made over sausages and beer, might have failed to sway him. In that event, Tyson could proclaim his impartiality, then come into court predisposed to his earlier stated position that *these mines have to go somewhere.* Worst of all, in my mind, he might come in thinking he understood the nature of the impacts on the Appalachian Trail, even though he had only seen the site from Little Hump. We had maintained all along that the impacts on the Trail at *Little Hump* were adverse, but probably not significant enough to warrant revocation. You could see the quarry clearing clearly from Little Hump, but it was over three miles away, and after seeing it, a hiker's gaze was drawn to the north, toward the New River headwaters, as the Trail made a sharp turn and Belview was out of sight again. The impacts on *Hump Mountain,* sometimes called Big Hump, were both adverse and significant. That was what Charles had found. But Tyson had not gone to Hump Mountain. He had only gone to Little Hump Mountain before turning back to Big Yellow. After weighing the risks, Forrest drafted a delicate letter addressed to Judge Tyson. He copied the letter to Paul's attorneys, saying that it was our duty to disclose "an unintentional ex parte contact" between the judge and a member of the plaintiff/intervenor group. Forrest proposed that if His Honor found that he would be unable to remain impartial, he recuse himself.

Trip, Ron, and Jim Gulick reviewed Forrest's letter, okayed it, and out it went.

The reply was swift in coming. Without explanation or elaboration Judge Tyson removed himself from our panel.


Leading up to our appearance before the Court of Appeals, I started to dream of ways to influence the outcome. In the 1970s a sports psychologist wrote a book called *Inner Tennis,* about visualizing success on the court. Players were encouraged to close their eyes and see themselves striking the ball cleanly, see themselves holding a trophy above their head. Golfers, too, gravitated to the approach of visualization. Now I adopted the technique. I envisioned what it would look like to win. In my dream Trip laid out our case with clarity and passion, and the judges on the panel fumbled over themselves thanking him for visiting such professionalism and expertise upon the bench. There stood Jim Gulick, grave in the face of the threat an adverse ruling would have on the state's ability to protect citizens from mistakes that could ruin their wells, their water, cost them their homes, or even endanger their health. In West Virginia that year, a child had been crushed in his bed when a boulder loosed from a mining operation crashed down the mountain into his bedroom. I wanted the judges on the panel to understand that Faye's house lay directly in the path of raining earth and rock. I could see Forrest, leaning forward gently, inviting the judges to sip his words as he delivered his smooth lecture on the sacred principle of notice to adjoining landowners, Ollie Cox's constitutional right to be protected from arbitrary agency decision-making just the same as every other citizen so situated. . . . Ron Howell, the Heel Hound, I could see him hammering the table before him, describing the sordid chain of events that had brought us to this point of contention. My mind swam with the possibilities. I could see myself climbing the deck stairs and knocking on the door of Ollie's house. There I was stepping into their living room to tell them that we had licked Paul. That we had succeeded in doing what had never before been done.

But my visions also strayed. I saw myself doing strange things now. I watched myself doing research on the Internet, finding out where the judges lived and giving all their neighbors STOP PUTNAM MINE T-shirts. Not the jurists themselves, that would be inappropriate. I knew that. Just their immediate neighbors. What would be wrong with that? I imagined slipping packets of news clippings from the case in the mailboxes of the Judges Wynn and McGee. I feared that in the fifteen minutes our side had to make our case, the judges would fail to understand, there in their hall of justice in Raleigh, far away from the nearest hill, much less the mountains, that real people were living to their west, folks whose hearts and lives were notched into steep mountain slopes, good people whose fate hung on the outcome.

On paper this case was complicated. But in human terms it was simple. Faye Williams had been cheated out of her right to contest the mine, and now her home was in danger of being inundated by liquefied dirt and thundering chunks of granite. Ollie was never given notice of her right to question the permitting process, and now she faced the end of peace and quiet at her home, and the threat that her very house would come apart. The Appalachian Trail, too, was willing to defend itself in hearings, to defend the experience of its users, but the hearings never took place. I wanted the judges to see that. To see all of it, the achingly beautiful views from Hump Mountain, the vast sea of treetops and dreamland valleys carved by rivers, this last best place to see this country much the way it looked in centuries past. And to see the faces of Faye and Ollie, and to see that good people had been violated when Paul and Randy drew their permit map with the deceptive buffers. Charles had let them. I wanted them to see that, too.

Ollie telephoned to report that Faye was going to attend the hearing.

"Good," I said.

"But I ain't."

"Ollie, you've got to come. You put a face on the thing that happened. I want you and Faye to sit next to each other."

"I'm not coming. I've already said that and I know you're not hard of hearing. That's one problem you ain't got."

"But I just told you, you have to. It's not a request, it's an order."

"Well, you can't make me."

"I might just try."

"I'd like to see that," she said, utterly unfazed. "Here, talk to Ashley."

"I don't want to talk to Ashley. I'm busy twisting your arm."

"Here." She passed the phone to Ashley.

Ashley told me that Ollie didn't believe me when I told her she would not have to testify.

"Is this about the hoboes again? I promise Raleigh is just as safe as Chapel Hill. Every bit as safe. You need to help me get her down here."

"She's still not yet recovered from testifying before Judge Downs," Ashley said. Freddy yelled something in the background, but I couldn't catch it. Something about his mother's foul mouth.

"I'm telling you, nobody testifies. It's a hearing, not a trial. It's a review of the Superior Court record. Did she have to testify in front of Bullock?"

"No. But she didn't go down for that either."

"And we lost." I congratulated myself for a line well delivered. How could Ollie dispute my reasoning?

"Just a minute." Ashley covered the receiver and hollered something at somebody in the house. "Freddy wants to know if Gulick is spying for Charles."

"What?"

"I don't know what the hell he's talking about. He was watching some movie about spies on some damn submarine last night when I went to bed."

"Is Ollie really not going to come? I'll drive her."

"Just a minute." Ashley forwarded my query to Ollie. "Nope. She says she's going to stay up here and make sure that flying squirrel doesn't get gone."

"I heard her."

# Chapter 21

The day before the Court of Appeals hearing I stood in front of the mirror and cut my hair. My hands trembled and I did a poor job. Every self-inflicted haircut was still an adventure. I loaded the dogs in the truck and drained the pipes to keep them from freezing while I was gone. I was driving down the mountain in a gentle snowfall when I lost control of the truck. My road is gravel except near the bottom, where state maintenance takes over, and as soon as I hit that pavement, I was a goner. I caught a glimpse of Biscuit roused from sleep behind my seat, now elevated in a corkscrew as we slid out of control toward a tributary of Birchfield Creek. Maggie remained stock-still. She fixed me with an accusatory glare. I punched the gas to grab the road because brakes are the wrong way to go on ice. Everybody in these hills knows that, and if you can muster the faith to go against your nature while hurtling out of control down a mountainside, you're wise to do it.

Not this time.

The maneuver and the fates sent us careering away from the creek, good enough, but we went wheeling instead into the deep ditch on the uphill side of the slope, nose down, with the left front tire snagging a culvert. I was already in four-wheel drive, but even in low range the road was too slick for me to get any traction. The frigid mud in the ditch sucked at the front tires as I goosed it. Worse, the angle at which I'd dived into the culvert left my right rear tire stranded an inch off the cursed pavement, useless. I opened the door and climbed out to assess the damage, skated to the uphill side, and promptly fell hard on my hip. I skidded under the belly of the truck. This was a startling but not altogether unfamiliar place for me to be. A few years earlier I had been in an icy back-road collision that had left me for a couple of long moments trapped underneath the bin of a four-ton snowplow. I scrambled out from under my own truck this time, wary that my vigorous search for purchase might cause the vehicle to slip farther into the ditch, with me under it, which could pin me to the asphalt, or worse.

Once free, I considered my options.

Luckily, down at the bottom of the creek there were any number of people who could help me. Johnny Grindstaff would have a chain, and he could pull me back onto the road. Or the Ollis boys could give me a tow. Rob Thomas would have a jack if my tire was flat. Of course if the axle was bent, I would be in a bigger fix. I walked down to the Grindstaffs, but Johnny was not home. And his boys, the twins, were at work. Johnny's wife, Tish, reported that Johnny was up on the mountain but he ought to be back in a while. I started to walk back up to the scene of the accident, and here came Joey Hodge. I hopped into his car and he gave me a ride back up to the culvert. He was apologetic that, no, he didn't have a chain. Joey was having a hard time, he said, without elaborating. I had known Joey since he was a kid. He was skin and bones now, his eyes hollow, his fingers like ragged claws on the steering wheel. Automotive accessories such as tow chains had disappeared from his life long ago. My next best option was Mr. Robert. I walked up his driveway, and he was already laughing by the time I swung open the storm door.

I have known Rob Thomas, Mr. Robert, essentially all my life. He was my father's fishing and hunting buddy. His drinking buddy, too. He knew every creek and rise of the mountain, was born right here. One summer day when I was ten, Mr. Robert's mind snapped. He slid into a delusional state that took the form of a World War II flashback. We all knew that Mr. Robert was a veteran of the war, that he had left Birchfield Creek as a teenage boy and traveled to the Norfolk navy yard, where he boarded a ship and went to France, where he saw things nobody should have to see. Before he left the holler, he had never seen the ocean, he had never seen a boat, but now he saw a battle-torn land. He saw cities on fire. He saw dead men in trenches along the front lines. It was rumored that he had killed Germans, that he had blown up bridges and brought down buildings in a unit of engineers. On the summer day his mind went, he set out with a purpose to kill all the Germans up on Birchfield Creek Road, and any Americans of German ancestry would do. That meant our neighbor John Hansen, and my father. Shots were fired on that day, at point-blank range an inch off the nose of John Hansen, then wildly over the head of my father, but miraculously nobody died on that long, hot day, no blood was shed. After the shooting Robert had passed out, drunk, spent. From that day to this I meet people who say, "I know you. Rob Thomas shot your daddy." But that was a past so distant we had all erased it. We had mastered the art of pretending it never happened. Mr. Robert was back in his right mind. He went to church and never touched white liquor or even beer anymore.

"Now, Jay," Mr. Robert said roundly, the way he'd greeted me every time I had ever seen him, as if we had just been talking and he had one more thing to add. "I've knowed I teached you to drive better than that." He had watched the whole sorry event from his window.

We visited for a while. Miss Stella offered me soup, then cake, and she had some beets she put up in the summer she wanted me to take home. I declined all, except for the jar of beets, and apologized that I had not come to visit on this day. I was in a hurry and I was in a fix.

Mr. Robert didn't do so well in the winter anymore. His airway seized on him, and for that he took hits of oxygen twice an hour. He had worked mines as a young man. Coal across the line in Virginia, rock here at home. His heart was going, the lungs, too.

"I wanted to come an' holp you, Jay," he said as the preface to an apology.

"No, Robert. You stay inside. It's too cold."

With his engineer's mind Robert could solve any mechanical puzzle. He could unbind chain saws and use a block and tackle to move a heavy load of lumber. The matter before him now presented little challenge. He would solve it with gravity. He explained to me how to turn my wheel, how to use the slope of the hill to my advantage. "Way hit's a'setting, hit wants to come out, Jay. You just have to kindly persuade it. Hit wants to go down the hill, but you fit it. You've got to let it *pull*."

I walked back down the hill with my instructions. He was right. I had fit it. *Don't fight it.*

Now Johnny Grindstaff showed up. He was coming down the mountain at a good clip. I noticed that he didn't have chains on his tires, and I braced myself for a collision as he neared my truck. But he glided around the scene of my little disaster with no discernible effort or difficulty, no slipping. He had his buddy Rick English in the car.

"Whar you doing, Jay, a-trying to kill them dogs o' yourn?" Johnny stroked his chin, making his assessment.

After we mused over my predicament, Johnny and Rick endorsed Robert's strategy. I was to back up, gently, with a downhill bias. They would put their shoulders into the back panel and persuade my rear end downhill, get my rubber back on the road, and that ought to pull the front tire out of the culvert. We would use the mountain itself, gravity, to pry me out.

"Only one problem," I said.

"What's that?"

"That's going to shoot me across the road and into the creek."

Rick turned to look at the creek, as if he had forgotten that it was there. "Aw?" he considered.

"Well . . ." Johnny thought on it. "Well, see then, you'll be backwards a-going down the mountain. Just put a tar on the grass next to the creek and back it down to Rob's driveway. That grass'll grab you if it ain't too bad froze. Wouldn't you say, Rick?"

"It ort to," Rick reasoned. "If them tars is any good."

"I wasn't having much success going down the mountain forward," I said. "You think I can do better in reverse?"

Johnny rubbed his chin. "I'd say it's questionable."

Rick added his bit. "I've always said a man's smart to try new things."

It was better to laugh than to cry, so I laughed.

I did as I was told. And just as predicted, my front tire popped out of the culvert and I sailed across the frozen road in reverse. Now Johnny and Rick were hollering for me to pull it hard. I pulled it with all I had, and the truck came to rest on the thin shoulder above the creek, two tires tearing through the icy grass crust to strewn gravel. I backed down to Robert's driveway and came to a tenuous halt.

This was pretty nice stuff. I got out and thanked the guys. We were all pretty pleased. Johnny and Rick because they were problem-solvers and genuinely liked to help a neighbor. Me because this had been a happy outcome to a rough start to the day. I checked the truck over, and the front end seemed to have made it out of the ditch unimpaired.

My friends were pulling away down the hill. I waved up at Mr. Robert's house that all was well. I was about to resume my trip, but this was not going to be my day. When I climbed into the truck, I could feel it shudder and drop. I got out to see that my left front tire had gone flat, down to the rim. Apparently when I came out of the corrugated-metal culvert, I tore the sidewall.

Back up to Robert's I went. He was shaking his head over me. Even Stella was tickled now.

She sang a good-natured admonishment: "You art not to mistreat your tars that way, Jay. When they've all you've got to rely on."

"I've got a spare," I said.

I borrowed the jack out of Rob's truck, which was parked in the barn. When I was a boy, Rob's barn loomed as a wooden pleasure dome. This orderly place of rubber hoses, hand sickles, chains, and braided ropes had every old tool a boy's mind could imagine. It had the warm smell of crankcases and fermented feed. I had always wanted to go up to the upstairs loft, to see what more the barn could hold—not hay—but I had never got up the nerve to ask. Guns and white liquor and apple wine, I figured. The things Mr. Robert didn't want Stella to see.

The temperature was now down to ten degrees. The storm had set in. I got up under my truck and got the jack set. But it kept slipping on the ice, dropping the chassis dangerously close to parts of me I would just as soon not have rendered useless. I did a little more cussing as that seemed to help my mood, and more important, the anger sent warm gushes of blood through me. I was now afraid that I was going to miss the hearing. My mind raced ahead to what I was going to do if I had a bent rim, or a cracked axle. I wondered if I could borrow a truck from somebody. But now the snow was piling up, the roads would soon be closing, and I realized people would be staying home. Who would want to send their own vehicle out with me or anybody else? Finally, I got the jack set, gave it a turn, and it lifted the chassis. My fingers were frozen stiff now, crusted with blood. I went around to get the spare tire off the back. I tried to unzip the cover on it, but it was brittle in the cold. In my effort to loosen it, the zipper shattered in my hand like a piece of glass. Now I went back up to Mr. Robert's to borrow a knife to cut the cover away. And thaw my hands.

"What did I tell you about leaving this mountain, Jay? There's nothing worth doing out there in the world. A man'd be smart to stay whar he's at."

I explained to Mr. Robert that the Court of Appeals hearing was in Raleigh the next morning and I had to get down to talk to the lawyers. I didn't need to tell him what hearing it was.

But he was surprised. "They give in the paper you'uns was whupped."

"We're not dead yet."

"Paul's mule-headed. And he's got a lot of money in it."

Like everybody else, Mr. Robert was on a first-name basis with Paul. And now I remembered. Mr. Robert had worked for Clark Stone. Years ago. Before Paul bought it.

"By now we've all got a lot in it," I said. "Money and heart."

Mr. Robert hummed and shook his head. "I told some boys, you know ever one of them, Jay, and they was talking. I said I'd knowed you since you was just little, and I said that you was a good boy."

I tried to warm my hands, coax some feeling into them as I fashioned my response. "All we're trying to do is make Paul follow the same law everybody else follows. You've got to follow it, and I think Paul should have to follow it, too. I don't care how much money he's got. The law is the law."

Stella shrank from the room. As if participation in this kind of talk was inappropriate for the women.

"They back Paul," Mr. Robert said, referring to the boys he'd been talking to. "But I don't care," he said, growing serious. "Paul knowed better. They'ves not any doubt about that, Jay. Paul knowed what he was doing when he went in at Sawdust, and he knowed when he went up there above Donnie's old store there."

"You're not going to tell me who you were talking to," I said, recognizing a reality, not pressing.

"You know them all, Jay, ever one. But I ain't putting them over you. You come and see me. Those boys, I don't never see them. I'd say Paul's big, and he's got a lot of money, but I know you know a lot of people down in Raleigh, the people that gets things done."

Mr. Robert had heard the stories, that I had political connections. He knew I was a lawyer, of course, the general misunderstanding. I had helped his son Gary with a legal matter, and I had tried to help his sister-in-law sort out her water rights on her spring. Not as a licensed attorney, just as someone who knows how to read a deed. Mr. Robert had probably heard what he knew about the case from Ollie. Stella was Ollie's half sister, after all. They were not close, not in the way of full sisters, but everything Ollie knew or said was likely to reach Stella within hours.

Now he grabbed my forearm and pressed with fingers that were like iron. "Lord, give Paul hell, Jay. You don't got nothing to be sorry for." All my life, as long as I can remember, Mr. Robert has used this gesture with me. Pressing my arm. When he tells a story, he likes to tap you on the shoulder or just hold your arm. He likes to shake your hand. He likes to exclaim with a quick grab of the arm just above the elbow. His hands have marked my years.

This was as good an endorsement as I would get. Mr. Robert has always been torn between two worlds. He and my father were hunting buddies, fishing buddies, and they drank beer and liquor together, for years, before Mr. Robert found the Lord. But if a disagreement arose between his neighbors on Big Yellow Mountain, even a drinking buddy, and his kin from down along the creek, we knew, even Dad did, that Mr. Robert would side with his kin every time. But not this time. Mr. Robert was taking my side over Paul's. I would never forget this because I knew that it cost him.

With the feeling returning to my hands, I took the knife and went back down to the truck. The dogs stared, eager that I might get them to safety. If your dog fears freezing to death, it's cold indeed. I cut off the tire cover, which fell away in sheets of vinyl ice. I loosened the bolts and lifted off the old tire. I got the spare tire loaded on. Once I had tightened the last bolt, I let the car down with the jack. But the spare didn't hold. As I continued to wind the jack down, the tire went completely flat, right down to the rim again. The rubber on the spare had cracked in the cold. Or it was just old. It didn't matter which.

Mr. Robert was already climbing into his coveralls.

"I'm going to take you down to Hugh's at Cranberry, and you can get you a new tar put on."

"I can't let you go outside, Mr. Robert. Just let me drive your truck to Hugh's and I'll bring the tire back."

But he wouldn't be swayed. He was taking me. We had shared a moment in which he had taken my side over Paul's. We were united. And when Rob Thomas is on your side, he's all the way on it. "We got to get you down to that hearing and you're not doing so good on your own, son."

We braced ourselves against the deadly wind and hobbled to Mr. Robert's truck. He took the wheel and we inched down the mountain.

We were all the way through the Cranberry Gap, plowing into the driving snow, slipping back and forth across the drift-strewn roadbed, Mr. Robert at the wheel, hunched in concentration, before I remembered that my old friend was now quite blind. In both eyes. For years he had treated his own cataracts by smearing Vicks VapoRub into his eyes, but it had finally come to blindness. On we went, though, generally sticking to the middle of the way.


I did not sleep the night before the hearing. As I lay in the bed at my mother's house in Chapel Hill, I was visited by every negative thought I could conjure or allow. I had run the numbers in my head a thousand times. We might get McGee. But we might lose Wynn. We were unlikely to get both Wynn and McGee. And we had no chance of getting Sanford Steelman, our replacement for Tyson. He was better on our issues than Tyson, Trip said, but not enough to matter. So, the most likely scenario was a loss, 2–1. Then we would appeal to the NC Supreme Court. Unless we failed to sway any of the three judges. The North Carolina Supreme Court has to take up split Court of Appeals decisions, while unanimous decisions are only taken up at their discretion. But the reality is, the Supreme Court rarely overturns the Court of Appeals, so this hearing was likely going to tell the tale of who would win. Paul or the Dog Town Bunch. The man or the mountain. Trip had explained it: "Most law gets made in the Court of Appeals." He said it would not be like with Judge Bullock in the Superior Court. "The Court of Appeals judges will have read the record. They write their opinions. They know their words might stand as the law of the land. This is the big time."

We felt the weight of it. Our Dog Town dustup had somehow earned the attention of the US Department of the Interior and national conservation groups and the best legal minds in the state. Now the brightest, most powerful judges were going to decide the outcome. If we fell, we would fall hard. But if we won, we would set a precedent, we would make history.

In the morning my mother and I picked up my sister in Durham and we drove the twenty-five miles to Raleigh. Down in the middle of the state there was no snow, no ice. When we arrived at the big gray Court of Appeals building, just to the south of the state Capitol, I asked my sister if she would park the car. I wanted to get out. I felt ill. And I felt late. We were an hour early, but I felt that if I could just talk to Forrest for a few minutes, and to Trip, maybe I could help ensure that they would drive home the notice issue. Or hammer away at Bullock's failure to fully consider the significant adverse effects on the purpose of the Appalachian Trail. I stepped into the lobby, and the first person I saw was Judge Tyson. I was not sure he saw me, or if he would recognize me if he did, but I flared off, down a hallway. I couldn't imagine anything more distracting right now than making small talk with the judge we had asked to step aside. I waited until he was on the elevator, then passed through the security station and went up by myself. I peeked through a swinging door into the main courtroom. A case was unfolding. I saw Trip. He was sitting with Faye, and they were taking in the matter on the docket before ours. I moved down the hallway and found Forrest and Jim Gulick in a conference room.

"So," I said, shoving my hands down in my pockets, rocking back on my heels in an exaggerated show of nonchalance. I couldn't think of anything much to say, words equal to the situation. Jim Gulick was still made nervous by me. Normally, I would be nervous around him, intimidated by the position he held, the authority of his bearing. But the Putnam Mine case, the violation of the mountain and my sense of righteousness, had emboldened me. Jim knew that I was constitutionally unable to let any point rest, and he knew that I was counting on him to advocate with expert skill and some appropriate measure of indignation. We both knew one more thing: that he was Charles's lawyer, not mine, and not Morgan's or Don's. We were all on the same side now, wanting to see the revocation upheld, but he had rebuffed us in our Avery County hearing. Ollie would not forgive him for his cross-examination of her in Judge Downs's court, and I was still trying to.

Now Jim introduced me to his wife. Suddenly I saw how big a case this was for all the players, not just for me and for Ollie and for the Appalachian Trail community. Jim's wife was here because this was among the more important arguments her husband would make in his career. She was here because he had talked about this case as they rode in the car, as they ate their dinner. Jim was known for his case preparation. He studied the record and he practiced. I imagined his wife had heard him run through his oral arguments in their living room, preparing for this moment. I had known it intellectually, had known the stakes were high, for my group, certainly, but I sometimes lost sight of the broader context of the fight, that on the issues now before the court, these stakes were, suddenly, terrifically high for the state and for the Department of Justice. If the state lost this case, if Jim did, state and county officials across North Carolina would have to rethink how much power they could exert in protecting the environment. Industry would flex its muscles and push the limits on everything from hog-waste disposal to mercury emissions to aerial spraying of pesticides. Rather than making me proud that our team had instigated a landmark case, I suddenly felt a long, smooth wave of nausea roll up through my gut.

Now Robert Crabill showed up. Robert is a lawyer and one of my oldest friends. He followed me to law school and I was the best man in his wedding. Seeing him file in, I was reminded that my friends had lived and breathed every moment of this case right along with me. I was grateful that he had cleared his afternoon schedule to lend his support.

I introduced him to Jim and to Forrest.

Forrest, noting the time of day, said, "You must be one of those lawyers who doesn't have to work too awful hard."

"No," Robert said. "I just figured it would be more efficient to see it in person than to hear about it from Jay after the fact. His telling will probably last longer than the actual hearing."

We stepped into the courtroom to watch the end of the case before ours. The room was chilly and impressive. Heavy, teal drapes hung from massive windows. Marble pillars soared to the ceiling. Intricate plaster ornamentation and polished mahogany furniture announced that the people of the Tar Heel State had invested this room with a sense of majesty. It spoke of authority. Here then was where the law got made.

In the case before ours, a young man was suffering some grave legal entanglement that escaped me. In this whistle-blower action, force had been used by an officer. Excessive force, perhaps. Then a trooper was fired, possibly in retaliation for . . . something. I tried to pay attention but I couldn't get my mind to land on any one thing for more than a moment.

Eventually everything that could be said in the defense of the defendant had been said, and the lawyer rested. The matter was taken under advisement and the judges rose to take a recess.

Our team huddled up and good wishes were rained upon the lawyers. Trip received the entreaties and moral support of my mother and sister, then hustled off to a far corner to finalize the strategy with Jim and Forrest.

In minutes the judges reappeared and took their places. Of the three judges on our panel, Judge James Wynn had been on the bench the longest. Seniority made him the presiding judge, so he sat in the middle. To his right was Judge Linda McGee. To his left, Sanford Steelman. Wynn was of stern countenance, with a tidy, clipped Afro and groomed beard. McGee had the appearance of a small-town school principal, pleasant but formidable. Steelman had a square jaw and a piercing gaze. He looked as if he had heard every argument a man could fashion, but had bought few.

Wynn called the hearing to order, and the floor rumbled with everyone taking seats. I liked Wynn instantly. He scanned the sizable crowd and said, "A lot of interest in this Trail, looks like." This as the attorneys were still finding their places. Trip, already in place at the lectern, nodded and affirmed that that was so. "Yes, sir, Your Honor. A lot." A. Bartlett White nodded across the aisle, as if granting that a point had been scored for our side. And this before the hearing began.

Housekeeping first. Trip and Judge Wynn sorted out who would speak when, what the order would be. Time was reserved for rebuttal.

Now Trip rose. Here began one last titanic effort to get the notice issue before the court.

But first, vested rights.

Clark Stone had claimed that once the state had issued mining permit 06-09, and once Paul had invested in the mine site, his reliance on the permit gave him rights that were *vested.* It was a stretch. States have sovereign immunity, even to do dumb things, and vested rights really only apply when a governing body *changes the law* after issuing a permit. But the vested-rights argument gave us an opening. Because Bart had raised it, Trip could use his refutation to address the heart of the matter, notice to the adjoining landowners.

I sat forward, straining to hear every word. The judges listened attentively as Trip glided easily from the specious vested-rights claim onto our favored ground: notice to Faye Williams and Ollie Ve Cook Carpenter Cox.

"Your Honor, if you don't notify Mrs. Williams and Mrs. Cox of their right to have a public hearing before the permit is issued, you don't ever learn the Appalachian Trail is right up the hill behind the Cox house, and you don't ever learn of Mrs. Williams's objections to the permit before it is issued. Without public hearings Mr. Gardner didn't have a chance to hear from either Cox or Williams before he issued the permit. And that is why we say the court must address the issue of whether the permit was valid." Unlike in Judge Bullock's courtroom, no objections to our notice claim were raised by A. Bartlett White or his co-counsel, Tina Frazier. It was as if objections were unseemly in this forum, beneath the dignity of this court.

It was easy to get swept up in the moment. The setting, the formality of the language. As Trip spoke—for one-half our allotted time, less the time reserved for rebuttal—I was overcome with a feeling of gratitude for the hearing, however brief, for the airing of our grievance. If we lost, and I suspected that we would lose, I was enormously proud that we had driven the issue to this point, that Ollie and Faye and the nation's favorite dirt path were having their day in the place where the law gets made. It was almost enough.

Wynn stroked his chin. "Isn't there a *presumption* that the permit is valid?"

"No, sir, Your Honor," Trip replied. "We do not believe so."

The judge warmed to his subject. "If I have a driver's license, which is a type of permit, there's a presumption that it's valid. Why do we not presume that this permit was valid?"

Trip steered the judge. "Your Honor, if Clark Stone raises vested rights, then they must show that the permit was validly issued. You don't get the benefit of the vested-rights argument if the permit is not valid. And the Superior Court erred by not ever considering whether the permit was valid, which is our contention."

"Is that your best argument?" Wynn leveled. "I want to hear your best argument."

Now Trip raised the mine map. This was his answer to the question, this mine map with the fifty-foot buffer drawn by Randy Carpenter.

"The applicant notified two people, Your Honor. It was a sham. He notified the gentleman he leased the mine site from, and he notified Charles Smith, who he bought twenty-five acres from. How did he avoid notice to the other twelve people living around the mine site?" Trip let his question hang in the air. "The agency allowed this to happen, but it doesn't give a vested right to the applicant. We say that you cannot have a valid permit if you violated the statute by failing to notify the adjoining landowners."

Now Trip directed the judges to the dot on the map, the ink dot in the crook of the permit boundary. "This is the home of Faye Williams. Surely the statute is designed for people like Mrs. Williams to have notice of her right to seek a public hearing, to object."

Without reacting to Trip's final assertion, Wynn nodded at Jim Gulick. Trip's time had expired.

Now Jim. He would have twelve and a half minutes to explain why states need broad authority to protect national parks. Why the Appalachian Trail must not be made to suffer because the Mining Act of 1971 is quite clear on when the head of the Division of Land Resources can *deny* a permit, but perfectly vague on when that head has the leeway to *revoke* a permit. Would Jim compare the Appalachian Trail to Yosemite and Yellowstone as I had suggested in e-mails and voice mails just that week and for several months prior to this moment? Would he stick stubbornly to the state's contention that the permit was validly issued, then revoked just as validly? We were going to find out.

Jim dug into his issues, but he was flat. He began to explain the protection afforded to publicly owned parks by the statute, but Judge Steelman interrupted.

"How far out from the Trail should the protection go?"

Jim paused to consider.

Steelman resumed. "Forty, fifty miles?"

Jim nodded. Now he understood the question. "No, I wouldn't say so, Your Honor. In this case, this spot is two miles from the Appalachian Trail, in a spectacular area prized for its scenery. This is an area where, ah, Kathy Ludlow, the scenery analyst from the United States Forest Service, says you should apply a standard where the activity does not have to be invisible, but should be *visually subordinate* to the forested area surrounding the site."

Jim struggled to recall Ludlow's name. The task is enormously difficult. Attorneys prepare their remarks yet know that the judges can interrupt the presentation at any time.

Judge Wynn had been lying in wait, he was about to speak, but now Jim seized a momentary pause in which Wynn was weighing whether Steelman had exhausted his line of inquiry. "What we have here is a record from the Superior Court that is filled with error. Judge Bullock ignored the findings of fact and substituted his own facts. This record is replete with evidence that these impacts are significant and adverse, but Judge Bullock ignored that. He ignored the Ludlow report and Pamela Underhill, from the National Parks Service, and the Hill landscape-architect report, finding that the impact would be significant and adverse on the purpose of the Trail."

Judge Wynn seemed impressed with Jim's round defense of the findings of fact. "The Superior Court said you can modify or suspend the permit," Wynn noted.

Jim leaned into his reply. "The precedent is clear, Your Honor, that when the public interest is involved, the proper reading of the word *may* will be *shall*. So the fact that the agency 'may' deny the permit should be read as 'shall deny the permit' in a case where the activity will have significant adverse effects on the purpose of the Trail, as is the case here. The General Assembly wants the purpose of publicly owned parks protected. That's clear and that's in the statute."

Judge Steelman was unmoved. "Why didn't the agency modify the permit? That's in the statute."

Jim did not hesitate to reply. "Your Honor, the department is supposed to issue a Notice of Violation. Mr. Gardner did that. Then the department is supposed to schedule a formal conference to discuss the violation. The department did that. The department can suspend or modify the permit. That is clear. In this case, as in other cases, it is then up to the mine owner, the very one who must carry out the modification, to suggest the modifications. They are supposed to engage appropriate experts. Clark Stone utterly failed to engage any expert advice." Jim paused now. "*No* landscape architect," he said, landing hard on the word *no.* "*No* acoustic engineers. The agency had to revoke the permit because Clark Stone failed to correct the violations. The Superior Court seems to say that once you get a permit, it's okay to do the things for which it could be denied and you can't have it revoked."

Now I saw more clearly what had happened. The videotape of Nasty dipping dirt may have gotten Charles's attention, but the state had revoked the permit in large part because Randy Carpenter had proven either unable or unwilling to take the state seriously. Randy had thought he could get away with minimal corrections of the violations, minimal modifications, and he had strutted his way through the public meetings. Rather than intimidating the state, Charles had taken Randy's antics and his disposition to mean that this company would never be able to operate under the terms and conditions of the permit. It suddenly seemed clear what had turned Charles: Randy.

Judge Wynn was still puzzling over the use of a denial criterion being employed in service of a revocation.

Jim was ready. "Your Honor, it could be a public-health impact, one of the other reasons for a denial. This time it was impacts on the Appalachian Trail."

A. Bartlett White got off to a rough start. He led by saying that vested rights was just a side issue. "To be honest we just threw that in," he said, addressing the judges. It was almost sneering at the court, at the sober responsibility of submitting a brief.

He pushed his snappy reading glasses down on his nose and raised one of his poster boards, but Judge Wynn stopped him. "Maybe twenty years ago I could have seen that board, but I can't see that far anymore. Just tell us." The remark drew laughs from the assembly, and Bart carried on, without his visual prop.

He began by pressing the case for modification.

Judge Wynn let him run for a moment, then offered a suggestion. "Do you want to work this out?"

White looked confused. Everyone in the courthouse seemed to lean forward. What was this?

Wynn was utterly conversational now in his tone. "I mean, it just seems the thing to do, is, if there's a chance, you should work this out."

White scrambled. "My client was issued the permit. Your Honor, there is nothing stopping the agency from going back to the statute and they can tell us what to do as far as modifying the permit. About screening the operation, and the little backup beepers . . . They should be doing it."

It was down to this. Clark Stone wanted the state to modify the permit, to tell it what to do, according to White, but the state wanted Clark Stone to take the initiative. I was beginning to see why Judge Wynn was perplexed. But that was not what this was about. We needed to get the judge off modification and this petty argument about who should have taken the initiative. The real problem was, I wanted to offer, that Clark Stone had cheated. They had used Randy's mine map with the fifty-foot "buffer" to deny Ollie and Faye their right to a public hearing, and everything that followed was poisoned by that failure, that misreading of the Mining Act.

Now Linda McGee entered the fray. "Why would you want the state to mandate the modification rather than coming up with your own proposal?"

Now Judge Wynn. "You just want to mine, right? If you can get this done, you don't want to be going in some place where everybody is going to hate you. Isn't that right? It seems like you could sit down and work this out. I believe you could do it."

I felt like leaping out of my chair and hurling oaths. *No, Your Honor! This cannot be worked out by talking about it. Not with Dear Ol' Dad and Randy Carpenter. A hearing at the Court of Appeals is our only line of defense. This is all we've got left!* I didn't want to work it out. I wanted to have a ruling.

But maybe this was the best we could do. A modification. It was stunning. After all this effort, all this hope invested in a ruling, the senior judge was trying to steer us to a settlement that would have Paul Brown pulling down Belview Mountain, albeit in a kinder, gentler way.

Now A. Bartlett White's co-counsel, Tina Frazier, took her turn. I had seen Tina at the other hearings, but I had not heard her speak. She quickly dispelled any thoughts Judge Wynn might have had about steering the parties to a settlement, or any idea that the Clark Stone side could be reasoned with. Instead she stuck her finger in Judge Wynn's eye. Wearily she said, "All this stuff about trying to work this out is a red herring." I immediately wondered at the wisdom of taking the judge's pet suggestion and dismissing it so roundly—even if I agreed with her. Every gaze in the room went to Judge Wynn. He stared downward, fixed on something on the pad before him. He was rapt in attention. Then, a few words into Tina Frazier's presentation, he shook his head so slightly that I could barely be certain I had seen it. Was it resignation at the delivery of a winning argument, or was it a flinch at an unexpected stumble into dangerous territory?

But Tina Frazier was just getting warmed up. Where had she been all this time?

"If anyone had been aware that the Trail was there, my guess is the permit wouldn't have been issued . . . ," she said, as if this were all quite simple. All watched in wonder as she spoke. "My client wouldn't have bought the land and wouldn't have spent two million dollars to put a mine there."

That was it. That was *our* argument, but it had just been made in all its elegant simplicity by the opposing counsel! The obvious inference to draw from Ms. Frazier's remark was that Clark Stone, with the submission of a mine map that cut out adjoining landowners from a possible hearing, had cost the state the knowledge of the location of the Appalachian Trail. I knew what Tina Frazier was trying to do. She was being zealous in defense of her client, trying to explain the frustration Paul felt, how he had wandered—innocently, in their telling—into this fix. She wanted to convey the outrage of Paul having spent vast sums of money on a mine that had now sat idle for three years. And she did that. But her words did far more. She did what we feared we had been unable to do: she made our notice case. And she made it on the record. While other judges in other courts had upheld A. Bartlett White's objections to the centerpiece of our argument, which the administrative law judge had gone out of her way to exclude, Tina Frazier waltzed our argument right in, uninvited. She had just spelled out exactly how important it was in Clark Stone's effort to secure a permit that nobody know where the Trail was. They may have thought they were just shutting Ollie Ve Cox out of her right to a hearing, and Mrs. Faye Williams, but in doing that, they had also shielded the state from knowing that a national park was just up the hill, a treasured linear greenway whose purpose was to provide a wilderness experience unimpeded by the sights and sounds of civilization.

Linda McGee got it. She pinned Tina Frazier. "So the location of this line allowed you to avoid notice?"

Tina seemed now to understand what she had done. The mistake she had made. "The line is supposed to be a barrier, a berm. The Mining Commission allowed it."

"But it lets you avoid notice?"

A. Bartlett White's face hardened through a fixed, neutral gaze. After nearly three years of litigation he had just watched his co-counsel serve up our case on a silver platter.

The truth seemed to crash in through the huge windows. A wave of truth that swamped White and his poster boards.

Judge Wynn wrapped up the hearing with a last plea for settlement. "I can see this is going to be a recurring thing," he said, weary at the very idea. He rolled his finger in the air to represent the string of battles he could well imagine between Clark Stone and the neighbors. His concern was clearly that Clark Stone was not welcome in the community and that the adjoining landowners were going to continually raise objections, valid and otherwise. I think this concern understated what was at stake, but I was beginning to see that Judge Wynn was not just suggesting that the parties try to mediate, he was issuing a warning. Somebody was going to lose, and lose big. It was either in our best interest to work toward a settlement because we were going to end up with an open-pit mine next to our national park, and next to the homes of Ollie and Faye, and we should try to get every modification possible, or it was in Clark Stone's best interest to concede to some radical modification of their permit and work toward that or they were going to be left with a revoked permit and an idle site.

Nobody spoke as we filed out of the courtroom. The nervous banter from earlier in the day was replaced by long faces and fatigue. We all had the sense that too much of our time had been spent vanquishing the curious vested-rights issue. Trip had argued with passion and clarity on our notice issue, but his twelve and a half minutes had flown by, with little time to explain how special the Hump Mountain section is to Trail hikers. Almost no time to explain who Ollie was, or what Faye would lose if Paul started crushing. Nobody compared the Appalachian Trail to Yosemite or to Yellowstone. Jim had mastered the complexity of the "significant adverse effects" aspect of the case, but Judge Wynn had dragged him off-topic to the long discussion on mediation. Clark Stone didn't have its best day either. Bart had admitted that the vested-rights claim was an afterthought. Judge Steelman had opened the door to their "zoning" argument, but no advantage was taken of it. And Tina Frazier had done better making our case than the case of her client.

My team streamed out onto the wet sidewalk in front of the courthouse. My sister has always had impeccable instincts. She wanted a word with Trip. "Did we just lose?"

Faye leaned in. She suspected the same.

My sister elaborated, "What was Jim Gulick talking about? I thought he was supposed to be in the environmental division at the attorney general's office, but all he did was talk about Charles."

I defended Jim. "It wasn't his fault. He represents the state, and the state had to deal with some of the technical stuff. All the authority issues. Charles is his client, not us."

Faye thought Jim should have been more assertive. "They pushed him around."

But Trip aimed to make himself clear. "Jim was good. He was. We did okay."

My sister was unmoved.

We all praised Trip. He had fought to get the notice claim in, and for that he would remain our hero. I was heartened that after all the wrangling about what approach to take, Trip now assigned Ollie's and Faye's claims equal billing to the Appalachian Trail claim. But would it win?

My mother expressed the feeling we all had. "I'm just glad it's over. I need to go home and read the statute and I need to lie down."

That was it. It was over. All the struggle to get press coverage, to put together a legal team and herd the conservation plaintiffs into line. All the work over the family dinner table, the effort to keep from falling into despair. The worries over money and mobilizing public pressure. It was over, and it would all come down to Wynn, McGee, and Steelman.

Somewhere in the middle of the journey, Robert Crabill had pulled me out of one of my pessimistic funks, saying, "The right side almost always wins."

"All evidence to the contrary?" I asked.

"I mean eventually. Not because the law is always on their side, there is a lot of bad law out there, but somehow the truth usually comes out and the right side usually wins if you can stay in court long enough."

"We're the right side in this one," I had said, stating it and wondering aloud at the same time.

"I think you are."

Was that what was happening? Was Robert's cosmic force for rational outcomes sorting itself out? Had Judge McGee found reason enough to rule for us, even though the statute was far from clear on our point? Or was something else in the works? Was money doing its talking and was the so-called progress of man going to continue unabated, devouring even the last best natural places? Was wrong rolling right? Were Ollie and Faye, the two women on the side of the mountain, just too small to win at something this big?

We let all the scenarios sink in. Trip explained that the judges were probably in chambers right now. "I think what they do is, they meet right after the hearing, vote one way or another, and then they will spend some time writing the opinion."

"So it will be over—" Faye started.

"My guess is they have already registered their votes," Trip said. "It's over now."

"When will we know?" my mother asked.

"Ninety days. Give or take."

We stood outside, unwilling to leave just yet, unable to let go of our day in court. The case had been our long, shared nightmare, but it was also now who we were. We were co-plaintiffs. We were a team, the Dog Town Bunch. And we didn't quite know what to do with ourselves now that it was over. We shook our heads and said small goodbyes and wandered off to our separate cars to return to the other parts of our lives.

We waited every day expecting news to come, a ruling. The days had warmed, summer came, but I didn't put in a garden. I fished a little, but not as much as was my habit in other summers. I spent a week in Raleigh, building a deck on the back of my brother's house. As always, I enjoyed the neat parameters of a carpentry task. My brother and I hauled the lumber, measured and cut, hammered nails in planks, and then it was done. I had some friends up to the mountain, on weekends, my brother's family, my sister's kids, we planned a family trip to the beach, but I generally stayed close to the mountain. I didn't make very good company. I had become bitter about politics and was prone to pick fights over the daily absurdities I encountered in the newspaper. War and famine and greed. Wrongheadedness.

I spent a lot of time with Ollie and Ashley and Freddy. Curly's job was no good. He was driving between home and California, hauling lettuce and other produce back to the East Coast. He told us stories, held us in thrall over the danger he faced on the shipping docks in California. He said the long-haul industry was closely tied to the drug trade. He wanted out of it, though the pay was pretty good. As Ashley said, "He's tired when he's home, and he's hardly ever home." In my distraction, my growing decline into cynicism, all I could think of was the waste of trucking lettuce from California to North Carolina, where we do, after all, have plenty of dirt in which we might grow our own lettuce if we weren't so busy growing condominiums and strip shopping centers. Why weren't we growing our own lettuce? I wondered. Why wasn't I? The answer served only to depress me further.

Freddy continued to collect cars and car parts. He would refurbish a car and sell it, then read about another car, a Hillman, for sale somewhere and go get it. "He's almost a businessman," Ashley said, paying her favorite cousin a rare compliment. Freddy was always busy with a project. He made hanging planters for Ollie out of old wagon wheels mounted on posts and planted a row of shrubs along the drive in clay chimney liners. His big project that summer was taking a four-door sedan, a Lincoln, and turning it into a stunted two-door menace. It's the art of the chop top and Freddy's reputation as a master was spreading beyond Cranberry Gap. He could drop the roof on a tall car and install custom glass in the new slivers of openings. He could turn a sedan into a wagon and buff all the pieced metal until there was no sign of his hand. Night after night, into the small hours, he welded and ground metal, morphing cars into new and unexpected and impractical shapes.

Ashley's health problems continued to dominate the household. She rarely ever slept through the night. She was constantly being put on antibiotics, then taken off them. She continued to get infections of the bladder, of the kidneys, of the eyes, and of the sinuses. Ollie spent her days carrying Ashley to specialists in Johnson City and Boone. Her bedside table looked like a tiny cemetery full of rounded headstones, pill bottles.

Ashley called me after one appointment she had with an immunologist.

"What did he say?"

"He said maybe we could move to Arizona."

"Why Arizona?" I asked with only mild surprise, now inured to absurdities when it came to Ashley's medical status.

"He said we could either take the house apart and see if it is leaking gases that I'm allergic to, or maybe we could move to Arizona where the air is dry." Without asking, she now handed the phone to Ollie.

369

"You ain't going to believe this," Ollie said.

"I heard you're moving to Arizona."

"New Mexico. Some damn place like that. I thought Ashley was going to strip a gear."

"Well, there are worse places, I guess."

Now Ashley came back on the line. "Can you believe that? I mean, maybe Dr. Big Bucks can defecate dollar bills, but I can't. We can't afford to move to Squirrel Creek, much less Arizona."

In spite of myself I laughed. "Ashley, you were raised better than to talk like that. Tell Ollie I want her to wash your mouth out."

Ashley scoffed at the idea she had been raised right. "Along with all the other things I'm allergic to, I'm probably allergic to soap. They'd put you in jail for criminally torturing a poor mountain girl."


In the long days of waiting for the ruling, I punished myself by reading the newspapers online. I had become a student of conservation battles in faraway places. Mostly I gorged on bad news. I felt a kinship with people living next to gas wells in the Powder River Basin in Wyoming. Timber companies were denuding mountains in Honduras, and hurricanes brought mudslides that buried whole villages. The planet's glaciers were melting at an alarming pace as people were using ever more electricity, burning ever more coal, driving ever more miles, using ever more petroleum—all of which exacerbated the problem of the melting glaciers, which, if you were inclined to believe in worst-case scenarios, could potentially lead to famine in China and India as the river systems in those places depend on reliable spring runoff from healthy glaciers to irrigate their rice and wheat fields. A man could do little about such pending calamities, the wanton destruction and yawning indifference to the natural world but it was compelling fare.

Every day brought a new opportunity to write letters in protest. On days when I felt up to it, I registered my opposition to clearcutting the Tongass National Forest in Alaska. I implored the US Senate to take a position on the fuel efficiency of the American auto fleet. I shared my dismay over proposals to open the eastern continental shelf to oil drilling, and at the US Supreme Court's failure to protect isolated wetlands under the Clean Water Act. I went through phases where I donated money, in small amounts—all that was left was small amounts—to conservation fights near and far. Other times I looked away, helpless in the face of coral bleaching in the world's oceans, and the shearing off of mountaintops in West Virginia. Frog populations were collapsing in the tropics. Zebra mussels were on the loose in the lakes of the Midwest, and the dead zone in the Gulf of Mexico was ever-expanding. Extinctions were on the rise. What could I, or any of us, do in the face of it?

Following the bad news was addictive, and like most addictions, it felt delicious and rotten in equal measure. At my worst I was given over to what a friend called conspiratorial misanthropy. I checked websites over and over, feeding my sick interest in politics. I expected something big to happen. Indictments of corrupt congressmen. I prayed for the resignation or arrest of the deputy secretary of the Department of the Interior. I followed energy legislation with an unhealthy fascination. Some days the small muscles in my fingers and hands ached from clenching the computer mouse, from hours spent at a low boil.

Mostly the news was of workaday greed and graft. Most days it didn't wreck me, it just steeled me. The US Forest Service proposed logging in the Sequoia National Monument, home of some of the world's most spectacular and beloved trees. This was nearly comic in its wrongheadedness, and I spent as much time delighting in spectacular and transparent stupidity as I did awaiting the end of the world as we know it. In our own Appalachian backyard, a new lax rule on stream protection in the West Virginia coal country was set to take effect, replacing a rule that actually protected streams. If those interested in ensuring water quality were horrified at the proposal, they could look to how the author of the new rule had boned up on mining law by serving as a highly compensated lobbyist and cheerleader for the coal industry in his prior career. Under the new rule coal companies would be permitted to smother streams under mine waste, as forbidden by the Clean Water Act, because soil overburden would now be called *fill,* and *fill* is not addressed in the Clean Water Act. Two thousand miles of headwater streams are currently buried under mine waste in West Virginia, the result of statutory dodgeball and limited budgets for investigating violations, but the administration sought to permit much more of this activity to help make the coal mines more profitable for their owners and to ensure a cheap supply of electricity. *Or some such bullshit,* as Ashley would say. Up was to be called down, in was out. The Clean Air Act, too, was slated for an overhaul. New rules were being scrapped, letting old coal-fired plants escape stricter air-quality rules and expand their output without having to consider negative impacts on public health and forest ecosystems. Lawsuits were filed. The world kept spinning, somehow, but I was not sure how, and in darker moments I wondered why.

Things were bad all across the land, and advocacy groups such as the Southern Environmental Law Center were busy racing to courtrooms to stem the worst abuses. One day my search through the war zone of current events turned up this gem: the Bureau of Land Management had sold the top of a landmark mountain in Crested Butte, Colorado, to Phelps Dodge, a huge mining company. For $875. That's $5 an acre for land next to one of the country's premier ski areas, where a single acre of land often sells for over a million dollars. Conservationists, and good-government types, were astonished and properly horrified, though it was getting harder and harder to muster indignation. The US Forest Service was under intense pressure to sell "isolated" tracts of land to private developers to raise revenue in lean times.

The Putnam Mine case was all about agency authority. About Charles's authority to issue permits, and under certain conditions, to revoke permits, to correct a mistake. So agency authority was the issue I was now most interested in. That spring and summer a lot of my reading focused on federal policy and how the federal agencies wield their power. I was following a case working its way up through the federal appeals process. In 1999 thirteen states had asked the Environmental Protection Agency to clarify their authority to regulate automobile emissions. The states were alarmed when, under the new Bush administration, the Environmental Protection Agency signaled that it had no such authority. When Massachusetts sued to force the agency to regulate pollution—the founding mission of the agency—the agency argued in court that it should be free *not* to regulate pollution. It was crazy. Had an agency ever gone to such lengths to dismantle its own ability to function? But the case was not an isolated one during the first years of the new century. The Interior Department had long held the authority to deny federal mining permits on public lands that would cause "unnecessary and undue degradation." But now, even as our case was unfolding in the state courts, the Interior Department issued a new rule rolling back these protections on federal lands, calling its own regulations "unduly burdensome." In the ensuing litigation the solicitor for the Interior Department argued that the agency did not have the authority to stop legal mining operations. Nor did it want the authority. Luckily, the federal court disagreed with the agency's plea to hamstring its own ability to function, saying that the statute gives the agency the authority and indeed the *obligation* to protect public land from undue degradation. Imagine it. The Department of the Interior, the body charged with stewardship over our most precious lands—lands that we all, as taxpayers, own—went into court hoping it would win the right to turn a blind eye to private degradation of that land. These were strange days, indeed.

It was hard to look at, but like a motorist gawking at a traffic accident, I could not look away. Perhaps most discouraging, the proponents of such extreme assaults on our natural heritage were acting in the name of greed, to be sure, which now seemed quaint and nearly humble in its familiarity, but also for the sheer sport of it. Because political victories enabled it, and a foreign war distracted from it. A prevailing notion across the land was now that industry and industry allies carefully placed at the regulatory agencies should take pride in *getting away with it*. There seemed to be a schoolyard belief that because one side of the political divide has made it a point to protect the land and water of the commons, the other side ought to make it a point to exploit, abuse, and even despise the commons. And the glee over their many "victories" was repulsive to me.

Occasionally I was distracted from my downward spiral into bad news on the national level by plain old weird news on the local scene.

Tammy Baker, our register of deeds, accused the clerk of court, Nub Taylor, of eavesdropping on the phone conversations of courthouse officials. Her evidence was that Nub somehow knew one day that she was having piggysticks for lunch. She had been telling a colleague, over the telephone, that she was going to be having piggysticks, the specialty of the local pizza place, for lunch, and then, when she saw Nub in the hall later that day, he asked her if she had enjoyed her piggysticks. The papers blared headlines about Nub and Tammy and piggysticks. How, Baker asked, could Nub have known what she was having for lunch unless he had been monitoring her phone conversations? The State Bureau of Investigation was called in. And they knew the way to the Avery County Courthouse. Eventually, a black-box recorder was found in the basement of the courthouse. It was an *aha!* moment. The press readied their pens to tell the story to a wider audience. But the tests on the box only confirmed what Nub claimed: the taping device was quite innocent—it played elevator music while callers to the courthouse were on hold. After much fanfare, and a rash of newspaper coverage, the charges in the piggysticks caper were eventually, mercifully, dropped.

As the summer wore on, things were almost back to normal. Ashley had a staph infection. She was taking high doses of antibiotics, but her doctors had to keep switching her to newer, more powerful drugs to stay ahead of the infections that took up residence throughout her body. That year alone she had been on Augmentin and Levaquin. She had done a course of Phenegan for nausea. She took Xolair for something she would rather not talk about. All totaled, she took thirteen pills at bedtime. One night Ollie collapsed on the floor and Freddy had to call 911. Her airway had seized up, and she might have suffered a mild stroke. She endured this medical setback with the same toughness she employed fighting Paul. She was badly bent but she would not break.

Down in the middle of the state, Trip's caseload was groaning. As the director of the SELC Carolinas office, he oversaw cases from Charleston harbor to the Tennessee line. One case in particular was drawing national attention. SELC had won a temporary stay before a federal judge to keep the navy from building an outlying landing field in a sparsely populated area of eastern North Carolina. Judge Terrence Boyle agreed with the plaintiffs that the navy had failed to take environmental impacts into account when making its decision to site the field right next to Pocosin Lakes National Wildlife Refuge, winter home to some two hundred thousand snow geese and tundra swans. Trip's team maintained that flying $81 million Super Hornet strike fighters so close to the refuge would endanger snow geese and tundra swans and Super Hornet jets alike—not to mention the pilots who fly them. Shorebirds would certainly be sucked into the jet engines, as they had been at domestic airports near nesting areas, bringing the mighty aircraft to the ground. The local community was galvanized by the fight. Farmers and retirees and bird-watchers were united. If the Department of Defense prevailed, thirty thousand acres of productive farmland would be seized by the navy using the power of eminent domain, and every citizen not driven off his or her land, and the newcomers who had flocked to the eastern rivers for recreation and the slow pace of life offered by the sylvan setting, would be subjected to the constant aural assault of maneuvers. Not to mention the daily threat of spiffy weaponry falling from the sky into yards and living rooms.

Of course Trip and the SELC team were thrilled about the preliminary court ruling in a landmark case that brought national attention to the organization. I was pleased, too, though I was a little jealous when any of the focus of the lawyers strayed too far from job one in Dog Town, USA.

# Chapter 22

We won the Putnam Mine case, carrying all three judges in the Court of Appeals. Writing for the panel, Judge Wynn rebuked the trial court, and Judge Bullock, on nearly every point in contention. He found that *contrary to the trial court's conclusion, the findings made by the agency in revoking the permit were supported by substantial, uncontroverted evidence that the mining operation had a significant adverse impact on the Appalachian Trail, a publicly owned and federally designated National Scenic Trail.* Further he found that the trial court erred in finding that an operation does not violate the Mining Act when it adversely affects the purposes of a publicly owned park, forest, or recreation area *to a significant degree.* The appeals court found it *does* violate the act, thus affirming the centerpiece of Jim Gulick's case. Wynn wrote that the violation was indeed *willful,* as evidenced by Paul's *inadequate steps to properly and effectively address the violation after being put on notice and despite guidance from DENR. That failure cannot be considered anything other than willful.*

As to the issue of vested rights, the court was merciless: *The doctrine of vested rights did not protect a mining permit where the permit was mistakenly issued in violation of an existing statute.* Further, *the vested rights doctrine arises from a validly issued permit, while this permit's validity has been specifically and consistently challenged.*

When the North Carolina Supreme Court refused to review the decision of the Court of Appeals the matter was closed, and the ruling became the law of the land.

---

This is how it ended for me. My phone rang one afternoon. It was Ashley. There had been an accident in Tennessee. Freddy was driving. He lost control of the car on a rain-slick road and they were already at the hospital.

"Was anyone hurt?"

"Yes," Ashley said, her voice checking. "My leg, and Ollie's in intensive care. I'm having surgery."

An hour later I approached the nurses' station at the hospital in Johnson City, slowly, reluctant to state my business out of fear that speaking the words would make this all too real. "Can I see Mrs. Cox?"

"Are you her attorney?" said the nurse.

I was surprised at the question.

The nurse elaborated, "Mrs. Cox was awake a while ago and she said her attorney was coming to see her. She may still be awake."

"Yes. That's me." I was Ollie's attorney. I liked the sound of it.

The receptionist nodded, her guess confirmed. "We only let family into the intensive care unit. Family and attorneys."

As I walked down the hallway, my thoughts were scrambled by what Ashley had told me. Freddy had been driving and it was raining so hard that the water was sheeting off Highway 19E between Roan Mountain and Elizabethton. Why were they in Tennessee? I was always giving them a hard time about going to Tennessee to eat lunch or to shop when we have perfectly good places to do both in Newland and Elk Park, on the North Carolina side of the line. But they liked to go to Tennessee.

The car had hydroplaned. It sailed off the road, wrapped around a locust tree.

Was there a guardrail?

There was no guardrail. Just a big locust tree.

Ollie had been on oxygen since earlier that year, unable to breathe right since suffering the seizure and stroke. When the car hit the tree, the oxygen tank hit her in the chest, then in the head. That's what Freddy

377

thought had happened. Ashley had reported all this on the phone, then she had put Freddy on. There was bleeding on Ollie's brain. Freddy couldn't remember exactly what had happened, but the story came out in a torrent. He was not speeding, and there had been several accidents in this same spot. The road might have been engineered wrong. I could hear the confusion in his voice.

I passed through the double glass doors into the interior of the intensive care unit, then into Ollie's room. Her thin arms lay on top of several sheets that hid her form. She stared sideways.

A nurse hovered by the window.

"That there's my attorney," Ollie said, turning her head slowly, introducing me.

I nodded at the nurse, she at me.

I tried to avoid betraying alarm. Ollie's face was a kaleidoscope of several different colors; a whorl of red bloomed beneath a green pallor. One arm was blackened. Was it burned? No. It was beat to hell.

"I'm all tore to pieces," Ollie said, finding just the right words.

"Yes, you are. I can think of easier ways to take down a locust tree."

Ollie tried to shift position under the sheets, but it brought too much pain. She lay back. "Locust makes a good fence post."

"That's what they say."

She was not quite lucid. Her eyes drifted, watching, but not seeing. "I got blood on the brain," she said simply.

"I heard that. Are you going to be all right?"

She did not answer. I'm not sure she heard me. "I was telling this nurse here that we licked Paul Brown." Ollie seemed to flicker with a new life, but it passed.

"We did."

Ollie looked at the ceiling, then closed her eyes to speak. "Paul's the biggest thing in these mountains, but we licked him good, and I'd say if he could, he'd ring our necks. Ain't that right?"

"We're too fast, Ollie. He could never catch us."

"I don't reckon he could. Paul's an old man," she said to the ceiling.

The nurse nodded. She caught my eye, gave a look of compassion, as if to thank me for enduring this nonsensical talk from her patient.

"Why don't you tell me how we done that," Ollie said.

"Done what?"

"Licked Dear Ol' Dad. We're just a bunch of damn hillbillies."

"You did it. You and Ashley."

"Tell me about it."

I told her about how I got the news from Trip one day that summer. After all the waiting. I told her how it felt on the day I got the news that we had won the Putnam Mine case. We carried all three judges at the Court of Appeals. Trip had left a message on my answering machine, and he sent me an e-mail at 7:02 in the morning. I would never delete it. The e-mail subject line read, *Home run on every issue!*

I had called Ollie on that day and woken her up, which is hard to do with an early riser. "What would you say if I told you we carried all three judges?"

She had paused for a long while. "I'd say it ain't nice to fool old ladies."

I told her now what she already knew, how we'd waited nine months before the NC Supreme Court issued their refusal to review the case.

"That was a long time," Ollie said, but I wasn't sure she was following me. Still, I told her. I kept talking because I didn't know what else to do.

Though she knew it as well as I did, I told her and the nurse that the Mining Act had been rewritten because of the case. That the notice provision was amended because of her. I didn't know what else to say so I just kept talking, saying words that came easily because I could talk about the Putnam Mine all day. I told her that we had the support of the US Department of the Interior. I told her about the first time we met Morgan because she loved Morgan. I told her that once she was out of the hospital, I was going to take her on a hike across Hump Mountain. She had never been to the top of the mountain behind her house. Little Hump Mountain, yes, but it was raining the day of our hike, and she had still not seen Belview Mountain from the highest point, from Hump Mountain.

She was asleep now but I kept talking. I told about the day we watched Janet Cantwell hunting for the burned debris in the haul road. The day the cat dragged in the flying squirrel. I talked about the county commissioners' meeting the day I met her and her family, and about the afternoon the bolt of lightning struck the crusher, the primary jaw. The nurse smiled as I told Ollie her own story. She lay still in the cloud of white hospital sheets while I told her what I could remember of how we licked Paul Brown and shut down the Putnam Mine. How Randy Carpenter had played chicken with Charles Gardner and lost.

I had embarked on an experiment in living. The Syrian Philoxenos praised those who dwell in solitude because the solitary live outside the law, and I suppose that is what I sought when I moved to the mountain, to live outside constraints, to live in silence for a while, to give myself the gift of time to think and be intentional about the things I do. I couldn't say if my experiment had been a success. I had not written the books I thought I would write, had not thought an awful lot about my journey or what I might do with myself. But I had been interrupted. I had been dragged into the world by the case, by these people. Still, I wasn't sorry. I said that to Ollie, too.

She was all tore to pieces, but she was asleep now, resting, and she was going to be all right. She was tough as a damn hammer.

When I was done talking, had said what I could think to say about the fight, about the mountain, more for me than for Ollie, I walked from the room to go see about Ashley. Her leg was shattered. It would be held together by pins, and Freddy and Curly were worried sick.

I didn't know it right then, at the hospital, but that was the end of one thing and the beginning of our lives after the case. Suddenly something was bigger than the fight over Belview Mountain. I didn't know it or I would have told Ollie as she slept. I would have told how it took three years, but the equipment was finally loaded onto lowboys and hauled off to some other run of rock, some other mountain. Randy wanted to open a quarry six miles down Highway 19E, up on Burleson Bald, off Hanging Rock Road, but he got into a mess down there with the local families—and another national park unit, the Blue Ridge Parkway. He had asked a young newlywed, Teddy Johnson, if he could travel up an old cartway through his land to put in a Christmas-tree farm. Johnson agreed, but when Randy hauled a drill rig up the mountain instead of tree seedlings, Johnson threatened to take possession of the drill, or to settle this another way that might hurt more, maybe both. Randy did eventually apply for a mining permit at the Burleson Bald site, but the Division of Land Resources denied it. Staff there cited his lack of timely and adequate notice to owners of record of land adjoining the site. They also noted potential adverse effects on groundwater, wildlife, and tributary streams, and inadequate measures to prevent impacts on fisheries. The state had apparently had enough of Randy's brazen lack of professionalism. After all that had happened at the Putnam site, Randy still found it too difficult to notify the adjoining landowners of their right to a public hearing.

I would have told Ollie about what happened to Randy after that. In subsequent years he would have his surveying license suspended and the North Carolina State Bar would disbar him for his role in the largest land-fraud debacle in state history. The disciplinary committee cited dishonesty, fraud, and deceit. When a federal grand jury indicted him for his central role in what amounted to a Ponzi scheme, the charges included conspiracy to commit mail, bank, and wire fraud; filing false tax returns; and making false statements to obtain loans. He faces thirty-eight years in prison. I would have told her that tens of millions of dollars had gone missing.

We didn't know all that yet, on that day in the hospital, but it would hold our attention soon enough. Ashley and Ollie reported the charges against Randy in regular phone calls. We were all interested, but this was not our fight, not our mountain. We didn't lose sleep over the Hanging Rock Road quarry or Randy's disbarment. I did offer advice to Teddy Johnson and the other neighbors, and I did read Randy's permit application and offer my opinion of it to the new secretary of the Department of Environment and Natural Resources, but I didn't do more than that. I didn't see any advantage in reopening old wounds.

It seemed far away from us that day in the hospital, but Ashley would move on with her life. She didn't like the idea of going away to school, living in a dormitory, so she enrolled at the local community college and took most of her courses online. She then enrolled at the University of North Carolina–Greensboro, where she maintained an "A" average. After the accident her ankle and foot gave her chronic problems, and her immune deficiency required constant monitoring. Still she managed to score perfect marks in nearly every class she took. She worked toward a degree in public health, with a minor in psychology.

Ollie took a stab at setting up an upholstery business, but her heart wasn't in it. After the accident she was in considerable pain. It was her back. In addition to the car accident, she had slipped on ice at the hospital one day when taking Ashley in for tests, and the two events conspired to ensure she would never have a day entirely free of pain. She sewed for neighbors and friends. She quit cigarettes after her seizure, and that made her ornery for about a year, but other than that she was herself.

Like Ollie, Belview Mountain bears scars, but it endures. It stands as it has for a billion years, having lost not an inch in elevation during the time we sought to save it. In a single growing season the clearing above the crusher greened up with a tangle of blackberry and blaspheme vine. The gash remains where the test blast heaved thousands of cubic yards of topsoil out of the ground. But even that will heal. Birds will leave seeds. Leaves will pool and rot against the banks, and tender plants will take root when there is enough soft ground to hold to. Opportunistic plants that specialize in openings and poor soils will exploit the disturbance.

Paul did not fare well after the case. He suffered a series of strokes but managed to keep at his work. One day, without taking the time to think hard about it, I called him to tell him I was writing a book about the case and the mountain. In that conversation he maintained that he had done nothing wrong. He said he had no interest in the Mining Act: "I never read it." That was Randy's job, he said. He called him "Carpenter" and did not seem to know him well. "Carpenter put that map together. That was his doing," Paul said. I told him that I hoped he didn't take the matter personally, that I had never wanted that. That I just wanted to see the law followed. He said he was mad at Charles, at "Gardner," as he called him. And he didn't trust the governor. "You shouldn't have called the governor," he said in a subsequent call. I told him the truth. That I didn't call the governor, but that I knew who did.

Paul was eighty-six years old when he died, in 2011. His obituary gave the sketch of a full life. His parents were Dewitt and Bessie Moody Brown. He was a former deacon at Cove Creek Baptist Church. He served on several boards in his community, including the Watauga County Board of Education and the Johnson County Hospital Board. He had been head of the Chamber of Commerce and served on the board of the Mountain State Health Alliance. He had numerous heirs, including four children, and they will continue the Brown name far into the future. He was a hard man, but by the accounting in the newspaper, he was a good man, too, a leader of his community.


"I'm writing a book," I tell Ollie, but she already knows this.

"I'm not going to read it." She doesn't want to read it but she wants to know what I'm putting in it. She wants me to tell the part about the Heel Hound and Forrest Ferrell at the hearing before Judge Downs. About how everybody in the courthouse wanted to know how she got the best lawyers in the mountains pleading her case. She wants me to retell the part about Paul out in the driveway, spinning up dust, when he found out about the lawsuit.

She doesn't think I should put her in it. "Nobody wants to read about some old mountain girl."

"You're probably right," I say. "You people talk funny."

She shakes her head at the memory of the case, as if that had to be some other life lived by some other person.

Since the accident she has slowed down. She walks as if her next step might bring a bolt of pain. But she doesn't stay still for long. She has taken up weaving. She wants to show me her latest creation. She can weave anything out of strips she cuts from plastic grocery bags. She makes looping knots with the deftness of a sparrow making a nest. I have seen her make a purse, a doily, a baby hat, all out of strips of plastic bags. The pieces are intricate and lovely. They are works of art, but she dismisses them: "I do this to keep me from going out of my mind."

"Can I buy one?" I ask.

"They ain't for sale."

"I don't have any money anyway," I say. "I spent it all on you."

"How'd I ever get mixed up with you?" Ollie marvels, frowning so convincingly I think she's suffering the pain that frequently races up her back. "You ruined my life."

"No, I saved your house. Don't you forget it."

"I taught you a lot of my tricks. You didn't even know how to trace a license tag before you met me."

"That's true."

Ollie hums low. "You know we love you, Jay."

"I know."

She runs a long strip of plastic through her fingers and ties a tight knot, cinches it down to join other knots. In her hands the plastic ribbons are becoming something useful, something beautiful.

"You ever seen anything like this?"

I never have.

I ask her to tell me again about her grandfather. The one who shot his own sister up on the mountain, out in the potato patch. I think by knowing this story, by learning what drove that man to do what he did, I will understand more about Ollie. More about the mountain and about Dog Town.

But she won't tell me, won't be baited. She is done telling me old stories.

"You're so smart," she says, weaving, sliding knots into place, "you tell me a story. A true one."

"All my stories are true."

"But don't put too many big words in it," she says now, concerned.

I nod. I promise her I will do as I am told. And we laugh.

# Acknowledgments

I would like to thank the following people who encouraged, assisted, and otherwise supported me as I wrote this book.

My sister fed and housed me, and took up the fight—and the publication of this book—as personal imperatives. She and my brother-in-law also gave me a cell phone and a laptop and told me when to park the car and rest. Eliza, Travis, and Sam put up with me and inspired me to tell stories that would last. My mother told me I was a writer, even when I wasn't writing. She is an editor and a writer and artist of the first order. I should have let her read the manuscript earlier than I did. My father shared tricks of the trade and suggested I try something easier than writing a book, which drove me forward. My brother's uncomplicated indignation provided clarity throughout.

Melissa Bond told me to write short stories, but accepted this alternative. Kate Whouley read the manuscript in its early stages and told me it was working. Knowing that David Ray was reading a draft with his discerning eye inspired me to focus and write better. Lee Smith read carefully and told me when I was finished. Woody Burns picked the right moment to put the manuscript in the hands of Shannon Ravenel, who in turn gave me a much-needed kick in the seat of the pants. Shannon also introduced me to my agent. Patrick McMillan's appreciation of the story made me want to tell it to a wider audience. Keebe Fitch assured me she could sell the book if I could finish it. Robert Crabill kept me from getting bogged down in details and remembered certain parts of the case better than I did. Tom Cors bailed me out more than once and provided emergency editing assistance on I-95. Edwina Tatum answered all questions on Dog Town genealogy, no simple task.

# ACKNOWLEDGMENTS

Tommy Holderness has provided wise counsel since 1986. John Wilson helped me tell the story with visuals. Carl Silverstein made it possible for me to hold the best job in America and write at the same time. David Brewer gave me leads that helped me immensely. My neighbors have been kind.

While I was writing the book I had the support and assistance of many people who appear in it. Forrest Ferrell and Trip Van Noppen continued to advise me and answer questions through the final edits. I enjoyed unlimited access to all case notes, files, and transcripts. Witt Langstaff fed me mountain rice and red wine, and gave me files, photographs, and his remarkable insight. Rick Middleton, Annie O'Leary, and Ann Oliver at Southern Environmental Law Center tolerated all the requests I made of them. At the conclusion of the case SELC presented me with a bill for $360,000, which, thankfully, I did not have to pay. They do not charge for their services, but the "bill" was a reminder of the time and effort they invested in the case. Jim Gulick, Charles Gardner, and Paul Brown gave generously of their time, submitting to interviews. Ashley, Ollie, Freddy, and Curley were involved in every step of the writing of this book and weathered countless phone calls, e-mails, and even, eventually, text messages. I also had the assistance of many others who do not appear in the book. They include Governor Jim Hunt, Governor Jim Martin, Bill Friday, Erskine Bowles, Hugh and Julia Morton, Richard Whisnant.

I want to thank my agent, Liz Darhansoff, who read the book in the shadow of the Appalachian Trail and chose the right path for it. The first time I spoke with Colin Harrison, I hoped he would become my editor and my friend. He has become both. I have tried to be worthy of the time he has invested in me. I would also like to thank the following at Scribner: Kelsey Smith, Mia Crowley-Hald, Susan Moldow, Roz Lippel, Nan Graham, Rex Bonomelli, and Ellen Sasahara. I am loath to cast aspersions, but in my opinion, they are without peer.

Finally, I would like to thank the heroes who have worked for decades to protect the Highlands of Roan landscape from ill-planned development and commercial exploitation. Southern Appalachian Highlands Conservancy (SAHC) was formed out of a committee of the

# ACKNOWLEDGMENTS

Appalachian Trail Conference (now Appalachian Trail *Conservancy*) for just this purpose. Thanks to SAHC and several partners, including The Nature Conservancy, North Carolina and Tennessee state agencies, the US Forest Service, Fred and Alice Stanback, and countless botanists, biologists, hikers, hunters, and outdoor enthusiasts, over 20,000 acres of this exceptional massif are now protected for the use and enjoyment of future generations. The Roan is still worth fighting for because of their foresight, talent, and effort.

# About the Author

Jay Erskine Leutze was born in 1964. He lives in the Southern Appalachian mountains of North Carolina. A graduate of the law school at the University of North Carolina at Chapel Hill, he has become a leading voice for state and federal funding for public land acquisition. He serves as trustee and secretary for Southern Appalachian Highlands Conservancy, one of the nation's most established land trusts.